MUSSOLINI'S DREAM FACTORY

Mussolini's Dream Factory
Film Stardom in Fascist Italy

Stephen Gundle

berghahn
NEW YORK · OXFORD
www.berghahnbooks.com

Published in 2013 by
Berghahn Books
www.berghahnbooks.com

© 2013, 2016 Stephen Gundle
First paperback edition published in 2016

All rights reserved. Except for the quotation of short passages for the purposes of criticism and review, no part of this book may be reproduced in any form or by any means, electronic or mechanical, including photocopying, recording, or any information storage and retrieval system now known or to be invented, without written permission of the publisher.

Library of Congress Cataloging-in-Publication Data

Gundle, Stephen, 1956-
  Mussolini's dream factory : film stardom in fascist Italy / Stephen Gundle.
    pages cm
  Includes bibliographical references and index.
  ISBN 978-1-78238-244-7 (hardback) -- ISBN 978-1-78533-041-4 (paperback) -- ISBN 978-1-78238-245-4 (ebook)
  1. Motion pictures--Italy--History--20th century. 2. Motion picture actors and actresses--Italy. 3. Fascism and motion pictures--Italy--History. I. Title.
  PN1993.5.I88G88 2013
  791.430945--dc23
                                                            2013020216

British Library Cataloguing in Publication Data

A catalogue record for this book is available from the British Library

ISBN 978-1-78238-244-7 (hardback)
ISBN 978-1-78533-041-4 (paperback)
ISBN 978-1-78238-245-4 (ebook)

'The life of Cinecittà began the moment the head of the government set foot in the studios. His presence started up the immense motor.'

Alberto Consiglio, *Cinema*, 25 April 1937

'Besides the Italy of Mussolini, there existed, just below the surface, the Italy of Vittorio De Sica.'

Stefano Vanzina, *Fotogrammi*, 10 August 1946

Table of Contents

List of Figures — ix
Acknowledgements — xi
Introduction — 1

Part I: Fascism, Cinema and Stardom
1. Italian Cinema under Fascism — 19
2. The Creation of a Star System — 40
3. Stars and Commercial Culture — 67
4. The Public and the Stars — 96

Part II: Italian Stars of the Fascist Era
5. The National Star: Isa Miranda — 123
6. The Matinée Idol: Vittorio De Sica — 144
7. Everybody's Fiancée: Assia Noris — 166
8. The Star as Hero: Amedeo Nazzari — 184
9. The Uniformed Role Model: Fosco Giachetti — 203
10. The Photogenic Beauty: Alida Valli — 224
11. The Duce's Whim: Miria Di San Servolo — 244

Part III: The Aftermath of Stardom
12. Civil War, Liberation and Reconstruction — 261
13. Survival, Memory and Forgetting — 278

Bibliography — 297
Index — 311

Figures

All images are from the author's own collection.

3.1	'Will all women wear lace collars because Isa Miranda wore one in *Malombra?*', asks the caption to a still published in *Cinema*, 10 August 1942.	78
3.2	Film actress Doris Duranti paying a morale-boosting visit to wounded soldiers, c.1941. Such visits were invariably manipulated for propaganda ends.	89
4.1	Avid film fan Nerio Tebano, who would later write a volume of memoirs, succeeded in getting his photograph published in *Cinema*, 10 November 1942.	105
4.2	'The ferocious Saladin', the rarest of the cards issued by the Perugina and Buitoni companies in a promotion tie-in with a radio show.	105
4.3	The '5,000 Lire for a smile' competition was one of several commercial initiatives that enticed entrants with material prizes.	108
4.4	A broad, movie-star smile from Adriana Serra of Rome, winner of the 1941 '5,000 Lire for a smile' competition.	109
4.5	Illustrator Gino Boccasile's pin-up, *Signorina Grandi Firme*, strides confidently towards Cinecittà.	110
5.1	Publicity brochure for Novella Film's *La signora di tutti* (Everybody's Lady) which launched Isa Miranda.	124
5.2	One of the first Paramount publicity shots of Isa Miranda, which appeared on the cover of *Stelle* magazine.	133
6.1	Charming everyman Vittorio De Sica, pictured with Maria Denis in the film *Partire* (Leaving).	147
7.1	A stylised Assia Noris on the cover of women's magazine *Piccola*. The caption describes her as the 'number one example of photogenic charm'.	168

7.2 Magazine advertisement for *Centomila dollari* (One Hundred Thousand Dollars), starring Assia Noris (top left) and Amedeo Nazzari (second from right, bottom row). 171
8.1 Amedeo Nazzari, Italy's Errol Flynn or Clark Gable, was the top star in the country by 1939. 186
8.2 Stars like Amedeo Nazzari were often inundated with fan mail and requests for autographed pictures. 197
9.1 Fosco Giachetti first made his name as the inflexible Captain Sant'Elia in *Lo squadrone bianco* (The White Squadron, 1936). 205
9.2 Fosco Giachetti signing autographs for fans in Florence, c.1941. 211
9.3 Fosco Giachetti relaxing at home reading a screenplay, c.1942. 217
10.1 Osvaldo Valenti and Alida Valli in the madcap 'white telephone' comedy *Mille lire al mese* (One Thousand Lire per Month). 225
10.2 Alida Valli (Kira) and Fosco Giachetti (Andrei) in a still from *Noi vivi* (We the Living), a controversial drama set in Soviet Russia (*Cinema*, 25 September 1942). 238
11.1 Miria di San Servolo (Myriam Petacci) photographed at the start of her brief film career. 247

Acknowledgements

I first realised the need for a book on the star system of Italian cinema during the Fascist period when I noticed that many historians of the time had never heard of once famous actors like Assia Noris and Fosco Giachetti. These and others acted in many films in the 1930s and 1940s; they featured regularly in the press, their images were reproduced on numerous postcards and by all accounts they enjoyed huge popularity. It is difficult, in my view, to form a complete view of Fascist Italy without taking account of their role and the meanings that were attached to them.

Many people have helped me to locate and consult the primary material for this book. Even before I saw many of the films, I spent long months in libraries and archives in Trieste, Bologna, Florence and Rome leafing through film periodicals. At that time I was grateful for the advice and encouragement of scholars who knew the cinema of the period far better than me: the late Alberto Farassino, Gian Piero Brunetta and Salvatore Ambrosino. Tracking down the films was more difficult in the early 1990s, when I first started researching this topic, than it is now, thanks to commercial DVD releases and YouTube. Chris Wagstaff allowed me access to his wonderful film archive, while Chiara Barbo and her friends at the Cappella Underground cine-club in Trieste copied many films for me. Franco Minganti also recorded several from television when it was impossible for me to watch them in the early hours. Over the years, Barbara Corsi, David Forgacs, Jacqueline Reich, Giorgio Bertellini, Katia Pizzi and Simona Monticelli have all offered me tips and insights that have been invaluable.

The book has benefited from two collaborations, the first a project I conducted in the early 1990s with David Forgacs on the cultural industries of the period between the 1930s and the 1950s, and more recently the AHRC project 'The Cult of the Duce: Mussolini and the Italians, 1918–2005' on which I worked with Christopher Duggan, Giuliana Pieri and others, including Simona Storchi, Vanessa Roghi and Alessandra Antola. Daniele Aristarco assisted me in the later stages of the research at the Archivo Centrale dello Stato in Rome.

I owe a specific debt of gratitude to Denis Mack Smith for first loaning me and then making a generous gift of his books and magazines on the cinema of the Fascist period, many of them now difficult to find. Simona Storchi watched with me over two summers a large proportion of the films examined in the text. I am grateful to her for sharing this not always pleasurable experience with me and for giving me the benefit of her always acute observations on the stars and their films. At Warwick, I have learned much from my colleagues, but none more than Victor Perkins, whose love of Max Ophuls' work was an inspiration when I was writing about Isa Miranda. Finally, I should like to thank Alessandro and Ilaria Giachetti, who very generously shared with me their recollections of their grandfather, Fosco Giachetti, and allowed me to consult his collected papers and cuttings.

Introduction

It is a dark, rainy night and a hotel sign is swaying in the wind deep in the countryside. A car pulls up at the garage that is annexed to the hotel and an attendant reluctantly appears. As he grumbles that every passing driver seems to stop here, sounds of music spill out from the hotel. There is a festive atmosphere due, it transpires, to the preparations that are being made for the wedding of the young niece of the hotel's owners. The girl concerned, Andreina, is trying on her wedding dress and showing it off to her excited friends. As her intended, a local mechanic, is expected at any moment, the group decides to play a joke on him. Quiet descends and the lights are flipped off. Someone cues up a gramophone record with the wedding march. When the door bell rings, young folk scurry into hiding. Andreina closes her eyes and sighs 'Franco!' As the door slowly opens, the music starts up and Andreina beams in anticipation. The friends throw confetti. As thunder claps, a man in a soaking wet trench coat crosses the threshold. Young faces peer out and someone whispers 'It's not Franco!'; one perplexed girl wonders out loud who it can be.

The first to realise who the stranger is is Andreina, who opens her eyes to find a tall, handsome man of sturdy build standing before her. He has confetti on his hair and shoulders and a look of surprise on his face. Her expression turns first to alarm and then to silent astonishment as she surveys his countenance. His eyes meet hers, causing her modestly to lower her gaze, only to raise it again a moment later and stare at him with evident pleasure. He, in turn, looks warmly at her and, addressing himself to the company that begins to emerge from behind chairs and curtains, begs forgiveness for intruding on a wedding. He is informed breathlessly by Andreina that he should not worry; he has merely been the victim of a prank intended for her fiancé who is due to arrive at any moment. 'Oh dear, I am a disappointment', he says. 'Far from it!', she exclaims.

Three older women appear in time to hear the visitor explain that his car has broken down and that he is in need of a room for the night. One, dressed severely in black and sour of face, responds brusquely that the hotel is closed for the season. The oldest woman, who is evidently in charge, interrupts her apologetically to say that he will have to make do with what they can offer. The third, the youngest of the three, pipes up enthusiastically to say that they will do everything possible to make him comfortable. As she comes forward and offers to lead him to the best room in the hotel, the mysterious stranger steps fully into everyone's view. He has broad shoulders and is strikingly handsome, with wavy, back-combed hair, a neat moustache and a charming smile. He looks around, absorbing the scene, takes out a cigarette, and catches Andreina's eye once more before starting to make his way upstairs.

As soon as he has gone, the youngsters gather in a huddle and a girl announces excitedly that the man they have been watching is 'Amedeo Nazzari'. The others cannot believe it. What would *he* be doing here? But the first girl is sure. 'Look,' she exclaims, 'he has the same eyes, smile and moustache!'

Upstairs, the older women set about preparing a room their unexpected guest. Two cover him with courtesies while the third, the least hospitable one, officiously places the hotel register on the table and asks him for his 'generalities'. The other women protest that this is not necessary, but she insists and takes him through a series of questions about his name, birthplace, place of residence and profession. The man obliges her and confirms that his name is 'Amedeo Nazzari'; he was born in Cagliari, lives presently in Rome and by profession is an artist – which he qualifies when the woman raises her eyebrows, as 'cinematic artist'. By this time the irritable black-clad woman is the only person in the establishment who does not know that the visitor is the most famous film actor in Italy. She even mispronounces his surname, placing the accent on the first instead of the penultimate vowel (an error that he promptly corrects), and openly boasts that she does not go to the cinema – an assertion that leads Nazzari to say that that is a shame. Not for her, he gallantly adds, but for the cinema.

Anyone watching the film *Apparizione* (Apparition) at the cinema in the mid-1940s would have identified the visitor from the moment he appeared on the screen. One of the best-known faces in the country, Nazzari had, by the time he shot this film in 1943, made some thirty-four films, several of which were huge successes. In a poll, held in 1939 and 1940 by the magazine *Cinema*, he emerged as by far the most popular male screen actor in Italy. With his handsome face and strong physique, not to mention the unswerving rectitude of his characters, he was the very incarnation of the popular screen hero. For some, he was a worthy local equivalent to Errol Flynn or Clark Gable. The failure on the part of some of the people in the hotel to recognise him immediately would have been, for the film's spectators, an improbable and therefore amusing situation.

What makes this film unusual is not Nazzari's charismatic presence, for this was a regular feature of many productions of the period, but the fact that the actor was, for the first but not the last time in his career, playing not a character but himself, or at least the public version of himself: Amedeo Nazzari, film star. Each of the personal details given in the hotel corresponds to the truth, except for one: Nazzari was not his real surname but a *nom d'art* that he adopted in place of his true one (he was born Amedeo Buffa in 1907). Nazzari's well-known and much-loved persona was signalled by the actor's familiar physiognomy, and also by the fact that he enters the scene dramatically and is illuminated more fully than anyone else. A series of close-ups give the audience chance to survey the eyes, smile and moustache that have been listed as his signature hallmarks.

Once Nazzari's film-star status is established beyond doubt within the diegesis of the film, he ceases altogether to be a private individual and becomes – in a comment on the nature of stardom – public property. The atmosphere of curiosity surrounding him turns first to excited reverence and then proprietorial control as the girls in the crowd of friends decide to harness his aura to stage another prank. Nazzari is dragooned into posing with Andreina as her groom. The 'wedding' shot of Andreina and Nazzari confirms the mutual attraction the two feel, which had manifested itself first in the seconds that followed the actor's appearance at the door. However, the brief idyll is disrupted by the sudden, belated entry of the real Franco, whose jealous displeasure is instantaneous. The rest of the film consists largely of Nazzari seeking to repair the damage he has unwittingly done by discouraging the attentions of the infatuated Andreina and persuading Franco that nothing improper was intended and that there is no reason his marriage should not take place as planned.

In the film, Nazzari is the star and Andreina, played by Alida Valli, is an ordinary, if beautiful, young woman who temporarily swoons in his presence. In this sense she acts as the conduit for feelings that the average filmgoer of her sex and approximate age might be expected to have. The paradox lies in the fact that Valli was herself barely less a star than Nazzari. Although aged only twenty-two in 1943, the year the film was made, she had already made twenty-four films and had played alongside Nazzari in three. She had established her popularity in a series of light comedies and consolidated it in costume dramas. Although she was a different sort of star to Nazzari – he was a heroic ideal figure who was seen as a sort of 'super-Italian', a screen embodiment of all the best qualities of the people, while she was closer to an idealised average: a typical middle-class girl distinguished only by her unusual beauty and vivacity – her celebrity at this time eclipsed that of all other female actors. When the official newsreel and documentary organisation, the Luce Institute, made a light-hearted film portrait of the Cinecittà studio complex in Rome, *Cinque minuti a Cinecittà* (Five Minutes at Cinecittà, c.1940), the two actors who were called on to briefly interrupt their work to greet the audience were Nazzari and Valli.

Films like *Apparizione* and *Cinque minuti a Cinecittà* do not by themselves tell us very much about the star culture of Fascist Italy. But they do establish that it existed. They show that there was a discourse about stardom and that stardom was seen to be an integral part of contemporary Italian cinema. Moreover, Italy could proudly boast its own stars, even if the self-referentiality of both films suggests an almost anxious self-promotion of Italian stardom. This reflected the climate of autarchy that obtained from the late 1930s and the awareness that Italian stars were in some measure stand-ins for the American stars whose films were no longer released into the Italian market after December 1938. On the other hand, the films show a degree of affection for home-grown talent that, according to most contemporary accounts and many subsequent ones, was real. Nazzari may in his career have been labelled an Italian Errol Flynn or Clark Gable, but he did not hail from the Olympus of Hollywood. As he spelled out in *Apparizione*, he was born in Cagliari, in Sardinia, and he lived in Rome. He was a local superman; half dream king, half man of the people. In the Italy of the time, the provinces dominated the cities and the star system reflected that. It was familiar and accessible, and its heroes and heroines seemed real rather than perfect.

Apparizione can be read as an unwitting final tribute to a star system that came to an end with the fall of Fascism. The film was barely finished in July 1943 when Mussolini fell and the director, a virtual unknown by the name of Jean de Limur, took flight. Like other films that were in production at the time, it could easily have finished up in a limbo. Instead, the negative was taken clandestinely from Cinecittà to safety, and the film was edited and completed for projection over the summer as circumstances permitted. Since no original exterior scenes had been shot, stock footage was inserted where necessary.[1] The film had a first release in the Nazi-occupied north of the country in February 1944, as bombardments were becoming a daily occurrence. After the war ended, with Italian cinema virtually inactive, it was released again in all major cities where it received an enthusiastic reception. The film received no official support when it was first proposed. Indeed, the General Directorate of Cinema found the theme so trivial and absurd that it discouraged its being shown in first-run cinemas. The positive audience reception it received was testimony to something the regime had encouraged but never been fully comfortable with, namely the popularity of the film stars. Although their creation had been thought necessary to the successful expansion of national cinema, they offered a reference point and role models that were in some measure beyond the control of the regime. In 1945 Nazzari and Valli were still surrounded by the aura that had been formed around them in the later Fascist period. However, the state-controlled film industry that had spawned them had ceased to exist, and their established images were on borrowed time. Neither had made a film since Mussolini's fall. Although their careers would resume and continue for three or more decades (and they would star together in three more films), they did not emerge unscathed into the postwar era. Both experienced setbacks and frustrations. To shake off the taint of having enjoyed fame under a repressive dictatorship would not prove to be an easy task.

* * *

What place did film stars occupy in Fascist Italy? On this vexed question there is no consensus. Historians of Fascism, who disagree over the extent to which the regime dominated society, have not paid very much attention to the mass media.[2] Stars, and actors and performers more generally, are ignored, suggesting that they are not considered at all significant. Historians of cinema have also for the most part paid little attention to them. Even Giulio Cesare Castello, who devoted a substantial book specifically to stars and stardom in 1957, and who was responsible for retrospectives of some of the work of Fascist-period stars on Italian television a few years later, dealt briefly with the Italian screen personalities of the late 1930s and early 1940s, granting them eleven pages at the start of a chapter concerned with the female stars of the 1950s.[3] In an article published in 1967, the sociologist Franco Rositi argued on the basis of an examination of the press of the interwar period that there had in fact been no star system since coverage was minimal.[4] In more recent decades, this outlook has changed, among film historians at least. Gian Piero Brunetta's monumental histories of Italian cinema bear witness to changing perceptions of the matter. His volume *Storia del cinema italiano 1895–1945*, first published in 1979, dealt with the stardom of the silent era but was dismissive of that of the 1930s. Referring to the appeal of American cinema, he wrote that the star phenomenon, 'in the absence of a strong Italian star system', had less impact on the popular masses than on the lower middle classes 'whose desires it fuelled, becoming the main vehicle for the expression of repressed thoughts and aspirations'.[5] He further observed that Italian stars were too modest 'to replace, at a popular level, the glamour of the great American stars and the mythology that the culture industry created around their lives. The Italian star system remained provincial in nature and was hampered by the way in which the film industry was run'.[6]

Twelve years later, in *Cent'anni del cinema italiano*, Brunetta dedicated a chapter to what he called the 'Divi in camicia nera' (Stars in blackshirts). Here, he wrote that the success of some comic actors had 'a propulsive effect in terms of the take-off of the entire national star system'.[7] He hailed Nazzari as 'captain and guide' of 'an ideal team [of stars] to counterpose to those of American cinema'.[8] Valli, for her part, was deemed to have 'won over the audiences of the whole of Italy' in light comedies before obtaining 'a striking personal success' in the dramas *Noi vivi* (We the Living) and *Addio Kira* (both by Goffredo Alessandrini, 1942). Soon, she was giving 'ample proof of her maturity and of her personality' in dramatic period roles.[9]

What can have induced Italy's leading film historian to have decided that the Fascist star system was now worthy of attention? One important factor is likely to have been the growing body of scholarly and journalistic work undertaken in the intervening period on the actors of the interwar period. Important contributions to the understanding of their role included the interviews with old stars conducted by Francesco Savio that evoked the world of Cinecittà in the 1930s and the testimonies published in Franca Faldini and Goffredo Fofi's oral history of Italian cinema.[10] The more general re-evaluation of the cinema of the Fascist period that began with Adriano Aprà and Patrizia Pistagnesi's *I favolosi anni trenta, 1929–1944* and which continued through other published works, as well as revisitations at festivals and television revivals, also probably had an effect.[11] In explicit polemic with those who dismissed more or less en bloc in the postwar years the products of the Fascist era, critics began to explore the films with fresh eyes. As Aprà and Pistagnesi put it, the impact of this revision was 'explosive', in that it showed 'Fascist cinema' was 'different and above all more complex than what might be called traditional historiography had led us to suppose'.[12]

Despite the acknowledgement the stars received as part of this revision, and the space given to them by Brunetta in his 2001 volume, scholarly attention to fame and celebrity in the Fascist period remains very limited. By far the majority of publications on this theme are of a journalistic nature. The most significant are the works issued by the Roman publisher Gremese dedicated to the careers of single actors, a number of whom began their careers in the Fascist period, and the encyclopaedic *Stelle d'Italia* by Stefano Masi and Enrico Lancia, which categorises and profiles all the female actors of the 1930–1945 period. To these may be added the mainly anecdotal books by Massimo Scaglione on the female and male stars.[13] Serious interpretative studies of groups of actors or of the star system remain absent, although studies have appeared of Vittorio De Sica, Clara Calamai, Roberto Villa and Amedeo Nazzari, while Alida Valli has been the subject of two biographies.[14] The most extensive coverage is offered by chapter length treatments in Brunetta and a chapter by Tullio Kezich in volume five of the Centro Sperimentale di Cinematografia's authoritative *Storia del cinema italiano*, as well as some contributions to volume six.[15]

Although it was unusual in Italy as elsewhere in the 1970s and 1980s for a scholar of cinema to address questions of stardom, this was less the case in the English-speaking world, where Richard Dyer's seminal work opened a whole field of study.[16] However, none of this affected the study of Fascist cinema, which was explored most systematically by James Hay in *Popular Film Culture in Fascist Italy*, and Marcia Landy in *Fascism in Film: The Italian Commercial Cinema, 1931–1943* and *The Folklore of Consensus: Theatricality in the Italian Cinema, 1930–1943*.[17] Not one of these works deals with the matter of stardom, although some issues relating to gender representation and, to a lesser extent, screen performance are addressed.[18] Nor, for that matter, is it tackled in an illuminating more recent study, Steven Ricci's *Cinema & Fascism: Italian Film and Society, 1922–1943*.[19] Stardom is ostensibly the subject of Landy's most recent text, *Stardom Italian Style: Screen Performance and Personality in Italian Cinema*.[20] However, the one chapter on the Fascist era deals with a range of directors and actors, identifies the star personae of the latter, and explores the way they are constructed and embedded in film texts. What is entirely missing is a wider sense of the phenomenon of stardom as a social practice. How was the public engaged by the stars? What forms of fandom emerged? What were the lifestyles of the stars and how did they relate to the regime?

In some of my previous writings, I have tried to begin to address these questions.[21] However, I have not had the space before now to devote more than a chapter to them. The aim of this book is to offer a more thorough and complete analysis of the phenomenon of film stardom in Fascist Italy. My intention is to explore especially those aspects that have hitherto received very limited treatment either in Italian or in English. These include: the relation between stardom and consumption, the popular reception of stars, their lifestyles and public images, the degree of engagement of different stars with the regime, the aftermath of Fascist cinema in terms of stardom, and the place of the stars in popular memory. Film texts are analysed in the book, while attention is also paid to the stars as social actors in a particular political and economic context.

My intention is to make a contribution to the historiography of Italian cinema but also, more widely, to Italian cultural history and to the historiography of Fascism. Achieving this necessitates the development of a perspective that is wider than most treatments of Italian stardom of any period and an engagement with the literature on Fascism and its legacies. It is striking that most historians of Fascism omit works of film history from their bibliographies while students of cinema whose focus is on film texts typically ignore the many historical works that have illuminated the Fascist period. Ruth Ben-Ghiat is one of very few historians who have sought to bridge this gap.[22] This book, it is hoped, will further foster a necessary encounter that hitherto has been largely lacking.

One key historiographical issue on which the study of stars may shed light concerns the supposedly totalitarian nature of Mussolini's regime. Once widely discounted as a way of interpreting Fascism, mainly on account of the latter's coexistence with the Church and the monarchy, this has been revived in recent times by Emilio Gentile and those who embrace his concept of Fascism as a political religion.[23] It has been disputed by historians including Richard Bosworth, and David Forgacs and myself,[24] who are more inclined to identify the presence alongside and even within Fascism of practices and processes that had little or nothing to do with Fascism itself. The present volume is intended to provide a close analysis of one of those areas where the regime sought to shape and control choices and decisions in order to harness a potential source of influence to its political project. But it did so in a context in which film production, distribution and exhibition were largely in private hands, and in which various commercial actors including magazine and book publishers, advertisers and record companies sought to use stardom for their own ends. Thus in its aim it encountered both cooperation and various sorts of resistance from commercial organisations, directors, actors, the press and the public.[25] It is well established in the field of star studies that spectators can read stars in many different ways and use them to articulate forms of resistance to dominant ideologies.[26] Opportunities for such readings may be limited under dictatorships but, on the other hand, a repressive atmosphere can turn stars into vehicles for secret or inexpressible aspirations. By studying closely this conflict between control and impulses of a different nature, it is possible to establish the extent to which film stardom was effectively incorporated into the system of social relations that directly or indirectly sustained the regime.

* * *

The first part of the book explores the way in which cinema featured in the politics and culture of the Fascist period. The emphasis is placed on the sound era, that is to say the period in which the state began to take a systematic interest in the film industry and serious efforts were made to increase production and attract public interest to it. In the 1920s, after the collapse of the industry that produced great silent divas and a few popular male stars, film stardom was largely an imported phenomenon. The Italian reception of the American stars of the post-First World War era is a key precursor to the emergence of domestic stars in the years that followed, but its basic coordinates are simple to establish and, in any case, Italian stars continued to compete with the Americans throughout the 1930s. The creation of a domestic star system, it will be shown, was the result of a variety of different political, economic and social impulses. Fascists were inconsistent in their approach, with some viewing stars as negative and others seeing them as crucial to the success of national cinema as commerce and as propaganda. Luigi Freddi, the most important single Fascist official in the area of cinema, disliked stars and rejected the need for them. He spoke instead of the need for a 'choral ethic' in Italian cinema.[27] Yet as the director of the state production company Cines in the 1940s, he placed many of the best-known names under contract and boasted about this in his memoirs.[28] Two key, and often neglected, factors in the development of domestic stars were commercial culture and the public. Each of these is examined in separate chapters.

The second part of the book is devoted to close analysis of the careers of six stars and one would-be star. The intention here is to examine the screen work of some of those who were acknowledged publicly as having star status; it is also to explore the critical reception their work received, their popular images, their political significance and the cultural meanings that were associated with them.

Isa Miranda was the only genuinely international star of the period. After making an important film in Italy with the Austrian director Max Ophuls, she appeared in French and German, as well as Italian, films before migrating to Hollywood in 1937 as a replacement for Marlene Dietrich. Her return two years later was marked by obstructionism on the part of those who disliked her independence of view and of action. Yet thanks to her early fame and international profile, Miranda probably exercised more agency than any other actor of the era.

Vittorio De Sica was the first new male star of the 1930s. If Mussolini can be said to have occupied the cultural realm of male stardom in the 1920s, thus retarding the process of forming new cinema stars in Italy,[29] the emergence of the charming, easy-going everyman De Sica suggested that various models of masculinity were possible under the consolidated regime. Fascism nonetheless sought to steer the development of male role models and to different degrees the rugged Amedeo Nazzari and the more cerebral Fosco Giachetti incarnated gender ideals that dovetailed with the dominant ideology without being entirely reducible to it. Their popularity stands as testimony to the regime's capacity to make its values resonate in popular culture.

Assia Noris, a Russian-born actress who starred in light comedies and costume dramas alongside all the leading male stars, was the top female star in the later 1930s. Often dubbed an ingénue, her smiling blonde persona was rarely fully submissive, even though ultimately it was never deployed to challenge dominant ideas about young women. It was the busy vivacity of many of her characters as much as their basic sentimentality that contributed to her success. Alida Valli was a more versatile actress and her characters, while sometimes breezy and charming, were often complex and melancholic. She made her name in comedy but soon also flourished in drama and melodrama. When the regime ended, she was at the peak of her fame, a national favourite whose modern personal style was widely imitated.

The would-be star included in this section is Miria di San Servolo, otherwise known as Myriam Petacci, the younger sister of Mussolini's lover Claretta. Her place in cinema is not important and only two of her films had been released by the time the regime fell. But she deserves more space than she is conventionally given precisely because the plan of the Petacci family, which Mussolini is likely to have personally endorsed, was to turn her into an overnight star. This did not happen, but as an experiment in star manufacture under Fascism her case is interesting not least because it relates to the issue, important in the controversy over totalitarianism, of how far stars could be manufactured from above. It may be argued that the debut of San Servolo, in 1942, came too late to bear on this, but it is the only case in interwar Europe of a dictator encouraging the creation of a star. It can be compared to other instances of actresses whose careers prospered thanks to the support of important figures in the regime. As far as Mussolini was concerned, he never expressed personal preferences among the stars (although his predilection for Greta Garbo is known) and only very rarely commented, in private, on single actors.[30]

The above list is not exhaustive. There are some actors who will be referred to in the book but who do not receive a dedicated chapter. These include some figures who have good claims to be treated as stars on account of the quantity and quality of their work, the leading roles they played, the popularity they enjoyed and the distinctiveness of their images. For example, Elsa Merlini, Clara Calamai, Luisa Ferida, Gino Cervi, Osvaldo Valenti, Doris Duranti, Massimo Girotti, Maria Denis and Roberto Villa can all be considered stars. In addition, the comics Macario, Totò, Renato Rascel and Aldo Fabrizi all brought the fame they had acquired on the stages of the peninsula to the screen. Some authors have extended the list far wider. Scaglione estimates that up to thirty actors could be said to have had star status, while Stefano Masi and Enrico Lancia, who consider only women, dedicate profiles to no fewer than 142 actresses, plus seven names from the silent era and sundry others whose appearances were too fleeting to merit more than a brief mention. Those featured are divided into several categories (for example, 'The four musketeeers of the regime', 'Fiancées of the Italians', 'Full-figured stars' and 'Stars in blackshirts') and are ranked in rough order of importance. But the application of the term *stelle* to all suggests a very loose idea of stardom that can be applied to more or less everyone who appeared on screen in anything more than a background role. I prefer a more restrictive notion of what a star is, that is related, first, to occupation of an acquired position of prominence in the film industry (established by levels of activity and earnings, box office success of films, the degree of agency exercised and so on) and, second, to Dyer's idea of 'structured polysemy', that is to say the way a star signifies.[31] Dyer was concerned to establish *how* this occurs, by arguing that the many meanings a star may have are contained by boundaries of gender, race, age, context and cultural contingency. What they signify in terms of individual identities is determined by their own characteristics as well as by the way their identities interact with the identities of other stars and with a particular historical situation. But it needs to be stressed that only actors of a certain standing and visibility can function in this way. Others may be good actors or known names but their cultural power is more limited.

The issue in Italy is confused somewhat by the fact that many commentators at the time, and some scholars today, regard the Italian star system as an ersatz one. In other words, actors were made to look like stars (and sometimes were chosen on the basis of a physical resemblance to an established name) and magazines treated them like they had treated Hollywood stars, but fundamentally they had limited resonance and no depth. Thus there was little to distinguish leading actors from supporting players. If this is true, then a loose application of the term 'star' may be justified. But, in my view, this is not the case. While it can be acknowledged that the star system, when compared to the American or even the French or German ones, was less systematically publicity-driven, due to the absence of large studios, and was less integral to the media system, there is ample evidence to suggest that at least some stars functioned in ways that are comparable to their foreign counterparts. Although mass culture was not fully developed, Italy's star system, influenced as it was by the Hollywood one and by the particular circumstances of the Fascist regime, was the product of a society in which forms of mass consumption and mediated experience were acquiring a significant place.[32]

The third and final part of the book is concerned with the fate of the stars of the Fascist period after the war. In contrast to Germany, few of the films in which they featured survived well into the postwar era. In West Germany, numerous Nazi-era films were exhibited or were broadcast on television from the 1950s. In some cases, they were regarded with great affection as national classics. Their lack of obvious propaganda traits was taken as a sign that they had nothing to do with Nazism. Even a critic like Eric Rentschler, who disputes this view, admits that 'Nazi film was traditional through and through'.[33] In Italy, the postwar rejection of the cinema of the Fascist era on the part of many within the film community and a significant portion of the public meant that many films disappeared (some of them to be lost forever). Only a handful, notably war films, were re-released after the late 1940s.

Many stars simply disappeared along with their films. Those who continued to work did so in second-rate productions or supporting roles. While German stars continued to act and enjoy public favour, despite their role in the entertainment apparatus of the Nazi state, their Italian equivalents, with just a few notable exceptions, struggled to find a place. This was a curious situation because in other respects the Fascist era was far more present in postwar Italy than the Nazi era was in the new state of the Federal Republic of Germany. There was a neo-Fascist political presence in parliament, the Mussolini family still aroused interest, the weekly press was filled with barely concealed nostalgia for aspects of life under the regime, and the built environment continued to bear ample traces of Fascism's determination to reshape Italian towns and cities. The film world itself was full of men who had begun their careers under the regime and who had in some cases actively supported it.

This situation can be explained in part by the fact that German cinema was already well established when Hitler came to power. No one could say that German cinema was a creation of the Nazis, even if emigration and Goebbels' interventions significantly reshaped it, whereas the resurrection of Italian cinema in the 1930s occurred entirely as a result of the active role played by the Fascist state. Thus the films of the period, even the most innocuous of comedies of manners, were all seen as being tarred with the brush of the regime. As the most visible face of cinema, and as individuals who had been pampered under the regime, the stars paid a price that very few directors and no producers did. In West Germany, the stars were one of few aspects of public life that provided a comfortable continuity in a situation in which not even the state survived intact. In Italy they were scapegoats; they were sacrificed along with many high officials (Freddi being the most prominent in the area of cinema) so that others could enter the new era without being held to account for their activity under Mussolini. The execution by partisans in April 1945 of Osvaldo Valenti and Luisa Ferida, two actors who threw in their lot with the Nazi-occupied puppet regime of the Italian Social Republic and frequented some its worst elements, was not sufficient sacrifice to permit others to live on professionally. Their execution was in large part a consequence of their fame. It was a demonstration that stars could, and in some cases would, be held personally and politically responsible for providing the regime with a deceptively attractive and engaging face.

This is not to say that the stars had no postwar life. The picture in fact is quite complex, and distinctions need to be drawn between the films and stars, and between actors who sought to shed or reconfigure their established star image, or were given opportunities to do so by directors, and those who hoped to continue to exploit a given image in a new context. The period between 1943 and 1947, when a much reduced number of films were produced, saw many exit the film industry. A few were able to find work abroad, a lucky handful in Hollywood. Nonetheless, in spite of the bracing wind of neorealism, there was a measure of continuity in the star system up to around 1950. After that time, new faces emerged who would lend a distinctive cinematic face to the postwar republic, and just three or four names from the previous era (notably Nazzari and Valli, but also De Sica and Gino Cervi) would continue to enjoy a following.

Although their lives would not always be easy, most of the once prominent actors did still enjoy some of the afterglow of fame. Their names meant little or nothing to younger generations of filmgoers, but illustrated magazines ran articles about them from time to time and a minor industry grew around their memoirs, autobiographies and biographies. A few forgotten films were shown on television in the 1960s and 1970s while others were revived in festivals and then entered wider circulation with their release on VHS. From the 1980s a wider range of titles were broadcast on both state and private television channels, mainly late at night or in the early morning, fuelling the fond memories of older spectators.

In later decades one-time stars were always assured of a warm reception at festivals, while stalls at antique and collectors' markets could always be guaranteed to have old magazines with their cover pictures as well as postcards and photographs. Their position in popular memory gradually became detached from the specificity of the Fascist dictatorship and was instead wrapped in nostalgia for a time when little was innocent – and perhaps least of all the madcap comedies and tear-jerking melodramas in which they starred – but much seemed certain and uncomplicated.

The final chapter explores these matters and considers three films made between the 1970s and the 2000s which evoke the film industry of the Fascist period and its stars. These are Dino Risi s Italian-style comedy *Telefoni bianchi* (White Telephones, 1976), Tinto Brass's meta-cinematic *Senso '45* (aka Black Angel, 2002), which transports the plot of Visconti's Risorgimento melodrama *Senso* (1954) (and above all of Camillo Boito's novella on which it was based) to Nazi-occupied Venice and the film world of Mussolini's doomed republic, and *Sanguepazzo* (Marco Tullio Giordana, 2009). The last film dramatises the rise and fall of Valenti and Ferida from their heyday in Rome to their squalid execution in Milan at the end of the war. In doing so, it restored them to their position as two of the most intriguing personalities of a cinema whose place in collective memory continued in some respects to be controversial.

Notes

1. For a detailed account of these events, see L. Freddi. 1949. *Il cinema*, Rome: L'Arnia, 490–91.
2. For many years, the only book on the media by a historian was P.V. Cannistraro. 1975. *La fabbrica del consenso: fascismo e mass media*, Rome–Bari: Laterza, a volume that, despite its author being an American, was never published in English.
3. G.C. Castello. 1957. *Il Divismo: mitologia del cinema*, Turin: ERI, 401–12.
4. F. Rositi. 1967. 'Personalità e divismo in Italia durante il periodo fascista', *IKON* 17: 62, 9–48.
5. G.P. Brunetta. 1979. *Storia del cinema italiano 1895–1945*, Rome: Editori Riuniti, 411.
6. Ibid., 482.
7. G.P. Brunetta. 1991. *Cent'anni di cinema italiano*, Rome–Bari: Laterza, 209.
8. Ibid., 212.
9. Ibid., 212.
10. F. Savio. 1979. *Cinecittà anni trenta*, Rome: Bulzoni; F. Faldini and G. Fofi (eds). 1979. *L'avventurosa storia del cinema italiano: raccontato dai suoi protagonisti, 1935–1959*, Milan: Feltrinelli.
11. Savio, *Cinecittà anni trenta*; Faldini and Fofi, *L'avventurosa storia del cinema italiano*; A. Aprà and P. Pistagnesi. 1979. *I favolosi anni trenta, 1929–1944*, Milan: Electa.
12. Aprà and Pistagnesi, *I favolosi anni trenta*, 28.

13. S. Masi and E. Lancia. 1994. *Stelle d'Italia: piccole e grandi dive del cinema italiano dal 1930 al 1945*, Rome: Gremese; M. Scaglione. 2003. *Le dive del Ventennio*, Turin: Lindau; and M. Scaglione. 2005. *I divi del Ventennio*, Turin: Lindau.
14. F. Bolzoni. 1984. *Quando De Sica era Mister Brown*, Turin: ERI; I. Moscati (ed.). 1996. *Clara Calamai: l'ossessione di essere diva*, Venice: Marsilio; G. Gubitosi. 1998. *Amedeo Nazzari*, Bologna: Il Mulino; S. Micheli. 1996. *Roberto Villa: attore e divo*, Florence: Manent; L. Pellizzari and C. Valentinetti. 1995. *Il romanzo di Alida Valli*, Milan: Garzanti; N. Falcinella. 2011. *Alida Valli: gli occhi, la bocca*, Genoa: Le Mani.
15. T. Kezich. 2006. 'Gli attori italiani dalla preistoria del divismo al monopolio' in O. Caldiron (ed.), *Storia del cinema italiano*, Vol. 5, 1934–39, Venice–Rome: Marsilio/Bianco & Nero, 383–403. See also chapters by Patrizia Pistagnesi and Bruno Di Marino respectively on male and female actors, and by Ernesto G. Laura on Alida Valli, in E.G. Laura and A. Baldi (eds). 2010. *Storia del cinema italiano*, Vol. 6, 1940–44, Venice–Rome: Marsilio/Biano & Nero.
16. R. Dyer. 1979. *Stars*, London: BFI.
17. Hay's book was published by Indiana University Press in 1987, Landy's respectively by Princeton University Press in 1986 and by State University of New York Press in 1998. Also of interest is E. Mancini. 1985. *Struggles of the Italian Film Industry during Fascism, 1930–1935*, Ann Arbor: UMI Research Press.
18. In *Fascism in Film*, Landy devotes one and a half pages to stars, despite admitting that from 1938 'Italian films increasingly became star vehicles', 20.
19. University of California Press, 2008.
20. Indiana University Press, 2008.
21. S. Gundle. 2002. 'Film Stars and Society in Fascist Italy' in J. Reich and P. Garofalo (eds), *Re-Viewing Fascism: Italian Cinema, 1922–1943*, Bloomington: Indiana University Press, 2005, 315–40. 'Divismo' in V. De Grazia and S. Luzzatto, *Dizionario del fascismo*, Turin: Einaudi, 439–42. Part of Chapter 5 of D. Forgacs and S. Gundle. 2007. *Mass Culture and Italian Society from Fascism to the Cold War*, Bloomington: Indiana University Press, 158–62.
22. R. Ben-Ghiat. 2001. *Fascist Modernities: Italy 1922–1945*, Berkeley: University of California Press.
23. Emilio Gentile's key writings on this theme are collected in *Fascismo: storia e interpretazioni*, Rome–Bari: Laterza, 2002.
24. R.J.B. Bosworth. 2005. *Mussolini's Italy: Life Under the Dictatorship, 1915–1945*, London: Allen Lane; Forgacs and Gundle, *Mass Culture and Italian Society*.
25. The history of Mussolini's own image and the uses to which it was put is bound up with the tensions inherent in this situation. See Gundle. 2008. 'Un Martini per il Duce: l'immaginario del consumismo in Italia negli anni Venti e Trenta' in A. Villari (ed.), *L'arte della pubblicità: il manifesto italiano e le avanguardie 1920–1940*, Milan: Silvana, 46–69.

26. Dyer, *Stars*, 18–22.
27. Freddi, *Il cinema*, 76.
28. Ibid., 395.
29. G.P. Brunetta. 1999. 'Divismo, misticismo e spettacolo della politica' in Brunetta (ed.), *Storia del cinema mondiale, L'Europa*, Vol. 1, *Miti, luoghi, divi*, Turin: Einaudi, 535–42.
30. Freddi, *Il cinema*, 392.
31. Dyer, *Stars*, 63. For a wider reflection on stars and 'sense-making', see P.D. Marshall. 1997. *Celebrity and Power: Fame in Contemporary Culture*, Minneapolis: University of Minnesota Press.
32. On this process, see Forgacs and Gundle, *Mass Culture and Italian Society*.
33. E. Rentschler. 1996. *The Ministry of Illusion: Nazi Cinema and Its Afterlife*, Cambridge, MA: Harvard University Press, 11.

PART I

Fascism, Cinema and Stardom

1

Italian Cinema under Fascism

On the morning of 29 January 1936, Mussolini travelled by car from his office at Palazzo Venezia to the outlying Quadraro district of Rome. The purpose of the trip was to lay the foundation stone of what would become the largest studio complex in Europe, eclipsing even the German UFA studios in Berlin.[1] The dictator liked to be associated with ambitious projects and his presence at the start of the process of construction of the planned new 'city of cinema' was carefully stage-managed. Mussolini performed the ceremony surrounded by senior officials including the director general for cinema Luigi Freddi and the Foreign Minister Galeazzo Ciano, as well as the president of the Cines company (and member of parliament) Carlo Roncoroni, and others. All the key participants were attired in Fascist uniform. Lining the path leading to the site of the laying of the stone on the Via Tuscolana were soldiers, young members of the Balilla organisation and representatives of other Fascist organisations. A large temporary wall behind them had been painted with the slogan that the Duce had appropriated from Lenin: 'Cinema is the most powerful weapon'. Atop the wall, the labourers who would build the city of cinema cheered and waved their spades high. Engaged on double pay, they were expected to work fast to complete the new complex in short order. Towering over them was a large cut-out image of Mussolini operating a movie camera. Although the Duce was more accustomed to posing in front of the camera rather than working behind it, the suggestion was that the regime would from now on be an active player in determining what Italians would see on their movie screens.

After years of crisis and tentative attempts to revive Italian cinema following its virtual collapse in the 1920s, finally the regime took the industry firmly in hand with the intention of establishing it on solid bases and harnessing it to its project of national development. The decision to create what would become known as Cinecittà was taken following a series of measures to develop institutions and measures to support cinema. Among those who had promoted these from at least the early 1930s were Giuseppe Bottai, the Minister of Corporations, Freddi, the director Alessandro Blasetti, and other film professionals. Before 1934 there were no state bodies responsible for propaganda in areas such as film, radio, theatre and literature.[2] However, in that year the press office of the prime minister was expanded and turned by Ciano, who headed it, into an under-secretariat for press and propaganda that was divided into directorates dealing with the domestic and foreign press. Directorates for cinema and tourism were added later that year, with an inspectorate for theatre being created several months after that. Subsequently, the under-secretariat was turned into the Ministry of Press and Propaganda. Under the direction of Dino Alfieri, this would be renamed the Ministry of Popular Culture in 1937.

Discussion about the possible construction of a film studio complex had not originally been seen as integral to these developments. Indeed, in the end, the commitment of vast sums of money, 'tens of millions' according to Blasetti,[3] occurred quickly. The event that precipitated this move was the fire that one night in September 1935 destroyed the four Roman studios of Cines, the largest production company in Italy. Dramatically reported by the newsreels of the Luce Institute, the fire was a deadly blow to the fragile structures of the Italian film industry. Virtually all the Italian films of any value that had been released in the sound era had been made in the Cines studios, which had been inaugurated in 1930. Freddi was the first to realise the need for a strategic response, and it was on his initiative that the first plans were drawn up for the modern studio complex he had dreamed of for Italy since he was invited to conduct a fact-finding visit to Hollywood. For the man who would be most responsible for developing and implementing the regime's priorities in relation to cinema,[4] it was essential that the state take an active and guiding role in promoting film production. A precondition of this was ensuring that facilities of sufficient quality and technical sophistication existed for films worthy of the Fascist era to be made.

Shortly after work officially began on Cinecittà, further foundation stones were laid. One of these was for the new buildings of the state-owned photography and newsreel service, the Luce Institute, which were located within the grounds of Cinecittà. The second, on the other side of the Via Tuscolana, was for the permanent home of Centro sperimentale di cinematografia (Experimental Film Centre), the official school for training actors, directors and technical personnel. Headed by Luigi Chiarini, the Centro had been in existence since 1935 but had been occupying unsuitable facilities.

The location of these institutions in close proximity to each other and scarcely a stone's throw from the centre of power (eighteen minutes by car from Termini station), in addition to the scale of investment in them, was proof of the regime's systematic involvement in a medium that until the early 1930s had not been deemed worthy of much attention. One factor in the radical change of attitude was the example offered by Nazi Germany's swift centralisation of all propaganda functions in a single ministry. This was a manifestation of an 'organic and totalitarian' approach that, the Nazis boasted, would now mark state policy. But it was also a sign of the developing perception that the expansion of cinema as a leisure activity and the cultural specificity of the medium in the sound era presented challenges that Fascism could not ignore. A regime that was concerned with the inculcation of an aggressive nationalist spirit in the population and with the promotion abroad of the idea that Italy would once again be a beacon of Western civilisation was compelled to face several issues. Among these were the role of cinema in spreading knowledge of the national past and cultural heritage, the contribution it could make to building a sense of national belonging through the spread of images of places, faces and customs, and its potentially controversial part in expanding familiarity with foreign cultures. The place of stars in this was not limited to one aspect, since, as bearers of a range of possible ideas and notions going from the nation to gender, or even simply how to speak, walk and dress, they could function in different ways. The question of stars will be tackled in the chapters that follow while, in this chapter, some broader issues about the nature of cinema in the Fascist period will be addressed.

The Role of the State

Fascists were accustomed to marking the birth of Rome on 21 April with the sort of pomp and ceremony that had become the regime's hallmark. That the creation of Cinecittà was seen from the start as an imperial project was evident from the fact that this very date was chosen to inaugurate the studio complex. The laying of the foundation stone had already proclaimed that the studios were being built 'so that Fascist Italy will spread more rapidly in the world the civilisation of Rome', as one of the first promotional posters announced. Just fifteen months later Cinecittà was completed. The speed of the work can be gauged by the fact that the Centro sperimentale – a much smaller project – was not ready until January 1940. In the end, Mussolini was unable to perform the inauguration until the end of April due to days of torrential rain. Even on 28 April, the appointed day, it rained in the morning leading to fears of a further postponement. Suddenly, at midday, the rain stopped and the clouds cleared, giving way to radiant sunshine. At 5.00 p.m. Mussolini arrived accompanied by party secretary Achille Starace, the president of the Luce Institute Giacomo Paulucci de Calboli Barone, Roncoroni and Freddi. There to greet them were the Duce's film-mad son

Vittorio, the technicians and officials who had created the complex, including the architect Gino Peressutti, and numerous members of a variety of Fascist organisations who, with their presence, turned the square in front of the main buildings into a parade ground. Mussolini spent several hours at the studios and witnessed work on *Scipione l'Africano* (Scipio the African, Carmine Gallone, 1937), a propaganda blockbuster set in imperial Rome that the government itself had financed since its theme of African conquest dovetailed with its own policy. Among the other films whose making he witnessed were the light comedy *Il feroce saladino* (The Ferocious Saladin, Mario Bonnard, 1937), starring the Sicilian comic Angelo Musco and a young starlet named Alida Valli. Far from being a propaganda project, this film was inspired by a craze for collecting illustrated cards set off by a radio comedy sponsored by the Perugina and Balilla companies.[5] Among the characters featured on the cards were the three musketeers and the 'ferocious Saladin' who gave the film its title. The contrast between the two films could hardly have been greater and the fact that Mussolini happily saw both attests to the variety of impulses and purposes that governed the Fascist approach to cinema.

Blasetti was among those who had called for a major investment and he was not disappointed. 'Freddi, Roncoroni and Peressuti, the three main executors of the order of the Duce that has given us Cinecittà, point of departure of decisive value to begin to work seriously, could not have beaten all the records they have beaten if they had not been able to spend millions without hesitation, millions as long as necessary', he noted.[6] The project was informed by Freddi's studies of the layout of Hollywood studios and Peressutti's own ideas, formed during a tour in November 1936 of the major European studios. Mussolini's own involvement in the project was considerable. Although he had never previously expressed much interest in cinema, he followed progress closely, calling in Peressutti for briefings on numerous occasions. The studio complex would become the jewel in Fascism's crown. Constructed in record time, it was a true city that included its own medical and postal services, fire station, restaurants, dwellings for portering staff, sports facilities, rest and recreational areas for actors and technical personnel, greenhouses and library. A new tram line, soon dubbed 'the train of the stars' even though it was mainly used by production crew, was established linking Rome's Termini station to the studios. In just thirty-five minutes it was possible to reach Rome's new Mecca of cinema by public transport.

'"Nothing has been spared" is the phrase that was heard most often on the day of the inauguration', Blasetti wrote. 'Nothing must be spared' should now be the watchword, he added, to ensure that film production quality improved. He warned that, if corners were cut, then 'in a couple of years, this prodigious Cinecittà will be seen as the most guilty effort of Sisifus of world cinema and will become simply an annexe of the nearby airfield'.[7] In fact, he need not have worried since government interventions to support production would be substantial and consistent. Soon, around half of all films made in Italy would use the new complex. Cinecittà saw the making of fourteen films in 1937, twenty-three the following year, twenty-nine in 1939, forty-six in 1940, fifty-two in 1941 and forty-four in 1942.[8] This expansion ensured that film-making, which had once been dispersed among Italy's major cities, became an almost exclusively Roman phenomenon. As production in Turin, Naples and other cities declined, the capital had become a magnet for technicians, writers and artisans. This trend was now confirmed. The intervention of the state created opportunities that were to prove important in extending patronage and thus the pattern of consensus around the regime. In his novel *Le due città*, Mario Soldati, a writer who would become a screenwriter and director, described how many of those who had once been convinced socialists or communists in Turin developed an attachment to Fascism out of a simple sense of gratitude: it was not right, they thought, as they settled into life in the capital whose development the regime was promoting, to 'spit in the plate from which they were eating'.[9] Numerous foreign dignitaries and film personalities were given tours of Cinecittà when they visited Rome and most of them were lavish in their praise. Frank Capra claimed the Columbia studios in Los Angeles were far inferior, while actors like Mary Pickford and Eddie Cantor were no less fulsome in their tributes. For Pickford, 'the city of cinema permits any type of production including the most ambitious, that which needs the most complete equipment. The Italians, as excellent builders, have outdone themselves'.[10]

The opening of the city of cinema marked the culmination of all the various measures that had been undertaken to support the national film industry and turn it into a tool for the enhancement of Italian greatness at home and abroad. Although steps had been taken in the 1920s, notably the founding of the Luce Institute, some bolstering of censorship and the creation of a para-governmental body to regulate distribution, the regime cannot be said to have had a policy on cinema before 1930. The advent of sound cinema raised issues of language and culture that had not existed, or had not caused concern, previously. For a regime that was seeking to shape the mentality of the population in line with its political project, the consumption of foreign-made sound films was an issue that had economic, political and cultural implications. The export of profits weighed heavily on the balance of payments, while constant exposure to foreign images and values risked undermining the efforts of the regime in areas such as custom reform. Fascists believed in the idea of Italian genius and they thought that national cultural expressions should be fostered and promoted abroad. As elsewhere in Europe, protectionism was one aspect of the game. But it was by no means the only one. The creation of the directorate of cinema was a sign that the state would become an active player in determining how the film industry would develop. Freddi argued that it had every right to directly influence 'this formidable social weapon that finds a parallel only in the press'.[11]

Many senior Fascists thought that cinema should be a focus of industrial policy; Freddi and others thought of it also in terms of cultural policy. From this point of view, it was not simply a matter of creating a system of support for private enterprise since the mentality of those involved in the business of cinema was dominated by 'commercial speculation'.[12] Italian production, in his view, was 'poor in content, immersed in artificial settings and atmospheres, devoid of any element of thought or originality, distant from life and from the reconstructive reawakening of contemporary Italy as well as from the spirit, taste, ideas and faith of our people'.[13] As Blasetti noted, most of the 'few little films' with low costs that went into production stood little chance against a Metro-Goldwyn-Mayer product or a London film; to screen them alongside such competition was like 'attacking a brigade with a battalion or offering just potatoes and beans at a formal lunch'.[14] Sustained intervention was needed to raise the average costs of production and promote quality.

For Blasetti, the support given by Freddi's directorate to a series of military and imperial films including *Cavalleria* (Cavalry, Goffredo Alessandrini, 1936), *Lo squadrone bianco* (The White Squadron, Augusto Genina, 1936) and *Il grande appello* (The Great Appeal, Mario Camerini, 1936) was a significant step in the right direction. Government action had raised budgets and ensured the making of films of 'national utility'. However, he lamented the 'enormous efforts' that had been necessary, including 'disproportionate and unnerving work' by the directorate itself and film directors to persuade reluctant industrialists to embark on making these films.[15] A keen believer in state action, Freddi expected that the opening of Cinecittà would make it easier for such films to be made. It meant that, at least some of the time, fiction films would be made to contribute to the cultural policy of the regime. The direct financing of two films, *Scipione l'Africano* and *Condottieri* (Luis Trenker), both of which would be released in 1937, suggested that propaganda would be one of the priorities of Cinecittà. Like the former film, *Condottieri* established its hero as a precursor of Mussolini. In this case, this was not the Roman general Scipio but the warrior-prince Giovanni de' Medici who, in the guise of Giovanni of the black bands, conducted a campaign in support of a unified Italy. Made with means that only official backing could bring, both films explicitly mobilised history to justify and legitimate the actions of the regime.

Does all this mean that Italian Fascism, like Nazism, was 'a totalitarian government that employed film as the most important vehicle in its media dictatorship, as a psychotechnology designed to channel the flow of impressions and information'?[16] For Eric Rentschler, the Nazis attempted to create a culture industry in the service of mass distraction. They engineered and orchestrated emotion, harnessing film to the project of remaking German politics and culture. In Goebbels' view, film's role was to 'map the universe in accordance with party designs, to provide a comprehensive lexical guide to the past and present, to account for all signs of life from the smallest atom to the mightiest being'.[17] 'Using different modalities (features, shorts, and documentaries that blended rabble-rousing agitprop, high drama, and escapist recreation)', Rentschler argues, 'films charted physical reality and occupied psychic space. Screen narratives often provided the illusion of room to move while remaining organised and administered by the state. And films did not exist in isolation, but indeed circulated and resonated in a state-regulated public sphere'.[18]

No one has suggested that film was such an integral part of the Fascist project or that it contributed in the same way or to the same extent to the maintenance of the pattern of consent that, most historians agree, was established in Italy by the mid-1930s. Indeed, Vito Zagarrio, in an essay dealing with film policy, asserts that cinema was 'in reality independent of the state' under Fascism.[19] However, although quite widely held, this view goes to the opposite extreme. Cinema may have corresponded to logics that in important respects were different from those of the regime, but it cannot seriously be denied that it made some contribution to the way society was organised and regulated. In his analysis of the content of selected films, Steven Ricci argues that the experience of cinema in the interwar years was marked by 'at least four major overlapping heuristic codes, a general codex that exists at the intersection between the state's public appearances and the positions of cinematic readership'.[20] These codes, he argues, are as follows: first, the social order is only ever depicted as a Fascist order; second, the past is always seen as Roman, the present and future as Fascist; third, contradictions between rural and urban ways of living are treated as reconcilable within the Fascist project; fourth, the public is always addressed as an undifferentiated national body.[21]

In fact, there were a number of points in common between Goebbels' project and the Fascist one. Like Goebbels, who wanted a cinema that would satisfy the domestic market and act as foreign emissary, Fascism wanted to enrol cinema in the service of national regeneration. Given this point of departure, there was considerable slippage between the position of those who thought the state should provide support and those who wanted more control. After a delegation headed by Giuseppe Bottai saw Mussolini in 1931 to discuss the state of crisis in which all areas of the film industry were languishing, some basic principles of government action were laid down. These consisted first of support for private industry through subsidies to producers and a tax on imported and dubbed films, then of more active interventions to shape the nature of the films made. Paradoxically, given the United States' attachment to free trade and private enterprise, it was the trip he undertook to Hollywood that persuaded Freddi of the need for cinema to be given pride of place in cultural policy and for the state to direct it fully. He was broadly in favour of 'a cinema under total state control' of the type that was taking shape in Germany, although, after a visit to Berlin in 1936, he expressed a preference for intelligent direction rather than violent coercion.[22] The latter may have been a distinctive hallmark of Nazism, but, as Rentschler argues, Hitler's regime used tourism, recreation and consumption as complements to law, order and restriction, and Fascism followed suit.[23] Leisure was a key part of the way in which a pattern of consent was constructed and space was granted to the articulation of the traditional aspirations of the classes that supported the regime. Goebbels wanted the film industry to appear both national and international, open and regulated, modern and eternal. Its task was to foster old forms of collective identity and offer a new tool of consensus-making. In all this, Fascism was scarcely different.

Where Fascism differed from Nazism in this matter was primarily in the way that Italy was different from Germany. It was a much less 'mediatised' society and the impact of cinema and the media was by no means as extensive. Nazism was a phenomenon of an industrial society in the way that Fascism was not. The movement may have been founded in Milan, which was the most economically advanced city in the country, and it may also have drawn much of its imagery and energy from the Futurists, but it won a mass following primarily in the rural areas of central Italy. Mussolini was well aware that abroad, especially in the United States, he was likened to a film star,[24] and he revelled in his appearances in newsreels, but at home live performance was his preferred idiom, and personal appearances and face-to-face encounters were crucial to the way his charisma worked.[25] Although cinema became more important in the course of the 1930s, the press remained the medium that the regime deemed most worthy of attention. Whereas newspapers were all, in different ways, controlled by the regime, cinema was never brought wholly within the public domain.

The State and Private Enterprise

Fascism tried to simplify the structure of decision making throughout the state and society. The creation of a one-party state with an ostensibly all-powerful dictator at the apex was accompanied by a system of corporations to govern the economic sector and a network of para-governmental organisations to regulate leisure, communications, health and other areas. For all this, decision making was often complex, with negotiations, lobbying and heel dragging on the part of a wide range of individuals and interests being a constant feature. As far as cinema was concerned, it is difficult to talk simply of a state-directed cinema, because the number of private companies and individuals involved was considerable, even if corporatism was intended to channel the articulation of interests. There were many types of interaction and interdependency, as well as conflict, between state institutions and the cultural industries.[26] State intervention in cinema involved a variety of different ministries, including not only the organs that were absorbed into the Ministry of Popular Culture but also the Foreign Ministry, the Finance Ministry, the Ministry of Exchange and Currency, the Interior Ministry and the Ministry of Communications. Each of these was concerned with different aspects of cinema as a cultural product, a business, a mass medium and a possible threat to public order. These different priorities and approaches led to actions that were not always coherent or consistent. Personal ambitions and rivalries on the part of officials sometimes interfered too, as ministers and others sought to establish their dominance, win the Duce's ear, or otherwise mark out their territory. Among Fascists, there were also policy differences such as those between Freddi and Mussolini's son Vittorio, who both, in their own ways, had an idea of the future of Italian national cinema that was informed by the American example.[27] There were others, like the former party secretary Roberto Farinacci, who believed that cinema should be bent to propaganda aims. In addition there were profiteers like Giuseppe Barattolo, founder of Caesar Film, who sought to turn state action to his personal business advantage, and men such as Giacomo Paulucci de' Calboli, president of the Luce Institute and Dino Alfieri, Minister of Press and Propaganda, who were more concerned with ensuring cinema made a full contribution to state revenues.

The regime actively shaped, organised and sustained the private sector. In keeping with the principles of corporatism, federations of producers, distributors and exhibitors were formed. These unified and granted a voice to key categories while also subordinating them, formally at least, to political imperatives. These structured associations did not prevent disputes of a commercial nature from emerging: for example, exhibitors were always far more favourable to American films than producers since they knew that the public always responded well to them. For this reason, they did not really want to reserve screen time for national products whose quality was uncertain. Distribution was the most complex category because the sector was composed not only of domestic companies but also of the Italian branches of the major American production and distribution companies. The state was neither a neutral referee nor a guiding influence removed from the fray; it was itself a part of the fray since it engaged in a limited degree of production through some ministries and the Luce Institute, and it was also a player in distribution and exhibition through ENIC (National Body of Cinema Industries), an entity that began as a minor distributor and which grew steadily by taking over failed private companies in the distribution and exhibition sectors to the point that Freddi was convinced it should act as a constructive stimulus to improve national cinema. Cinecittà itself began as a partnership between the state and the strongest actor in the private sector, the Cines company, but, following the death of Roncoroni in 1938, his heirs sold out to the state which became the sole proprietor. Later the nationalised Cines company engaged directly in production, setting, as Freddi (who was its president as well as president of Cinecittà) saw it, a benchmark for commercial producers.

Freddi always took the view that weak companies had no place in the production sector and what was needed was a limited number of well-established ones.[28] The support given to producers was always linked to box office receipts, an approach that was intended to reward the strong and successful. Freddi's preferred method of day-to-day intervention was censorship. As far as foreign films were concerned, his actions were informed by a cultural agenda. He generally approved American films, which he found had the same positive and forward-looking values he hoped to foster in Italian cinema, while often finding fault with French products that were deemed corrupt and morally damaging.[29] As for domestic production, censorship was not seen as a punitive or negative activity but rather as one of stimulus and encouragement. Freddi instituted the practice of preventive censorship, forcing producers who wished to receive state aid to submit scripts to him before production started. In this way, he was able to shape cinema and directly influence the way films were made.

A second area in which he intervened was publicity. He took credit in his memoirs for establishing a press service within the directorate of cinema.[30] This provided newspapers and magazines with a vast quantity of 'lively and varied' material on single films and on Italian cinema more generally. The main task, as he saw it, was to draw a distinction between productions of a certain minimum quality that deserved to be brought to the attention of the public, and exploitative quickies that frustrated and annoyed filmgoers. He was particularly concerned to exclude from this service poor quality films that in his view had no right to benefit from official support. Traditionally, Italian production companies undertook little promotion – 'out of a misplaced sense of economy',[31] Freddi claimed – with the result that their films had lost out to better-supported foreign competition.

Freddi approached advertising and publicity by 'seeking to disconnect it from a publicity-driven focus on stars and audience-pleasing gossip'.[32] He called for serious and properly trained personnel to use all available techniques to provide films with original and compelling launches. Good relations needed to be maintained with the critics while material was supplied to magazines to arouse the interest of the public. Posters and illustrated material needed to be produced according to artistic criteria.[33] In 1935 he organised an event to mark the fortieth anniversary of the birth of cinema, with the aim, he later claimed, to 'raise it to a higher and more noble plane'.[34] Specifically, a bulletin was published that offered news about upcoming productions and releases, including material provided by production companies but excluding 'the usual, ready bluff with which elements of dubious value and dubious morality sought to sustain initiatives destined to sure failure'.³⁵ Photographs of approved quality were distributed of Italian films and cinematic events to the domestic and international press; and radio promotions were initiated.

As a result of the changes, cinema became a significant factor in the news media as magazines and newspapers started to devote far more pages to it than they had done previously. In consequence, more people associated with the industry became well known. Actors were the main beneficiaries, but directors, cinematographers and some critics also became, albeit to a lesser extent, part of the sphere of recognition. The fruits of this shift were reaped fully after the decision in 1938 to grant ENIC a monopoly on the distribution of foreign films in Italy.³⁶ This led directly to a boycott of the Italian market by the major American studios, which could no longer sell their films to the highest bidder but had to accept the price offered by the state.³⁷ No one in Italy had expected the boycott, and the American studios, which took the step hoping to force the Italian government to back down, were surprised when the gap in the market was successfully filled by increased domestic production and imports from other sources. In understanding the market's positive response to Italian films in this phase, acknowledgement must be given to the efforts that were made to create a climate of expectation and interest around them.

The steady increase in the importance of the film industry in national life, and the multiplication of agencies, departments and news media dealing with it, turned it into a key tool in the Fascist patronage structure. As Ruth Ben-Ghiat has shown, the regime saw culture as an integrative device that would bind Italians to the state and bolster the normative behaviours it promoted.³⁸ Instead of demanding conformity from intellectuals, it used opportunities, subsidies, flattery and other incentives to draw artists and writers into patterns of collaboration. The extent of state or para-state activity was such that few intellectuals did not 'become entangled in Fascist cultural enterprises and institutions'.³⁹ Cinema had technical and commercial dimensions, but it was also closely related to literary culture and journalism. Many of the men who wrote scripts for films, and in some cases took up directing, came from conventional literary backgrounds. The large number of screen adaptations of plays and novels that were made in the 1930s and 1940s reinforced this connection. As criticism became a distinct and widely practised activity – not only, as Ben-Ghiat points out, because the critic's role is necessarily magnified in a dictatorship, 'where the acts of interpretation and contextualisation take on heightened importance', but also as a consequence of cinema becoming a recognised branch of national culture – the entanglements further multiplied.

It is not easy to gauge how many people saw themselves as actively contributing to a politically run cinema rather than simply working in an industry. Precisely because Fascism was so good at putting its stamp on institutions and areas of activity, and absorbing ordinary practices into ostensibly larger schemes for national renewal, distinctions are difficult to make and are even, in some respects, pointless. Most film workers, of whatever category, were involved equally with the films that were regarded as worthy and commercial products that had no substantial official approval. While propaganda features were few, occasional invitations to collaborate on them or other official projects were issued to many directors. Even Mario Camerini, who is often regarded as having had no Fascist sympathies at all, was obliged to make one propaganda film, the colonial-themed *Il grande appello* (The Great Appeal, 1936). If any distinction is worth making for the period prior to 1942–43, when war setbacks eroded confidence in the political leadership, it was less between anti-Fascists and Fascists than between ideological Fascists and the quietly conformist majority.

Ideological Fascists were not numerous. Of directors, Alessandro Blasetti was the most prominent to align himself with Fascism in the 1920s and early 1930s. As an organiser and promoter of cinema's development he had frequent contact with high officials and he made a number of films, including *Terra madre* (Mother Earth, 1931), *Sole* (Sun, 1929), *1860* (1933), and *Vecchia guardia* (The Old Guard, 1934) that were conceived as propaganda. Other directors, including Gioacchino Forzano, who pursued a number of film projects at his own Tirrenia studio in collaboration with Mussolini, made important contributions to cultural policy. The director of *Scipione*, Carmine Gallone, as well as Goffredo Alessandrini, Augusto Genina, Roberto Rossellini and Francesco De Robertis, who all directed anti-communist, colonial or military films, were also closely implicated in developing a type of cinema that had broad, if not unanimous, official approval. None of them, however, can be said to have contributed conceptually or originally to Fascist cultural policy.

Most artistic personnel were not particularly political and their behaviour was that of people who mainly thought of themselves as working in an industry rather than under a regime. They made films with the public in mind more than the Fascist state. It was only when pressures were brought to bear during the war years that they were obliged to tailor their work more to official expectations. Among the bones of contention were matters concerning the appearance of actors, their earnings and lifestyles, and their personal lives. In addition, there were pressures to make films that dovetailed with the idea of the nation in war and particularly with the idea of the national purpose that Fascism itself had. But even actors, like Amedeo Nazzari, who were identified as bearers of Fascist ideas of the new Italian, always viewed themselves more as independent professionals than as tools of Fascism.

For obvious reasons, it was customary in the years that followed the end of the war for emphasis to be placed on the ways in which cultural spaces, some of them institutional, witnessed the circulation of anti-Fascist ideas.

While this was undoubtedly true to a limited extent as far as the Centro sperimentale and the magazine *Cinema* were concerned, this point should not be over stressed. Cinecittà had begun as a collaboration between the state and private interests but ended up as a branch of the state. Commercial films may have accounted for most of what was produced there, but the Fascist presence was impossible to ignore. There was a party section and, from 1940, a Dopolavoro (afterwork leisure organisation). Fascist ministers and other officials often visited, as did Freddi even before he became president of the complex in 1940. Although he only wore uniform on ceremonial occasions and preferred where possible to engage in good-humoured persuasion and advice rather than issue heavy-handed ultimatums, there was no tolerance of active dissent. The secret police OVRA had its informers everywhere and Cinecittà was no exception.[40] On the occasion of Mussolini's major speeches, such as the declaration of war in June 1940, studio workers were taken off set and bussed to Piazza Venezia to provide enthusiastic approval while actors and other personnel stopped work to listen to loudspeakers. Against all this, the oft-cited example of Visconti's debut film *Ossessione* (1943), which was made by a group of committed anti-Fascists largely on location in and near Ferrara, with the clear intention of challenging the aesthetic and thematic norms of Fascist cinema, weighed lightly. The film, in any case, only had a limited, much contested, release in the Spring of 1943 and several of those involved were arrested in the course of its being made.[41] Rather than anti-Fascism, it is better to think of a hollowing out of Fascism to the extent that its capacity to involve and mobilise those beyond the ranks of the committed was reduced. The coercive apparatus remained in place even if it ceased to function effectively.

Shaping National Film Culture

Fascist cinema was often dismissed in the postwar years as unsubtle propaganda – a view largely based on the Luce newsreels and a handful of features including *Scipione l'Africano*.[42] The typical entertainment features, dubbed 'white telephone' films, were deemed pure fluff, providers of a smokescreen of light entertainment that obscured entirely the truth of life under the dictatorship. In fact, as has long been recognised, the output of Italian cinema was much more varied than this. While some propaganda features, such as the three war films made by Rossellini from 1941 to 1943 (*La nave bianca*, The White Ship, 1941; *Un pilota ritorna*, A Pilot Returns, 1942; *L'uomo della croce*, The Man with the Cross, 1943), which were directly produced by government ministries, were more or less direct emanations of the regime,[43] others produced by Fascist enthusiasts were received coldly by at least parts of the political leadership. Just as Goebbels preferred indirect to direct propaganda in cinema, Freddi was strongly opposed to the making of films that had an explicit propaganda purpose. Like Giuseppe Bottai and other more sophisticated Fascists, he sensed that these would be counterproductive. The aim rather was to find oblique and indirect ways of harnessing film to Fascism's general project. He deplored films like Blasetti's *Vecchia guardia* or former National Fascist Party (PNF) secretary Roberto Farinacci's pet project *Redenzione* (Redemption, Marcello Albani, 1943), both of which glorified the movement's origins in the violent *squadrismo* of the early 1920s, and was not keen even on *Scipione l'Africano*.[44] It was ideologues in the Fascist press who championed political cinema rather than leading officials.

Perhaps inevitably, Italian cinema was profoundly shaped by the example of Hollywood, which dominated Italian screens up until 1938. It has been argued that a 'Hollywood myth' 'took shape in Italy in the 1920s and had its zenith and decline in the 1930s, thereby traversing the whole of the Fascist period'.[45] Mario Soldati suggested that Italian cinema of the 1930s was 'a minor version of American cinema'. He had in mind not only comedies like *Darò un milione* (I'll Give a Million, 1936) and *Centomila dollari* (One Hundred Thousand Dollars, 1940), both directed by Camerini, with whom Soldati worked as an assistant before himself becoming a director. Some historical and war films owed debts to American ideas of spectacle, character and narrative. Even blockbusters like *Scipione l'Africano* were made with an eye to Cecil B. DeMille's films of scale.

However, the genre system was not the same as the American one. In the United States, movie genres had developed as a feature of industrial filmmaking and had become central to the way in which the public understood the experience of cinema. They were closely related to the studio system and the commercial context of film-making as mass culture.[46] It was virtually impossible to think of Hollywood cinema without reference to the western or the gangster movie. In Italy, there were no westerns, few gangster and no horror films, virtually no children's films, and no cartoons or science fiction. There were by contrast musicals or films in which music featured significantly, historical films, sophisticated comedies, light comedies, war films, literary adaptations, and biopics. The Italian system was shaped by factors including a higher degree of improvisation, the expressed preferences of the regime for certain types of film, national tastes in matters of comedy and music, and the fact that the audience for film was mainly northern, urban and middle class. In contemporary films, urban settings and themes dominated, as would be expected, but there were frequent excursions into an idealised rural world that reflected the regime's attachment to an ideology of ruralism as a core component of national identity. This especially applied to films that had a more or less explicit Italian setting.

Comedy worked as an umbrella genre in Italian cinema in so far as it was presented in many variants. There was even variety within the 'Hungarian-style comedies', that were dubbed 'white telephone' films after the war. The urban world featured more as myth than reality in these films. Often set in some European location such as Budapest, Vienna or Berlin, as well as, occasionally, New York – if the location was identified at all – the films occupied a limbo space in which normal ties, values, roles and relations were suspended, as much for the audience as for the characters. In his *Popular Film Culture in Fascist Italy*, James Hay explores this 'pseudogenre', as he calls it, through some of its tropes including the grand hotel and the department store.[47] Modern leisure, economic ease and style are the features of these films, although the lower-class figures who are catapulted into this ethereal realm are usually disenchanted and return to their point of departure. Some films revelled in petit-bourgeois delusions of mobility or grandeur while others ridiculed them. As Hay writes, 'Camerini's comedies (with the possible exception of *Darò un milione*) always reject the upper-crust lifestyle. In so doing they decry the false magic of that lifestyle and promote the social and political idealism of petit-bourgeois ideology'.[48] In the meantime, however, they afforded the audience the pleasure of an escape into a world of luxury, refinement and cosmopolitanism. Utterly removed from the reality of everyday life in Italy, they featured actors dressed and polished up to the ninth degree who live in impossibly luxurious homes and move with ease in fantasy night clubs, while exteriors are often completely absent. This genre worked well commercially because it employed motifs, locations and character types that were well established in international cinema and which were identified especially with Hollywood. The substance of the drama was usually frivolous and repetitive. Moreover, many screenplays were simply translations of foreign ones, with the result that the situations and dynamics were often unfamiliar. These films may have served the interests of the regime in some way, and had they not it is very doubtful that they would have received regular ministerial financial support or have constituted such a large percentage of the films produced. But, by the same token, it is beyond dispute that these films, even if Ricci is right to argue that they did not contradict the basic presuppositions of Fascist order, did nothing to support the ethic of heroism and sacrifice that the regime was seeking to instil in the Italians. Freddi was on record as expressing his distaste for them and they were regularly judged negatively by most critics in the press and specialist magazines.[49] They satisfied the requirement that entertainment cinema should not comment on or even represent Fascism and its place in day-to-day Italian life, but that is all.

Much more suitable were the historical films which constituted approximately 20 per cent of the 720 films made in Italy between 1930 and 1943.[50] Films of this type were part of the tradition of Italian cinema and many more had been made in the 1910s. Thus it would be a mistake to see films of this type as being necessarily a consequence of Fascism's concern with Italian history. Fascism championed some films, and the regime financed a small number of blockbusters and some films dealing directly with Fascism itself. But Hay points out that historical films were 'basically ... commercial enterprises'.[51] They were suitable vehicles for the relaunch of national cinema that offered, certainly, opportunities for the injection of propaganda in some instances, but which were often devoid of explicitly political motifs. Of the periods employed for settings, the Belle Epoque was the most popular, followed by the nineteenth century, the Renaissance, the Risorgimento, the seventeenth and eighteenth centuries, the ancient period, the First World War and the Middle Ages. In their themes the films quite regularly invited the drawing of parallels between past and present, in keeping with Fascism's idea of itself as 'embodying the immortal primacy of the Italian spirit' and of Mussolini as 'the history maker'.[52] They offered ample opportunities for audience identification with heroic lead characters and scenes of conflict and battle. Spectacular moments and nationalistic themes were readily fused.

Hay links historical films not so much to a genuine interest in the national past as to the needs of the present: 'modernization in Italy offered the ideal climate for the historical film and Italian Fascism's affinity for it'.[53] Blasetti noted that the historical film was a powerful means of cementing popular culture.[54] Asserting or defending cultural traditions against alien values or forces is a key motif. War and imperial films were significant extensions of the historical genre. The spectacular exploration of exotic, remote and fascinating milieux, the presentation of unusual characters, as well as the establishment of Italian superiority, and the clash of Italian values and forces with alien elements all provided opportunities for inspiring stories of endeavour and heroism. To add to the patriotic impulse, the films stood as testimony to the skills of costume and set design in Cinecittà.

As in Hollywood, the sound era saw the birth of the musical film. These came in different forms: biopics of the composers Bellini and Verdi, opera films, films featuring opera singers or popular music performers, films with a theme song or in which diegetic musical moments contributed to their appeal. Although virtually all films employed music to create atmosphere and aurally render situations and characters, the place of music in Italian culture and identity ensured that films with a musical character enjoyed a ready appeal to domestic audiences. In terms of exports, Italy's identification as the land of music and song meant that these films had a sales point that foreign distributors could exploit.

Mussolini and Cinema

Few things in Fascist Italy happened without Mussolini approving them or knowing about them. In contrast to the detached style of government practised by Hitler, the Duce delegated as little as possible and intervened in every imaginable sector. Although Richard Bosworth has recently challenged the established view that 'Mussolini was always in charge', suggesting that 'a dictator's attention span is not always long' and that his power was 'incomplete and elusive',[55] there can be no doubt that he cultivated the impression of absolute control and that, in order to achieve this, he concerned himself to some degree with everything. In the 1930s, cinema was added to the matters that came to his attention.

Freddi gives the impression that the Duce did not watch movies with an expert eye but rather with the personal preferences of a common spectator. 'He let himself go completely with certain comedy films, before which he behaved like any member of the audience, without mental reservations, aesthetic or philosophical reflection, or moral, political or intellectual pretensions; he enjoyed himself and that is all,' he wrote.[56] His favourites were Laurel and Hardy, while he disliked gangster films, excessive intimacy or over-long kisses, and interracial mixing. He preferred films with a social content and musicals, although Disney's *Snow White and the Seven Dwarfs* (1937) enchanted him.

Mussolini's expertise in matters cinematic grew as he took a close personal interest in the presentation of his own image in newsreels.[57] Every Tuesday, he was accustomed to review the material that was destined for the country's cinemas. On Fridays, he often watched a feature film. These were either films he had asked to see or films Freddi urged him to view. Freddi noted in his memoirs that Mussolini 'was the "sole" spectator in the broadest sense who, with his exclusive judgement, could decide the fate of works which were destined rather for the public'.[58] In addition, from 1937 his day typically ended with the viewing of a new film. Even if, according to his son Vittorio, who set up the cinema at the family's residence at Villa Torlonia, the Duce rarely made it to the end without falling asleep,[59] he developed a general familiarity with current film culture. Usually he was only approached over important decisions, but his judgement was also sought from time to time over single films, especially if there was a difference of opinion between officials.

On some issues, he was firm. He thundered in November 1938 against the drain that American films were on the economy and was defiant before the embargo that had been announced by the studios.[60] He was particularly alert to politically dangerous representations. A few comments he let slip confirm that he was aware of the social dangers of cinema and that he had an instinctive feel for its possible impact on behaviour. He was stricter than his officials in terms of representing bad examples. Freddi cites the case of *Passaporto rosso* (Red Passport, Guido Brignone, 1934), a film of patriotic content that he had personally championed, in which some rebels in Latin America are seen to prepare for an insurrection by recovering previously hidden weapons. Mussolini demanded modifications to eliminate the lesson in revolutionary technique that was thereby imparted. He required the removal of a scene in *Modern Times* (1936) in which Chaplin inadvertently takes cocaine with comic results, believing that public attention should not be drawn to narcotics. 'Only once did I witness a violent explosion on Mussolini's part', Freddi wrote, adding that this occurred before his appointment as director general.[61] This occurred over *Il cappello a tre punte* (The Three-Cornered Hat, Mario Camerini, 1934), a comedy set in the eighteenth century starring the Neapolitan brothers Eduardo and Peppino De Filippo. A scene in which comically righteous indignation against taxes and regulations results in an incitation to revolt against a government accused of starving ordinary folk so angered Mussolini that he demanded that the film be stopped. 'Is it worth working like a beast to be paid back in this way by the Italians?' he protested to the perplexed officials present at the screening before storming out. After some minor changes, the film was duly released.

Freddi's portrait of Mussolini's tastes and interventions is confirmed by entries in his lover Claretta Petacci's diaries, which were published for the first time only in 2009. Claretta was a keen filmgoer and occasionally films formed the basis of exchanges of views between them. He advised her to see *Scipione l'Africano* but otherwise he mainly responded to the accounts she gave him of the films she saw, usually in the company of her sister. Occasionally, he was more forthcoming. He told her that he had abandoned the screening of a French comedy before it had finished because its utter triviality exasperated him.[62] In March 1938 he informed her that he had banned a Marlene Dietrich film (*Knight without Armour*, by Jacques Feyder, later released in Italy as *La contessa Alessandra*) as it dwelt on the oppressive rule of the Tsar,[63] and he announced to her in October of the same year that he would view a Garbo film, *Marie Waleska*, and make a judgement about it. It had been brought to his attention since it ridiculed Napoleon, 'showing him as a common man'.[64] In the political culture of the regime Napoleon was not only regarded as Italian but also as a precursor of the Duce.[65]

The dictator's responses to films often surprised officials but they understood that, beyond showing particular attention to any possible disruptive impact that films might have on the political order, he approached cinema in a way that was in tune with the feelings of ordinary spectators. Far from being dismayed by this, they took it to be a proof of his charisma. It was a sign not of his ordinariness but rather of his genius for interpreting the popular mind.

Although light comedies were not to his personal taste, Mussolini does not seem to have objected to them, seeing them simply as harmless entertainment. This may help to explain why producers made such films in large numbers. The market calculations of producers and distributors, and the demand from exhibitors for Italian films that could stand up against American imports, played a part in determining the kinds of film that were actually made, alongside the sometimes conflicting directives of different parts of the state and the National Fascist Party and the structures of censorship.[66] Although the regime became more cinematised over time, and the role of the state expanded, the degree of control over production was less than in Nazi Germany where Goebbels seemed even to make the mistake of confusing cinema with reality in Nazism's last desperate weeks. For all Freddi's fervour, Mussolini had no intention of upsetting private interests and, despite the expansion of the role of the state,[67] film production, like distribution and exhibition, remained predominantly a commercial activity. Moreover, only very occasionally did Mussolini comment on matters relating to film stars. Despite his well-known dislike for anyone stealing his limelight, he never seems to have thought of them as serious rivals for public affection.

Notes

1. See L. Freddi. 1949. *Il cinema*, Rome: L'Arnia, 199–201.
2. D. Forgacs and S. Gundle. 2007. *Mass Culture and Italian Society from Fascism to the Cold War*, Bloomington: Indiana University Press, 215.
3. A. Blasetti. 1982. 'La cinematografia è l'arma più forte' (1937) in Blasetti, *Scritti sul cinema*, ed. by A. Aprà, Venice: Marsilio, 159–62, 161.
4. For an assessment of Freddi's role, see V. Zagarrio. 2006. 'Schizofrenie del modello fascista' in O. Caldiron (ed.), *Storia del cinema italiano*, Vol. 5, 1934–1939, Venice–Rome: Marsilio/Bianco & Nero, 37–61. For a critical analysis of his memoirs, see A. Catania. 1996. 'Luigi Freddi e il libro della solitudine' in M. Biondi and A. Borsatti (eds), *Cultura e fascismo: letteratura, arti e spettacolo di un Ventennio*, Florence: Ponte alle Grazie, 291–308.
5. E. Detti. 1989. *Le carte povere: storia dell'illustrazione minore*, Florence: La Nuova Italia, 78–80, 93–95.
6. Blasetti, 'La cinematografia è l'arma più forte', 159.
7. Ibid., 159.
8. All the films made at Cinecittà in these years are listed in F. Mariotti (ed.). 1989. *Cinecittà tra cronaca e storia 1937–1989*, Vol. II, *I film*, Rome: Presidenza del Consiglio dei Ministri, 8–134.
9. M. Soldati. (1964) 1979. *Le due città*, Milan: Garzanti, 262.
10. Mary Pickford, untitled note, *Cinema*, 25 April 1937, 300.
11. Freddi, *Il cinema*, 20.
12. L. Freddi. 1935. 'Arte per il popolo' in *40 anniversario della cinematografia*, Rome: Sottosegretariato di Stato della Stampa e Propaganda, 14. It is worth noting that Stefano Pittaluga, the leading film producer and head of Cines until his death in 1931, was not held in universal high regard. An official briefing note from 1929 on the 'men of cinema' described him as 'a former yachtsman camouflaged as an industrialist, a man without either scruples or sensibility who is politically corrupt and utterly inferior ...; he is one of the most typical and most grotesque bluffers of Italian business'. Archivio Centrale dello Stato (ACS), Ministero del Interno, Direzione generale publica sicurezza, Divisione polizia politica 1927–1944, b. 175 bis, f. M 39/1 Ente nazionale per la cinematografia.

13. Freddi, *Il cinema*, 42.
14. Blasetti, 'La cinematografia è l'arma più forte', 159.
15. Ibid., 160.
16. E. Rentschler. 1996. *The Ministry of Illusion: Nazi Cinema and Its Afterlife*, Cambridge, MA: Harvard University Press, 16.
17. Ibid.
18. Ibid.
19. Zagarrio, 'Le schizofrenie', 60.
20. S. Ricci. 2008. *Cinema & Fascism: Italian Film and Society, 1922–1943*, Berkeley: University of California Press, 160.
21. Ibid., 160–63.
22. Ibid., 45–46, 50.
23. Rentschler, *The Ministry of Illusion*, xi.
24. Cf. G.P. Brunetta. 1989. 'Il sogno a stelle e strisce di Mussolini' in M. Vaudagna (ed.), *L'estetica della politica in Europa e America negli anni trenta*, Rome–Bari: Laterza, 161–76; S. Gundle. 2013. 'Mass Culture and the Cult of Personality' in S. Gundle, C. Duggan and G. Pieri, *The Cult of the Duce: Mussolini and the Italians*, Manchester: Manchester University Press, 72–99.
25. See S. Gundle. 2013. 'Mussolini's Appearances in the Regions' in Gundle, Duggan and Pieri, *The Cult of the Duce*.
26. Forgacs and Gundle, *Mass Culture and Italian Society*, 198.
27. In *Il cinema*, Freddi devotes a whole chapter to his differences with the Duce's son; see 297–322.
28. Forgacs and Gundle, *Mass Culture and Italian Society*, 204.
29. Ibid., 224–25.
30. Freddi, *Il cinema*, 408–11.
31. Ibid., 409.
32. Ibid., 395.
33. Ibid., 74.
34. Ibid., 395.
35. Ibid., 409.
36. Ibid., 207–8.
37. See Forgacs and Gundle, *Mass Culture and Italian Society*, 151–52; B. Corsi. 2001. *Con qualche dollaro in meno: storia economica del cinema italiano*, Rome: Editori Riuniti, 28–29.
38. R. Ben-Ghiat. 2001. *Fascist Modernities: Italy, 1922–1945*, Berkeley: University of California Press, 9–10.
39. Ibid., 10.
40. See N. Marino and E.V. Marino. 2005. *L'Ovra a Cinecittà: polizia politica e spie in camicia nera*, Turin: Bollati Boringhieri.
41. On the making of *Ossessione*, see B. Torri. 2010. 'Il caso "Ossessione"' in E.G. Laura and A. Baldi (eds), *Storia del cinema italiano*, Vol. 6, 1940–1944, Venice–Rome: Marsilio/Bianco & Nero, 176–84.

42. G. Nowell-Smith. 1986. 'The Italian Cinema under Fascism' in D. Forgacs (ed.), *Re-thinking Italian Fascism*, London: Lawrence & Wishart, 142–61.
43. Although it has been argued that Rossellini subverted his brief by focusing on the weak, the marginal and the wounded in his films. See R. Ben-Ghiat. 2000. 'The Fascist War Trilogy' in D. Forgacs, S. Lutton and G. Nowell-Smith (eds), *Roberto Rossellini: Magician of the Real*, London: BFI, 20–35.
44. Freddi, *Il cinema*, 399.
45. L. Albano. 1979. 'Hollywood: cinelandia …' in R. Redi (ed.), *Cinema italiano sotto il fascismo*, Venice: Marsilio, 219.
46. S. Neale. 1999. *Genre and Hollywood*, London: Routledge, 9.
47. J. Hay. 1987. *Popular Film Culture in Fascist Italy: The Passing of the Rex*, Bloomington: Indiana University Press, 40.
48. Ibid., 47.
49. See S. Parigi. 1991. 'Commedie in rivista: la critica nella stampa specializzata 1930–1943' in M. Argentieri (ed.), *Risate di regime: la commedia italiana 1930–1944*, Venezia: Marsilio.
50. Ibid., 153.
51. Ibid., 154.
52. C. Fogu. 2003. *The Historic Imaginary: Politics of History in Fascist Italy*, Toronto: University of Toronto Press, 56 and 74.
53. Hay, *Popular Film Culture in Fascist Italy*, 155.
54. Ibid., 155.
55. R.J.B. Bosworth. 2009. 'Dictators Strong or Weak? The Model of Benito Mussolini' in Bosworth (ed.), *The Oxford Handbook of Fascism*, Oxford: Oxford University Press, 259–75; 265, 270, 272.
56. Ibid., 392.
57. See E.G. Laura. 2000. 'Cinegiornali e mito del "Duce"' in Laura (ed.), *La stagioni dell'aquila: storia del Istituto Luce*, Rome: Ente dello spettacolo, 101–6.
58. Freddi, *Il cinema*, 388.
59. See R. Renzi. 1992. 'Intervista con Vittorio Mussolini' in Renzi (ed.), *Il cinema dei dittatori: Mussolini, Stalin, Hitler – immagini e documenti*, Bologna: Grafis, 13–17.
60. Freddi, *Il cinema*, 460.
61. Ibid., 395.
62. C. Petacci. 2009. *Mussolini segreto: diari 1932–1938*, Milan: Rizzoli, 61 and 171.
63. Freddi, *Il cinema*, 263–64.
64. Ibid., 420.
65. See A. Campi. 2007. *L'ombra lunga di Napoleone: da Mussolini a Berlusconi*, Venice: Marsilio, Chapters 1–2.
66. Forgacs and Gundle, *Mass Culture and Italian Society*, 199–200.
67. F. Bono. 2010. 'Verso un gruppo di Stato: Cinecittà, ENIC and Cines' in O. Caldiron with A. Baldi (eds), *Storia del cinema italiano*, Vol. 6, 1940–1944, Venice–Rome: Marsilio/Bianco & Nero, 365–82.

2

The Creation of a Star System

As the issue of the rebirth of Italian cinema came to occupy a place in economic and cultural, and then political, debate, it was inevitable that the question of stars and stardom would be raised. Stars were not only a central feature of many successful films and the focal point around which entire Hollywood studios were organised, but also the main selling point of American movies at a time when these held a dominant place in the international market. Italians did not need to be very old to remember that their cinema had once had its own stars and that these, in their time, had been no less, and in some respects more, compelling than the stars of Hollywood. Thus there was an issue of whether Italy possessed some specific primacy in this field which, although lately obfuscated, could be drawn on to situate stardom at the heart of a revived national cinema. Some thought that stardom was in any case a useful promotional tool, and that ideas about Italy and the Italians could be communicated via stars to domestic and foreign audiences. Others were more wary. They saw that stardom that in the United States had become a weapon of big capital. Stars had been reshaped in the American era in ways that could not easily be harnessed to Fascist Italy's cultural and political ambitions. Thus if Italian cinema was to be reborn on new bases it needed to avoid replicating this model.

The stars that were soon formed in the revived Italian cinema were shaped by both political and industrial factors. Luigi Freddi was not very favourable to stars and stardom but, once they had emerged, he could see their uses. As Roberto Burchielli and Veronica Bianchini have written:

> The Fascist regime understood the enormous power of cinema ... in relation to its propaganda aims – and the national stars, who were cultivated within the confines

of Cinecittà, were a key aspect. The star system became 'Hollywoodian' too: the popular actresses were few and the fortunes of many films were based on their fame. With their 'ordinary' gestures, their way of smiling, of riding a bicycle or driving a car, of singing or dancing, the new protagonists of Italian cinema made the screen into an accomplice of the country's dreams.[1]

There were historical reasons in Italy why stars were thought of in terms of actresses rather than actors, but in fact some of the most significant screen idols would be male. This shift was due both to the development of a more rounded star system in the sound era and to the specific requirements of a regime that needed male role models.

In this chapter Italian screen stars will be explored in relation to debates about stardom and the efforts that were made both to learn from Hollywood and to be different from it. These will be considered in the context of the drive that was made in the Fascist period to turn cinema into a powerful national industry. First, however, something must be said about the Italian stardom of the silent era and the impact in Italy of Hollywood stars.

The Legacy of the Silent Era

By the time Mussolini came to power in 1922, many of the stars who had excited the fantasies of early filmgoers had disappeared. By 1925, the year Fascism became a dictatorship, they had all gone. Mussolini, the dynamic new prime minister, the man of the people with a past on the left who promised to restore order and dignity to the country, to some extent filled the gap. In his analysis of the personality cult of Mussolini, Dino Biondi argued that the leader of Fascism was the first beneficiary of the decline of the first screen stars. Having become a compelling political figure on the eve of the First World War, he filled the gap when other celebrities fell away.[2] But the memory of the special attractions of the divas of the 1910s remained strong. The early stars were indirect protégées of D'Annunzio, the writer and poet whose decadent aesthetic of excess and refinement had an impact on everything from fashion and interior decoration to the attitude towards Italy's artistic heritage and politics. Lyda Borelli had appeared on stage from the age of sixteen in his plays alongside the great actress Eleonora Duse. Like the other leading screen actresses of the 1910s, Francesca Bertini and Pina Menichelli, who were both in their early twenties at their height, she emerged in a context in which the Art Nouveau or Liberty style was the rage and there was a diffuse artistic involvement with feminine beauty. Borelli belonged to the spirit of her time, Ettore Zocaro noted, by 'interpreting a specific style according to which women covered their bare shoulders with ostrich feather boas and wandered across the stage carelessly dragging a mink coat behind them'.[3] She achieved stardom through the transposition of a theatrical repertoire and performance style to cinema. Her influence was cemented in the twelve films she made between 1913 and 1918.

As Angela Dalle Vacche writes, the cinematic diva did not have the advantages of the point of view shot or the shot-reverse shot that were cardinal features of classical American cinema.[4] But she did benefit from close-ups and these brought an intimate intensity of experience to the cinematic spectacle that was unknown in theatre. The diva drew audiences into her torments and her ecstasies and swept them along in a frenzy of corporeal expressivity. Duse's contortions had been a trademark of her theatre but cinema was able to work more intensely on the senses by highlighting a single gesture, glance or object. Audiences knew that they could expect to be transported into alluring milieux in films and experience with their diva of choice a range of emotions that would be expressed through signature physical movements and gestures. Before, typically, finishing badly, she took spectators on a psychological and experiential journey of unusual intensity. 'The sparkle of a goblet of champagne, the smoke of a cigarette, the hint of a fragrance ... the revelation of an ankle, the caress of a flower: a wealth of messages is communicated through the exchange of glances and the presence of objects', Brunetta notes.[5] The spectator was consequently sucked in, to the extent that he or she experienced 'the loss of perception of space and time'. 'A piano, a couch, flowers ... the appearance of a coach or a chauffeur-driven car, the possibility of entering noble palaces by means of staircases, of being invited to parties and the rites of the aristocratic and high bourgeois worlds: all this works together and makes visible and tangible things that had previously been confined to the imagination or restricted to the few.'[6]

The literary antecedents of the screen diva shaped every aspect of her being and confirmed her as a cultural emblem. This has led some to argue that 'the world represented on the screen had virtually no links with the real country ... but many with the literary world and that of the figurative arts'.[7] 'The diva's unusual contribution to the history of stardom stems from the cultural specificities of Italian modernity', Brunetta argues.[8] Among these was the fact that modern urban culture was confined to a limited number of large cities and the audience for cinema was much smaller and consequently more bourgeois than in other industrial countries. Despite this, the diva's stardom was constructed through repetition and predictability. As a fact of modern communication, it belonged to what Walter Benjamin would call the age of mechanical reproduction.[9] In contrast to historical films, which presented different situations and characters each time, the diva was both constant and mobile in the sense that her character was readily identifiable and guaranteed to evolve. Famously, Antonio Gramsci anticipated Benjamin's reflections on the decline of the auratic aspect of culture by denying Borelli's art, affirming that she 'cannot play anyone other than herself'.[10] Unwittingly, he identified what would become a key characteristic of screen stardom. As Vittorio Martinelli confirms: 'Malevolent or transparent, fatal or ingenuous, it was always her; she was unmistakeable because she carried in her blood the lively fascination of her heroines'.[11] Although the idea of the screen goddess was originally imported from Scandinavia, in Italian cinema it acquired a special resonance.

At a time when female roles were more subject to change than at any time in the recent past, Borelli's attitudes and gestures offered a template for imitation. Between the early war years and 1920, young women copied her looks and gestures, dressed like her, did their hair like hers, and affected attitudes similar to those of the characters she played.[12] This practice was not encouraged by the numerous popular and women's magazines that were published at this time. A close study of the coverage received by Francesca Bertini in some fifty publications has revealed that the attention granted to cinema and its stars was sporadic and irregular.[13] It was rather a spontaneous response, the expression of a desire for acknowledgement and emancipation. The critic Alfredo Panzini described Borelli's particular performance style as 'borelleggiare' (Borelling, one might say), and 'borellismo' soon became a phenomenon. In 1921, three years after her final film, Tito Alacci commented in a volume entitled *Le nostre attrici cinematografiche* on its impact on Italian cinema and on actresses including Bertini and Menichelli. The way *borellismo* impacted on urban culture is an indicator of cinema's power and of the suggestiveness of early stardom.

Most Italian stars were women. Such male stars as there were, were figures whose roots were in popular rather than high culture. Moreover, it was mainly the characters they played that were of interest. The performer Emilio Ghione was far less well known than his creation, the character Za la Mort, who appeared in some features and several series in the period between 1914 and 1924. A dark, ambiguous outlaw, who was conceived as an Italian response to such French figures as the gentleman thief Arsene Lupin, his adventures took him up into high society and down into the depths of urban squalor.[14] A delinquent with a sense of morality, whose mission was to right blatant wrongs and injustices, he was a cinematic transposition of the serial novel or *feuilleton* who recalled Robin Hood and Zorro. Like the divas, Ghione used his eyes and face to convey moods and intentions. Sharp lighting and make-up gave his creation an unsettling charisma. His faithful female sidekick, Za la Vie, served to humanise him.

Another character who enjoyed widespread popularity was the strongman Maciste. He first appeared in *Cabiria*, a historical blockbuster by Giovanni Pastrone for which D'Annunzio wrote the intertitles, coining his name along the way. Played by Bartolomeo Pagano, a one-time dock worker, Maciste featured in some twenty films from 1914, including no fewer than four in 1926 alone.[15] In them, he was inevitably pitched against evil forces, whether the setting was ancient or modern, and would offer spectacular demonstrations of strength such as breaking chains, keeping enemies at bay with a chair leg or lifting men above his head like sticks. He was fast and agile but it was his physical power, courage and goodness that caused audiences to grow attached to him. Maciste bore a resemblance to Hercules but had no actual background in Greek or Roman myth. Rather he was the cinematic transposition of the circus strongman, a giant with the capacity to resolve problems by the use of brute force. From the moment he first appeared on screen, fifteen minutes into *Cabiria*, he became a popular favourite and he was an off-screen personality too.[16] For years, his name was a guarantee for producers who were obliged to think up ever more outlandish or exotic situations in which to place him. In his final film, *Maciste contro lo sciecco* (Maciste against the Sheik, Mario Camerini, 1926), he engaged in an underwater fight with a shark.

A number of observers have noted an interrelation between the Duce and the male stars. Like Za la Mort, he was forceful and tainted with violence; he had, like Ghione's character, an outsider aura and an unsettling stare. The link to Maciste was stronger. Brunetta has dubbed Mussolini 'a dressed-up strong man who from a distance could be mistaken for Pagano'.[17] If the founder of Fascism seemed like a real-life Maciste, and possibly employed gestures and poses trademarked by Pagano, then the relationship was not only one way. The screen giant in turn became over time more like the man who became prime minister in 1922. In particular in *Maciste imperatore* (Emperor Maciste, 1924), he adopted Fascistic poses and set himself up as the defender of order against the disloyal, the violent, and vested interests.[18] Both Mussolini and Maciste regarded violence as a legitimate means of setting things to rights. At one level, this aligned the strongman with the new order in the country, but a cartoon featured in the brochure of the Pittaluga production company suggests that the two might, for a period, have been competitors. It commented ironically on the suspicion with which anyone who sought to dispute Mussolini's primacy was regarded. Positioned atop a large barrel of castor oil, which Fascists were accustomed to administer forcibly to their enemies, Mussolini addresses Maciste, who is attired in imperial uniform, saying, 'So you want to be emperor? Well, watch out ... because there is enough for you too'.[19]

In 1922, the American journalist Walter Lippmann published his influential book *Public Opinion* in which he stressed the importance of fictions and narratives in contemporary life.[20] People not only wanted hero figures to occupy the public sphere, they wanted to see them too. 'Photographs have the kind of authority over the imagination today, which the printed word had yesterday, and the spoken word before that. They seem utterly real', he remarked, adding that moving images were even more persuasive because the construct was so rich and complete that 'the imagining has been accomplished for you'.[21] Writing in 1926, the Italian Aldo Varaldo placed similar stress on the visual: 'We live today solely for rushing and seeing: it is above all the eye that rules us and drags us along. The domination of the eye is present among all publics and can be seen in complex forms of female staging, various scenes, cosmoramas and other marvels'.[22] 'By seeing, observing and indulging in visual abandon', the public laid itself open to new seductions. 'That is why the beautiful actress is such a persuasive phenomenon' and why, 'among all the beautiful actresses of Italy', Lyda Borelli, 'the youngest, the most refined and perhaps the most intelligent, if intelligence is taken as being the awareness or intuition of one's own power', had triumphed. The public found itself 'enslaved in an instant by the best and most worthy of forces: that of the aesthetic'.

Mussolini's unique position on the political scene was expressed in a highly visual way, through poses, sartorial choices, constant travel and a strong media presence. A man of the people who was turned by close associates into a figure of exception, he captured the imagination of contemporaries and pioneered a type of spectacular politics that filled the press and held the attention. This was able to occur because Italian cinema had grasped the idea of seriality, Brunetta notes, 'without elaborating any project for the construction of solid bases of support. Everyone seemed to live from day to day in both the phase of ascent and decline'.[23] Precisely the inability to create a solid production and distribution system would contribute to the crisis that would strike the film industry during and after the First World War. Borelli had left the scene and the public eye completely by 1918, while several other female stars of this era, including Bertini and Menichelli, finished their careers in the early 1920s. While the female stars withdrew, the men either went abroad or, like Pagano, who did not enjoy good health, retired. However, not even a politics so geared to the tastes and expectations of the mass age could satisfy all the needs that film stardom did. By his occupation of the stage, Mussolini may have retarded the emergence of new Italian male stars, but he could do little to stem the appeal of the glamorous idols of Hollywood.

American Cinema and Its Stars

When Italian cinema stumbled, the American companies were ready to exploit the demand for product. They first attracted audiences in Italy through films featuring the comics Charlie Chaplin, Laurel and Hardy, Buster Keaton and others, as well as the hugely popular adventure films of Douglas Fairbanks. Where Italian cinema had been a hit-and-miss affair, with no stability and little real regularity of supply, American cinema had a consistency that constituted a guarantee for both exhibitors and the public. The industry's ability to recruit the best talents from across the world contributed to its ability to deliver product that went over with audiences. This showed no sign of declining as the years passed. Audiences around the world shared the same fascination with the glittering and irresistible Hollywood star images which offered vehicles of escape, fantasy and desire. Even a cursory glance at the advertising material that was employed by distributors and exhibitors in Italy, or at the leading fan magazine *Cinema illustrazione*, confirms the variety and visibility of the Hollywood star system.

The consolidation of the studios and the onset of sound coincided with a significant change in the nature of the star system. Writing thirty years after Lippmann and Varaldo, Edgar Morin argued that the development of the illustrated press, greater synergy between different cultural industries and the expansion of the cinema audience, led to a new emphasis on realism. As American hegemony was established, the gods and goddesses of early cinema were replaced by recognisable types in a process of embourgeoisement of the imaginative world of what had once been a lower-class entertainment. 'The bourgeois imagination appropriates the real by multiplying the signs of verisimilitude and credibility', he argued.[24] Plausible stories took the place of improbable ones, and stars increasingly blended 'the exceptional and the ordinary, the ideal and the everyday ... offering ever more realistic points of possible identification'. Morin saw this trend as one manifestation of the way the urban masses were demanding not just collective entertainments but forms of individual psychological satisfaction: 'Improvements in living standards, limited social conquests (paid holidays, reduction in the length of the working week), new needs and new opportunities for leisure reinforce ever more a basic demand: the desire to live one's own life, that is to say to live one's own dreams and to dream one's own life'.[25]

The studios had their share of ups and downs and faced numerous challenges,[26] but the 1930s overall were a very positive period for Hollywood cinema. The advent of sound film was a source of problems but it also drew new audiences and created the new genre of the musical as well as breathing new life into existing ones, by means of the addition of dialogue. People wanted to hear the stars speak and were fascinated by the sounds of their voices. It was this fascination rather than the invention of sound technology that compelled the studios to embrace sound and movie theatres to undergo costly conversions. But the process took several years and was not easy; indeed many early sound films were depressingly static due to unsophisticated recording technologies.[27] If the studios produced stars in large numbers – and Adrienne McLean argues that in Hollywood in the 1930s there were 'arguably a greater number than in any other decade of the twentieth century' (some eighty-five in total, excluding the Marx brothers)[28] – it was because at a difficult time they proved to be the main hook, the most reliable way of tying filmgoers irresistibly to the movies to the extent that an entrance ticket was often the last thing people gave up rather than the first.

The American star system was promoted in Italy by local agencies of the major American studios and distributors, and by the film press, which was kept supplied with a regular flow of publicity material. Posters were commissioned to adorn street hoardings and cinema fronts. By means of an established code of colours and styles, these indicated genre and setting while also making the faces and names of the stars part of the everyday environment.²⁹ Soon the American stars eliminated nostalgia for the Italian silent stars by forming tastes in such a way that the idea of the star corresponded to the very figures that were the calling card of American cinema. Some critics noted a certain similarity between Borelli and Greta Garbo, who negotiated better than many the transition to sound. This was because she was in origin a star of the silent era who recalled the remote, fantastic goddesses of that age, whereas the American stars of the 1930s were more realistic. Gary Cooper, Errol Flynn, Clark Gable and Ronald Colman, Joan Crawford, Jean Harlow, Carole Lombard and Myrna Loy conformed to types and were the products of a marketing process that was meticulous and scientific. Audiences in Italy, as elsewhere, loved them and admired them, even if they had difficulty pronouncing their names and the process of dubbing levelled out some of their individuality.

The regularity and diverse nature of these contacts meant that over time a gradual shift occurred. Hollywood decisively shaped the way people understood stars, who, instead of being extreme creatures, were typically defined by the widely appreciated attributes of beauty, youth (or, for men, youthful maturity), a good physique, excellent grooming and tailoring, attractive moral qualities, wealth, happiness, a leisure-oriented lifestyle, good humour, charm, and so on. The magazines provided many clues to their personalities which were invariably matched to the types they played and the film genres in which they were habitually cast. Photographs lent a strong visual appeal to the experience of stardom and soon regular readers of magazines could identify a series of recognisable lifestyle traits, poses and typical eccentricities. Although American stars were remote and frustratingly out of reach, save for the rare occasions when they visited Italy for promotional or vacation purposes, they seemed like neighbours and friends. 'The crowd got used to thinking of American actors as friends of the family and to pitying Italian actors as presumptuous losers', observed the director and critic G.V. Sampieri.³⁰

The extent of the engagement with American star culture can be gauged from the Italian press. The studios always supplied a mass of promotional material but most publications preferred to use this selectively. Journalists specialised in the coverage of Hollywood and acted as mediators between stars and their fans. Cesare Zavattini indulged in fantasy pieces that purported to be on-the-spot reports from the Mecca of cinema.³¹ Some, however, got to visit Hollywood. The journalist Arnaldo Fracciaroli offered in 1929 a first-hand description of the life there, while Marco Ramperti, a Milanese writer and film critic of the paper *L'Ambrosiano*, was even photographed strolling arm-in-arm with Jean Harlow. A collection of his highly personal comments on the attractions of the female stars was published in volume in 1936 under the title *L'alfabeta delle stelle* (The Alphabet of the

Stars). His note on Garbo was one of the longest. 'Everyone has dreamed of her, yet no one has managed, even in a dream, to approach her', he observed; 'She is now the Idol, the Sybil, the Muse, the mystical aura, the totem of the two hemispheres'.[32] By contrast to the mystery of Garbo, the main attraction of Carole Lombard to him was her full breasts.[33] He included just four Italians in his alphabet, one of whom was the long-retired Lyda Borelli (remembered as a divine, regal figure who preceded Garbo and whose gestures remained unsurpassed, her memory surviving even the destruction of her films). The other three were two stars of the comedies of the early 1930s, Elsa Merlini and Milly, and Isa Miranda.

All of this caused dissatisfaction among the cultural elite. Not a few intellectuals looked down disdainfully on the naivities and enthusiasms of Hollywood from the high point of a superior and certainly older civilisation. For those who were concerned with the rebirth of Italian cinema, the extraordinary way Hollywood occupied the mental world of spectators provoked concerns of a different type. The dominance of Hollywood meant that there was no place for 'our beautiful girls and handsome young men', as Sampieri put it, and this offended national pride.[34] In order to make a place for them, it was necessary to find ways of making stars whose names would resonate appropriately in Fascist Italy.

Italian Actors or Stars?

Pittaluga's Cines company, with its new sound-equipped Roman studios inaugurated in 1930, showed that in some way Italian cinema could acquire a place in the sound era. However, most of the actors who featured in the productions of the Cines company were recruited from the theatre. In Italy, as in the United States and other countries, the arrival of sound demanded a new type of screen performer, in brief one who could deliver dialogue in addition to gestures. However, Freddi did not believe that the theatre was an appropriate recruiting ground for new faces, 'first of all because [stage actors] consider cinema to be a true fount of plenty that gets them through the dead season'.[35] Their attitude towards cinema work, which they undertook in the summer for relatively high pay, was less than constructive: 'they hate and despise it, thinking it an inferior art, perhaps because they do not feel in it the warmth of a live audience and its applause'. In his view, the importation of performers with established modes of delivery and mannerisms, and who refused to adapt their craft to the needs of a different medium, was a wrong turn.[36] The genre in which Cines specialised was sophisticated comedy and many of its screenplays were adaptations either of stage plays or foreign-language successes.[37] What would later be disparaged as 'white telephone' films were its typical output. Actors 'contributed with energy worthy of a better cause to the flowering of that vacuous and bastard genre that was the so-called "white telephone comedy"', Tullio Kezich has written.[38]

In Freddi's view, the two arts of stage and screen were to be considered completely separate; indeed, their needs were often opposed. 'So', he went on, 'we need to create actors' for the screen. But he argued that it would be absurd to try and replicate a model of stardom that, in his view, appeared to be on the point of decline even where it had triumphed. However, 'that does not mean that the problem is insoluble or even difficult. It would be enough to follow the opposite method to the one that has been followed up to now ... and give preference wherever possible to the presence of the masses.'[39] Mass scenes, he argued, confer 'a suggestive and powerful choral ethic on a film and could easily be harnessed to the modern concept of a new Italian cinema'. Interviewed in *Cinema illustrazione* in June 1934, Alessandro Blasetti responded, when asked if there could ever be an Italian phenomenon of stardom with the same hold over the public as that of the foreigners: 'Goodness! Why not!'[40] He went on to say: 'certainly our diva of today and tomorrow cannot be either an aristocrat or a refined bourgeois, but rather a woman of the people, who is loved by the audience not on account of her mysterious charm'. His response is interesting not just because of the optimism it betrayed but because it immediately set up a distance from the divas of the past on the one hand, and the artifice of Hollywood on the other. In his view, a potential Italian stardom needed to find a new way that was accessible and down to earth.

It was quite commonplace among Fascists to talk of the need for a star system that would consist of authentic and recognisable Italian types rather than the shiny cosmopolitans who populated the Cines comedies. Although well made and in their own way stylish, these often lacked an Italian flavour on account of their fidelity to their German or Hungarian origins.[41] In the report he prepared for Mussolini in 1934 following his study visit to Hollywood, Freddi spoke of the need to copy America and Germany in recruiting technical specialists from other countries but he rejected any idea of using foreign actors, 'equally for a question of self-esteem, for the requirements of sound cinema and for the desirability for production to be typically Italian'.[42]

The new brand of screen actor was given a distinct profile. Actors, Freddi argued, needed to be selected on a continuous basis from among 'the middle, educated classes who are distant from banal, snobbish and parvenu-type habits'. He lamented the fact that known names were used to dupe the public into patronising poor films. 'The players, and it becomes monotonous to repeat it, were always the same and, what is more, lots of films were based on their names and their credit with the audience which had no artistic value or original physiognomy.'[43] To ensure that standards were maintained, selection needed to be ongoing. 'There should be regular purges of the least remunerative, adaptable and typical elements', he recommended. Perhaps confusing actors with the parts they played, he set up a provincial ideal-type that was infused with patriotic pride and respectability. 'Special attention should be given to pronunciation. Preference should be accorded to healthy, spontaneous, open Italian physionomical types devoid of sophistication or exotic mannerisms.'[44]

Freddi was convinced that actors should be drawn from the educated middle classes. These had been reluctant to contemplate the cinema as an appropriate field of activity, he felt, because of the 'bad reputation that, mostly wrongly, was attributed to the cinema milieu'. This had prevented the recruitment of 'elements who either belonged to the educated classes or who had lived in moral circles'.[45] The intervention of the state in creating new institutions and bringing the industry into the sphere of public control and regulation was intended to have a moralising effect and to create a situation in which it was regarded with a certain prestige and importance.

Freddi's personal campaign against stars bypassed the fact that stardom was not simply a false imposition on cinema, the product of the narcissism of actors or the short-term outlook of producers. It was also a promotional tool that was crucial in rooting cinema in the popular mind. It was a means whereby actors were transformed into ideals and cheerleaders for the films in which they appeared. Given that Fascism had no intention of abolishing commercial film-making, it was ingenuous to imagine that stars could be done away with; because, through them, cinema had also shaped human perceptions and values.

One of the areas in which such shaping had been dramatic and was ongoing was that of physical beauty. There had been a view, articulated from 1930, when an unsigned article entitled 'Per l'attore italiano' appeared in *Cinema illustrazione*, that cinema should act as a vehicle for the promotion of typically Italian physical specimens. Cinema was called on to 'boost systematically its Italian qualities' by 'seeking among our varied and beautiful people its sources of inspiration':[46]

> Our actresses should give us our best, most pleasing, most delicately charming and most seductive images of Italian womanhood, which is the world's favourite, and our actors should be fine examples of Italian masculinity, from the gentlemen of the noblest stock on earth to the peasants who maintain the purest lines of the most classical virile beauty: every region, every district of our country offers magnificent examples which should be used just as the sculptor or the painter use models – not to copy them but to re-create them.

Yet this was not necessarily easy to achieve. Writing in 1936, the critic Giacomo Debenedetti argued that:

> one of the most salient aspects of the industrial history of cinema is the progressive and intensive perfecting of feminine beauty. All technical conquests, even if they were born for other purposes, converge in the task of improving the star: ever

lighter and more subtle make-up, modelling of the body in clothes that reveal ever more of the person, abolition of all underwear that disturbs the flow of the body line, magical and flattering lighting, close-ups.[47] ... And let no-one tell me that some of these are due to fashion not cinema; fashion today is invented in Hollywood. All Paris does, like other capitals, is to launch its products. ... In this way, film has brought beautiful women into a direct, immediate and almost sensual contact with the public, exciting it to insist that they should be ever more beautiful. For the perspective of the stage, which rendered the 'less beautiful than reality' acceptable, we have reached the stage of 'more beautiful than reality', that is to say we have passed from convention to realism and from realism to a super-realism.[48]

This was a matter of great concern because it touched on a core issue in national identity. Italian intellectuals, who conventionally took pride in their country's reputation as the home of feminine beauty had watched the progressive advance of modern beauty with dismay. Since the early post-First World War years, they had waged war against artificial and unconventional femininity, labelling it unnatural and un-Italian.[49] This position had been turned into dogma by Fascism. Debenedetti's assertion that 'the manufacture of a diva can be perfectly adapted to the preferences of the moment without this necessarily meaning that it becomes poetic' was a recognition of the triumph of a practical logic.[50] In other words, for all the admiration he expressed for cinema's ability to perfect and present beauty, there was a feeling that something was being lost. Cinematic beauty was cold and uninviting. An article in *Lo Schermo* on 'the beauties of Hollywood' deemed that theirs was 'the beauty that you obtain in the studios, cinematic beauty, chemically pure beauty'.[51] In other words, it was synthetic and inhuman. Jean Harlow was 'a masterpiece of embalmment', or sculpted marble. 'In that bland museum, the synthetic, chemically pure beauty of the Hollywood studios expresses the suggestive warning that is emanated by masterpieces: do not touch'. This was something that was extraneous to Italian culture since 'no one, in fact, who is not a boy whose senses have just awakened or a sad pervert, has ever fallen in love with one of those women we see at the cinema, just as no one has ever been erotically aroused by a beautiful statue'. Even though 'the process of decantation is unknown to us', the article's author sadly admitted, 'the result bears an unmistakable, typically American, brand, and reworked in this way it appeals even to our audiences'.

The women who featured in Cines films in the early 1930s presented appeals that were not primarily visual. Indeed Elsa Merlini and Milly were better known for their musical qualities, while Dria Paola, Isa Pola and Lia Franca were quite modest, unexceptional types. Merlini was an interesting case of a well-known stage performer who took well to cinema and who based her appeal more on vitality than beauty. Her exuberant performance as a young woman aspiring to an office job in the popular film *La segretaria privata* (The Private Secretary, Goffredo Alessandrini, 1931) struck a chord.

With her round face and chirpy singing voice she brought verve to a film whose German origins were apparent in several of the situations and locations. As with many early sound films, the musical element was a critical part of the appeal and Merlini's pleasant singing voice turned her into 'the favourite of bourgeois audiences' who 'busied herself in a whole series of artificial and silly comedies usually of an imported type'.[52] Ramperti found her melancholic despite the busy good humour of her exterior attitude. Milly, by contrast, was pure joy: 'every film sung by Milly is a rustic festival where warbles and firecrackers end up being a single thing, happiness itself', he waxed lyrically.[53]

Only Isa Miranda was hailed both as a cinematic beauty and an authentic Italian woman. She was seen as a mixture of Hollywood and the Italian Renaissance: 'her cheekbones recall Hepburn or Dietrich's but more directly they recall the women that the Tuscan [Leonardo da Vinci] painted in the guise of young Marias or adolescent saints in northern Italy'.[54] Miranda, in fact, was the only actress to benefit from a proper commercial launch. Cast by Max Ophuls as the lead in *La signora di tutti* (Everybody's Lady, 1934), the film with which the Milanese publisher Angelo Rizzoli began his career as a producer, she was heavily promoted in the company's magazines and treated as a fully fledged star.

The magazines always put a positive gloss on the fact that Italian stars were different. Over a period of years they ran a continuous commentary on Italian performers, urging that lessons be learned from Hollywood without going too far. A case in point is an article published in *Cinema* in 1937 on actresses' hair.[55] The author called for hairstyles that corresponded to the spirit of an actress, noting that the Americans paid attention to many aspects of a performer's presentation, including nails, hair, face, teeth and dress. But Italian actresses were warned to take care not to take this too far since American cinema 'bears the mark of an excessively rigid fetishisation of "beauty"'; 'sometimes American hairstyles seem like metallic helmets ... like something superimposed and absent, devoid of that lively fascination that is demanded of all feminine traits'. This discourse was not without its contradictions. While simplicity was widely seen as a virtue, performers were warned not to 'overdo a realism that sometimes borders on neglect'.

Something was found wanting in virtually every Italian actor who took to the screen in the early to mid-1930s. If they were not lacking in looks, they were found to be short on style and originality; if they were fashionable then they could be deemed static and theatrical. The point of comparison was almost always Hollywood. Dria Paola, for example, was urged to stop wearing her hair like Greta Garbo, while Germana Paolieri was reproved for exhibiting her body in a swimsuit without having undertaken any regular exercise ('By now Hollywood has made us more demanding in the matter of nudity', was the comment).[56] Looking back on the stars of the early 1930s, Giulio Cesare Castello found them to be 'domestic and provincial'.

'There were lots of female creatures of a full-figured or downbeat type (the young Isa Pola, for example) who were unmistakeably and sometimes rather depressingly ordinary, and certain young chaps who now and again were capable players but who invariably were unsuitable as candidates for the conferment of a mythical aura'.[57]

In the early 1930s, male stars were few and far between. One was Vittorio De Sica, who Castello dubbed 'the first real example of stardom in that modest Italian cinema in search of an identity'.[58] Despite his undeniable charm, easy way with songs and the label of 'local Rudolph Valentino' that an American movie professional gave him, he was not conventionally good-looking; he was 'ugly' and possessed of 'a less than irreprehensible nose'. Good looks were not a strong suit either of two men mentioned by Kezich: Nino Besozzi, whose lazy, relaxed playing contrasted with the energy of Merlini; and Armando Falconi, an older actor whose cheery manner brought a familiar and avuncular air to many films. Although the men were by no means exempt from scrutiny, it was mainly women who were seen to embody the idea of the star.

In 1935 Mario Soldati published under a pseudonym a work of fiction that was hailed as the novel of Italian cinema of the 1930s. He was clearly writing for a public that was intrigued by the cinema and especially by the people who appeared on the screen. His novel offered an informed peep through the keyhole that was intended to serve as a warning to those who thought luck or ambition were sufficient qualities to become a star. As his title *24 ore in uno studio cinematografico* suggests, he chose to focus on 'a day in the life of a star'. Inevitably, the star was female.[59] The novel begins with a woman waking up early in the morning and preparing to leave home by taxi. 'Who is this woman who seems to live in ease and wealth but whose day begins at the same hour and with the same angry rapidity as that of a worker or a hunter?', the narrator asks, before it is revealed that she is 'a film actress ... a so-called screen diva or star'.[60] Soldati knew the world he was describing. Yet there is something impressionistic about his text that suggests he was designing an ideal type, imagining what the life of a fully fledged star might be rather than conveying the reality of an existing category. Not by chance, the book is littered with references to Hollywood and meditations on the fabricated nature of cinema ('artifice, always, is at the basis of cinema'). Stars, he claimed, needed to possess many qualities, 'which rarely are all found in the same person'. These included 'beauty, a photogenic quality (which is a different thing from beauty), good pronunciation, temperament, a certain intelligence etc.' A young woman might have all of these but her chances could be ruined by some other defect, 'bad teeth or, worse, a bent nose', he concluded.[61] The problem was that by 1935 Italy did not yet have a stable star system and the imagination was the only sphere in which it existed. The true star, as he saw it, had still to be created.

The Formation of a National Star System

'The period ... between 1934 and 1939 can be defined as one of a desperate and often discouraging search for homemade stars', Tullio Kezich has written.[62] Brunetta agrees, stating that, 'if we were to measure, even purely in quantitative terms, the light emitted by the halos of the few autarchic stars of the year following the inauguration of Cinecittà, basing ourselves on infinitesimal bits of stardust, we should have to note the almost complete absence of radiations and autonomous and self-sufficient energy'.[63] What changed the situation was the withdrawal of the American majors from the market at the end of 1938 in protest at the creation of a state monopoly on the purchase of foreign films. This led to a most significant expansion in production and in the domestic standing of Italian cinema. 'There is a great deal to be done to create a true, genuine Italian star culture', Sampieri wrote some months after the withdrawal.[64] Three things needed to be done. First, the circulation of news and photographs about American stars needed to be stopped since it was defeatist and inappropriate after the majors' withdrawal; second, photos of Italian actors had to be circulated to make them desirable and interesting. Third, actors had to be persuaded to stop getting angry if they were approached to do bathing costume shots or if news and gossip was circulated about imaginary love affairs, since this sort of publicity generated interest. This last point was controversial, not only because actors were sensitive, but because official opinion took a dim view of the sort of gossip that occasionally appeared in the press.

By 1939, only a handful of names were established, among them Isa Miranda and De Sica. Others included Assia Noris, a Russian-born actress who married the director Camerini and starred in several of his films alongside De Sica, the tall and rugged Sardinian Amedeo Nazzari and the taciturn Fosco Giachetti. Elsa Merlini, Nino Besozzi, Dria Paola and Lia Franca had faded already. The increase in the production level in the years that immediately followed and the virtual absence of new American films of note meant that a critical mass existed for which more names became more regular features and more familiar to audiences. It was in this context that Gino Cervi, Clara Calamai, Alida Valli and many others got their chance.

As these new figures asserted themselves, the press ceased to lament the absence of a group of fully fledged stars able to bring lustre and commercial appeal to national cinema. Previously, general discourses had often been disparaging about Italian actors. Now there were a number of indicators that film stardom was no longer entirely a derivative phenomenon. For Scaglione, the crusade against Hollywood 'imposed on directors the need to valorise that human typology that will be defined as "Italian" and that sometimes would create unease and questionable artistic results'.[65] The demand for physical types that were fine examples of the Italian race was voiced among others by Vittorio Mussolini who called for 'a racist consciousness in Italian cinema',[66] 'that is a highlighting of the characteristics that correspond physically' to the biological and aesthetic sense of race. Even extras whose bodies did not fit should be eliminated, he argued.

In this crucial phase, the collective discussion around national cinema found a new theme. Once movie stars had been made a legitimate object of reflection, the right to comment on them was open. In *Cinema* in April 1939, Anton Giulio Majano, a future television director, pronounced his dissatisfaction with the screen images of a number of stars he identified by name.[67] Leda Gloria was branded 'too exuberant and lower class', Maria Denis too petit bourgeois, Laura Nucci too decorative, Alida Valli immature and Assia Noris pretty but doll-like. Other critics, however, were happy to leap to the defence of this or that actress. Paola Barbara, who in Majano's judgement was too unrefined, was deemed 'spontaneous and instinctive' in *Cinema* later the same year. She was, it was observed, 'in her physique and temperament, the genuine type of Italian woman'.[68]

Although the majority of comments concerned women, the rise of a variegated category of male stars also occasioned comment. The strongest and longest lasting star of the period, Nazzari, was immediately hailed as positive, while Fosco Giachetti also was the bearer of a conventional notion of male heroism and sacrifice that in some features was given a Fascist inflection. The regime attempted to profit in some way from the successes of actors by association or by using them in propaganda productions. Although Nazzari and Giachetti both made many films with no propaganda content, they were repeatedly hailed as representatives of Fascist heroism and masculinity. By contrast, De Sica and Gino Cervi were more commonplace types better suited to everyday roles, while Massimo Girotti and Rossano Brazzi were young pin-ups and Roberto Villa the shy boyfriend. For cultural reasons, and because of the gender of most critics, the women were still scrutinised more closely, but it was the men who were the main bearers of ideals of custom reform, aspirations to change in national character, raised national prestige and collective image.

In his memoirs, Freddi looked back proudly at the great steps forward that Italian cinema took between 1934 and 1937. Writers, musicians and technicians had been brought into cinema in large numbers and many new faces had been given a chance before the cameras. Every year new names joined their ranks and many were successful. All the work and efforts at consolidation that had been made, he claimed, led to a situation

> in which we were able to create new splendid constellations, in the light of which waves of fresh, new talent could step forward and find recognition; talent that sprang not from the boards of the stage but from real, true life and that was endowed with fresh spontaneity and fertile creativity. A practically trained company was thus created that for long [was] able to respond to all the needs of the screen.[69]

Freddi was alluding to the opportunities offered by expanding production and the role of the Centro sperimentale in forming new cadres for the industry. In typically boastful fashion, he associated the innovations of his own period as director general with the triumphant re-emergence of Italian cinema.

The Centro sperimentale, founded in 1935, was expected to take a major role in cultivating new talents for the industry. Some did graduate from it, including Mariella Lotti, Carla Candiani and Roberto Villa. The most famous student was Alida Valli, who in fact never finished her course. However, most of the established young women, including Assia Noris, Maria Denis, Doris Duranti and others, had been handpicked by producers and directors, and new faces were still discovered by chance, in the street, in holiday resorts, or among the generic personnel of prose and variety theatre.[70] Isa Miranda and Elsa De Giorgi had sent photographs of themselves to production companies and were invited to take screen tests. Leda Gloria, Laura Nucci, Orietta Fiume, Luisa Ferida, Dina Sassoli and Laura Solari all won competitions. Men continued to be recruited from the theatre, although a small number, among them Massimo Girotti, were drawn from sport.

In terms of the process of turning an actor into a star, the role of the director was crucial. It is difficult to think of a single actor who achieved star status without the backing of an established one. De Sica and Noris, for example, owed their popularity in large measure to their roles in the popular comedies of Mario Camerini. Denis trod water in run-of-the-mill light comedy before emerging more strongly in the dramatic Spanish civil war film *L'assedio del Alcazar* (The Seige of the Alcazar), directed with customary flair by Augusto Genina in 1936. She consolidated her position with a moving performance in the costumed tear-jerker *Addio Giovinezza* (Goodbye Youth, Ferdinando Maria Poggioli, 1940), in which she played a love-struck seamstress who is cast aside by her student beau. Luisa Ferida would have remained a minor supporting actress had Blasetti not cast her alongside Gino Cervi in *Un'avventura di Salvator Rosa* (An Adventure of Salvator Rosa, 1940), after which she appeared in a string of passionate, compelling or tragic leading roles in *Fedora* (Camillo Mastrocinque, 1942), *Nozze di sangue* (Blood Wedding, Goffredo Alessandrini, 1941), and *Fari nella nebbia* (Headlights in the Fog, Gianni Franciolini, 1942). Massimo Scaglione has argued that most actresses struggled to achieve an identifiable screen personality as they were thrust into the most disparate roles by directors working in a hurry without regard to quality.[71] Giachetti and Nazzari owed their initial successes to a series of quality military films that enjoyed official prestige: *Lo squadrone bianco* (The White Squadron, Augusto Genina, 1936) and *L'assedio del Alcazar* for the former, *Cavalleria* (Cavalry, Goffredo Alessandrini, 1936) and *Luciano Serra pilota* (Luciano Serra, Pilot, Goffredo Alessandrini,

1938) for the latter. The relative homogeneity of these roles was crucial in forging their personas.

A single big hit was often decisive in establishing a star's image in the public mind. Assia Noris had made some fourteen films, often playing capricious but engaging socialites, before she was cast as the servant girl Lauretta in Camerini's *Il signor Max* (Mr Max, 1937). It was that role that endeared her to middle-class audiences and turned her into a national favourite. Alida Valli was picked out from the start of her career as having great promise, but it was her first film with Nazzari, *Assenza ingiustificata* (Unjustified Absence, Max Neufeld, 1939), that made her truly stand out from other young actresses. Clara Calamai's popularity as a dark lady owed much to her role in the rumbustious Renaissance drama *La cena delle beffe* (The Jester's Supper, Alessandro Blasetti, 1941), in which Nazzari's loutish character rips off her dress to momentarily expose her breasts. Despite the large number of films he made, Nazzari's own image was always heavily determined by his performance in *Luciano Serra pilota*.

Some directors were known for their attention to actors. Camerini, Blasetti, Genina and Poggioli were thought to be capable of bringing the best out of them and consequently many were eager to work for them. But ongoing working relationships were the exception rather than the rule. Camerini married Noris and supported her career as long as their marriage lasted. Blasetti often gave the leading female role to his wife, Elisa Cegani. De Sica was Camerini's preferred male lead while Soldati worked with Valli whenever he could. Doris Duranti's star vehicles were all produced by Eugenio Fontana and directed by Flavio Calzavara. Beyond these instances, most actors were left to their own devices. Although the general directorate and, later, Cinecittà supplied ample photographic and written material to the press, publicity build-ups occurred around films rather than players.

Specific casting choices were given ministerial consideration when films were deemed to have a propaganda purpose or connotation, or when there was concern that a casting option might damage an established benefit. The Minister of Popular Culture, Alessandro Pavolini, expressed disapproval of the decision to cast Giachetti as a Communist political commissar in *Noi vivi – Addio Kira* (We the Living – Addio Kira, Goffredo Alessandrini, 1942) but did not impose an outright ban.[72] In general terms, the regime – sometimes through officials, sometimes through official critics – was more concerned that stars should offer gender representations that accorded with its own view of male and female roles. It also intervened to try and Italianise aspects of the star system which, ever since the heyday of Cines in the early 1930s, had included an exotic element. In the 1940s a number of female stars' names were brusquely Italianised in title credits and in the press, with Doris Duranti's first name becoming Dori, Irasema Dilian's being turned into Eva Maria. This followed criticism in the press of new starlets. 'Quite often we are presented with a new face', *L'Eco del Cinema* commented in

January 1941, but the spectator inevitably asked: 'Haven't I seen her somewhere before? But where? They are all too similar right down to their silly names: Rubi, Vivi, Elli, Jole, Jone ... Enough, please! Do all these blessed cinema girls all have to be so beautiful and smooth, beautiful and smooth like porcelain dolls? And do they have to go and choose names that don't belong to the earth or the sky?' the anonymous author protested.[73]

There are numerous testimonies from the period which suggest that actors, and especially actresses, were accustomed to demanding to see ministers or officials when they had failed to do obtain roles by conventional means. Actors were aware of the context in which they were working and sought to use political connections to seek advancement or simply satisfaction. But there is no evidence of any systematic intervention in response to appeals of this type. Most actors avoided close identification with the regime out of a desire to preserve their independence and to avoid risks to their popularity. Production companies could play an important role in casting but their power was very limited compared to that of the major American studios. The only companies that at any point employed a casting policy were Cines, Lux, Scalera, Excelsa and Italcine. Before Cines systematically signed up many of the best names in the 1940s,[74] most actors were never placed under contract for more than one film. Two exceptions were Isa Miranda, who was signed to Lux, and Alida Valli, who was contracted first with Exclesa and then Minerva. The chronicles of the period are filled with accounts of tussles between directors and production companies over casting. Powerful directors often seem to have got their own way. For example, Blasetti succeeded in casting Luisa Ferida and Rina Morelli in *Un'avventura di Salvator Rosa* against the production company's preference for Valli and Denis. Soldati, by contrast, had Miranda imposed on him for *Malombra* whereas he would have preferred Valli.

The Workings of Star Culture

By the early 1940s, Italian cinema was working largely in the manner of a proper industry. The quality of most technical aspects of film-making was high, the volume of production had increased, Italian films dominated the internal market and actors had succeeded to some extent in supplanting the missing Americans in the public's affections. Among the innovations boosting the standing of actors were: the star billing accorded to them in film publicity and title credits; the impact on box office of casting and the consequent increase in actors' pay; evidence of growing public involvement through fan letters and letters to the press; the coverage of stars in illustrated and women's magazines; some, albeit limited, indications of a star lifestyle including access to elite events and circles; the multiplication of commercial and promotional initiatives around individual stars, and yearnings for celebrity. With the active role of government institutions, ranging from the Centro sperimentale to the Venice Festival, the coordinated action of producers and studios, the development of a dedicated film press consisting of several titles, and the support of the mainstream press, for the first time a discourse came into being around the subject of the national star system.

Of course, the Americans still conserved a place in the memories of critics and spectators alike. But, no matter how derivative the Italian stars had once been, by this time they had acquired profiles of their own. The tendency to label Italians 'the American this' or 'the American that' persisted, but was not really justified. An oft-cited cartoon published in *Cinema* in 1941 entitled 'Ameni paralleli' (Amusing parallels) matched up many prominent Italians with their supposed Hollywood counterparts. Caricatures of, amongst others, Elsa Merlini, Alida Valli, Roberto Villa and Doris Duranti were paired, respectively, with those of Claudette Colbert, Loretta Young, Tyrone Power and Dorothy Lamour – that is to say, the proper stars of whom they were supposedly the derivative local versions. In fact, this exercise was no more than what it claimed to be – an amusing diversion – rather than the revelation of a hitherto secret template. Many of the pairings had little rhyme or reason, or were based on no more than superficial physical resemblances. The actors who were most repeatedly and insistently seen in relation to Hollywood stars – Isa Miranda and Amedeo Nazzari – were notable by their absence.

Italian stars were assumed to conform to the tastes, social norms and aesthetic values of their society. This theme, which found authoritative support as Fascism strengthened its racial ideas, was taken up repeatedly through the decade. *Cinema* argued in 1936 that, since the United States had persuaded everyone to live in their world, 'why don't we try to get others to live under the influence of Italy and Rome, by promoting a cannon of beauty, a sense of balance and a way of life to which the world today, through struggles and contrasts, is tending to return?'[75] Two years later *Cinema illustrazione* suggested, on similar lines, that American cinema had done much to give the world an image of the American as a paragon of beauty, strength, and moral and physical health. Italian actors, it argued, should also be physical ideals of the race. One good example was Amedeo Nazzari, who was deemed to have 'handsomeness plus physical harmony and spiritual calm'.[76] Actors who were deemed to embody identifiable national characteristics could be sure of special praise. The women's magazine *Grazia* announced that 'Paola Barbara is one of our actresses who most corresponds to the common ideal of the healthy, beautiful, intelligent, restful woman, whose plump grace transmits such a sense of peace as to make optimists of even the most determined grumps'.[77]

The corollary of praise was criticism. In contrast to the American stars, who were treated in the press as remote beings, unreal entities who were regarded with wonder and viewed from a certain position of inferiority,

Italian actors were down to earth and familiar. They were 'ours' and deemed to be expressions of 'us'. As such they were subject to praise, criticism, encouragement and advice of a quite different order. They were homely idols, everyday Italians writ large. They were often depicted in gently mocking caricatures in the press and were also the target of personal judgements. Gino Cervi was a particular target on account of the very ordinariness that he deployed so effectively in some of his screen roles. 'Gino Cervi is ugly!' *Film* pronounced, deriding his 'bureaucratic hair', 'chubby ruby cheeks' and 'waddle'.[78] The magazine *Si gira* felt he had let himself go physically: 'A film actor has a duty to keep in shape physically and maintain a lively, curious spirit for as long as possible. It is not right that he should allow himself to get tubby like any bourgeois pushing forty or allow a sense of monotony and boredom to creep into his art.'[79] Even Mussolini very occasionally commented on the appearance of actors, but only privately to Claretta Petacci, to whom he remarked that Orietta Fiume was 'racchia e brutta' (scrawny and ugly).[80] In public discourse, criticism was usually cast in more general terms but in certain areas could be quite damning. The performing talents and beauty of actresses was not always deemed to be up to the mark by male critics, and it was occasionally remarked that better-looking women could be seen on the country's streets.

These expressions of dissatisfaction never disappeared completely but they certainly diminished as the star system took on a definitive shape and patterns of allure were woven around the leading names. It is striking that the continuous public discourse about the physical qualities of actors and their suitability or otherwise as representatives of the Italian race was not matched by any debate about the particular cinematic qualities or values that needed to be mobilised in relation to them. Whether it was due to the centrality of the physical body in Fascist aesthetics, and in the classical ideals that the more cultured Fascists appropriated and championed, or to the lack of a developed cinematic culture is unclear, but it does not appear that any discourses were elaborated in print about the way Italian stars should be lit and shot in order to highlight their exemplary qualities. Nor is it possible to identify any consistent practice. Where there was perhaps a more marked sense of the national specificity of screen performers was in the treatment accorded to their voices. Great stress was placed on the way their spoke Italian, the clarity of their diction, and the texture and timbre of their voices. Stars may sometimes not have looked completely original but they always sounded distinctive – a reason their appeal was also harnessed by radio.

In this respect Fascist Italy differed from Nazi Germany, where Erica Carter draws attention to what she calls a 'curious visual underemphasis, even of Germany's most favoured stars'. Lighting, she notes, was crucial in Hollywood to bring out and reinforce the star's inner worlds. Lighting was gendered, with multiple lights being used to accentuate the beauty of women in close-ups and to highlight the character of the individual in the case of men.[81] 'Star lighting in Hollywood famously lent to the faces of Garbo, Dietrich and their contemporaries a shimmer that fractured the realism of the film image, and drew attention to the star as fabrication, surface image and show', she argues; 'in [Zarah] Leander's films, by contrast, the rejection of Hollywood star aesthetics in the visual construction of her screen image went hand in hand with a narrative repudiation of visual excess'.[82] 'So-called ensemble lighting was the preferred German alternative to the American habit of back and top lighting for "halo effects" in star representation in particular'.[83] An anti-star aesthetic thus prevailed in Nazi cinema that manifested itself in a rejection of key traits of Hollywood practice. As a result, Carter argues, it would be more accurate to consider a figure like Emil Jannings an 'actor-personality' rather than a star in the American sense.[84]

In Italy, as in Hollywood, a number of cinematographers were of Central European origin, including most notably Vaclav Vich, while others like Ubaldo Arata and Anchise Brizzi were locally trained. Lighting practices could be described as conventional rather than ideological. Gender differentiation was marked, with men always being lit more realistically and women more aesthetically. The soft-focus, top-lit close-up became de rigueur for young actresses. Sometimes such techniques had a diegetic justification; at other times, it is the spectator alone who is the intended target. Such shots (which in Hollywood were sometimes set up by still photographers) impressed themselves on spectators and recurred in their memories of films. Moreover, in the presentation of some male stars, the influence of Fascist aesthetics was evident. The low-angle three-quarter shots of Amedeo Nazzari and Fosco Giachetti respectively in *Cavalleria* and *Lo Squadrone bianco* (notably in the key establishing shots of the latter film) served to underline visually the literal and moral position of leadership that their characters occupied within the narrative. By obliging the spectator to look up to the men, the *mise-en-scène* was arranged in such a way as to establish the authority of a certain type of heroic masculinity. The same model was employed by Luce Institute newsreel photographers in portrayals of Mussolini and leading Fascists. The actors of course appeared in many non-military films where they were photographed differently, but some of their aura undoubtedly derived from the way they were set up as figures of authority – and implicit examples of Fascist masculinity – in these films.

The Fascists generally preferred simplicity over excess but it would be difficult to argue, as Carter does for Germany, that visual excess was 'un-Italian'. Indeed, an obsession with the visual and with surfaces was a key part of Italian culture from which neither Fascism nor cinema was exempt, despite the attempts made in the early 1920s in the arts to promote a return to classical order.[85] If the fracturing and surface emphasis of star images which Carter links to Hollywood was less developed, this was due to a conception of lighting as art rather than commerce, and the conviction that the

Italian quality of stars had to be manifested in warmth and spontaneity, in contrast to the cold, manufactured stars of Hollywood.

Nevertheless, the regime and its various aesthetic requirements were not the only factors bearing on the way actors were photographed. The star system itself produced pressures for certain types of lighting effects. Stars were sensitive to matters of image and were often caught in bitter rivalries over matters of billing, size of part or visual presentation. Some demanded preferential treatment from cinematographers and costume designers. For example, Assia Noris was very aware of her idealised screen image and actively insisted on back and top lighting for halo effects.[86] Alida Valli, by contrast, was an actress whose interiority was explored more through different lighting effects and greater use of shadow. Vich and Brizzi worked with both of them and tailored their work to their preferences as well as the parts they played.

The rise of the star system was marked by an exponential increase in the use of close-ups. Some observers deplored this as a deleterious development. In a significant article, the theorist and critic Guido Aristarco drew a distinction between what he termed the 'functional close-up' and the 'narcissistic close-up'.[87] He observed that the latter was a degenerative form that had become a hallmark of a cinema that was in thrall to its stars, to the extent that it completely dominated some films, such as Alessandrini's *Noi vivi* in which three stars (Valli, Giachetti and Brazzi) were cast as the leads:

> If the diva shrieks, it is because she wants a close-up (and I am thinking of the shrieks of Assia in doll-like mode, of the fatal Miranda, of the 'girl' Merlini, of Lili [Lili Silvi] the untamed shrew). If the actor threatens to break his contract, it is not because he wants original and inventive parts but close-ups (and I think of the threats of the 'cynical' Rossano [Brazzi] or, better, of his 'human' smile or of the 'wavy' hair of the handsome Amedeo [Nazzari]). And the director, faced with these aristocratic and divine shrieks, these aristocratic and divine threats, gives in. Besides – as I have said before – theory does not count. It is practice that counts; in a film what counts are the names of the actors, or rather of the artists, of the *divo*, the *diva*, the star. It is their close-ups that matter, not the theories devised by the aesthetes of cinema on close-ups.

Narcissistic close-ups failed to use the visual expressiveness of the human face to its full potential, Aristarco argued, because the stars always spoke during them. Words thus gained the upper hand over the image and cinema lost a vital lyrical tool.

In the early 1940s various episodes of star tantrums and temperament were reported and close-ups were by no means the only cause. For example, *Film* ran an article entitled 'Maria, the tyrant' which announced that Maria Denis was refusing to work early mornings. 'That little flat nose of hers has made her, almost naturally, the typical heroine of cinema's bourgeois sentimentalism ... The more she is small and contrite, the better she is on screen. But for some time now in real life, that little ordinary nose is raising itself towards demanding attitudes and queenly pettiness.'[88] There were anxieties of various order in relation to the stars, and these could be found as much within the film industry as beyond it. Cesare Zavattini noted in his diary in November 1941 that Merlini, Lili Silvi and others had all given vent to signs of temperament and needed to be put in their place. Examples of 'nervous' behaviour, he argued,

> force me to conclude that our generation has not trained actors correctly. We have spent our lives complimenting them. Some of them as a result expect the constant admiration of the air, of things and of men. They live without suspicions, they are greedy for our eyes, indeed they almost pop them out of their sockets; their apparent happiness is humiliating, but more humiliating still is their way of granting themselves particular rights. In fact they have not got any, especially not today. I hope that nostalgia for the time when spectators used to drag carriages from theatre exits will disappear forever, along with autograph hunting. We agree that in Italy we have actors great and small who live naturally, cross the road at a normal pace, read the odd book and know they are not immortal. But what I am against is the aura, whose growth all of us have contributed to out of weakness or ingenuity.[89]

Mario Soldati, author of *24 ore in uno studio cinematografico*, was the director of the only film that satirised the tantrums of the stars while exposing their utter replaceability. *Dora Nelson* (1939) cast Assia Noris in a double role: as a temperamental diva named in the title who, on a whim, abandons the set of a film she is making, and as an ordinary girl resembling her who is called on to stand in so that the film can be completed. A remake of a French film directed by René Guissart, the action was adapted in every particular to the Italian context. Some of the real staff of Cinecittà featured as themselves, including the irascible porter Pappalardo, and numerous real locations were used. The sweet ordinary girl was a reflection of the screen image of Noris but insiders knew that it was the unbearable Dora Nelson who was closest to the truth.

It is worth noting that these comments were largely directed at actresses and reflected the viewpoint of male writers and directors. The disruptive behaviour of a Nazzari, who often refused to follow the instructions of directors, escaped comment. A gendered reading of the issue, instead of accepting the comments at face value, might suggest that, by making demands, actresses were trying to establish a degree of agency in a process that took it for granted that they would not assert any subjectivity. Such tensions were a feature of the stardom that was becoming a decisive factor not only in Italian cinema but also in the nascent consumer culture of the interwar years.

Notes

1. R. Burchielli and V. Bianchini. 2004. *Cinecittà: la fabbrica di sogni*, Milan: Boroli, 38.
2. D. Biondi. 1973. *La fabbrica del duce*, Florence: Valecchi, 88–89.
3. E. Zocaro. 1993. '"Prima donna" del teatro italiano' in J. Pantieri (ed.), *Lyda Borelli*, Rome: MICS, 12–23, 31.
4. A. Dalle Vacche. 2008. *Diva: Defiance and Passion in Early Italian Cinema*, Austin: University of Texas Press, 1.
5. G.P. Brunetta. 2001. *Cent'anni di cinema italiano*, Rome–Bari: Laterza, 99.
6. Ibid.
7. Ibid.
8. Dalle Vacche, *Diva*, 1.
9. W. Benjamin. 1970. 'The Work of Art in the Age of Mechanical Reproduction' in Benjamin, *Illuminations*, ed. by H. Arendt, London: Fontana, 219–54.
10. On Gramsci's cinema writings, see Dalle Vacche, *Diva*, 52–55.
11. V. Martinelli, 'La Borelli' in Pantieri, *Lyda Borelli*, 27–28, 28.
12. L. Paciscopi. 1986. *Cinefollie: miti e sregolatezze del "muto"*, Milan: Lucini, 44.
13. C. Caranti. 2003. 'La diva e le donne: Francesca Bertini nella stampa popolare e femminile' in G. Mingozzi (ed.), *Francesca Bertini*, Genoa: Le Mani, 112–24.
14. See D. Lotti. 2008. *Emilio Ghione – l'ultimo apache: vita e film di un divo italiano*, Bologna: Cineteca di Bologna, 153–54.
15. See S. Dagna and C. Giannetto (eds). 2009. *Maciste l'uomo forte*, Bologna: Cineteca di Bologna.
16. See J. Reich. 2010. 'Slave to Fashion: Masculinity, Suits, and the Maciste Films of Italian Silent Cinema' in A. Munich (ed.), *Fashion in Film*, Bloomington: Indiana University Press, 236–59.
17. Brunetta, *Cent'anni*, 118.
18. Dagna and Giannetto, *Maciste l'uomo forte*, 17.
19. Ibid. On Mussolini and mass culture, see S. Gundle. 2013. 'Mass Culture and the Cult of Personality' in Gundle, C. Duggan and G. Pieri (eds), *The Cult of the Duce: Mussolini and the Italians*, Manchester: Manchester University Press.
20. W. Lippmann. (1922) 1949. Public Opinion, New York: The Free Press.
21. Ibid., 61.
22. A. Varaldo. 1926. *Profili di attrici e di attori*, Milan: Barbera, 53–54.
23. Brunetta, *Cent'anni*, 100.
24. E. Morin. 1972. *Les stars*, Paris: Seuil, 23.
25. Ibid., 24.
26. A. McLean. 2011. 'Introduction: Stardom in the 1930s' in McLean (ed.), *Glamour in a Golden Age: Movie Stars of the 1930s*, New Brunswick: Rutgers University Press, 1.
27. R.B. Jewell. 2007. *The Golden Age of Cinema: Hollywood 1929–1945*, Oxford: Blackwell, 95–96.
28. McLean, 'Introduction', 6.

29. On film posters, see L. Ventavoli (ed.). 2001. *Il cinema del ventennio raccontato dai manifesti*, Turin: Bolaffi.
30. G.V. Sampieri, 'Divismo', *Lo Schermo*, July 1939, 18–20.
31. See C. Zavattini. 1991. *Cronache da Hollywood*, Rome: Lucarini.
32. M. Ramperti. (1936) 1981. *L'alfabeta delle stelle*, Palermo: Sellerio, 77–78.
33. Ibid., 115.
34. Sampieri, 'Divismo', 18.
35. L. Freddi. 1949. *Il cinema*, Rome: L'Arnia, 76.
36. T. Kezich. 2006. 'Gli attori italiani dalla preistoria del divismo al monopolio' in O. Caldiron (ed.), *Storia del cinema italiano*, Vol. 5, 1934–39, Venice: Marsilio/Bianco & Nero, 383–403, 387.
37. See V. Buccheri. 2009. *Stile Cines: studi sul cinema italiano 1930–1934*, Milan: Vita e Pensiero.
38. Kezich, 'Gli attori italiani', 401.
39. Freddi, *Il cinema*, 76.
40. Quoted in Kezich, 'Gli attori italiani', 383.
41. On Cines see Buccheri, *Stile Cines*, and R. Redi. 2009. *La Cines: storia di una casa di produzione italiana*, Bologna: Persiani.
42. Quoted in Freddi, *Il cinema*, 75.
43. Ibid., 252.
44. Ibid., 74.
45. Ibid., 279.
46. Anon. 'Per l'attore italiano', *Cinema illustrazione*, 29 October 1930, 5.
47. G. Debenedetti. 1983. 'Dive, maschere e miti del cinema' (1936) in *Al cinema*, edited by L. Micciche, Padua: Marsilio, 155.
48. Ibid., 157.
49. S. Gundle. 2007. *Bellissima: Feminine Beauty and the Idea of Italy*, London and New Haven: Yale University Press, 86–87.
50. Debenedetti, 'Dive, maschere e miti del cinema', 155.
51. G. Marescalchi, 'Bellezze di Hollywood', *Lo Schermo*, January 1936, 28–29.
52. G.C. Castello. 1957. *Il divismo: mitologia del cinema*, Turin: ERI, 433.
53. Ramperti, *L'alfabeta delle stelle*, 136.
54. Ibid., 137.
55. A.P. Cades, 'La capigliatura', *Cinema*, 25 February 1937, 142–44.
56. Quoted in Kezich, 'Gli attori italiani', 386.
57. Ibid., 401.
58. Castello, *Il divismo*, 402.
59. M. Soldati. 1981. *24 ore in uno studio cinematografico*. Palermo: Sellerio; first published 1935, under the pseudonym Franco Pallavera.
60. Ibid., 12–13.
61. Ibid., 24.
62. Kezich, 'Gli attori italiani', 386.
63. G.P. Brunetta. 1989. *Buio in sala: cent'anni di passioni dello spettatore cinematografico*, Venice: Marsilio, 126.

64. Sampieri, 'Divismo', 19.
65. M. Scaglione. 2003. *Le dive del ventennio*, Turin: Lindau, 101.
66. Vittorio Mussolini in *Cinema*, 10 September 1938. Quoted in Scaglione, *Le dive del ventennio*, 85.
67. A.G. Majano, 'Evoluzione della diva', *Cinema*, 10 April 1939, 223–35.
68. Puck, 'Paola Barbara', *Cinema*, 10 September 1939, 178.
69. Freddi, *Il cinema*, 281.
70. Jori, 'Come "nascono" divi e stelle?' *La Domenica del Corriere*, 9 February 1941, 5.
71. Scaglione, *Le dive del ventennio*, 54.
72. B. Di Marino. 2010. 'Gli interpreti maschili tra commedia, drama, film storico e realismo' in E.G. Laura and A. Baldi (eds), *Storia del cinema italiano*, Vol. 6, 1940–1944, Venice–Rome: Marsilio/Bianco & Nero, 267.
73. Emmeci, 'Parliamo un po' delle nostre attrici nuove', *L'Eco del Cinema*, January 1941, 3–4.
74. Freddi explained he had signed up many actors to Cines on exclusive contracts 'not for publicity reasons, that is solely to link the name of an actor to a brand, but to guarantee that the company had a solid group of actors at its disposal to permit the development of strategic production'. See the interview with him in Anon., 'La terza Cines', *Tempo*, 5 February 1942, 23.
75. G. Vigolo, 'Roma e Hollywood', *Cinema*, 25 November 1936, 373–74.
76. Anon., 'Il tipo italiano nel cinema', *Cinema illustrazione*, 12 October 1938, 7.
77. Anon., 'Paola Barbara e il suo nome', *Grazia*, 13 March 1941, 16–17.
78. Tabarrino, 'Gino Cervi è brutto?', *Film*, 23 March 1941, page unnumbered.
79. E. Giovannetti, 'Qualche franca parola: Gino Cervi', *Si gira*, January 1943, page unnumbered.
80. C. Petacci. 2009. *Mussolini segreto: diari 1932–1938*, Milan: Rizzoli, 461 (entry of 17 November 1938).
81. E. Carter. 2004. *Dietrich's Ghosts: The Sublime and the Beautiful in Third Reich Film*, London: BFI, 118–19.
82. Ibid., 185.
83. Ibid., 74.
84. Ibid., 129.
85. On the 'return to order' in the arts, see S. Storchi. 2006. 'Valori Plastici 1918–1922: le inquietudini del nuovo classico', supplement to *The Italianist*, 26.
86. S. Masi. 1991. 'Il controluce nei cappelli' in M. Argentieri (ed.), *Risate di regime: la commedia italiana 1930–1944*, Venice: Marsilio.
87. G. Aristarco, 'Primo piano funzionale', *Si gira*, July 1943, page unnumbered.
88. E. Giovanetti, 'Maria, la tiranna', *Film*, 9 January 1943, 5–6.
89. C. Zavattini. 1979. *Diario cinematografico*, Milan: Bompiani, 23–24.

3

Stars and Commercial Culture

The Fascist regime did not actively promote private consumption since it preferred public investment in industry and infrastructures, such as roads and buildings, as well as foreign conquest. Moreover, it often engaged in ideological battles against modern consumption and its supposedly deleterious effects in terms of promoting a cult of things foreign, undermining conventional gender models and making Italians soft. Mussolini himself often denounced the ideology of comfort and individualism that was associated with consumption. Yet in the post-First World War era, urbanisation, the specialisation and division of labour, the expansion of the category of dependent workers, the erosion of links between city and country, and of traditions that privileged self-sufficiency over spending, all brought changes in patterns of living. Technological innovation impacted on the range and availability of products as well as on communications, culture and entertainment. All of these factors brought Italy into line with other European countries, even though they occurred in a context in which freedom was curtailed and power centralised as never before. As Bianca Gaudenzi has observed, hostility to consumption was never translated into outright repression since Mussolini entertained 'fundamental connections ... with Italian big business and the middle classes, which strove for a modernisation of the production process and, more generally, for that same "comfortable life"'.[1]

Although Fascist propaganda railed against cosmopolitanism in language, behaviour and consumption, the development of the consumer economy in Italy was inevitably shaped by the experiences of more advanced countries.[2] From the mid-nineteenth century, France had been the primary reference point for innovations in Italian retail, distribution and marketing.

The first big stores were modelled on French examples while several Italian commercial artists who played a part in the growth of advertising culture worked in Paris and other capitals. In the 1920s, the influence of American methods and approaches was apparent. Marketing campaigns were launched by Italian branches of American advertising agencies for a number of American branded goods. Fascism understood the advantages that accrued in terms of consent by allowing, and therefore taking credit for, the expansion of limited forms of consumption. Moreover, in supporting industry at a time of world economic crisis, it promoted a form of consumerist patriotism that bestowed approval on the purchase of all national goods and merchandise. There was an explosion of patriotic language in advertising that had the paradoxical effect of 'raising consumption to the status of being a full contributor to the nation's development'.[3]

In the United States, a tight connection existed between film stardom and marketing.[4] In Italy, where modern marketing was less advanced, stars, whether American or Italian, did not function in the same manner. Nonetheless, it is important to understand the ways in which the star system in Italy was embedded in, or related to, the development of mass consumption and, then, how it was affected by the restrictions of the war years. Cinema was an aspect of commercial culture and connections, both implied and structured, existed between the shopping practices and everyday lives of the urban population and the films they watched on screen.

The Role of Cinema

In the United States, the histories of cinema and of consumerism were intertwined. The development of the exhibition sector and indeed of the film industry as a whole was part of the chain store revolution.[5] According to Charles Eckert, 'in the 1910s and 1920s Hollywood assumed a role in the phase of capitalism's life history that the emerging philosophy of consumerism was about to give birth to'.[6] The type of films that were made was driven by the pressures of sales and publicity people in New York, and these pressures led in the direction of contemporary set films that were filled with sumptuous clothes, desirable objects, lavish sets and exciting action.[7] In Italy, the connections that obtained in the United States between moviegoing and consumption were not so strong. Although many cinemas, especially those located in the centres of large cities, bore names like Lux, Excelsior, Smeraldo, Moderno, Eden and so on that implied luxury and modernity, few were purpose-built and even those that were, such as the Grattacieli and Supercinema in Rome, were unlike the fabulous dream palaces of the exotic or Art Deco type that flourished in the United States and Britain. Many were converted theatres or anyway unobtrusive buildings that blended with the urban environment. Nevertheless, by the

1930s, cinema had become a part of the texture of urban life in the more economically developed parts of the country, and in large cities and towns in the centre and south too. In the north, filmgoing was not spread evenly; it was concentrated in provincial capitals and large towns. But larger villages often had cinemas and some churches (more after the Second World War) had dedicated film theatres.

The difference between town and country therefore lay not so much in the existence or not of opportunities to go to the cinema as in the choice and quality of experience. Rural audiences were presented with films on a 'take it or leave it' basis while urban dwellers could choose from a number of options offered by cinemas within easy reach of home or work. While keen filmgoers with enough ready cash would follow the new releases and attend a range of first-run cinemas located in town and city centres, less well-off audiences in outlying residential areas were more likely to go to one of perhaps two or three second-run cinemas located in or near the quarter where they lived. Those who lived at a distance from commercial centres in the outer suburbs were faced with third-run cinemas where end-of-run films could be enjoyed in less than comfortable conditions for a very modest ticket price. The Fascist Afterwork organisation offered regular free film shows to mainly northern audiences who were happy to accept whatever film was provided. All village theatres were second or third run and some could be very primitive, such as the one in an unidentified location in Piedmont where the auditorium was described in *La Domenica del Corriere* (March 1940) as 'a barn that originally must have been a storehouse for grain or something similar, turned into a cinema by means of the addition of a screen, a cabin and a single projector, and rows of benches and chairs'.[8] Reels were often biked back and forth between villages as in the manner shown in Giuseppe Tornatore's *Nuovo Cinema Paradiso* (New Cinema Paradiso, 1988). Locations lying even further out benefited from occasional visits from the mobile cinema vans which the regime instituted in order to ensure that the whole population was reached by Luce documentaries.

In cities, class was the primary basis on which audiences were organised. Well-appointed first-run cinemas charged 1.5 lire per ticket in the mid-1930s, a price that deterred the less well-off while still being cheaper than the theatre. They offered comfortable environments in close proximity to shops, bars and cafes. Lower-middle-class people attending second-run cinemas could expect to see new films a few weeks after their debut in cinemas that were often no smaller than first-runs and which were usually possessed of cushioned seating. Third-run cinemas catering to workers were spartan, invariably being fitted with wooden seats and lacking heating in winter. As a commentator in *Lo Schermo* remarked in June 1937, films were served 'on a silver platter' in first-run theatres, on pewter plates in the second-runs, on ceramic dishes in the thirds and on 'earthenware, usually cracked' in the remainder.[9]

Films were consumed in different ways at different times of the day and week as well as in different categories of cinema. Weekend shows in the villages tended to be family experiences, while regular afternoon and evening shows in the towns and cities were frequented by a variety of different audiences: single men, groups of women or men, courting couples, married couples and so on. Even given these varieties of spectatorship, higher end cinemas contributed to the creation of a climate that was favourable to the promotion of, and aspiration for, material goods. Cinema-going spread the idea that free time was properly spent consuming goods and services and consequently fed into the commercialisation of leisure. Moreover, films presented scenarios that were eminently material. Hollywood's sophisticated comedies, with their stylish urban settings and easy representation of luxury, provided an example. So too did the German and Hungarian films that were often remade in Italy. Through them, modern, upscale environments became a cinematic koine, a visual trope that drew spectators into a world of unproblematic escape. The sets of the Italian comedies that would after the war be dubbed dismissively as 'white telephone' films had a distinctly improbable air to them. Houses and apartments were huge, cars top of the range, and domestic staff numerous. Critics noted the regular appearance of the domestic bar, a phenomenon that in Italy simply did not exist. Many films featured at least one scene in a *tabarin*, that is a night club-come-restaurant that again was more of a cinematic trope than a real place.

Given the American experience of commercial pressures leading to the production of sophisticated comedies, it is legitimate to ask if the fact that around half of the films made in the Fascist period can be classified as comedies of a similar type was similarly the result of pressures to produce films that encouraged consumer appetites. It is tempting to dismiss this question by observing that commercial interests simply did not have the power to shape films, and film companies did not have the strategic nous to realise that an alliance was possible or might work to their advantage. The consumer market, moreover, was not yet a mass one; it was fragmented regionally and stratified by class. But if this is so, why then were so many films made that superficially resembled the upscale Hollywood fare, and whose interests did they serve? The fact is that among the various reasons that require evaluation are 'commercial motivations'. Sales and publicity men (but not departments, which did not exist) did not provide the impulse; rather it was producers who understood the appeal of commercial culture, wealthy environments and luxury objects. In an interview, Camerini revealed that the producer of *Grandi magazzini*, Giuseppe Amato, told him to be sure, when filming scenes set on the shop floor, to include close-ups of products and brand names.[10] Whether this was because deals had been struck, or to lend authenticity to the studio reconstruction of a store, or to lure spectators with a visual festival of desirable goods, was not made clear.

There is very little evidence of explicit product placement but the feel of opulence was informed by the modernist interiors and furniture of elite design magazines like *Casabella* and *Domus*. Indeed, the interiors and furniture on display were supplied by real companies, as they were to theatres whose repertoire was composed of sophisticated Italian and international comedies and dramas. When these were adapted for the screen, as they often were, they required opulent sets, props and costumes. Well-to-do spectators would have recognised the source of design motifs and objects. For wider audiences, the issue is more complex. Were they attracted, repelled or left indifferent by the insistent use of wealthy settings, modern furnishings and cosmopolitan practices? *La Domenica del Corriere* observed in April 1940 that spectators in centrally located cinemas liked escapist society comedies.[11] However, it noted that these did not go down well in peripheral districts, where people disliked films that showed an unrealistic standard of living; they preferred dramas.

I have argued elsewhere that the absence in Italy of the sort of regular structural connections that existed between the film industry and producers of consumer goods in the United States meant that the argument put forward by Brunetta to the effect that entertainment film pushed individual aspirations away from collective political goals and in the direction of fully fledged prosperity cannot really be tested, and therefore is impossible to accept as anything other than a possible hypothesis.[12] However, since then Emanuela Scarpellini and Bianca Gaudenzi have advanced the understanding of interwar consumerism. Imagining the reception a city audience in Fascist Italy might have accorded a prestige American film (she uses the example of the 1932 Metro-Goldwyn-Mayer film *Grand Hotel*), Scarpellini evokes 'the effect on the male and female audience in the stalls, carried away as they are by that enchanted world'.[13] Then she poignantly describes the return to reality at the end of the evening, when 'the old caretaker [of the cinema] has to shoo everyone out and so the youths crowd towards the exit in their homemade clothes of coarse cloth, imitation leather shoes, and fashion accessories from cheap chain stores. They go away on foot; some take the tram. The caretaker wheezes himself astride his old Bianchi and starts to pedal squeakily homeward. Every evening it is the same story'.[14]

The spectators she conjures up are both distinctly external to the realm of comfort and consumption ('coarse' cloth, 'imitation' leather shoes, 'cheap' stores; public transport to get home) and, at the same time, marginally incorporated within it ('cheap chain stores' suggests an advanced system of retail distribution; 'fashion accessories' implies a pattern of taste and personal styling; a 'Bianchi' bicycle – no matter how squeaky – denotes the presence of brands). In this context, it would be difficult to deny the power of films to harness material aspirations. The question is whether this means that they effectively led, as Brunetta argues, in a direction incompatible with Fascism. Every scholar who has addressed this theme has drawn mainly, if not exclusively, on film texts. The contribution of extratextual factors has been ignored. They have, however, reached different conclusions. In contrast to Brunetta, several authors have embraced what might be termed the 'fold-back hypothesis'. This has been most fully elaborated by historians of Nazi cinema who have argued that films offered consumerist, cosmopolitan, excessive visual material that 'gently reminded viewers of attractions beyond the domain of ideological mobilization and yet at the same time assisted in blowing the vessel of everyday culture into the harbor of an autonomous German distraction industry'.[15] They bore witness to the 'Americanist inclinations and perplexing syntheses of the Nazi culture industry' – the way it allowed hybridity and ambivalent representations to enter the heart of a cinema whose ostensible function was to assist integration of individual into community through modern modes of diversion.

In his discussion of *Grandi magazzini*, James Hay stresses the way the film's narrative ultimately 'does much to project the image of corporate society'.[16] By the way it interweaves events in and outside the store, as well as the various compartments of the store itself, it creates 'the illusion of an organic bond' between all of these and suggests that social problems may, through this, be surmounted. To support his view that the film dovetails with the purposes of Fascism, he highlights the way the festivities to launch the new shopping season, which close the film, parallel the agrarian ritual of the planting season: 'Just as an agrarian ritual ensures the success of the harvest, this commercial spectacle infuses the corporate system with a sense of *organicism* or organization; employees and employers participate in the success of the system through their cooperation and commitment and through a momentary recognition of their place in the organization'.[17]

Hay's argument is not dissimilar to those advanced more recently by Steven Ricci, or by Eric Rentschler in relation to Nazi cinema. According to these authors, films such as *Grandi magazzini* did not create a clash with the prevailing, politically supported value system, but rather presented a spectacle of consumption that captured and articulated the desires of audiences only to fold them back into the Fascist project. In relation to this specific film, Hay finds much evidence in the film to support his view. The 'organicism' of the world portrayed on screen is contrasted with the dishonesty, moral displacement and spiritual emptiness of untrammelled commercialism. Certain consumer objects (for example, the director of personnel's car, and the lavish furnishings of the manager's apartment) serve to symbolise modernity and upward mobility, but, at the same time, the people who own them are exposed by the film's lower-class protagonists as racketeers. The latter, a driver named Bruno and a shop girl called Lauretta, are tempted by dishonest behaviour when they borrow goods from the store to go on a weekend ski trip. It is only when they decide to marry and set up a home, presumably with the aim of having a family, that their desires for items of furniture and domestic equipment are endowed with legitimacy. As in other

Camerini films, lower-class people are tempted by superior lifestyles but only find happiness when they spurn these and are reconciled to their humble but decent situations of origin.

Hay is basically right in his analysis of film texts for there is precious little, if anything, in the films of the period that overtly encourages anything other than the achievement of modest prosperity within the context of social order and social convention. Nevertheless, he does concede that both imported and imitative domestic films 'placed Italian audiences in the presence of models of "modern" and cosmopolitan lifestyles – ones that, due to the growing ubiquity and accessibility of the cinema and to the mimesis of film imaging, appeared to be seductively plausible'.[18] This suggests that some connections nonetheless obtained with the real world of consumption. If this was so, then the matter of the possible impact of such films cannot be entirely resolved by means of analysis of the film texts.

In his essay, Eckert listed three ways in which American cinema was integral to the historical development of consumption. The first was a general coincidence of purposes in a specific economic conjuncture. Industry pressure led movie studios to develop product that fitted with the ethos and needs of manufacturers.[19] Second, he details a number of tie-ups between large studios and established manufacturers that provided for the display of goods in films, and press campaigns with endorsements, or radio ads, from stars. Such tie-ups, or sponsors, were actively pursued by studios which even framed scripts on the basis of them.[20] Third, stars became, in this process, sales agents with a quantifiable merchandising value. For a brief period, the 'fusion of products and performing stars' took the form of specific pairings, for example of Eddie Cantor and Texaco, and Bing Crosby and Kraft.[21]

The Americans tried to export commercially packaged stardom. U.S. government agencies, as well as individual film companies, studied foreign audience tastes, and their reports, although quite general in content, give some feel for consumption patterns. The January 1930 edition of the Department of Commerce, Bureau of Domestic and Foreign Commerce's bulletin, *Motion Pictures Abroad*, suggests that Italian audiences were thought to be susceptible to commercial suggestions:

> The average Italian theatre goer shows a marked preference for American films on account of their more brilliant technique. Sex appeal and star value both count for much with the local public but they are not sufficient in themselves entirely to captivate Italian taste. In contrast to the Anglo-Saxon public, the Italian likes, in love passages, elemental passion rather than delicacy of sentiment; above all, the Italian likes vigorous action and dynamic quality. Sumptuous interiors of hotels, liners, and millionaire homes exercise extraordinary fascination for him, because being generally accustomed to a lesser standard of living, he is curious to see how the other half of the world lives. The pastry-like lightness of the typical American production and its intimate touches of tragedy and comedy are better adapted to Italian taste

than the more distinctly cerebral qualities of German and Russian films, concentrated as they are on the elaboration of original, fantastic or revolutionary themes as in 'Metropolis' or the 'Battleship Potemkin'.[22]

Consequently, distributors sought to create a commercial buzz around films. One of very few examples of a tie-in involving a department store occurred when the La Rinascente store in Milan, and possibly other cities, launched a line of little girls' clothes and dolls in 1936 to coincide with the release of a Shirley Temple film. Loudspeakers in the store broadcast the voice and songs of Shirley, posters and photographs were distributed, and announcements were placed in the press and on the radio. In addition, four publicity vans carried news of the event out into the provinces.[23] The fact that this does not appear to have been followed up suggests that it was not very successful. Most work concerned the merchandising of films themselves. In keeping with ballyhoo tradition, press books and bulletins suggested ways of turning films into events. For example, in 1936, Twentieth Century Fox proposed that for the launch of *Music in the Air* (Joe May, 1934), an operetta set in Bavaria, cinema foyers should be decorated in the style of a mountain village. Radio announcements, locally commissioned advertising posters and competitions of one sort or another all featured too. What the Americans knew better than anyone was that films did not market themselves and that the most powerful marketing device was stars. The commercial connotation of American film was grasped by Italian companies which continued to derive benefit from it even after the withdrawal of the majors from the market. The Motta shop in Piazza Duomo in Milan was well known for experimenting with novel forms of display and advertising. In 1941 one window display featured a table with a *panettone* Christmas cake, bottles of sparkling wine and cardboard cut-outs of Hollywood actors, including Jean Harlow, in evening dress.

For the most part Italian distributors and exhibitors did not go in for U.S.-style ballyhoo. Most films relied for advertising on some press coverage, promotional material on forthcoming presentations, radio slots and, most crucially, posters. But, to draw attention to the opening of *Re Burlone* (The Gay King, Enrico Guazzoni, 1936), a train which had appeared in the film was placed in Piazza Barberini in Rome. In Milan, a miniature model of the Dolomites was erected under the porticos of Piazza Duomo to arouse public interest in *Scarpe al sole* (Shoes in the Sun, Marco Elter, 1936), while old soldiers were engaged to promote the film by patrolling the city accompanied by characteristic trumpet bursts. An Alpine regimental choir greeted spectators of the film at the cinema. *Darò un milione* (I'll Give A Million, Mario Camerini, 1935), a comedy starring Vittorio De Sica and Assia Noris, was promoted by a singular tie-in involving the month-long circulation of fake 1,000 lire banknotes featuring the actors' faces, while their caricatures adorned giant posters afixed to public buildings.[24]

The appeal of modern commercial culture was captured in a number of films, particularly the small but significant number that were filmed on location in Milan. Mario Camerini's *Gli uomini, che mascalzoni!* (What Scoundrels Men Are! 1932) offered a highly – perhaps exaggeratedly – modernistic picture of Italy's leading industrial city. It presents a contrast typical of the director's oeuvre between dignified lower classes and their frivolous and coarse betters, while featuring the commercial dynamism of the Milan trade fair, billboards and posters on the streets, inventive advertising lining out-of-town thoroughfares, a modernistic perfume store, restaurants and dance halls, extensive public and private transport, and popular illustrated magazines. The Rome-born Camerini stressed the novelty of Milan's modernity, and a very similar picture of the city was offered in the adoptive Roman Mario Mattoli's *Tempo massimo* (Full Time, 1933). Nearly ten years later, the city's image was only moderately different in a minor comedy about a middle-class family, *La famiglia Brambilla va in vacanza* (The Brambilla Family Go on Holiday, Carl Boese, 1941) and the melodrama *È caduta una donna* (A Woman Has Been Run Over, Alfredo Guarini, 1942), both of which used the city as a realistic backdrop. The glimpses of contemporary Rome in films such as *La bisbetica domata* (The Taming of the Shrew, Ferdinando M. Poggioli, 1942) and *I bambini ci guardano* (The Children Are Watching Us, Vittorio De Sica, 1943), while not so immersed in the texture of modern life, also suggest that commercial culture was intertwined with urban patterns of living. In rural Italy and much of the south, many of the practices normalised in Milan were completely unknown. But their appearance in films which had real, identifiable locations brought them down to a level that was more accessible and plausible than the studio-bound dreamworlds of the 'white telephone' films.

Italian Stars and Glamour

The quality that was most often associated with the Hollywood stars was glamour. Glamour had a long history in nineteenth-century commercial culture but it enjoyed more widespread success in the 1930s, when the term itself first became widely used.[25] In one of the most quoted of definitions, Margaret Thorp, who identified it as 'a very important stock in trade of the movie business', dubbed it 'sex appeal … plus luxury, plus elegance, plus romance'.[26] In brief it was a veil of make-believe that persuaded spectators that they were sharing in the lives of the beautiful, the rich and the fashionable of the world's metropolises, when in reality they were watching regular men and women acting out pretend scenarios on sets constructed on studio lots in Los Angeles. The whole process of creating stars, by transforming individuals into something more compelling and alluring than reality, was a calculated and cynical one in which, not by chance, the publicity departments took the lead. Italians were aware of glamour as a Hollywood product. To a degree, they were fascinated by it as the manufactured allure of a more mobile and developed society. Its meaning was debated, while photographic images presenting examples of it were often featured on the covers of women's and popular film magazines. One of the most striking of all appeared on the cover of *Eva* in 1934 with the simple title 'Fascino',[27] the word that was taken to be the nearest translation of glamour, although the English word was also employed in press articles about cinema.

Glamour was, to a large extent, about commerce and publicity. Although Eckert does not mention the concept directly, it is clearly an aspect of the marketing of stardom. Even though all the structural mediations and relations present in an advanced industrial society like the United States were much less strongly present in Italy, the distilled glamour of Hollywood was a powerful, if not always fully understood, allure. The attempt to replicate it proceeded through some of its most important components even though some of these were not well-established commercial activities. The role of the state needs to be taken into account because in some areas it, more than private industry, took the lead in exploiting the promotional potential of cinema.

Two industries identified by Eckert as crucial were fashion and cosmetics. The first of these was more important in Italy. That cinema was seen as a force for promoting Italian products as well as qualities and values is evident from the very first issue of the official magazine *Lo Schermo* in 1935. Cine-actresses, wrote 'Marta', are 'the queens and arbiters of elegance': therefore they could help to revive Italian fashion if the fashion industry were to make use of cinema to promote goods, as occurred in the United States.[28] By this time, the government had committed itself to the development of the fashion sector and was seeking to reduce the consumption of foreign goods and undermine foreign styles and influences, in much the same way as it was with cinema. The Ente nazionale per la moda (National Fashion Council), based in Turin, organised short films made by the Luce Institute to promote collections, and it placed some garments in films. Cooperation between the sectors was urged by Mussolini himself in April 1937 in a speech demanding the primacy of Italian clothes in Italy.[29] In the aftermath of this, the general directorate of cinema and the fashion council engaged in coordinated action to promote national fashions. The sense of cinema as a 'shop window for fashion, decoration and furnishings' was established. *Lo Schermo* ran a regular column, entitled 'Il cinema e la moda', in which various aspects of the question were addressed. One feature, Blasetti's *La contessa di Parma* (The Countess of Parma, 1937), a story of a fraught romance between a fashion model and a footballer, was made with the official sponsorship of the fashion council. One of its themes was the patriotic struggle to free Italian fashion of its subordination to Paris. Promotional material announced that all the best designs of the best Italian fashion houses would be paraded on screen as in a classic presentation.

In December 1938 it was argued that producers had to understand that not only was inelegance bad; it was boring or annoying for the spectator to see on screen the sort of clothes that any woman might wear. Since the screen offered the public the image of an ideal life 'it cannot bear to see all the things that belong to its daily torment and sacrifice':

> A magnificent dressing gown, a beautiful evening dress, a gracious and original sports outfit, worn with verve and grace, can lift the tone of an entire scene and complete it; fine underwear, particular touches, that give a lift and make the overall effect of an outfit perfect have the effect of making an artist nicer and more pleasant for the audience. Even in the most modest films the female wardrobe must always be considered with every care and always be perfectly in tune with the context and personality of the artist.[30]

Producers must avoid 'gaffes and inelegance', it was argued; 'certain absurd little hats, certain banal frills, certain operetta eccentricities that give the impression of poverty, neglect, must absolutely be abandoned'. [31]

The press in the early 1940s often featured comments on the appearance of stars. These were a mixture of helpful advice and patronising criticism. The popular weekly *Film* ran a series by the fashion commentator Vera under the title 'Come dovrebbe vestirsi ...' (How [a named star] should dress). Each week a different actress was subjected to scrutiny. Paola Barbara was seen as a typical Italian beauty with a sunny disposition. As such, she could never add elegance to clothes; rather clothes needed to give it to her. Care was needed over the cut and the accessories used, since if a costume was too tight, as had been the case in *La peccatrice* (The Sinner, Amleto Palmieri, 1940), it made her seem fat.[32] Maria Denis was a pretty girl who was simply unsuited to elegance. She should never be dressed in rich or complex clothes.[33] By contrast, the tall and athletic Vivi Gioi, an actress of Swedish family origin, was regarded as a beacon of elegance and Vera went to visit her in her dressing room. Gioi lamented the fact that film costumes sometimes arrived only at the last minute. However, she was looking forward to her next film since all her costumes were coming from Biki, a designer she admired.[34] Vera also interviewed Doris Duranti, an actress who specialised in femme fatale parts. She lamented the fact that no one created clothes especially for actresses, who were forced to choose their wardrobes from normal collections.[35] It was striking that these comments concerned established actresses. *Cinema illustrazione* in 1936 had only complained that newcomers often dressed badly; established names were left in peace.

Fig. 3.1 'Will all women wear lace collars because Isa Miranda wore one in *Malombra?*' asks the caption to a still published in *Cinema*, 10 August 1942. (Author's own collection)

Costume designer Nino Novarese argued for a type of star dressing that was not subordinate to fashion but which worked within its general tendency, softening or exaggerating details, lines and lengths as appropriate. Feature films could not use current fashions since these tended to be already out of date by the time the films reached the screen and could be the object of ridicule in first-run cinemas.[36] Like other, less well-informed observers, he wanted to learn lessons from Hollywood without losing sight of the Italian tradition of taste and style. When critics sought to distinguish between the Americans and the Italians, it was not always to the detriment of the latter. For example, in 1939, *Cinema illustrazione* praised the fact that Italian actresses were not American 'stars'. 'They do not have "fans" and do not need police cordons; they are not theatrical and extravagant', the article went on. We have never seen actresses like Evi Maltagliati or Elsa Merlini 'wrapped in those very rich and slightly tasteless kilometres of silver lace, nor in gold armour that makes them seem a very elegant Unica or Perugina chocolate'. They are not dummies but women and actresses, 'and it is really this lack of perfection that makes the elegance of our actresses vibrant'. The following year, *La Domenica del Corriere* deplored the style of American films and the 'debatable clothes that clash with the sobriety of our Latin taste'.[37]

The rejection of showy, eye-catching dressing had a downside. For *La Domenica del Corriere* even films with society settings did not set the tone or lead trends in matters of fashion and elegance.[38] It lamented the fact that no actress's personality was defined or completed through specially studied fashions. Here, it might be added, Merlini was the exception. Her earning power rocketed as soon as she started making films. As a theatre performer she earned 30,000 lire per month, whereas she was paid double that for two weeks' work on *La segretaria privata*.[39] She immediately set about making sure that whenever she appeared in public she dressed like a star. It was revealed in the press that she had her own dress designer, Gori. Isa Miranda was another actress who invested in constructing a stylish public image (see Fig. 3.1). She modelled Italian clothes on various occasions, including long elegant dresses for *Lo Schermo*. Nonetheless, the general point held and the blame for this situation was laid squarely at the door of fashion houses, which were accused of failing to understand cinema's potential and therefore not investing in it. The magazine urged that the suppliers of costumes should be given more explicit credit and that designers should be encouraged to bring more verve and fantasy to the creations that would figure on the screen. They were also encouraged to create some dresses exclusively for particular features.[40] By the 1940s, some fashion producers were becoming better known. Women's magazines like *Eva* ran articles on the Milanese designer Biki and Ventura furs of Casa Dellera. Film credits frequently listed established houses and contributed to making the names of Italian couturiers and furriers more familiar. The state provided support, for example by organising a fashion show in 1941 to tie in with Venice festival. Yet the only known case of an Italian tie-in was the collection Gion Guida designed in 1936, inspired by Alessandrini's historical film *Cavalleria*. Essentially, Italian fashion at this time operated on an artisan basis and had little interest in trying to reach a wide market.

Cosmetics was a further area in which Hollywood exercised a key influence, even though most of the major houses, with the exceptions of Max Factor and Perc Westmore, were based in New York rather than Los

Angeles. 'The cycle of influence made up of films, fashion articles, "Beauty hints", columns featuring the stars, ads which dutifully mentioned the star's current film and tie-in advertising in stores, made cosmetics synonymous with Hollywood,' writes Eckert,[41] adding that the same was true for brands of soap, toothpaste, hair preparations and other toiletries. Stars were absolutely central to this since 'no more potent endorsements were possible than those of the women who manifestly possessed the most "radiant" and "scintillant" eyes, teeth, complexions and hair'.[42] In this sphere, the Italians could not even hope to compete with Hollywood, for not only were there no large cosmetics companies but the whole idea of artificial beauty was still far from having won legitimacy. In America too, there was opposition from various cultural forces to the use of lipstick and other products by young women,[43] but their power was less than in Italy. Nevertheless, one or two companies used film themes in their advertising and one secured testimonials from leading actresses. Guizzo for the lips and Guizzociglia for the eyes 'are always preferred by great actresses', ran advertisements featuring pictures of Alida Valli, Vivi Gioi and Clara Calamai. Oretta Fiume endorsed To-Radia face cream and powder crème, claiming that 'they make me calm and happy because they lend freshness and luminosity to my skin'. Leda Gloria endorsed (with a signed picture) a skin treatment called L'acqua Alabastrina by Dr Barbei. Diadermina face cream and powder was advertised with movie-star types rather than actual stars. Male endorsements were rarer but Vittorio De Sica, who was known for his broad smile, did one for a toothpaste company.

It is worth observing that through the 1920s and 1930s many companies and individuals wrote to Mussolini seeking permission to use his endorsement for this or that product. In a few instances permission was granted. The example of Perugina chocolates is the best known. For the most part they were refused, as were most requests for autographed photographs.[44] Like some figures in Hollywood, he was wary of destroying his aura of exclusivity by being too accessible and associated with products and places that lacked prestige. Stars were useful alternatives and were obviously more appropriate choices for the promotion of a variety of products mainly aimed at women. Paola Barbara and Isa Miranda both endorsed sewing machines, while a company from Como made silk cloth with Assia Noris's signature as a design motif. A cigarette case with a cover featuring an image of her face was also put on sale.

Publicity and Private Life

In the United States, it has been argued that 'stars established the value of motion pictures as a marketable commodity' and 'by virtue of their unique appeal and drawing power stabilized rental prices'.[45] Star publicity was a crucial feature of the way in which Hollywood studios built up interest in actors. Publicity departments knew exactly how to shape an image and get it over to the public through the media. They organised events, photo shoots, interviews, and coverage of stars' off-screen lives. In contrast to the silent era, when actors were given exotic names and personas, from the 1930s a dose of realism was mixed with the enviable aspects of the stars' lives.[46] Embellishment took the place of invention. The backgrounds of European stars were almost always played up, while ordinariness was often a feature of the presentation of U.S.-born stars.

Most of the publicity material was also used in foreign markets. Readers of Italian film and women's magazines were supplied with extensive information about the way of life of the stars of Hollywood. This was presented in a way that matched expectations deriving from the environments and relations they enjoyed in film. The stars were a privileged group who lived a life that was configured as thoroughly enviable. Their beauty, clothes, homes, hairstyles, lips were all discussed. For official opinion, however, the publicity given to the stars' lives in the press was inappropriate. In May 1936, an article in *Lo Schermo* denounced the constant flow of trivial snippets and pictures of stars, who were seen in evening dress and daywear, in sports gear, in casual mode and even in their underpants and slippers, with or without a dog, with a cat or a monkey, with a cigarette or a racquet.[47] They pretended to know how to play golf, ride a horse, fry an egg, grow flowers, love children, read a novel and be happy. Tittle-tattle about their private lives was particularly deplored. 'Often there are articles signed by them, young men and ladies, that pretend to reveal how many lovers they have had and which tell us about their sex appeal or other rather delicate themes. Sometimes these are followed by other pieces of information or various "indiscretions" that become the bread and butter of the seamstresses and shopgirls of the whole world', it thundered. 'We – we can swear it – will not do this. We will do something completely different. We will abolish stars,' the article piously concluded.

Such rash optimism proved unfounded. Although the briefings issued by the Ministry of Popular Culture frequently instructed the press to ignore this or that actor or to mention foreigners less, these were mostly reactive.[48] If Italian actors were not given a publicity boost they could never hope to share or appropriate the limelight of Hollywood. As *Cinema* noted, 'it is strange, but more precise things are known about the far off actresses of Hollywood than about the much closer ones of Cinecittà'.[49] The process of star grooming and presentation in fact was not absent, but it lacked the systematic science of Hollywood. While some commentators and industry insiders would have liked to see the emergence in Italy of American-style stars, the infrastructure was almost entirely lacking. Film actors were moulded by producers and directors rather than big studios with a strategic commitment to building and promoting stars, bringing on new talent and testing it out gradually. Rarely was there a consistency of engagement with their careers. In many cases, little was done to package an actor beyond endowing him or her with a new name that carried either an alluring or vaguely exotic appeal. For example, Amedeo Buffa became Amedeo Nazzari, while Maria Belmonte became Maria Denis; Luisa Manfredini adopted the name Luisa Ferida and Alida Maria von Altenberger became Alida Valli, while Assia von Gerzfeld, who was born to a Swedish father and a Russian mother, was given the name Assia Noris. Others retained names that had down-to-earth, even rustic, connotations, like Gino Cervi and Clara Calamai. Some, such as Fosco Giachetti and Massimo Girotti, were lucky enough to have names that resonated on their own.

Publicity in fact was a thorny issue. In the battle that was fought through this period between those who believed that advertising should inform and educate the public and those who preferred to seduce it with noise, sensation and unfulfillable promises, Freddi was unequivocally in the former camp. His idea of publicity was serious and high-minded. It had nothing to do with the American idea of ballyhoo that had been so important in turning cinema into the most popular leisure activity in the United States. The aim was always to ensure that cinema, as a medium of national importance, was treated with dignity. Bad publicity was simply unwelcome.[50]

Nevertheless, as he recalled in his memoirs, 'the general directorate oversaw the creation of photographic material concerning our actors and actresses, material that Italian production companies, out of a misplaced sense of economy, had always ignored and without which it was impossible for the public to acquire a full knowledge of our players'.[51] In the period following the withdrawal of the majors, publicity around stars was at last employed in a systematic fashion. The primary intent was to boost their standing so that they would be able to substitute for American stars in public affections. Freddi and other knew that Italian films would do consistently better business if the public recognised and loved the stars. The Cinecittà press office performed the main function here. Its task was to publicise all the activities of the production complex and ensure that forthcoming films received due coverage. Among the things it did was 'sending on a weekly basis ... close-up photographs of actresses and actors' and arranging exclusive interviews for leading press organs.[52]

The press office of Cinecittà thus took the place of studios in distributing photographs of the stars. Rome's leading society photographers also took an interest in them as they emerged as personalities, and it was through their work that the glamour of Italian actors was constructed. Rome's photographers were established names, frequented by the elite of society and the regime, whose studios were situated in prestigious locations. Elio Luxardo, Ghitta Carell and Arturo Ghergo were known for their flattering formal and informal portraits of the prominent. Luxardo was a Brazilian who had lived in Paris and first came to Rome to study at the Centro sperimentale before giving up his desire to direct for photography, while Carell had arrived from Hungary and won introductions to the elite before producing portraits of Mussolini and his daughter Edda.[53] Both specialised in making portraits that were imprinted with a distinctive style that owed something to Hollywood but more to their own mixture of cultural influences. Ghergo's manner of capturing the beauty and charisma of his subjects owed more to international fashion photography, which was exemplified at the time by Cecil Beaton.[54] He used luminous backlighting and costuming, but not sets or props, as well as a personal knowledge of his subjects to create images that were seductive. His photographs were worlds unto themselves, divorced from reality; they were soft-focused and romantic, very stylised and with a marked emphasis on the eyes.

The critic Giuseppe Turroni suggests that Luxardo took over the Hollywood custom of using props and scenic backdrops to forge an alluring look, 'albeit of a homely and autarchic nature'.[55] In fact, many star photographs by Luxardo and the others were striking, and they remain so today even if they were intimate and measured rather than hyperbolic. Sex appeal of the type that Hollywood photographer George Hurrell deliberately worked to achieve through what he termed a 'bedroom look' was largely absent,[56] but the sensual appeal of the surface textures of skin, hair, lips and eyes is undeniable. Luxardo took up the American taste for ironical poses, stunt photos and, in diluted form, the sexed-up image, but he used more shadow than was customary in the United States, adding depth and reducing the euphoric air that marked Hollywood, especially in the war years.[57] All the Roman photographers engaged in retouching as part of the process of elaboration of the image in order to reduce their subjects' weight, eliminate imperfections, and generally enhance them, but without standardising or homogenising them. In their portraits the stars never became ciphers or general bearers of a pre-existing allure; they remained individuals who at most were shaped by the identifiable signature of a photographer.

The magazines published these photographs with a certain pride in the fact that Italy could give rise to a star system of such allure. All editors understood that stars were visual treats and that pictures of them, especially but not only on covers, lent aesthetic and commercial appeal. Newsstands in the interwar years were decked out with innumerable brightly coloured or attractively presented weeklies. Camerini was so taken with them that they often featured in his films as markers of urban modernity.

The real sticking point was gossip. Stars were happy to sit for the best photographers but they were much less keen on allowing public speculation about their love lives. They knew well what the official view of this was, even if it was sometimes contradicted. In July 1939, Samperi urged in *Lo Schermo* that a fantasy element was needed in the stars. 'A tone for the public' was required to counteract the impression that they were 'bourgeois', all hard work, discipline and dignity. 'Try to indulge the fantasy of reporters', he admonished the stars:

> There is nothing wrong with allowing it to be said that you, my dear girls, have touched the heart of a maharajah, or that a beautiful American has lost her head for one of you, my friends; nor indeed that you, beautiful XY, are romantically involved with director YX. These are all things that cause no ill to anyone, neither to he who lets them be said nor to he who says them. That a camera lens catches you in a bathing costume when you take a dip in the sea or the swimming pool, or while you chat with friends, what can be bad about that, so long as the costume suits you?

In fact, the stars would never relax their guards about their personal or romantic lives. In general, actors were not keen to give their whole lives over to publicity and there was no organisation strong enough to force them to do so. The women's magazine *Grazia* noted that Luisa Ferida, who at the time was living with the actor Osvaldo Valenti, refused to reveal anything at all about her private life.[58] Assia Noris, it was observed, notoriously refused to reveal particulars of her romantic and mysterious childhood. Various factors came into play here, from a sense of privacy to a desire to avoid censure. Moreover, in Italy, stars worked harder than they did in the United States, making more films per year, and they generally believed that they were entitled to spend their leisure time as they wished.

The Lifestyles of the Stars

Magazines in the early 1930s had inserted Italian stars and starlets in photographic spreads featuring Hollywood stars, thus giving the impression that they belonged to the same imaginary community. Swimsuit shots of stars, usually relaxing by the sea in the summer, became a minor trope. Dria Paola, Silvana Jachino, Germana Paolieri, Nelly Corradi and Isa Pola all posed for pictures of this type.[59] Star tastes were unambiguously modern. In 1931, nineteen-year-old Laura Nucci, starring in Blasetti's *Palio*, said:

> I love jazz. I could spend hours lying listening to jazz. I adore modern dances, fine lunches, cars and planes. I drive every type of car and I go flying as often as I can. I don't like poetry, I don't like theatre, I don't like novels. I adore cinema. I wear red and black, which are my favourite colours. My perfume is Origan. I love violas and roses. And I am happy.[60]

Despite being known for lusty peasant parts in films including Blasetti's *Terra madre* (Mother Earth, 1931) and Camerini's *Il cappello a tre punte* (Three-Cornered Hat, 1935), Leda Gloria also revelled in her success. Masi and Lancia observe that 'like all the divas of the period [she] owned a huge car that she drove with sporting dash around the roads of Rome'.[61] Unlike most others she also took to the skies: 'When I realise that everything is getting on my nerves and life starts seeming to be grey, I rush in my car to the Littorio airport and order them to bring out my aeroplane. Flying has a relaxing effect on my nerves and makes the tension disappear as if by magic.'[62]

The material resources of many actors increased markedly as a result of their film work. In 1939 *La Domenica del Corriere* reported that there had been a boom in pay since the early 1930s.[63] In the previous two years it had increased, depending on the individual, by 50–200 per cent. Their rewards, of course were less than those of the Americans but in the context of the Italian economy, not to be disdained. The adoption of exterior symbols of wealth went hand in hand with this. In the Luce documentary *Cinque minuti a Cinecittà*, Amedeo Nazzari drove into the frame in one of the large open-top cars for which he was famous. Most stars dressed well, travelled widely and enjoyed the fruits of their success.

Later, publicly revealed tastes and pastimes were more conventional. *Film* magazine in 1940 ran numerous 'stars at leisure' pictures, with Maria Denis on roller skates, Vivi Gioi at the swimming pool and so on. The result was a healthy, outdoor look. Stars' hobbies were varied but conventional. *La Domenica del Corriere* reported in 1941 that Silvio Bagolin collected stamps, Giacinto Molteni and Roberto Villa played chess, Elsa De Giorgi painted ceramics, and Assia Noris adored spending time at home. The article was accompanied by pictures of Maria Denis skiing, and De Sica and Melnati boxing.[64] 'Nothing exceptional can be noted in the off-screen activities of our cinema actors; none of the hundred bizarre things that the American stars had got us used to can be seen in them. They appear rather as nothing other than fine girls and good boys. But is this not perhaps a reason why we like them?' it asked. In February 1943, the same magazine informed readers that Carla del Poggio was studying for her school certificate, while Assia Noris played tennis, Isa Miranda liked gardening, and Clara Calamai and Elisa Cegani enjoyed reading; Maria Denis was keen on flower arranging, while Vivi Gioi and Lilia Silvi loved to go cycling.[65] Women's magazines also ran leisure features that, if anything, were even more domesticated. *Grazia* showed Maria Denis on her bicycle, on the phone, ironing, and signing autographs. The message, the magazine spelt out, was that she was just like any middle-class Roman girl. Laura Solari was seen doing the ironing and sitting reading in a refined domestic environment. The once-modernist Laura Nucci was depicted at home and at the hairdressers.

Little beyond these publicity snapshots reached the media, which was sometimes a problem for those whose job it was to build public interest. 'The day of the stars is not very varied, at least as far as the part that is concerned with daily work is concerned', wrote *Cinema* in a feature illustrated with photos of actors on and off set, adding that 'the other, what can be called the private day, is like a secret life that takes place for most behind closed doors'.[66]

The veiled 'secret life' of the stars was in fact quite varied. Many actors' leisure time was spent in the company of other actors and film people in the more informal of public establishments. Carousing occurred in Rome as it did in Hollywood, with hard living and womanising being favoured by a clique of male actors. A number of film actors cultivated friendships among the artistic community of Via Margutta. Amedeo Nazzari enjoyed the relaxed atmosphere of this bohemian environment, while Isa Miranda happily posed for the numerous portraits that the artists made of her. Others gravitated towards the more moneyed, ostentatious circles. Osvaldo Valenti, a prolific actor of wide range who, despite never speaking on screen with his own voice, played leading men, villains, weaklings and numerous character and supporting parts, was notorious for his fast living. A man of enormous vanity, an exuberant exhibitionist and a cocaine addict, he was fond of pranks and was often out on the tiles in the hotels and clubs of the elegant Via Veneto, frequenting the brash and heterogeneous night-owl society of ambitious financiers, fashionable lawyers, actors and rich wastrels.

Others, however, were drawn towards higher social circles. Fascism did not adopt a consistent approach towards high society, though to some extent it was forced to embrace old rituals as well as forging new ones – for, as Fabrice d'Almeida has argued, 'high society shows the ability of a government to live with the elites of its country, to achieve a synthesis of the power principle with the pleasure principle'.[67] Just as the regime sought to create mass rituals for the new era, so it aimed to annex cultural life and forge a new aristocracy that reflected the ideals and value system of Fascism. The dominant ethos may have been spartan, but luxury was permitted to an elite that blended the socially distinguished with those whose upward mobility had been facilitated by the regime. Famous actors were ornaments who could be dragooned into attending diplomatic receptions and other formal occasions. Some of them, like Maria Denis, Doris Duranti and Assia Noris, who all lived in the Parioli district, were in any case at home in the higher social and cultural circles of the capital. Noris later boasted that she had met Hitler, Goebbels and Mussolini.[68] She got to know Princess Mafalda of Savoy well when both stayed at the same hotel in Cortina. She was invited to Quirinal Palace to take tea with Queen Elena, where she later recounted that she was shown to a room where she found the king's spouse standing on a table replacing a lightbulb. Duranti too claimed that 'my world was made up of marquises and countesses'.[69]

Despite the attempt to moralise the entertainment sector, there was more sexual licence in the artistic community than any other quarter of society. When the actress Maria Mercader arrived in Rome from Spain, aged twenty, she was still a virgin. This fact, she recalled in her memoirs, was discovered by Vivi Gioi, who regarded it as hilarious and absurd. Sex was necessary for good health, she informed her. The news of Mercader's purity spread fast and Gioi's then companion, Amedeo Nazzari, subjected her to a lewd gesture.[70] Before long, she began what would become a stable, if adulterous, relationship with the married Vittorio De Sica.

Needless to say, no scandal reached the media at this time, unlike the 1950s when they became almost routine, but the behaviour of some actors caused ructions at the top of the regime. Senior Fascists were known to covet affairs with actresses and could often be seen on visits to Cinecittà that had no official justification.[71] The only instance of a lasting, albeit turbulent, relationship, was that between Doris Duranti and the man who from 1939 was Minister of Popular Culture, Alessandro Pavolini. Papers conserved in the Central State Archives reveal that Duranti leaned heavily on the minister, who called with his car to take her to Cinecittà in the morning and pressured the director of cinema, Eitel Monaco, to grant her special favours.[72] She ostentatiously phoned him several times a day from public places, regarding the relationship as a badge of status. On occasion she obliged the fiercely jealous Pavolini to wait for her at the hairdresser's, exposing him to potential ridicule. If reports are accurate, however, she was not faithful and was caught in a tryst with the actor Andrea Checchi. While well known in political and cinema circles, even though the couple did not appear officially in public together, this relationship was the source of some embarrassment. Mussolini allegedly ordered Pavolini to leave her and was met with a refusal.[73] According to the actress, the Duce told him he understood after seeing her on screen.

Autarky and Modesty

As domestic conditions grew more difficult and shortages impacted on everyday life, the pressure on stars to set an example of modesty, which was often branded as an appropriately Italian way of being, increased. The pride in simplicity entailed an expectation that actors should embody a social ethos of sacrifice. Freddi demanded discipline from all, asserting that 'actors should be at the service of cinema and not serve themselves from it'.[74] Offensive displays of wealth were anyway regarded with great disapproval. As one of the first stars of the sound era, Elsa Merlini was, for a period, paid better than anyone else in Italian cinema. As a result, she indulged in gestures of dubious taste. One day she was said to have purchased a whole roast chicken in the Cinecittà refectory and fed it to a hungry stray dog before the eyes of workers whose lunch consisted of an egg sandwich and some tomatoes.[75] The gesture caused outrage, and news of it spread fast. Freddi heard of it and word even reached Mussolini, who indignantly raised the matter with his director of cinema, in the presence of Ciano. In his memoirs, Freddi noted that 'Mussolini spoke in a calm and detached way, addressing me. But

I was under the impression that his comments were really directed at Count Ciano'. Freddi probably missed the point here. While Mussolini did not approve of his son-in-law's sophisticated tastes and upper-class friends, he disapproved even more of actions that might fuel discontentment or unrest. He evidently intended to make it clear to Freddi that it was his job to ensure that certain extravagances on the part of actors were avoided.

To bring such excesses under control, in July 1939 the Corporazione dello spettacolo introduced a pay cap, fixing the maximum at 80,000 lire for ninety days work. In addition, 4–8 per cent of reward payments over 300,000 lire and 4–15 per cent of export earnings could be distributed among players. Often these rules were not fully respected.[76] Nevertheless some restrictions were real. In August 1939, a popular weekly tuned in to the prevailing mood to express disapproval of the 'long shiny cars, often foreign, in which the stars are accustomed to travel along the boulevards of Rome and of Cinecittà, from one studio to another' (several of which can be seen in the documentary *Cinque minuti a Cinecittà*).[77] Stars and movie personnel were no longer ferried by car to and from work after the practice was abolished in 1941. Alida Valli won praise for taking the tram that hitherto had mainly been used by studio workers, minor performers and students at the Centro sperimentale.[78] Paola Barbara told the women's magazine *Grazia* that she liked fast cars but now 'takes the tram like a woman of the people'.[79]

Some actors made a point of embracing austerity. When Elsa De Giorgi was asked about her lifestyle, she responded:

> When I receive an invitation from a fashion designer to attend her presentation, I almost have the impression – excessive, I don't deny it – that it would be irreverent towards those who are short of money or are active at the front to go to those places and indulge myself. It would be useless anyway in fact because, after all, even if I were to commit the mortal sin of emptying my handbag spending Lit. 300 for a hat and Lit. 2,000 for an outfit, where and when would I have the opportunity to show off all that elegance?[80]

Film magazine announced that stars were donating subscriptions for servicemen, while Laura Nucci, Maria Denis and Luisella Beghi were photographed knitting for soldiers at the Dopolavoro of Cinecittà. Paola Barbara boasted that she was one of first to respond to the 'wool appeal' by knitting garments for soldiers every Thursday.[81]

The female stars were regarded as fodder for soldiers. There were no American-style pin-ups in swimsuits, but the idea of the attractive girl, the potential future spouse of the tired combatant fighting far from home, was widely used as a morale-booster. The young actresses of Cinecittà encapsulated better than anyone else this ideal. De Giorgi wrote that as soon as Italy attacked Greece in 1940, 'the female stars started to receive thousands

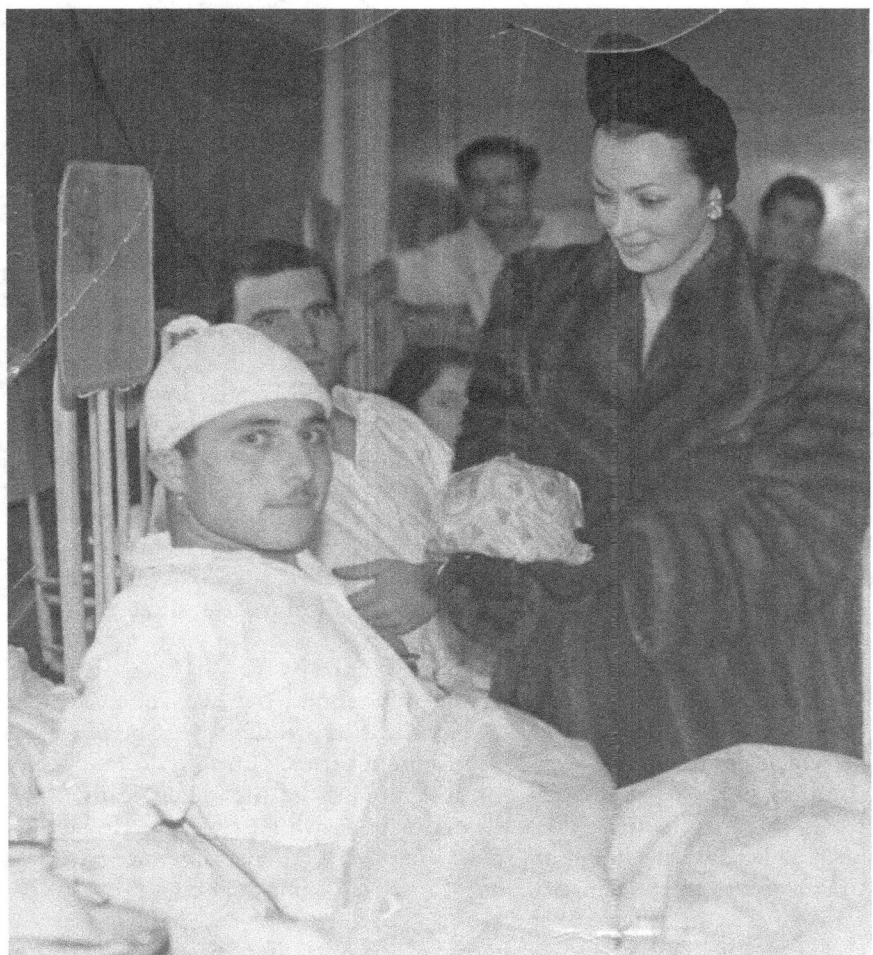

Fig. 3.2 Film actress Doris Duranti paying a morale-boosting visit to wounded soldiers, c.1941. Such visits were invariably manipulated for propaganda ends. (Author's own collection)

of military postcards from soldiers who requested autographed photographs to keep in their tents or to carry with them into battle'.[82] The actresses set about 'signing thousands of portraits in which their faces smiled and their lips, eyes and hair were illuminated in a flattering way'. De Giorgi's maid was detailed to spend her free time addressing envelopes and reading the admiring words that the soldiers wrote, interwoven with apprehension for the destiny that awaited them. What began as a spontaneous demand was, according the De Giorgi, quickly harnessed by the Ministry of Popular

Culture. The stars were obliged to make Sunday visits to military hospitals where their encounters with wounded soldiers were discreetly filmed for use in newsreels (see Fig. 3.2). Typically, the visits were made to convalescents but one week the plan was different. 'We had already been ordered peremptorily to go to Celio and two other hospitals. On a cold and damp Sunday in December, they came to get me in a battered old taxi in which I found, already on board, Valli, Jachino and others', wrote De Giorgi.[83] She went on to recount that they found themselves taken to an out-of-the-way hospital where they were obliged to act the part of visiting stars according to a precise screenplay, and to move and speak according to the instructions imparted by a director. Studio-style lights had been installed and the wounded, who – in contrast to past experience – were in a very bad way, had been assembled to play in what the women quickly realised was 'a veritable propaganda film complete with actresses and directors'. Horrified by the ordeal and shaken by the evident hostility with which they were received by the men, the women were indignant at the 'sinister clownery' of the experience. De Giorgi went directly to Via Veneto to demand a meeting with the minister, Pavolini, to whom she vigorously complained. Somewhat overestimating her influence, the actress later recalled that 'from that day for the duration of Fascism all visits by the female stars to military hospitals were suspended'.[84]

In his discussion of the functions performed by stars in Nazi Germany, Lutz Koepnik has argued that they 'gently reminded viewers of attractions beyond the domain of ideological mobilization', while aiding the processes by which dominant values were subtly reinforced'.[85] In Italy, stars did not conform to the contradictory political typology of the ideologically mobilised but fundamentally domesticated woman while never overtly holding out an alternative. Their main role, as far as the regime was concerned, was to contribute to the construction of a sense of national community. This was achieved in different ways through performance and public intervention. Like cinema more generally, and also advertising, they played a role in maintaining an illusion of normality through the war years.[86] These all held out a promise of a future of prosperity and well-being for all, at a time of hardships and suffering.

There was also a possible political intent here. If it is true that Mussolini's stardom 'was more luminous than any other male or female Italian movie star at that time', then by the end of the 1930s the institutionalisation of his personality in popular film culture was resulting in a loss of political focus. This, for Hay, was an unforeseen consequence of the build-up of the dictator as a star. Thus, after steadily increasing through the 1930s, there was a sharp drop of around 50 per cent in Mussolini's appearances in newsreels in 1939–40.[87] It may also be argued that the problems that the regime was beginning to encounter in public opinion counselled a certain removal of the Duce from the sense of day-to-day life under the regime.[88] As Pasquale

Chessa has remarked, 'after two decades of over-exposure the image of the Duce was worn out', and those who were charged with shaping public opinion were aware of this 'process of mediatic degeneration'.[89] Film stars now provided attractive emblems of the present that were both functional to the regime and in important respects external to it.

There was a marked increase at this time in the number of films starring comics who were well known for their stage work. Erminio Macario first took to the screen in the early 1930s, but, towards the end of the decade, others made the transition, including Aldo Fabrizi, Renato Rascel, Carlo Dapporto and Antonio De Curtis (Totò). The sure-fire box office appeal of such performers is likely to have been the main factor in their recruitment but the promotion of comic distraction probably received official blessing. There is no evidence to suggest that their continued appearance in films through the war years was the result of an official policy of distraction, but the hypothesis cannot be discounted.

However, the climate of hardship also strengthened the hand of those who were not favourable to the stars. In June 1942 the Ministry of Popular Culture placed restrictions on the publication of star biographies, which had mostly taken the form of supplements to magazines, pamphlets and small books. The Catholic *Rivista del cinematografo* rejoiced and called for further action 'to defend the people from the cult of stars'.[90] Stardom was an American import, it asserted, that had a bad influence on private life through its celebration of divorce, unorthodox behaviour, scandal, corrupt lifestyles and easy earnings. Thanks to the massive influx of American images, American-style oddities had become norms; biographies of the stars were eagerly devoured and had become spiritual guides for girls. 'Our people need something better than this frivolous press that sows illusions of an easy life, easy earnings and easy glory! Life is hard and it will be hard for many years', the magazine thundered. Cinema should transmit responsibility and morality. In the months that followed, the *Rivista* broadened the attack. Actors were even criticised for posing for the cameras at the Venice Film Festival in 1942, some of them in swimsuits on the beach. In an uncompromising article, cinema was deplored as a subversive force, which both worked on exterior appearances by fetishising hair and other physical features and affected the interior spirit by transmitting wrong-headed ideas to the young and the poor. 'Cinema continues to transmit to the most humble or unhappy classes ... [images of] beautiful houses, rationalist furniture, fine clothes, lucky lives, the success of the daring.'[91] All this was damaging and illusory, it concluded.

In early 1943, Mino Doletti, the editor of *Film*, the biggest-selling fan magazine, was summoned to the Ministry of Popular Culture to be told by the director general of cinema, Eitel Monaco, of 'the need to reduce the space accorded in the magazine to polemics, indiscretions and titbits that did not always correspond to a serious appreciation of the cinematic industry and art'.⁹² Doletti provided assurances that he would comply. He also compiled a report addressed to the minister in which he defended the role of *Film* as a serious magazine that had always sought to differentiate itself, in its five years of life, from 'the light and frivolous press, based only on the most clamorous indulgence of stardom'. It had collaborated with many ministerial initiatives and had contributed, he wrote, 'to the formation of an Italian star system'. A note on the report written by Monaco repeated the expectation that the magazine would adopt a more serious tone. By this time, some at least must have had an inkling that it would not be the dispositions of the ministry that would contain the influence of the stars but rather the serious setbacks the country was undergoing in the war. As the space for consumption was curtailed, there were fewer opportunities for stardom to function as a factor in commercial culture or for it to encourage the young to indulge in improbable fantasies.

Notes

1. B. Gaudenzi. 2011. 'Commercial Advertising in Germany and Italy, 1918–1943', University of Cambridge, Ph.D. thesis, 56.
2. S. Gundle. 2001. 'Visions of Prosperity: Consumerism and Popular Culture in Italy from the 1920s to the 1950s' in C. Levy and M. Roseman (eds), *Three Postwar Eras in Comparison: Western Europe 1918 – 1945 – 1989*, London: Palgrave, 151–72.
3. E. Scarpellini. 2011. *Material Nation: A Consumer's History of Modern Italy*, Oxford: Oxford University Press, 87–88.
4. C. Eckert. 1991. 'The Carol Lombard in Macy's Window' in C. Gledhill (ed.), *Stardom: Industry of Desire*, London: Routledge, 30–39.
5. D. Gomery. 1992. *Shared Pleasures: A History of Movie Presentation in the United States*, London: BFI, 34–56.
6. Eckert, 'The Carol Lombard', 30.
7. Ibid., 33.
8. *La Domenica del Corriere*, 10 March 1940.
9. a.b., 'Il sonoro e I cinema della periferia', *Lo Schermo*, June 1937, 39–41.
10. S.G. Germani. 2001. 'Entretien avec Mario Camerini' in A. Farassino (ed.), *Mario Camerini*, Locarno: Yellow Now, 112.
11. *La Domenica del Corriere*, reported in issue of 25 April 1940.
12. G.P. Brunetta. 1991. 'Mille e più di mille (lire al mese)' in M. Argentieri (ed.), *Risate di regime: la commedia italiana 1930–1944*, Venice: Marsilio. For my discussion, see 'Visions of Prosperity', 165–66.
13. Scarpellini, *Material Nation*, 83.
14. Ibid.
15. L. Koepnick. 2002. *The Dark Mirror: German Cinema between Hitler and Hollywood*, Berkeley: University of California Press, 161.

16. J. Hay. 1987. *Popular Film Culture in Fascist Italy: The Passing of the Rex*, Bloomington: Indiana University Press, 109.
17. Ibid., 108.
18. Ibid., 101.
19. Eckert, 'The Carol Lombard', 35.
20. Ibid., 36–37.
21. Ibid.
22. National Archives and Records Administration (NARA), U.S. Department of Commerce, Bureau of Domestic and Foreign Commerce, Motion Picture Division, *Motion Pictures Abroad*, 29 January 1930, page unnumbered.
23. *Bollettino 20th Century Fox Film*, September 1936.
24. G.V.S., 'Come si lancia un film', *Cinema illustrazione*, 8 January 1936, 4.
25. See S. Gundle. 2008. *Glamour: A History*, Oxford: Oxford University Press.
26. M.F. Thorp. 1939. *America at the Movies*, New Haven: Yale University Press, cited in J. Richards. 1984. *The Age of the Dream Palace: Cinema and Society in Britain 1930–1939*, London: Routledge, 157–58.
27. Issue of 15 September 1934.
28. Marta, 'Il cinema e la moda', *Lo Schermo*, 44–45. Fashion commentators often wrote under single-name pseudonyms like Marta or Vera.
29. S. Grandi and A. Vaccari. 2004. *Vestire il ventennio: moda e cultura artistica in Italia tra le due guerre*, Bologna: Bonomia University Press, 201–2.
30. Roffi, 'La moda per le attrici cinematografiche italiane', *Lo Schermo*, December 1938, 41.
31. Ibid.
32. Vera. 'Come Paola Barbara dovrebbe vestirsi', *Film*, 16 November 1940, 10.
33. Vera, 'Come dovrebbe vestirsi Maria Denis', *Film*, 30 November 1940, 10.
34. Vera, 'Come dovrebbe vestirsi Vivi Gioi', *Film*, 15 February 1941, 10.
35. Vera, 'Come dovrebbe vestirsi Doris Duranti', *Film*, 1 February 1941, 10.
36. N. Novarese, 'È più difficile vestire le "stelle" che …', *Lo Schermo*, June 1937, 14–15.
37. *La Domenica del Corriere*, 10 July 1940.
38. *La Domenica del Corriere*, 10 March 1939.
39. Kezich, 'Gli attori', 389.
40. *La Domenica del Corriere*, 10 July 1939.
41. Eckert, 'The Carol Lombard', 35.
42. Ibid.
43. See K. Peiss. 1988. *Hope in a Jar: The Making of America's Beauty Culture*, New York: Metropolitan.
44. This aspect of Mussolini cult is discussed in Gundle. 2013. 'Mass Culture and the Cult of Personality', in S. Gundle, C. Duggan and G. Pieri (eds), *The Cult of the Duce: Mussolini and the Italians*, Manchester: Manchester University Press.

45. K. Klaprat. 1985. 'The Star as Market Strategy: Bette Davis in Another Light', in T. Balio (ed.), *The American Film Industry*, Madison: University of Wisconsin Press, 351.
46. T. Harris. 1991. 'The Building of Popular Images: Grace Kelly and Marilyn Monroe' in C. Gledhill (ed.), *Stardom: Industry of Desire*, London: Routledge.
47. M. Buzzichini, 'Antidivismo ovvero non rifaremo Hollywood', *Lo Schermo*, May 1936, 23.
48. For a reasonably complete list of the briefings or *veline* issued by the ministry, see S. Raffaelli. 1997. 'Le veline fasciste sul cinema', *Bianco & Nero*, 4, 15–63.
49. *Cinema*, 10 December 1937.
50. L. Freddi. 1949. *Il cinema*, Rome: l'Arnia, 395.
51. Ibid., 409.
52. Ibid., 282.
53. See A. Antola. 2011. 'Ghitta Carell and Italian Studio Photography in the 1930s', *Modern Italy* 8, 249–73.
54. See C. Domini and C. Ghergo (eds). 2012. *Arturo Ghergo, fotografie 1930–1959*, Milan: Silvana.
55. G. Turroni. 1980. *Luxardo: l'italica bellezza*, Milan: Mazzotta, 8.
56. J. Kobal. 1993. *George Hurrell: Hollywood Glamour Portraits*, London: Schirmer, 15.
57. On Luxardo, see B.L. Randone. 'I fotografi del cinema: Luxardo', *Film*, 26 October 1940, 8.
58. Anonymous note, *Grazia*, 19 June 1941, 16–17.
59. Dria Paola in *Cinema illustrazione*, 7 October 1931, 12; see also 'Stelle di mare', in issue of 1 July 1936, 6–7.
60. Anon., 'Vita e miracoli di Laura Nucci', *Cinema illustrazione*, 28 October 1931, 2.
61. Masi and Lancia, *Stelle d'Italia*, 16.
62. 1934 interview, cited ibid.
63. *La Domenica del Corriere*, 10 August 1939.
64. *La Domenica del Corriere*, 13 April 1941.
65. *La Domenica del Corriere*, 28 February 1943.
66. Anon., 'La giornata dei divi', *Cinema*, 25 March 1942, 162–63.
67. F. d'Almeida. 2008. *High Society in the Third Reich*, Cambridge: Polity, 6.
68. Noris quoted in O. Ripa, 'Ho perso il mio piccolo angelo', *Gente*, 6 August 1969, 53.
69. Enzo Magrì, 'Doris Duranti: il primo seno nudo del cinema italiano', *L'Europeo*, 22 November 1973, 80.
70. M. Mercader. 1979. *La mia vita con Vittorio De Sica*, Milan: Mondadori, 22–23.
71. See E. De Giorgi. 1992. *I coetanei*, Milan: Leonardo.
72. Archivio Centrale dello Stato (ACS), Segreteria Particolare del Duce, carteggio riservato, B. 48, Pavolini Alessandro. The folder contains various

letters and reports on the relationship, mostly dating from the early months of 1942.
73. Magrì, 'Doris Duranti', 80.
74. Freddi, *Il cinema*, 74.
75. Ibid., 396.
76. Thirty years later, Noris recalled that 'in my house I had a magnificent Steinway piano on which producers used to place hundreds of thousands of Lire at the start of every film. Of course, this was additional to the ministerial Lit. 80,000' (*Gente*, no. 34, 1969, 55).
77. *La Domenica del Corriere*, 10 August 1939.
78. Anonymous note, *Lo Schermo*, July 1941, 24–25.
79. *Grazia*, 13 March 1941.
80. *Film*, 8 March 1941.
81. *Grazia*, 13 March 1941.
82. De Giorgi, *I coetanei*, 55.
83. Ibid., 55–56.
84. Ibid., 61.
85. Koepnik, *The Dark Mirror*, 163.
86. The role of newsreels in preserving a sense of normality is noted in E. Cicchino. 2010. *Il Duce attraverso il Luce*, Milan: Mursia, 689.
87. Hay, *Popular Film Culture*, 232.
88. See P. Corner. 2009. 'Fascist Italy in the 1930s: Popular Opinion in the Provinces' in Corner (ed.), *Popular Opinion in Totalitarian Regimes: Fascism, Nazism, Communism*, Oxford: Oxford University Press, 122–46.
89. P. Chessa. 2008. *Dux: una biografia per immagini*, Milan: Mondadori, 304.
90. G. S. Ch., 'Difendere il popolo dal divismo', *Rivista del Cinematografo*, June 1942, 77.
91. G. S. Ch., 'Saggio di divismo', *Rivista del Cinematografo*, May 1942, 101.
92. ACS, Ministero della Cultura Popolare, Gabinetto, Fasc. Cinematografia, sottofasc. 17 'Film' giornale.

4

The Public and the Stars

The matter of popular opinion under Fascism has been approached in a number of ways by historians. The debate that followed Renzo De Felice's controversial assertion in 1974 that the Fascist regime rested on wide consent among Italians inspired efforts to apply new methods to the study of life under the regime.[1] Victoria De Grazia used social history to explore the role of organised leisure, while Luisa Passerini and Maurizio Gribaudi used oral history to explore popular memories of the period.[2] Studies of women's experience of the regime, of young people, as well as life in a range of specific cities, added further layers of understanding.[3] Most recently, Paul Corner has addressed directly the issue of people's attitudes in the provinces to larger political themes and personalities and smaller local issues and the problems of everyday life.[4] The intention here is not to address directly the question of whether and to what extent people supported Fascism. It is rather to explore an area of individual and collective expression that for the most part lay outside the official public sphere and only very partially was affected by the official rhythms of public life. In other words, it is to look at a focus of attention and interest that was different from, though not necessarily in conflict with, Fascism itself.

The practices associated with film fandom were quite varied. Star worship consisted principally of assiduous viewing of the films of the elected favourites. It extended, in some cases, to the collection of images and press cuttings, and discussion of the stars within peer group settings. Less frequently, it manifested itself in imitation of exterior gestures, attitudes, personal styles and attire. These practices had precursors in the admiration of opera and theatre stars in the nineteenth century. Then, it was typically educated young urban people, mainly males, who became caught up in the phenomenon; those, in other words, who had access to the media concerned and the press, as well as sufficient free time to entertain dreams and fantasies. Cinema brought certain specific innovations that derived from the mass nature of the medium and the development of the broader communications apparatus. Wider groups, including the upper stratum of young workers and those living in the provinces, were involved. In the sound era, relationships changed again and so did the ways in which men and women understood and interiorised stardom.

The first question that this chapter will ask is: who made up the groups that were most prone to cultivate relations with stars and render these relations concrete in practices of the self? Next, the aim will be to explore how stars, first foreign and then Italian, were experienced by spectators; this will involve considering a number of media parallel to cinema that operated in conjunction with it, including radio, the press and postcards. Finally, the chapter will explore a variety of rituals and practices that were associated with star worship and which were variously promoted or criticised by the authorities. Most of these practices were registered by the press, which encouraged some of them and channelled others. The close attention the film press paid to public responses to films and stars means that, although inevitably partial, it is possible through it to reconstruct some aspects of the way cinema impacted on everyday life, aspirations, desires, models of appearance and behaviour. Additional information has been taken from memoirs, oral history testimonies and social histories.

Film Audiences in the 1930s

The public first developed an interest in film stars in the silent era when practices of star worship developed, especially around Lyda Borelli and Rudolph Valentino. In later years, it was mainly the American stars who attracted interest and envy. The category of filmgoer most susceptible to the appeal of the stars was the young urban dweller with a minimum of disposable income: school pupils, university students and young workers. For such people, cinema was the primary leisure experience at a time when the forms of leisure were undergoing change. The invention of radio, the development of professional sports, the expansion of the daily and periodical press, the establishment of commercial dance halls and the growth of travel all redefined experience in a way that cried out for new models. Urban culture produced opportunities and enticements that were often articulated through cinema. For young people cinema was a part of their experience in a way that it had not been for earlier generations and thus they paid special attention to the ideas and suggestions that it provided.

Writing in 1931, Lucio Ridenti, a theatre critic and editor of *Il Dramma*, noted that 'the allure of celebrity is not a force that is unleashed by the famous person to be spread over those who celebrate him but something that flows from the crowd of celebrators to the one who is celebrated'.[5] It was, he argued, an aspect of the modern, machine world and its relentless anti-individualism. The widespread desire to escape normality and break free of the crowd found expression in identification with, or interest in, the famous. For this reason, he continued, people accepted behaviour in the famous that would otherwise be unacceptable. However, certain basic things were expected of the famous that mostly had to do with visual impact. These included an elegant demeanour, possession of the latest fashionable clothes, physical beauty, openness about feelings and moods, and a willingness to be discussed and judged by others.

In Italy, the appeal of film stars lay in the fact that they offered an alternative to the conventional roles that were held out, especially for women, by the Church and the regime. Both these sources of authority stressed the traditional calling of women at a time when larger numbers than ever before were working in factories, shops, offices and workshops, or were attending school or university. Victoria De Grazia has shown that the only modern models available to young women in the areas of beauty, courtship, behaviour and dress were supplied by magazines, advertising and cinema; the stars were the human bearers or embodiment of these.[6]

Film stars provided raw material for young people: role models, life guides, models of appearance and behaviour. They were embodiments of the sexes, they offered ideals of beauty and were exemplars of widely supported values (or occasionally subverters of them). They were leaders of style and functioned as a focal point for aspirations for social mobility, luxury and self-realisation. The film star was not in this sense simply a known screen actor, but a figure who resonated beyond the screen, impinging on values, tastes and cultural models. For the young it was exterior appearance and mannerisms that mattered most, and magazines were obliged to dispense advice on this score. *Cinema illustrazione* ran a column 'Lo dica a me e mi dica tutto' (Tell me and tell me all) in which the 'super-revisore' (the Neapolitan writer Giuseppe Marotta, editor of the magazine) dispensed advice to readers. More than other magazines which employed similar devices (letters' columns were run by such exotically named characters as Aladin, Knight of Hearts and Dona Dolores de Panza) this particular 'agony uncle' was cinematic in orientation:

> Your life is a film and you are the leading actor in it. But not always is your performance successful. Why is this? Because the film of your life lacks a super-revisor. The super-revisor in film studios has the job of correcting scene by scene the imperfections and sometimes he can even turn a mediocre film into a good film. You too will make use of a super-revisor. Tell him what in the film of your life is going badly or makes you feel bad and the super-revisor will instruct you what to do. You can also ask the super-revisor news about things, events and people that have to do with film.[7]

Under his pseudonym, Marotta responded to hundreds of readers of *Cinema illustrazione* who wrote in every week demanding the addresses, dress and shoe sizes, and personal tastes of their favourites. Film fans became accustomed to reading about the love and family lives, homes, leisure activities and tastes of the stars. The frequency with which Marotta was called on to provide details of the marital or relationship status of this or that star suggests that they were seen both as objects of personal desire and as public property.

The illustrated periodical press attended to a number of needs.[8] First of all, it provided visual and written information about the world. It also provided spectacle, distraction and pleasure. Cinema featured regularly in family weeklies and women's magazines in terms of cover illustrations and photographs, news, comment, biographies and so on.[9] The popular film magazines catered most of all to the interest in stars. They furnished material, responded to queries and requests for information, maintained a discussion around star figures that included playful speculation and gentle mockery (caricatures especially); they also catered to the yearning for stardom that was a feature of the engagement of many with cinema. The American stars formed an unrivalled focus of interest through the 1930s before circumstances altered. For Lorenzo Pellizzari, 'up to 1939 (but something had changed) there was still admiration; in the years after that, a sort of respect remained, despite everything. It was a true love affair, to which Hollywood responded in the form of interviews, visits, messages and photographs with dedications'.[10] The evidence suggests that Italian stars also were the object of admiration and love, especially once Italian cinema's recovery was well established. The magazines' role could be seen as policing, bringing secret dreams and private behaviours to the surface and making them visible. Once this occurred they could be discussed or corrected. They also performed a service in providing an outlet that existed nowhere else for the need for advice on romance and personal issues. For De Grazia, 'Mass culture offered advice that mothers could not: about types of men, kinds of kisses, how to flirt. At base, it offered advice on how to negotiate with the opposite sex'.[11]

As Jackie Stacey found in her study of British women and American stars, Hollywood had a special ability to capture aspirations and unleash desires with its gallery of players and masterful display of them.[12] Their appeal stemmed from their status as extraordinary beings; they were lifelike fantasies that seemed to be ideal versions of everyday people. They were independent, stylish and enviably fulfilled. In Italy, as elsewhere, preferences for this or that star were often shared. Girls talked about cinema in trains, streets, trams and living rooms. Inevitably, one of the topics was 'Come si diventa attrici' (How you can become an actress).[13] This sense of the average young spectator as a potential star was captured by Gino Boccasile in one of his cover illustrations for the magazine *Le Grandi*

Firme. His idealised heroine, a curvaceous middle-class girl who throws herself enthusiastically but not always ably into all manner of activities, including day-dreaming over the photos of male actors, is depicted marching triumphantly towards the gates of Cinecittà while an audience of ordinary folk applauds (see Fig. 4.5).

Spectators developed close identifications with the stars. They thought of themselves in relation to them and formed complex mental worlds that were infused with dreams and aspirations. For a lucky few, these dreams came to fruition. Several of the young stars of the 1940s emerged from this milieu of dedicated fandom. The actress Luisella Beghi, for example, who grew up in Parma and went to the cinema every day in her teens (the early to mid-1930s) was especially keen on American films and consequently her preference was for American stars. 'There were those films with Greta Garbo, and then Ronald Colman', she told Francesco Savio in the 1970s;[14] 'I was crazy about Ronald Colman. There was Lilian Harvey, Clark Gable, Bette Davis, there was Katherine Hepburn. I liked her a lot and I said (you know what young girls are like?) "How I'd like to play her parts"'. Evident in these remarks is an attraction to an actor of the opposite sex and identification with one of the same sex. The latter is emphasised in star studies, even though there is ample evidence that the former was a dynamic of equal power. Another young actor in the 1930s, Roberto Villa, told Savio: 'I was particularly crazy about Barbara Stanwyck. I thought she was fabulous, she had this femininity, this unbridled sexuality, I liked her a lot'.[15] Even at a distance of several decades, certain names resonated, as David Forgacs and I found when we conducted a series of oral interviews in the early 1990s.[16] One of the key divisions in star preferences was between foreign stars and home-grown ones. Although the Americans would occupy the dominant place in popular memory, in fact there were others too. Some Italian spectators were drawn to the foreigners because of both the cultural and cinematic properties that characterised them, although few were able to verbalise this with the skill of novelist Italo Calvino, who, as a teenager in the 1930s, regularly went to the cinema alone in his home town of San Remo:

> French cinema was as heavy with smells as American cinema smelt of Palmolive, of shiny, sterile places. The women had a carnal presence that fixed them in your memory as both living women and erotic spirits (Viviane Romance is the figure who comes to mind here) whereas in the Hollywood stars the eroticism was sublimated, stylised, idealised (even the most carnal of American actresses of the time, Jean Harlow, was made unreal by the dazzling whiteness of her skin).[17]

The sense that is given in all three of these testimonies is of new worlds of experience and desire opening up before the eyes of young people, alerting them to horizons beyond those of their family and community. Among the witnesses interviewed for the Forgacs and Gundle project, such observations were common. 'Regardless of whether the film was good or not, you saw performances by extraordinary actors. Bearing in mind that they were edited, they probably were not quite at that level, but they really knew how to hold their place as stars', said one man, born in Turin in 1927;[18] while another added, 'The American actor was more spontaneous. You could see he fitted the part, he really seemed to have lived it'.[19] The admiration expressed in these remarks is a little more distant than that noted by Jeffrey Richards with reference to Britain in the 1930s. He observed that one of the functions of stars was 'simply to distract attention from reality by allowing the viewer to opt out into a total fantasy world'.[20] But, even if 'opting out' was problematic in Fascist Italy, it is just as true that, as Richards adds, 'For many cinema-goers America was that fantasy world and American stars the ultimate self-projection'.

The Dialogue with the Stars

Writing letters to Hollywood could be a frustrating experience for Italians, but the local film press played an active part in seeking to provide the sort of information and involvement that spectators sought. The relationship with Italian stars was not necessarily better as actors varied in their attitudes to fan letters. Broadly speaking, the men ignored them. Both Fosco Giachetti and Vittorio De Sica confessed this quite candidly. The women often took more interest. Isa Miranda responded personally to many letters, while Assia Noris employed secretarial staff to respond to fans' letters and requests for photos. Others relied on the Cinecittà press office to do the job for them. Leda Gloria regaled a journalist with tales of the bizarre letters she received proposing marriage, business arrangements or foreign trips. Perplexed by the scale of the phenomenon, she devised a method for puncturing inflated hopes: 'To some of the nicest authors, I send a really ugly photograph that I have had reproduced in a thousand copies. It is a photo of me at school aged sixteen. When I send the photo I write to the man concerned telling him that that is the real Leda Gloria and that the blonde actress to whom he has directed his flattering proposal is a creation of cinematic tricks'.[21] When she was asked, in 1965, to comment on the public reaction to stars in the Fascist period, Alida Valli responded, 'Well, they asked us for autographs and they wrote us letters. But there was not the hysteria of today. The biggest star of all was Amedeo Nazzari. Rossano Brazzi was idolised by young girls, followed directly by Roberto Villa and Massimo Serato, as well as Fosco Giachetti. Doris Duranti was a real diva.'[22]

In her study of a published volume of fan mail sent to Claudia Cardinale – mostly in the 1960s – Reka Buckley found that a considerable number of people wrote asking for money, material goods or some form of practical assistance.[23] There is no equivalent resource for the 1930s or early 1940s, although film journalist Alessandro Ferraù wrote a series of articles for *Film* in 1941 in which he discussed the fan letters of several actors (none of them top stars). His analyses suggest that the public of the pre-war years was less demanding, perhaps because the wealth of actors was less flaunted, but also perhaps because the audience did not yet routinely include members of the lower classes, who in any case at that time would scarcely ever have written a letter. He found that schoolgirls wrote to Roberto Villa, often in groups, usually shortly after seeing him in a film. Launched as the adult son of former aviation hero Luciano Serra in *Luciano Serra pilota*, who had followed his father into the air force, his boyish appearance and cordial manner endeared him to girls who wrote 'al più simpatico attore del mondo' (the nicest actor in the world), 'gentilissimo grandissimo attore' (kindest, greatest actor), 'illustre attore' (illustrious actor) or simply 'a Roberto' (to Roberto), one or two of them confessing that they were doing so during lessons.[24] There was a particular desire to see him in modern dress, without wigs, swords or costumes. Lots of soldiers wrote to actresses asking for photos, and some confessed that they had been tempted to steal posters. Some fans, following the policy of encouraging Italian-looking actors, stated that they did not want to see on the screen blonde actresses 'like their American colleagues'; 'now we want to see stars of our own, from our country, brown-haired, beautiful, endowed with the charm of our peninsula, of which you are the ideal prototype', one wrote.[25] One actress who fitted this bill, Carla Candiani, received letters from soldiers, autograph hunters and lovelorn admirers.

Judging from these surveys, there seems to have been relatively little of the type of personal identification that Lucio Romeo noted in 1956 when he discussed fan letters in *Cinema*.[26] At that time fans mainly wrote to stars who resembled them physically, with Jennifer Jones being a favourite on account of her long dark hair and vaguely Mediterranean appearance. But, as in the earlier period, desire was expressed in romantic, delicate tones. Hollywood actors were still seen as demi-gods who lived on a remote Olympus, whereas Italian actors were local and could be seen out and about in the capital. The local agencies of American companies were engaged in responding to letters from fans to their players, while Italian actors, if they responded, did so individually. Nevertheless, anecdotal evidence suggested that the numerous adolescent female stars who flourished in the wake of the Canadian Deanna Durbin, including Chiaretta Gelli, Carla Del Poggio, Irasema Dilian and Valentina Cortese, were embraced by their peers as ideal projections of themselves, and their careers were followed with keen interest.

The film press expanded markedly from the mid-1930s. The oldest magazine, *Cinema illustrazione* (published in Milan by Rizzoli from 1925), was joined in the later 1930s and 1940s by many more. Some, like *Lo Schermo* (published in Milan from 1935), *Bianco e Nero* and *Cinema* (published in Milan by Hoepli from 1936) were more or less official organs of the film establishment, the first-mentioned being associated directly with the general directorate of cinema. Others, including *Stelle, Si gira, Intercine, Cinemagazzino* and *Film* were geared more to the interests of readers, while *Primi piani* (a glossy monthly, published from 1941) was pitched upmarket. Women's magazines and weekly illustrated magazines also gave cinema coverage. Regular features in all of these on the processes of film-making and the people engaged in this enviable activity encouraged the growth of interest. Articles drew a picture of Cinecittà as a home-grown dream factory where the fortunate few who had been selected to appear in the movies worked.

Italian stars were a spasmodic presence in the film press before the late 1930s and it is fair to assume that they had little impact on the public. Later, however, a range of innovations served to increase their visibility and potential allure in the eyes of audiences. The creation of Cinecittà and the transfer of the Centro sperimentale film school to new premises on the Via Tuscolana did not just take the quantity and quality of film production to a new level but also provided an opportunity to construct a mythology around Italian cinema. The more official magazines ran regular stories intended to romanticise the school and turn actors into an enviable open elite. Although films with plots that involved cinema itself were few, documentaries were commissioned that presented the work of the city of cinema. The Luce Institute's *Cinque minuti a Cinecittà* (Five Minutes at Cinecittà) was a playful excursion into the various aspects of film-making that might have intrigued or delighted spectators. At least ten well-known actors were presented by name in the voiceover to the documentary, including, most prominently, Amedeo Nazzari and Alida Valli. Like Mario Soldati's film *Dora Nelson*, it featured the deco-style entrance over which letters forming the word Cinecittà stood. Both also featured the real porter of the establishment.

In the process whereby spectators turned the film-going experience into something much more continuous and personal, a number of factors counted. Among these was the adoption of an attitude of dreaming that Gian Piero Brunetta, borrowing from Calvino, has referred to as 'mental cinema'.[27] This could be elaborated from fragments of experience and memories or even be stimulated in someone with little familiarity with cinema, by means, say, of a photograph or a poster. To some extent this was manipulated by the producers of films, who knew that memorable moments or phrases could stick. Garbo's 'I want to be alone' line, uttered in *Grand Hotel* (Edmund Goulding, 1932), encapsulated the star's reluctant publicity image. In Italy, two catchphrases were associated with Nazzari. The first and the most famous, 'Chi non beve con me, pesce lo colga!' (A plague on anyone who refuses to drink with me!), was spoken in *La cena delle beffe* (The Jester's Supper, Alessandro Blasetti, 1939), while his response to a mispronunciation of his surname in *Apparizione* (Apparition, Jean de Limur, 1943) also found its way into popular banter. Several stars were known for trademark features or styles: Nazzari's moustache and wavy hair, De Sica's smile, and Valli's shoulder-length hair which partially covered her face. Few costumes acted as prompts to memory although Noris's little hats won attention and her daring two-piece circus costume in *Darò un milione* caused a minor scandal. The actress later reported that, after she appeared in it, she received lots of letters offering to marry her to save her from perdition.[28]

Publishers knew that fans liked to collect pictures of their favourites. Images of stars were available from various sources: magazines published photographs of all sizes from the full-page poster to the small-format; there were postcards of stars, and series of photographs included with confectionary. In addition, *figurine*, or cards and stickers, were attached to various types of products. Little evidence has been gathered about how fans started to collect images and cuttings or what uses they made of them. Indeed, the most important work on the postcards of the period concerns not a film star but Mussolini.[29] The Duce's image, which was reproduced on thousands of postcards, was unquestionably the most sought-after and collected of the period. Film star collections, of which there were certainly some – Brunetta for example, mentions one begun by the Florentine Anita Frizzi in January 1937 – worked in a different way since collectors had a choice of subject.[30] They could choose to focus their attentions on one star or construct personal galleries of their own.

One collector, Nerio Tebano, lived with his parents and many siblings in a hotel in Taranto, Sicily (see Fig. 4.1). He cultivated a keen interest in cinema and wrote to many stars, including Isa Miranda, to whom, he later recalled, he began to write long letters after her screen debut in 1934 ('she replied immediately, seeking my opinions and judgements, that I expressed dispassionately', he later claimed).[31] 'I used to isolate myself in the afternoon in one of the empty rooms from a situation that seemed to me like a Tower of Babel', he wrote. 'In that room I used to play at cinema with a collection of postcards of film stars (I had collected more than two hundred of them). It was a feeling that was fantastic and professional at the same time'. One day, a guest left with the cards, leaving the young man bereft. 'With that theft finished a game that I often used to play with the relatives who came to visit us', he later recalled. 'The game consisted of a sort of guessing competition. They used to lay out all the postcards before me, one after another, and I had to guess the name of each actress or actor. I knew them all by heart, so I always won.'[32]

Several companies, particularly manufacturers of confectionary, issued numbered small-format cards, in the manner of American and British

Fig. 4.1 Avid film fan Nerio Tebano, who would later write a volume of memoirs, succeeded in getting his photograph published in *Cinema*, 10 November 1942. (Author's own collection)

Fig. 4.2 'The ferocious Saladin', the rarest of the cards issued by the Perugina and Buitoni companies in a promotion tie-in with a radio show. (Author's own collection)

cigarette cards, and young people went to some effort to complete collections. An initiative like the famous Perugina–Buitoni card-collecting campaign, promoted through the radio programme *The Four Musketeers*, was conceived in a context in which consumers were already engaged in gathering visual ephemera (see Fig 4.2). No promotion involving film-star cards provoked such passions or conflicts,[33] but the level of commitment to personal collections should not be underestimated. More personal albums were filled with press cuttings and postcards. The latter often featured the stunning photographs taken of the stars by Luxardo and Ghergo. Far more alluring than almost any film performance, including close-ups, they distilled the glamorous essence of the star into a single image. Owners, or collectors, of them could consume these images in private daydreams or share their fantasies and possibly swap cards with their friends. The 'girl peer culture' that De Grazia has analysed was matched in this respect by a no less enthusiastic mass cultural boy peer culture.[34] On this plane at least, if on few others, the Italian stars proved to be the equal of the superlative American stars who had been removed in 1939 from Italy's screens, but not from spectators' hearts and minds. Fanatics continued to adore their idols in secret, Viniccio Marinucci confessed in August 1944; they whispered items of news to each other and passed postcards around.[35] They also lovingly leafed through their collections of past issues of film magazines.

Getting into the Movies

American film companies and their backers in government always felt that they had a found a special connection with foreign film audiences. 'American pictures, I hardly need say, continue to maintain their immense popularity abroad', declared Nathan Golden, chief of the Motion Picture Division of the Department of Commerce in 1937:

> Theatergoers are enthusiastic about them – in Norwegian coastal cities and in high Andean capitals, in the teeming Oriental centers and in the sophisticated, metropolitan theatres of Western Europe. That is only natural, of course, when one considers the engineering genius, the artistic ability, and the business acumen that go into their making. Foreign peoples like them and demand them, because they realize their incomparable excellence.[36]

However, companies made wide use of publicity to arouse interest and cultivate audience involvement. Numerous interviews, visits, messages and photographs with dedications all served this end.[37] Starting with Douglas Fairbanks and Mary Pickford, who were given a tour of Roman tourist sites, many stars toured the country. Visits on the part of movie personnel were written up in such a way as to flatter Italy, with stars expressing their love for the country and its past and, sometimes, admiration for its present direction.[38]

Production companies eager to cultivate the personal engagement of spectators launched competitions on a regular basis. In Italy, the most famous was probably Twentieth Century Fox's to find a new Rudolph Valentino following the actor's early demise. It was won by Alberto Rabagliati, who went to Hollywood and subsequently, despite his failure to make a mark, wrote a book about his experiences there.[39] In biographies of Sophia Loren, it is always recounted that her mother, Romilda Villani, won a Greta Garbo lookalike contest and would have gone to America to work as the actress's stand-in had personal circumstances not prevented her.[40]

The Americans knew the publicity that initiatives like these could generate, but they were never quite sure that foreign spectators could be persuaded to live through the stars to the same extent as Americans. When an unnamed American publicity man from one of the Hollywood majors, who was passing through Rome, was interviewed in *Cinema illustrazione* in 1932 he said that 'the American public is a public that is very greedy for gossip ... To enthuse spectators the smallest thing is enough. Being a fan, that is someone who is fanatical about a star, is a source of joy for a young American who never forgets to write regularly to his idol. For them the opening of a new film is as important as a boxing match between world champions.' As if to express his uncertainty about whether the same dynamic operated abroad, he added, cautiously, that only the stars who had already won recognition at home were launched in Europe.[41] Nonetheless, the press and stores were all involved in campaigns to arouse audience interest. In 1933 *Stelle* announced a 'matrimonial competition' in which readers were invited to guess which actors had been chosen as suitable husbands for a string of unmarried Hollywood actresses. The prizes – a manicure set, a perfume spray, a make-up set, soaps and so on – were offered by the La Rinascente stores.[42]

Promotion competitions of the Hollywood type were held from time to time. From the early 1930s, *Cinema illustrazione* published pictures of 'fotogenici', that is photographs of young men and women adopting 'photogenic' attitudes reminiscent of film stars. In autumn 1930, it launched its 'Siete voi fotogenico?' (Are you photogenic?) competition, which was open to all except professionals. Articles about the promotion were illustrated with photographs of American starlets. Readers were also asked to vote on the degree of likeness achieved in the shots. There were lots of examples of plucked eyebrows, hair brushed back, American-style open smiles, cigarettes dangling from mouths, made-up women, intriguing glances, and cocked hats. A lot of emphasis was placed on the styling of hair, while some entrants sent in swimsuit shots. Then, for several weeks in summer 1931, the magazine ran a competition of readers' photographs expressing 'hate'.

The implication of all these initiatives was that out there among the filmgoers there were cinematic talents waiting to be noticed or discovered. In keeping with the emphasis on self-styling, cinema magazines featured many advertisements for all manner of beauty products such as machines for waving hair, powder, nail varnish, face cream, perfumes and bust enhancers. In 1933, *Stelle* held a competition called 'Volete diventare artisti?' (Do you want to become an artist?), for which readers were invited to send in photos. In keeping with a common attitude towards American mass culture, it was claimed that people in Italy had more personality and were less standardised than in America.

Some publications collaborated with Italian production companies. *Lo Schermo* reported in January 1940 that Nelly Morgan had won a Sovrana film competition entitled 'Perchè nasca una stella' (So that a star may be born). Later that year, the Lux company launched a search in conjunction with *Film* for a young woman to play Manzoni's virginal heroine Lucia Mondella alongside Gino Cervi as Renzo in a film version of the novel *I promessi sposi*. The vagueness of Manzoni's descriptions of his heroine allowed the company to ask not only 'Who will it be?' but also 'Will she be blonde or brown-haired?' Thousands of photographs sent in by 'the beautiful girls of Italy' were judged by a commission; many of the subjects were attired in peasant costume. Fourteen finalists were selected and brought to Rome; however, none of them satisfied the director Mario Camerini. Determined not to give up, Lux engaged the photographer Elio Luxardo and sent him on a tour of Italy.[43] It was announced that he would photograph all-comers who presented themselves at Lux's offices in eight cities in the course of June 1941. All beautiful girls were invited to respond. In the end Camerini cast Dina Sassoli, a 21-year-old from Rimini who had won a *Film* magazine competition for new faces in 1938.

Beauty contests enjoyed a brief heyday in the 1920s. They were eventually banned, although pictures of American contests continued to appear in the Italian press. Competitions were anyway still staged in holiday resorts. *Cinema* reported in September 1941 that a swimsuit competition in Riccione had been concluded.[44] From 1939 the '5000 Lire for a smile' competition, sponsored by the Chlorodont toothpaste company and *Tempo* magazine, became an annual event (see Fig. 4.3). Although heats were held

Fig. 4.3 The '5,000 Lire for a smile' competition was one of several commercial initiatives that enticed entrants with material prizes. (Author's own collection)

Fig. 4.4 A broad, movie-star smile from Adriana Serra of Rome, winner of the 1941 '5,000 Lire for a smile' competition. (Author's own collection)

in resorts, it was mainly a postal competition. In 1942, ten thousand photos reached the organisers. Although the competition was in theory open to anyone, be they young women or men, children, babies or old folk, the emphasis clearly fell on the young, the photogenic and, given the competition's postwar evolution into the Miss Italy pageant, the female (see Fig. 4.4).[45] Among the prizes were twenty-five screen tests.

Le Grandi Firme, edited by Cesare Zavattini, also launched a competition, in April 1938, to find a young woman who resembled the pert *Signorina Grandi Firme* drawn by Boccasile who adorned the magazine's cover (Fig. 4.5). The winner was promised a film career. 'The Amato production company is committed to grant a regular contract for one year, to be paid at Lit. 2,000 per month, to the first winner who will also be cast in one of its films', read the announcement. Although the magazine was closed down before the competition finished, the promise was maintained and the result announced in another publication, *Il Milione*, also edited by Zavattini.[46] The winner was one Vanna Borea who, however, immediately renounced her prize. The competition was relaunched the following year and a winner found who eagerly accepted the offer of the Amato company.

Fig. 4.5 Illustrator Gino Boccasile's pin-up, *Signorina Grandi Firme*, strides confidently towards Cinecittà. (Author's own collection)

Competitions like this worked because young people knew well from the press that many Italian stars had found their way on to the screen through competitions or by being talent-spotted. *La Domenica del Corriere* reported that Maria Denis had been discovered on the street and Assia Noris in the foyer of a Rome theatre, while Elsa De Giorgi had sent her photo to production companies. Leda Gloria, Laura Nucci, Oretta Fiume, Luisa Ferida and Laura Solari had all won competitions.[47]

Numerous youngsters wrote directly to production companies, without waiting for the occasion of a competition. The publicity agent Vittorio Calvino analysed some of them for *Primi piani*.[48] He found that the cinema was seen as an Eldorado where money and fame could easily be acquired. For others it was a possible escape from pressing problems. One young widow wrote, 'I have no means and I don't know how to do anything, so I can't find employment. I would work willingly for the cinema and I am available for anything. It would be necessary to cover the cost of my journey to Rome.' The owner of a small hotel in the Veneto region that was not doing well had decided, 'I think that I have no other way forward except the cinema. I could be an actor adapting even to secondary parts at first (waiter, artist, butler etc.)'. A young man from Foggia conveyed his enthusiasm as follows:

> I know that you don't become an actor just like that but I have the talent, the passion, a lively intelligence, limitless will and firm intentions. I would certainly succeed; the mirror, my master, has convinced me that I am right to pursue my desire, my precocious instinct. I will be capable of combating obstacles; facing discomforts, overcoming all difficulties and winning every battle. Mine is the intention, believe me, of a man determined to reach his goal and realise his sweet unique dream.

At the foot of his letter, he added, almost as an afterthought, 'If I am not photogenic, I wish to do everything possible to acquire photogenic qualities'. Some authors described themselves in detail: 'I am 25; tall, nice and charming', wrote one. 'My hair is brown and wavy. I have a high forehead and thick eyebrows. My eyes are black and big, lively, expressive and speak volumes. My nose is Roman and regular. My mouth is small, the lips full and clever [sic]. My laugh is genuine and my voice manly.' Others, like a 23-year-old woman from a small village near Catania in Sicily, had little or no familiarity with the cinema, even as spectators, but had clear ideas about what it could mean for them in terms of personal emancipation: 'From childhood I have been living the monotonous life of a little gossipy village that does not offer even the smallest of distractions. My parents keep me shut up indoors, without ever visiting family friends or holding gatherings even among relatives. There are no family dances and no opportunities to watch a film – that would be a scandal! I have resolved to break out of the chrysalis and take a decisive step towards the cinema that so attracts me and for which I feel a great desire!'

The biggest advantage that Italian stars had over the Americans was that they were more readily accessible, physically as well as culturally. Their voices, each with their own distinct tones and pronunciations, were important calling cards. Unlike the remote stars of Hollywood, they could actually be seen in Rome and on select occasions in other locations, at least by those who lived in the capital or were able to travel. In 1939, Vittorio Mussolini organised, with the contributions of the magazines *Cinema* and *Film*, an encounter of stars and the public in the Adriatic resort of Riccione, where the Mussolini family vacationed. *Film*'s editor, Mino Doletti, argued that this was an important event, 'contributing to the formation of an Italian star system'.[49] To judge by its success, occasions of this type generated considerable excitement. Holiday resorts were thought of as typical of locations where the stars might be found. 'Oh, delightful stars of the sea, wherever there is ample space we see you, wherever there is sea, sand and sun: in Riccione, Viareggio, Venice or on the Riviera', remarked *Cinema illustrazione* in 1936 in an article adorned with photos of actresses in bathing costumes,[50] adding that American stars would be doing the same things thousands of miles to the west on the beaches of California. Swimsuit shots of actresses in Italy normally required some seasonal or locational justification. The Venice Film Festival was one of these. Stars and cinema personnel converged on the Lido in late August, where they invariably found numerous autograph hunters lying in wait for them. Years later Assia Noris recalled: 'I remember the line of policemen to protect me when I arrived at the Venice Festival and my appearances at the balcony were repeatedly demanded. It was a time of balconies then.'[51]

Location filming was relatively rare but the knowledge that famous actors were in a locality was guaranteed to draw crowds to the hotels where they were staying. When Alida Valli was filming *Piccolo mondo antico* (Little Old World, Mario Soldati, 1941) near the northern lakes, a large crowd gathered outside her hotel and noisily demanded her appearance, even though they had been told that the actress was not present at the time.[52] To the delight of fans, in August 1940 *Film* published on its back cover a map of Rome with the faces and addresses of the stars, indicating where they lived.

For those who lived far from the capital and were unable to vacation in fashionable resorts, the radio provided the best vehicle for a live encounter. Between 1942 and 1943, actors could regularly be heard on the radio in a programme entitled 'Attori italiani al microfono' (Italian actors at the microphone). As Franco Monteleone observes, radio and cinema audiences were one and the same: 'Shop assistants, white-collar workers, teachers, shopkeepers, artisans, low-level state employees, students and housewives, maids and soldiers: this was the majority of Italy that listened to the radio, that went to the cinema, that read – when it read – mass circulation magazines'.[53]

The scale of interest among young people for film careers was not deemed to be healthy by many of those concerned with cinema. It might have helped to keep enthusiasm for Italian cinema up but it manifested a worrying tendency to think of cinema as little more than play. Film fans were often under the impression that the Italian stars lived well. One reason so many desired to get into the movies was precisely because they imagined it would lead to a life of ease and material comfort.

Freddi commented on all those women who sigh 'Lucky her!' thinking of the film star. In fact they faced a life of hard work, getting up at six, spending up to two hours in make-up, engaging in serious work in the studio all day, even up to 10 P.M. or midnight. In all seasons they had to perform under harsh lights and make no complaints about it. Despite this, an actor needed to be fresh and well rested as the camera would pick up on the slightest sign of tiredness. The 'comfortable' life of the 'diva' or 'divo' is not really so enviable, he insisted.[54]

'It is not true that Italian producers are ready to launch any girlie so long as she satisfies their desires', he wrote in his memoirs:

> A film in those days cost something like one or two, or up to three or four million lire to make, and these are not figures that you throw to the wind on a whim for some small and too hasty gratifications. It is not true that the female stars are absurdly frivolous and fatuous floozies. Many of them are women who are passionate about their trade, ready to sacrifice every convenience, satisfaction and pleasure for the sake of cinema, and the others, because there are in fact others and it would be silly not to admit it, are for the most part those who do not count for anything. It is not true that directors try to seduce inexpert young girls who want to get into the movies. As far as I know, by contrast, directors are actually afraid of only one thing: the naive young girl who wants to get into the movies. It is not true that female supporting actors are easy to please floozies. Many of them (and I could even cite their names) are excellent wives and mothers who are only worried about the family budget and helping their children to find a position in life. Almost all of them are women who need to work even at the cost of considerable effort. It is not true, in other words, that the cinema is a world in which it is easy to earn money, no one does much work and there is a lot of corruption. Money at the cinema requires a lot of hard work, more than in many apparently more serious and taxing professions. And corruption in the world of cinema is not, in percentage terms, either more or less than that which exists in all the fields of life of a big city, which, in Italy, where a certain honest and active sense of tradition is present among the majority of citizens, means, basically, very little indeed. The exception is not the rule.[55]

Official media were vigilant in ensuring that misleading suggestions were quashed. A note in *Lo Schermo* in November 1940 called for the interruption of a series of articles published in the Trieste daily *Il Piccolo* under the title 'Storielle dello schermo' (Tales from the screen), because it had suggested that 'a manicurist with good legs was promoted to the level of star thanks to her love affair with Commendatore X'. Such tales brought cinema discredit in the eyes of the public since 'real actresses are not born on the knee of Commendatori'. Efforts to correct the firmly held but mistaken convictions of impressionable filmgoers could occasionally be found even in films. In *Apparizione*, it is Amedeo Nazzari himself who acts against type to shatter the infatuation of film-fan Alida Valli who has ditched her fiancé to run away with him. The actor feigns himself a cynical seducer to scare the girl into believing that her virtue is in peril in his company. When she begs him to take her away with him, he drives her to his apartment, where before her eyes a flimsy negligee is laid out on his bed for her by a manservant. She is horrified, but the audience knows that he has no real interest in the girl, who he returns chastened but intact to her family who are in on the act. This scene represented the culmination of a pedagogical narrative trajectory. Earlier in the film, Nazzari had delivered a lecture to an older woman who doubted the seriousness of actors, saying that they may earn well but their popularity can be temporary and work is not guaranteed. In the end, the spectator is assured that in reality he was a morally upright, hard-working professional who lived alone and had little time for a private life. Alert observers would however have made a mental note of Nazzari's car, comfortable apartment and personal staff.

Disapproving articles about fandom appeared with a certain regularity in the Catholic press and even in the film press. Youngsters who indulged in unrealistic fantasies about cinema and its stars were often subjected to admonishment or pity. However, despite evidence to the contrary, there was often a belief that Italians would never indulge their desires to the same extent as the naïve Americans. In 1941, Antonio Ghirelli, who would become a leading journalist in the postwar years, observed that people liked to fix their aspirations on to other people; they wanted to know names and recognise faces. Even intellectuals did it with directors, he wrote, and so ordinary people do so with actors. He suggested that there was no need to be concerned: 'we have enough good sense not to found "fan clubs" comprised of the deluded, to be moved by Giachetti's red braces, or get sad because De Sica is no good at billiards'.[56] Italians, he implied – somewhat curiously, it might be said, given the extent of the Mussolini personality cult – could be trusted not to indulge in more than moderate enthusiasm for their screen heroes and heroines.

Stars and Ideology

In his work on stars, Richard Dyer highlighted how stars could play against dominant values, capturing and articulating unacknowledged desires and practices and providing a means through which these could take shape and acquire some citizenship.[57] In a situation of dictatorship, such as that prevailing in Fascist Italy, there were many barriers to the presentation of dissonant voices or models of behaviour, and the eclectic nature of Fascism could cover over a variety of different impulses and provide some illusion of resolution. But there were spaces in which Fascism coexisted with impulses that, while not necessarily openly conflictual, were certainly different. The popularity of American cinema testifies to the appeal exercised by images of a freer, more mobile and prosperous society. The Hollywood stars appealed on many levels, but above all they held out an idea of the possibilities of human realisation that was more private and material than anything Fascism offered. De Grazia has shown how important American films and the stars were in terms of shaping modern ideas of behaviour, dress, romance, work and enjoyment among young women. While official opinion and media presented a traditionalist idea of women's roles, Hollywood held out exciting alternatives. Italian cinema was much more closely aligned with the regime's preferences, programmes and prohibitions. But inevitably modern themes and aspirations were given voice in films. Stars such as Elsa Merlini, whose chirpy working girl in *La segretaria privata* (The Private Secretary, Goffredo Alessandrini, 1931) was imitated in numerous comedies, presented a model of female independence that could only be found in commercial culture. Even where narratives punished female independence or transgression, the airing of difference or variety could open horizons. Despite pre-censorship and its control of the press, the regime could not channel modes of spectatorship that went beyond film texts. If films catered to the audience's consuming glance, spectators could engage in the sort of textual poaching that potentially subverted or nullified a moralistic narrative. Fascism aimed, through film and other media, to use mass culture to cast a mythic spell over masses, to address modern modes of experience (such as the demand for distraction and visual pleasure), and to transfix audiences with the aim of achieving their subordination. But stars only keyed in with this to a point.

In the case of some Italian stars, multiple roles were performed. As the leading Italian star, Amedeo Nazzari was called on to perform in several films with a militaristic or propagandistic bent. In these, he became the quintessential Fascist star, the embodiment of an ideal of masculinity that was perfectly aligned with the regime. In addition, however, he embodied values of rectitude, loyalty and justice that were not necessarily so aligned and which in some instances clearly conveyed, albeit obliquely, a sense of justice that concorded badly with dictatorship. Furthermore, in his embodiment of the popular idea of the film star, he exhibited a lifestyle that was comparatively opulent and more in tune with commercial culture than the austere model held up by Fascism's strategy of custom reform. Stars were contradictory figures who exemplified different aspects of dominant social values through various aspects of their images.

One of the most significant areas in which stars culture conflicted with the basic values of dictatorship was in offering choice and opportunities to express preferences and change opinions or loyalties. Between 1939 and 1940 *Cinema* magazine conducted a poll among its readers to establish the popularity of Italian actors. Nazzari came top among the men, with 19,020 votes, while 5,481 voted for Giachetti and just under 5,000 for De Sica. Regarding the women, 9,250 readers preferred Assia Noris, while Alida Valli scored 8,991. Paola Barbara, Isa Miranda, Luisa Ferida and others followed. The results were announced at a big party held at the Hotel Excelsior in Rome. Directors, actors and technicians joined the stars in a great celebration of Italian cinema. Thousands of members of the public mobbed the winners and the famous in what Brunetta has described as 'the first and also the last [party] in honour of a cinema that was working at full pelt ... Europe may have been in flames, but in the little Roman oasis the flashes and noises of war still seemed a long way away and everyone celebrated, feeling himself happy, protected and safe'.[58]

This poll was one of very few opportunities that were offered for a free and competitive affirmation of opinion under the regime. To be sure, people could choose every week between this or that magazine, or this or that film, but the casting of a vote had a slightly different connotation. In terms of the interpretation of Fascism, such a poll could be seen as a harmless outlet; allowing a simulacrum of democracy in a sphere remote from political power did not in any way undermine the regime. Yet it is difficult not to see in the practice of voting, albeit by a relatively small number of people and within the context of a promotional campaign, a type of behaviour that was external to those encouraged and theorised under the regime.

Star culture may have served some purposes under Fascism but there were a powerful range of institutions and individuals who opposed, deplored or rejected it. Families could oppose the cinematic passions of young people in the same way that they regulated leisure, acquaintances and romantic affiliations. In some sectors, as shown above, even seeing a film was deemed undesirable. In others, it was other, more intense manifestations of interest or engagement. Nerio Tebano found that, while his father indulged his passion for cinema and its stars, his mother took a different attitude: 'In addition to the postcards that I had collected as a boy, my interests were directed to film magazines', he later wrote. 'That invasion of paper did not go down well with my mother who disapproved of my cinema mania that, she said, distracted me from my studies. Every day there were lively discussions on the theme. "You'll see one day or other, where that rubbish will finish up" was the end point of those discussions ... Unfortunately, the daily threat became reality':

> Coming back from school one day I found the cupboard empty. My world fell in, but to console myself I thought at first that it was a joke or that the space was being

cleaned. My mother was not at home at that moment. I turned to my father to ask where my magazines had gone. With much hesitation, he told me that two men from the Red Cross had come with bags to take away all that paper. My mum had called them 'for my own good', he said, trying to cover for her and justify what she had done, while admitting in his heart that she had committed a *sopruso* [abuse of power] and that he had done nothing to stop her. I hated my mother for two weeks; then I closed myself off in total silence. I never forgave my father either, on account of his role as the Pontius Pilate of the situation.[59]

The intensity of these feelings, and the place they maintained in Tebano's memory of his adolescence, suggest that young men and women made a great investment in cinema and its imagery. 'I think we expressed the Italians of that time,' the actress Maria Denis said later, 'and in those days the consciousness of the individual was a bit underdeveloped. We did nothing to try and say anything new; we were not encouraged to say new things.'[60] Fans, however, wove the stars into the texture of their own lives and through them found personal spaces and vehicles for dreams and fantasies that did not exist anywhere else.

Notes

1. R. De Felice. 1974. *Mussolini*, Vol. 3. *Mussolini il duce*, I. *Gli anni del consenso 1929–1936*, Turin: Einaudi.
2. V. De Grazia. 1981. *The Culture of Consent: Mass Organization of Leisure in Fascist Italy*, Cambridge: Cambridge University Press; L. Passerini. 1987. *Fascism in Popular Memory*, Cambridge: Polity Press (Italian edition 1984); M. Gribaudi. 1987. *Mondo operaio e mito operaio*, Turin: Einaudi.
3. See, for example, V. De Grazia. 1992. *How Fascism Ruled Women: Italy 1922–1945*, Berkeley: University of California Press; P. Willson. 1993. *The Clockwork Factory: Women and Work in Fascist Italy*, Oxford: Oxford University Press; and 2002. *Peasant Women and Politics in Fascist Italy: The Massaie Rurali*, London: Routledge; T.H. Koon. 1985. *Believe, Obey, Fight: Political Socialization of Youth in Fascist Italy, 1922–1943*, Chapel Hill: University of North Carolina Press. The best-known city study is P. Corner. 1975. *Fascism in Ferrara: 1915–1925*, Oxford; Oxford University Press.
4. P. Corner. 2009. 'Fascist Italy in the 1930s: Popular Opinion in the Provinces' in Corner (ed.), *Popular Opinion in Totalitarian Regimes: Fascism, Nazism, Communism*, Oxford: Oxford University Press, 122–46. His work builds on earlier research into popular responses to the regime in S. Colarizi. 1991. *Le opinioni degli italiani sotto il regime, 1929–43*, Rome–Bari: Laterza.
5. L. Ridenti. 1931. *Il traguardo della celebrità*, Milan: Ceschina, 16.
6. V. De Grazia, *How Fascism Ruled Women*, 130–36.
7. Anon., 'Per l'attore italiano', *Cinema illustrazione*, 29 October 1930, 5.

8. See I. Piazzoni. 2009. 'I periodici italiani negli anni del regime fascista' in R. De Berti and I. Piazzoni (eds), *Forme e modelli del rotocalco italiano tra fascismo e guerra*, Milan: Monuzzi, 83–122.
9. See C. Bisoni. 2010. 'Il cinema italiano nelle riviste e nei settimanali popolari' in E.G. Laura and A. Baldi (eds), *Storia del cinema italiano*, Vol. 6, 1940–1944, Venice–Rome: Marsilio/Bianco & Nero, 509–21.
10. L. Pellizzari. 1982. 'Introduzione a una storia d'amore: il fuoco e le ceneri' in Pellizzari (ed.), *Hollywood anni trenta: le pratiche produttive e l'esibizione del private*, Venice: la Biennale di Venezia, 72–74.
11. V. De Grazia, *How Fascism Ruled Women*, 133–34.
12. J. Stacey. 1994. *Star Gazing: Hollywood Cinema and Female Spectatorship*, London: Routledge.
13. Anon., 'Come si diventa attrici', *Cinema illustrazione*, 10 June 1931, 3.
14. F. Savio. 1979. *Cinecittà anni trenta*, Rome: Bulzoni, 84.
15. Ibid., 1134–35.
16. D. Forgacs and S. Gundle. 2007. *Mass Culture and Italian Society from Fascism to the Cold War*, Bloomington: Indiana University Press. On the methodology of the oral interviews, see 281–305, including an essay by Marcella Filippa.
17. Ibid., 48.
18. Ibid., Gualtiero, interview no. 5.
19. Ibid., Gustavo, interview no. 75.
20. J. Richards. 1984. *The Age of the Dream Palace: Cinema and Society in Britain 1930–1939*, London: Routledge, 159.
21. Quoted in S. Masi and E. Lancia. 1994. *Stelle d'Italia: piccole e grandi dive del cinema italiano dal 1930 al 1945*, Rome: Gremese, 16.
22. O. Fallaci. 1965. 'Lo specchio del passato', interview with Alida Valli, *L'Europeo*, 10 January 1958.
23. R. Buckley. 2009. 'The Emergence of Film Fandom in Postwar Italy: Reading Claudia Cardinale's Fan Mail', *Historical Journal of Film, Radio and Television* 29(4), 523–59.
24. A. Ferraù, 'Lettere d'amore a Roberto Villa', *Film*, 27 February 1941, 11.
25. A. Ferraù, 'Lettere d'amore', *Film*, 5 April 1941, 8.
26. L. Romeo, 'Paradisi artificiali per sognatori di stelle', *Cinema*, 1 June 1956, 251–53.
27. G.P. Brunetta. 1989. *Buio in sala: cent'anni di passioni dello spettatore cinematografico*, Venice: Marsilio, 127.
28. See Chapter 7.
29. E. Sturani. 2003. *Le cartoline del duce*, Turin: Edizioni del Capricorno.
30. Brunetta, *Buio in sala*, 127.
31. N. Tebano. 1983. *La scatola magica: tra i fantasmi del cinema e della memoria*, Bari: Dedalo, 100. Tebano's photograph was printed in the readers' correspondence pages of *Cinema* of 10 November 1942, 659.
32. Ibid., 331–32.

33. In the film *Il feroce saladino* (The Ferocious Saladin, Mario Bonnard, 1937), the Sicilian comic Angelo Musco, down on his luck, stages a show based on the characters of the Perugina–Buitoni promotion. The film offers a snapshot of the passions the promotion engendered. During the show audience members stand up and fight each other for ownership of the precious cards, of which the ferocious Saladin was the rarest.
34. De Grazia, *How Fascism Ruled Women*. Chapters 5 and 7 on 'Growing Up' and 'Going Out'.
35. V. Marinucci, 'Cinema proibito', *Star*, August 1944, page unnumbered.
36. N. Golden, 'Safeguarding and Developing our Film Markets Abroad', *Motion Pictures Abroad*, 15 October 1937, 4.
37. Pellizzari, 'Introduzione a una storia d'amore: il fuoco e le ceneri', 72–74.
38. 'What a man!', Gary Cooper was reported to have said, as he viewed the statue of Garibaldi on Rome's Gianicolo Hill (E. Prudenti. 1931. 'Mezz'ora con Gary Cooper a Roma' in Pellizzari, *Hollywood anni trenta*, 103–4). Others voiced their desire to be admitted to the presence of the Duce. Several, including child star Jackie Coogan, had their wish granted.
39. A. Rabagliati. 1932. *Quattro anni fra le stelle*, Milan: Bolla.
40. See W.G. Harris. 1998. *Sophia Loren: A Biography*, New York: Simon and Schuster, 10.
41. E. Roma. 1932. 'Il "tifo" inventato a Hollywood' in Pellizzari, *Hollywood anni trenta*, 121.
42. 'Bando di concorso matrimoniale', *Stelle*, 16 September 1933.
43. I. 'Elio Luxardo ambasciatore del cinema alla corte della bellezza', *Film*, 14 June 1941, 6.
44. Anonymous note, *Cinema*, 10 September 1941, 165.
45. See S. Gundle. 2007. *Bellissima: Feminine Beauty and the Idea of Italy*, London: Yale University Press, 116–21.
46. See P. Biribanti. 2009. *Boccasile: la Signorina Grandi Firme e altri mondi*, Rome: Castelvecchi, 97–103.
47. Jori, 'Come "nascono" divi e stelle', *La Domenica del Corriere*, 9 February 1941, 5.
48. V. Calvino, 'Speranze e illusioni', *Primi piani* 1(3), July 1941, 36.
49. Archivio Centrale dello Stato (ACS), Ministero della Cultura Popolare, Gabinetto, Fasc. Cinematografia, sottofasc. 17 "Film" giornale.
50. Anon., 'Stelle di mare', *Cinema illustrazione*, 1 July 1936, 6–7.
51. Quoted in O. Ripa, 'Ho avuto cinque mariti ma ero tanto bambina', *Gente*, 21 August 1969, 55.
52. Bort, 'Alida Valli trova un personaggio', *Film*, 19 April 1941, 5.
53. F. Monteleone. 1992. *Storia della radio e della televisione in Italia*, Venice: Marsilio, 65.
54. Freddi, *Il cinema*, 301–2.
55. Ibid., 300–1.
56. A. Ghirelli, 'Il divismo', *Cinema*, 25 November 1941, 326–27.

57. R. Dyer. 1979. *Stars*, London: BFI, 27–8.
58. G.P. Brunetta. 1991. *Cent'anni di cinema italiano*, Rome–Bari: Laterza, 214.
59. Tebano, *La scatola magica*, 63–64.
60. Quoted in Savio, *Cinecittà anni trenta*, 468.

PART II

Italian Stars of the Fascist Era

5

The National Star
Isa Miranda

Between the early 1930s and the early 1940s no Italian film actress achieved the degree of national and international recognition that befell Isa Miranda. 'Isa Miranda represented in that brief cycle of years the only great phenomenon of female stardom of Italian cinema', Orio Caldiron and Matilde Hockhofler have written, identifying her stardom as one of the key factors in the affirmation of cinema as a mass spectacle in Italy and as a catalyst of emotions, aspirations, desires and ambitions.[1] The film that launched her and made her name was Max Ophuls's *La signora di tutti* (Everybody's Lady, 1934), a film that was conceived and realised by the publisher Angelo Rizzoli, who wanted to replicate in Italy the Hollywood phenomenon of the publicity-driven star launch. The film was not a big box office success in Italy; as a melodrama it had some claim to mass attention but, as Gian Piero Brunetta has remarked, ultimately it was 'a work too sophisticated and distant from the models of popular culture and from any sort of projection-identification at all'.[2] Nevertheless, the film contributed decisively to Miranda's star status and the particular position she would occupy in the international star system. It was a complex film that won the prize for cinematic technique at the Venice Film Festival on account of its ample uses of dissolves, montage sequences, tracking shots and voiceovers.[3] 'The praise for the film's technical aspect is highly ironic', Susan White comments, 'in that the subject of the film is the alienation of woman through technology – including the camera, the printing press, and the auditory devices of telephone, telegraph and radio'.[4] The tragic development of the narrative leaves the film's protagonist, played by Miranda, 'fragmented, frighteningly disunified'.

The film's complicated plot focuses on Gaby Doriot, a young film star whose new film cannot start shooting because she is nowhere to be found. Eventually, she is located unconscious following a suicide attempt. Transported to a clinic and placed under anaesthetic, she relives in a form of dream the events that have led to her desperate act. We are then taken back to her youth, spent motherless with a strict father. She is expelled from school and is locked up at home after a teacher who has fallen in love with her runs away, abandoning his job and family. After some time she is allowed out and comes into contact with the wealthy family of Roberto, a young man who lives with his parents. While he is away, Gabriella – not yet Gaby – becomes the companion of Roberto's disabled mother and develops an attachment to his father, Leonardo, who falls in love with her. After the sudden accidental death of Roberto's mother – who had been searching for her while she, unaware of the fact, was in the garden with Leonardo – the latter becomes an obsessive lover. The weight of guilt and Leonardo's obsessive behaviour, which leads to his ruin, drive Gabriella away. She flees to Paris where she eventually becomes the star of a film. Leonardo decides to try and make contact with her but, on his exit from the cinema where Gaby's first film (also entitled *La signora di tutti*) is premiering, he is run over by a car. The incident leads the press to evoke the earlier tragedy of the schoolteacher, tinging the actress's image with scandal. Gaby meanwhile, learning that Roberto has returned, hopes to be reunited with him but, after hope is briefly rekindled, she instead learns that he is married to her sister and has two children. It is this disappointment that leads her to attempt suicide. The operation fails to save her, and when the film's narration of her past life is complete, she dies.

Fig. 5.1 Publicity brochure for Novella Film's *La signora di tutti* (Everybody's Lady) which launched Isa Miranda. (Author's own collection)

The film lends itself to a variety of readings about female subjectivity, the tragic fate of the star unable to achieve a balance between fame and love, and the medium of cinema. As White has noted, there is a typically Ophulsian contrast between music as a source of female pleasure and fulfilment (Gaby is also a singer) and the interruption and interjection of the visual, except that in this film the two dimensions are 'hopelessly intertwined'.[5] Concern with modern technology is conjoined with a conventional construction of Gabriella as a fatal woman. Like two previous films by the Austrian director, *Liebelei* (1932) and *Divine* (1935), *La signora di tutti* explores the story of an ordinary and innocent woman who, unaware of the effect she has on the people and world around her, is then catapulted into a medium and an industry in which her appearance, voice, gestures and capacity for expression are magnified, exploited, projected and sold. Authentically aural, she is no longer herself when packaged as an image. Indeed still as well as moving images of Gaby punctuate the film. However, as White explains, some of the flashback images appear more personal than others; the unconscious Gaby is not quite as passive as she may appear.[6] She is mainly objectified in the film but the frame narrative struggles to endow her with some subjectivity and thereby disrupt the main thrust.

Gaby's physical attractiveness constitutes the source of her fatal influence, as well, of course, of her success as a star. White notes that, unfairly, 'the woman is held by the film to be necessarily responsible for the damage done by her compelling presence', adding 'or perhaps, the film shows us that contemporary society holds her thus responsible'.[7] Either way, she is the victim of a patriarchal order that is both abstracted and specifically incarnated in authoritarian older men. Ophuls, Mary Ann Doane observes, 'had a predilection for stories about passionate women and doomed love affairs played out in a bourgeois setting'.[8] However, this film was about cinema and its technology, and the way in which a particular woman becomes the object of desire of all men. This occurs through a process which differentiates her from all women. For Doane:

> Gaby becomes the image of Woman because no other – ordinary – woman is like her. The image is characterised by a lack of resemblance. Nevertheless, she somehow represents all women through her incarnation of a generalized femininity, an abstraction or ideal of femininity. The monolithic category of Woman here is not even an alleged average or distillate of concrete women but their abstraction, their subtraction (in its etymological sense, abstraction is a 'drawing away from'). Not like other women, Gaby becomes Woman. *La Signora di tutti* chronicles the expropriation of woman's look and voice and consequent transformation of the woman into Woman, a position inaccessible to women. This is not only the process of the narrative trajectory of *La Signora di tutti* but of the cinematic institution as well, in its narratives, its star system, its spectacle.[9]

Gaby exercises a fatal attraction on those around her, but, unlike the femmes fatales of film noir, she is passive rather than consciously manipulative or scheming. She appears to float in a passive state and wreaks havoc unawares. In this respect, Doane argues, she is 'reminiscent of the tradition of the diva in the silent Italian cinema'.[10] A woman of exceptional beauty who causes catastrophe simply through her presence, the diva often met an end as tragic and final as her lovers, and this is the case with Gaby. But this reminiscence is a matter of echoes since the age of the diva had passed and her exaggerated gestures were deemed absurd. Doane argues that the gestural excess of the diva was replaced by 'the hyperbolic strategies of the Ophulsian style – in camera movement, *mise-en-scène*, and music, which take up in their repetitive *straining*, the thematic of the fatal inevitability of history'.[11] Indeed, the film can be seen as 'an investigation into the birth of a star (in contrast to the diva of the teens)'.[12] In Miranda's performance there was a dose of romantic pathos in the Garbo mould. Her persona glances backwards to the idea of the diva while incorporating a sense of the ordinary girl.

La signora di tutti was Miranda's first major film, and its theme, the rise and fall of a young film star, immediately wove into her yet-to-emerge screen persona a star narrative. Miranda played the ordinary beauty who wreaks havoc on those around her and who loses herself in the interstices and mechanisms of mass culture. Inevitably, over the years, this tragic narrative came to be read back on to Miranda herself, even though there were few biographical overlaps between her and her character. Gaby Doriot was born as a fictional invention of Salvatore Gotta, who wrote *La signora di tutti* as an instalment novel for Rizzoli's popular magazine *Novella*. So successful was the series that the print run of the magazine rose from 180,000 per week to 250,000, an event that so impressed Rizzoli that he held a banquet for all his workers and decided to turn the story into a film, to be produced by himself.

Novella launched a competition to find the woman most suited to playing Gaby, and Miranda was selected from the hundreds who took part. She was not in fact a complete greenhorn. She had sent pictures of herself to production companies in the early 1930s and had been summoned to Rome by the Cines company. After passing a screen test she was cast in two films. Although some accounts say that Rizzoli personally chose her, it seems more likely that it was the more experienced Ophuls who cast her, seeing in her not a figure of identification but a woman who could be moulded into an object of male desire.

The marketing of the film began with the search for the protagonist and proceeded from the start of the shoot to the film's release (Fig. 5.1). Miranda's body was made the centre of the promotion. Publicity material gave her vital statistics and listed her weight. This aroused expectations that could not be met. 'When such a lot of fuss – this sort of fuss – is created around an actress, the public is justified in concluding: "well, show us your legs". And since this anatomical detail was not worthy of all the publicity, the public did not like the film. It was liked instead by the critics, who look not at legs but at the spirit' wrote an anonymous author in *Film* in 1938.[13] Miranda's legs were never revealed, he continued; rather, audiences were treated to the melancholy that was 'her colour', the sadness that was 'her essence': 'we know all her sobs, we know the damp of her tears, and we love above all the perfume of her melancholy'. This, he continued, should not be contaminated with publicity, with excessive details about her physique, advertising for skin creams and stockings, puffery telling us that she plays all sports and that she is paid lucratively and receives so many thousands of love letters. All this was of no interest. The audience was only interested in knowing that she was a woman who was inclined to sadness and an actress of sober temperament who preferred hints to histrionics, and sighs to sobs.

It was the narrative of the film, but more importantly the positing of two Gabys – the ordinary but still dangerous girl, and the star – combined with the processes of casting and promotion of the film, that established Miranda as a star. Even the pre-star Gaby gazes at herself in the mirror as if she were fascinated by her own image or preparing for a performance. Within the diegesis of the film, she has the qualities of a star before becoming one. She is mechanically reproduced and that production is placed in inverted commas by the process itself, thus creating a platform for discussions that went beyond the normal criticism and commentary of the press. Paradoxically, it is the 'non-starish' aspects of Gaby (Michael Walker says 'it is very difficult to imagine Gaby as a film star – she is simply too meek and withdrawn') that assist this.[14]

For all its virtuosity, the film in fact received a mixed response from critics. Anton Giulio Majano and Paolo Negro referred in 1935 to 'the deeply anti-human and anti-Italian immorality of the subject of *La signora di tutti* of which we do not know which should be condemned more strongly, the decidedly nineteenth-century and fin-de-siècle taste or the chaotic and grand Guignol-esque absurdity, with its mix of femmes fatales and ruined men with the addition of the usual tentacular city'. It was shocking, they argued, that an enlightened figure like Rizzoli should have taken such material for his debut in film production.[15] Luigi Freddi too dismissed it as 'a film whose ethical conception is to say the least dubious'.[16] Nevertheless, it established Miranda's name beyond Italy's borders and it was enough of a success at home for Miranda to receive many letters from women. As testimony to her growing fame, in three years (1934–37) it was said she received twenty-eight thousand fan letters. 'After *La signora di tutti* ... I received hundreds of letters from young brides who asked me to be godmother to their babies that they planned to call Miranda', the actress later recalled. 'In those years, thanks to me there were a good number of Mirandas in Italy'.[17] Critics may have seen Gaby as a poorly defined character but she incorporated a range of established female types including friend, daughter, sister, centre of desire, lover, starlet and vamp, which enhanced the actress's appeal to women.[18]

From this moment, the Miranda persona was a star persona. The film and its launch projected her unambiguously as a star, and a discourse around stardom stuck to her for the rest of her career up to at least 1943 and in lesser form persisted long afterwards. She became, Morando Morandini later remarked, 'La Miranda – the domestic equivalent of the American femmes fatales, a home-made Greta Garbo'.[19] Against this star persona, two other Mirandas struggled to come to the surface: the actress and the woman.[20] Over time, as she matured as a performer, the actress would complement, and in certain moments displace, the star persona. But every Miranda performance was taken in some way to be about stardom, about the possible forms of Italian stardom, about the foreign conditioning of Italian stardom and the controversies around the star phenomenon. This was a time, the 1930s, in which stardom seemed in Italy to be a remote and in some respects undesirable and inhuman thing. She was in this sense marked by the modalities of her first consecration as a star.

There was a Cinderella element in her story. Indeed, in 1942, *Film* magazine even recounted her life story in the form of a fable.[21] For Caldiron and Hockhofler, she 'incarnated from the start the myth of the actress who comes from the audience, a sort of "self-made girl" who scales the empire of cinema by force of will and application, obstinate tenacity and unbreakable determination'.[22] Born Ines Sampietro in Milan in 1905, her parents were peasants who had moved to the city on their marriage. Her father worked for the tram company while her mother was employed in a tailor's workshop. Ines had various jobs and had posed as a model for artists and for postcards. After attending acting school in the evenings, she was employed by a theatre company and performed under the adopted name of Ines Casali. She decided to send her photographs to Cines in Rome and was called for a test. She auditioned several times before winning small film roles. By the time she was cast in her first role as protagonist, in *Tenebre* in 1933, she had adopted the name by which she would become famous. 'Isa Miranda is not only the actress of melancholy; she is, also, the actress of will. She wanted to make it and she has made it', *Film* commented in 1938.[23]

Miranda was not generally seen as beautiful. Her angular face and square nose were never held up as ideal. There was 'a touch of coldness' to her appearance that assisted an able director like Ophuls in highlighting her photogenic qualities.[24] For this reason, it was often said that there was something enigmatic about her – or about her image. But she was unquestionably possessed of spirit and her performance style was understated and romantic. Although the heritage of the silent-era divas was lurking in the background, her acting over time became more realistic. She was important because she represented the desire in Italy to create an actress with qualities in common with Garbo and Dietrich. For Caldiron and Hockhofler, she was 'a sort of Italian reply to Hollywood, something between the openly sexual provocation of Marlene Dietrich and the openly spiritual depth of Greta Garbo, the long legs of Marlene and the disturbing eyes of Greta'.[25] Throughout her career, and many decades after her debut, she would still be referred to in the press as 'the Italian-style Garbo', 'Our Garbo' or 'the Italian "Marlene Dietrich"'.[26] Her image, in this sense, always followed that of bigger stars. Whereas Zarah Leander was chosen to fill the void left in Nazi Germany by Dietrich and Garbo, and thus was always an entirely ersatz figure,[27] Miranda was Italian cinema's autarchic reply to the American star system. As such she was the bearer of an authentic nationalist discourse even if the type of visual pleasure she offered was in part derivative. For Caldiron and Hockhofler, she had an unparalleled impact on the cinematic imagination of Italians between the early 1930s and the end of the 1940s. At a time when Italian audiences were completely taken with the big names of American cinema, she represented 'the only great phenomenon of female stardom in Italian cinema', and as such she contributed to the affirmation of cinema as a mass spectacle.[28]

Nevertheless, the idea of Miranda as a confectioned image modelled on the myths of international cinema was one that was challenged and subverted almost from the moment of its establishment. In the two films she made following *La signora di tutti*, directed respectively by Mario Camerini and Guido Brignone, her brilliant blonde hair, elegant wardrobe and sophisticated air were exchanged for a simpler, darker-haired demeanour. In *Come le foglie* (Like the Leaves, 1935), she played the part of Nennele, a bourgeois girl whose family members are forced by financial ruin to exchange high living for simpler ways. While the others fail or are diverted, Nennele finds a job and persists, feeling increasingly alone and helpless. She rejects a marriage proposal that could ease her situation and, in a desperate gesture, attempts suicide. She is saved at the last minute by her father and a would-be husband. In 1945, Miranda recalled, 'Mario Camerini wanted me brown-haired, modest and simple to completely cancel out my previous role, in the belief that only I could have conveyed the limpid character of Nennele'.[29] She disliked the efforts made to remove her beauty and downplay her photogenic qualities, but later recognised that Camerini had been right. This was picked up immediately by the critics. Filippo Sacchi in the *Corriere della Sera* approved: 'Camerini has done the right thing by immediately cancelling in her the traces of that publicity pre-formation to break the bridges between Nennele and *La signora di tutti*, presenting her to us without the embellishments of the camera, in all the hard irregularity of her true features'.[30] In this film, he added, Miranda imposed herself 'gradually with a sincerity, humility and power of emotion and passion that (and you feel it) has the effect of moving the audience deeply'. In the Genoese paper *Il Lavoro*, Guglielmina Setti urged cinematographers to cease 'presenting her to us like a porcelain statue'. With due work and application, she argued, Miranda would soon lay just claim to the title of 'queen of our screens'.[31]

The same year, in the epic film *Passaporto rosso*, she played a woman who was emigrating with her father to South America. Set between 1890 and 1918 (the voiceover at the start makes it clear that the events take place before 1922), the film explored the trials and tribulations of the thousands of Italian emigrants in the period, it is implied, before Italy was redeemed by Mussolini. Miranda plays a teacher who is courted by a young doctor she has met on the boat, but she is also the object of the attentions of a Mafioso-type named Don Pancho. After her father dies in an epidemic, Maria is forced to sing in a society cafe to earn money to pay off her debts. Although the audience knows by now that she is a moral, upstanding girl, for a scene in the cafe she wears a revealing stage costume. The other singers and dancers, who appear to be prostitutes, gawp and paw her. She complains of feeling 'so very alone' and evidently her virtue is under threat. Eventually, she is freed of this destiny and finds fulfilment helping other emigrants who contribute to the building of a railway. She marries the doctor and has a son who becomes a civil engineer. In a forward jump in time, he in turn marries and has a son of his own. When his father, moved by news of the outbreak of war, contemplates volunteering, the son overcomes an initial indifference to the homeland of his parents and volunteers to fight. He does not return and a silver medal is awarded to his memory. In the final scene of the film, set in 1922, a figure evidently intended to convey the idea of Mussolini pins the medal to the chest of Miranda's character's grandson and kisses his cheek.

The film was of the patriotic type that Freddi liked. It had an epic quality and was deeply inspiring. Reviewers praised Miranda for the skill with which she brought the tragic and suffering Maria to life. Her rendition of the song in the cafe was done with an understated tragic air that put Marlene Dietrich to shame, commented *Il Giornale d'Italia*.[32] Mino Doletti, in *Il Resto del Carlino*, compared her performance to that in *La signora di tutti* in which she was a 'sinister and sick creature, with a disturbed and disquieting sensibility (not stuff of ours, for goodness sake, but imported stuff!)'.[33] 'Here she is simply a woman, calm and human, who loves and suffers. We dare to underline: an Italian woman of the type who plotted during the Risorgimento, one of those women who know how to be sweet and uncorrupted wives, who dress proudly in mourning when they give up a son to the Fatherland. Isa Miranda should be just as she is, calm and measured, gentle and sweet'. 'We thank in her name the Almighty for not having made her beautiful and for having omitted to endow her with "sex-appeal" (a debatable quality that cancels the distinction between women and females). We thank her directors for never having insisted that she show us her legs', wrote one enthusiastic reviewer. Instead she had simplicity and a transparently Italian quality.[34] She played with subtlety and was very good at conveying suffering. After this film Miranda was to all intents and purposes established; her range and her merits were beyond dispute. She was universally hailed as an interesting and valid actress.

Her career developed a significant international dimension thanks to Alfredo Guarini, who produced *Passaporto rosso* and subsequently managed and directed her, guiding her away from Italian cinema towards foreign opportunities. Between 1936 and 1937, she made films in Austria (*Il diario di una donna amata/Maria Baschkirtseff*, Hermann Kosterlitz, 1936 – an Austrian film made in German and Italian versions), in France, including Pierre Chenal's adaptation of Pirandello's *Mattia Pascal* (1938) and *Nina Petrovna* (Victor Tourjansky, 1938), in which she played a Russian-born courtesan. Set in imperial Vienna, the story had strong echoes of Dumas fils's novel *La dame aux camélias*. The renunciation of love on the part of the lead character and her ensuing sad death once more offered the actress the chance to display her gift for controlled suffering.

Italian critics did not take to Miranda's European films, feeling that her roles, as doomed sophisticated types, were clichéd. As Adolfo Franci wrote in *L'illustrazione italiana*:

> Imagine a sort of *Dame aux camelias* transported from the Paris of Louis Philippe to the Vienna of Franz Josef and you will have an idea of the content of this film where Fernand Gravey ... is a graceful and elegant actor and Isa Miranda, as usual, impersonates Marlene Dietrich or Greta Garbo. Let us hope that this is her last 'femme fatale', her final goodbye to a cloying and mannered character in which European directors had forced her after the success of *La Signora di tutti*.[35]

They much preferred the alternative Miranda that was developed in *Come le foglie* and *Passaporto rosso*. In these films, she cast aside the Dietrich-style mask and revealed a more authentic, uncomplicated personality. Many years later, Guarini claimed that he told her, during a private screening of *La signora di tutti*, that she should rebel against those who wanted to make her into a copy of Dietrich and expose 'her true personality'.[36] But the same Guarini also promoted her first in European cinema and then in Hollywood, where the down-to-earth Miranda was of little interest. The identification of Miranda with Dietrich began in the French press, which knew that the star of *The Blue Angel* (Erich von Sternberg, 1930) was in decline and that a younger version would soon be needed. Mario Gromo in *La Stampa* wrote that, 'In *Come le foglie* our actress was unambiguously Italian. Now a sophisticated "standard" is beginning to take her over. Hollywood will probably end up transforming her completely'. However, he added that, 'In any event we are happy that it will be an Italian name that will shine among the stars and starlets'.[37] Ultimately, Miranda's two faces gave her a versatility that few others had, although part of her mythology was that she retained the tastes and habits, as well as the innocence and hopes, of 'one of us'.

After a short German parenthesis in which she starred in one film with the tenor Beniamino Gigli, she was approached by Paramount, who were looking for an actress to replace Dietrich as the German actress's box office appeal declined. As negotiations began, she requested a passport. However, while the matter was considered, it was suggested to her that she might accept an invitation to join the cast of *Scipione l'Africano* (Scipio the African, Carmine Gallone, 1937), a film strongly supported by the regime. Many leading actors took part in this vast historical epic; in Miranda's case out of fear that retribution might follow a refusal. Given a choice of parts, she selected that of a patrician woman, Velia. After this, she left for Hollywood, embarking on the *Rex* cruise ship in Genoa in August 1937. Although journalists attended her departure, there was no official send-off and no official expression of good wishes. It was evident that her decision was regarded as a sort of betrayal.

Nevertheless, her recruitment completed her internationalisation since she became the first established Italian screen actress to cross the Atlantic. In consequence, there was much curiosity about what would happen to her. 'Will she be transformed? Will the legs pop out? We know she has given out her address and gives out photographs, and that she counts the letters that she receives in order to galvanise the efforts of her publicity office', commented *Film*,[38] adding that such dedication was to be regretted. 'You should not have done this to us, Isa. Those who love you most — did you know? — are those who do not write to you'.

Although Italians would not have chance to view Miranda's Hollywood screen work until much later, Paramount ensured that publicity material reached Italy. Superb glamour photographs appeared in Italian magazines, including the cover of *Stelle*, 27 November 1937 (Fig. 5.2), in which her face was turned into a glistening charm object. Italian reactions were divided. On the one hand, the extraordinary transformation of the actress at the hands of the costumiers, make-up artists, hairdressers and photographers of Paramount revealed just how far behind Italian cinema was. On the other hand, her reduction to 'a dehumanised sexual emblem' provoked unease. For Giulio Cesare Castello, writing in 1957, 'admiring amazement for the metamorphosis gave way to perplexity dictated by the shiny artificiality of those images which cancelled any human warmth'.[39]

In January 1938, G.V. Sampieri wrote of the visit to Rome of Murray Bois-Smith of Max Factor. He was presented as the man responsible for making over Miranda. 'Her face in Italy was only capable of producing tears. We have made her expression luminous', he announced. Sampieri commented that Italian directors from *Tenebre* through to *Scipione l'Africano* had given the public a Miranda who was astonished, pained, tearful or afflicted by the most desperate of problems. This was an ecstatic, strained and false face. 'Then one fine day, touched by grace, the actress goes to Hollywood and here we are, immediately the miracle occurs — that fine betrayed face acquires finally a

Fig. 5.2 One of the first Paramount publicity shots of Isa Miranda, which appeared on the cover of *Stelle* magazine. (Author's own collection)

light, its own light and is illuminated by a marvellous smile. We here, in her native land, in her natural atmosphere, were not capable of this', he added. The reason for this, Sampieri affirmed, was the ongoing resonance of the femme fatale in Italian cinema. Miranda was a prisoner of an old bourgeois culture that had degenerated into a cliché. Italian cinema continued to be shaped by practices that were twenty years out of date. The Hollywood portraits were splendid and made her look young, luminous and alive. In America, he said, there were just a couple of screen femme fatales of a superior type. The rest were smiling, pleasure-seeking women, and that is why they were successful. 'So when a Miranda arrives on the other side of the ocean, miraculously rejuvenated by the sea breeze that has freed her of the make-up imposed on her by national and international films, Max Factor and his collaborators make her over, remove the sheen of antiquity and uncover finally her true face. In this way, it is not so much a star that is born in Hollywood, as a woman'.[40]

By no means everyone took such a positive view. In February 1938, *Cinema illustrazione* noted that Miranda had always been seen as a younger Marlene, but remarked that in the United States she risked becoming simply a lookalike:

Indeed, the first photographs 'made in Hollywood' of this actress make her look so much like Marlene as to leave us open-mouthed. Where will this manipulation lead that allows the Americans to reproduce in series the same type of woman? Why, in this case, not opt to attempt to discover the true Isa Miranda 'type', instead of doing everything possible to cancel those physical traits that can in some way make her similar to her celebrated original? Since no matter how fascinating all this may make her she will in the end be no more than a copy. Unfortunately the film that Miranda will make for Paramount under the direction of Cukor has a title that by itself speaks volumes: 'The Lady of the Tropics'. Oh dear! The Americans will return a Miranda to us wrapped up in extreme fatal garb, feathered, scheming and vampish, a substitute Marlene who will make us long bitterly for the unkempt and sad actress of *Come le foglie*.[41]

The Americans, following a standard model, painted the actress as socially well-connected, a friend of D'Annunzio and aristocrats. Miranda herself was not happy that her publicity launch was so conditioned by her physical resemblance to Marlene. 'That was a big mistake that led to me resisting every effort that – even in good faith – tended towards a modification of my aesthetic characteristics', she said later.[42] Her film experience in Hollywood was scarcely more satisfactory. She was engaged to shoot *Zaza* with George Cukor but, three days into the shoot, a minor road accident was used as an excuse to oust her from the film and replace her with Claudette Colbert. In another version, it was her imperfect English that was to blame, while in another it was the risk of a debutante to the American screen.[43] It has also been said that her fiery temper on set led to her being dropped.[44]

Although Adolph Zukor, the head of Paramount, pledged his support for her, she then made two films of low calibre, in which her roles were of the typical sort reserved for European actresses.[45] *Hotel Imperial* was a remake of a 1927 film of the same title, starring Pola Negri. It was a First World War melodrama of Austrian and Russian spies in which Dietrich had been slated to play. Miranda played a hotel maid determined to avenge her sister, who has been seduced and abandoned by an Austrian officer. A routine film for which she won praise, it has been said that her English was so poor that she had to recite her lines phonetically.[46] The film never had an Italian release. *Adventure in Diamonds* (George Fitzmaurice, 1940), which would be released in Italy as *La signora dei diamanti* only in 1947, followed. American critics noted a similarity between this film and *Desire*, a Dietrich vehicle, and more generally with the Garbo films of ten years or so previously. Indeed the director, a known Italophile, had directed Garbo in *Mata Hari* and the Pirandello adaptation *As You Desire Me*.

Writing in the *New York World-Telegram* of 4 April 1940, William Boehnel went so far as to dub Miranda 'the blonde venus of Mussoliniland', a comment that might appear negative but which was accompanied by an acknowledgement that she 'not only fascinates with her beauty but shows herself to be an actress of the very first order'. In the film Miranda played Felice Falcon, an adventuress and jewel thief who rejects her ways for love of the suave George Brent. Miranda acknowledged that Fitzmaurice was the first director to believe she could do light comedy. The actress recalled in 1945 that she had argued with him, insisting that she could only do drama. The tone and speed of the dialogue in English frightened her.[47] In fact she conveyed well the light tone required of her part, and wore with panache the elegant costumes designed by Edith Head. Her English though fell short of the fully comprehensible; and the cinematography was far less flattering than the test stills, her angular face and square nose depriving her character of the head-turning beauty the plot attributed to her.

Following these two films, Miranda returned to Italy after preparations to film the life of the nineteenth-century courtesan Lola Montez, directed by John Ford, dragged on. She expected to travel to the United States once plans were finalised, but the sudden death of its producer, Douglas Fairbanks, put paid to such hopes. Her arrival home in December 1939 was greeted with absolute silence. Miranda and Guarini (who had married in Texas in 1938) had been warned by the journalist Mino Doletti that nothing would happen on their return but that no one would be there to receive them. Guarini soon worked out that an order had gone out from the Ministry of Popular Culture not to grant the actress any coverage.[48] An interview she had given shortly before leaving the United States in which she expressed sympathy with the Jews of Danzig, who were suffering at the hands of the Germans, had caused disapproval in high places. Although the order would be revoked, suspicions remained and work was lacking. Despite the persistence of an adoration that echoed some of the hyperbole of the diva era, that was reflected in her being painted by many of the leading artists of the day including De Chirico and De Pisis, various projects in which she rested hopes remained unrealised. Guarini said that they found a desert around her.[49]

During several months forced inactivity, she spent every morning signing photos and responding to letters. She also undertook pilgrimages to Fascist hierarchs to implore them to allow her to work. One of these, she later claimed, asked for sexual favours. When she attempted to renew her passport, the Minister of Popular Culture, Pavolini, informed her that she was Italy's best actress and was needed at home. In the meantime the police conducted checks on her. Reporting in August 1940, they found that there was little to note.[50] The actress was said to be living quietly and cultivating her dream of making a big international film in Italy. This was taken to reflect her view that Italian cinema was inferior to foreign cinemas. More seriously, it was observed that her husband had a past as a subversive and had been a member of the Communist Party of Italy before

Fascism. In 1926 he had tried to enrol in the PNF but had been rejected because of his political precedents and bad reputation. Miranda's own father had been an anti-Fascist and a reader of the Socialist paper *l'Avanti*.

In the end Miranda was able to resume her career, according to Guarini, thanks to the support of two producers, Riccardo Gualino and Vincenzo Genesi, who were disinclined to conform to the unofficial boycott, and of the critics Filippo Sacchi and Sandro De Feo, who backed the actress's desire to return to the sort of role she had played in *Passaporto rosso* by asserting that she felt hard done to and wanted to make a good Italian film to teach the Americans a lesson. Writing in *Lo Schermo*, one critic said she held up the good name of Fascist Italy in a politically hostile setting. The article was entitled 'Isa Miranda has stayed Isa Miranda'.[51] More than thirty years later, Guarini simply said, 'I found friends who lent us the capital anonymously and in 1941 I made three films with la Miranda'.[52] In fact, as Miranda herself would later admit, she was allowed to work again only after a meeting with Mussolini at which she was invited to declare that she was better off in Italy. To Oriana Fallaci, she offered more details:

> I don't remember exactly where the meeting took place. Certainly in Rome, at the laying of some stone. I remember only that at a certain point, a big noise of shoes was heard, then a whispering of excited voices: he's coming! he's coming! And then Mussolini stopped in front of me, nose in the air and hands on his hips – what manners! 'Well, who are you?' 'My name is Isa Miranda, excellency'. 'Ah! It appears you have returned from America.' 'Yes, Excellency.' 'Ah! How do you feel to be back in Italy?' 'My heart is content, excellency.' 'Good!' Then I bowed to him and he left as everyone around him made the Fascist salute. I was not very brave, I admit, but my heart was content in fact: in Italy there was my mother.[53]

She made three films directed by Guarini: *Senzo cielo* (Without the Sky, 1940), *E' caduta una donna* (A Woman Has Been Run Over, 1941) and *Documento Z-3* (Document Z-3, 1942), all of which were mediocre tearjerkers. In the first, she plays the white queen Regina of a tribe of Indians in the Mata Grosso, Brazil. Kidnapped as a child, she has grown up among the Indians, who worship her as a goddess. In this fable, she is attired in two-piece costumes, sarongs, exotic headdresses, leopardskins and other garments of Hollywood derivation. She herself retained certain Hollywoodian features, speaking with an English accent that was compared to the Italian spoken by Laurel and Hardy in dubbed versions of their films. Critics attacked her for donning such skimpy costumes and flaunting her body. She looked like a sort of Dorothy Lamour, 'a Tarzan in a skirt'.[54] Ramperti intervened, defending her as a universal beauty and equating her with Manzoni's heroine Lucia Mondella. Others relished the pin-up quality of the promotional photographs. Before, her body had been absent and she was almost immaterial, but now, a certain G.P. wrote in the weekly *Tempo* (no. 71, 1940), 'Judging by the photographs (we have not yet seen the film) nudity regains in cinema, perhaps for the first time with such substance, a chaste, animal and fully spontaneous beauty, that sculpture or painting once had'.⁵⁵ Her sex appeal, the critic added, had been re-elaborated through a refined, mature performance.

Miranda did not mix much with her colleagues in the cinema environment. 'No, [I had] only work relations during shoots ... I remember fondly Memo Benassi, Andrea Checchi, Fosco Giachetti, Claudio Gora. But I cannot speak of friendships; I respected everyone and I expected to be respected', she later said.⁵⁶ Her relative isolation rendered her vulnerable to envious ambushes and subterfuges that further complicated her relaunch in Italy. Her experience over *E' caduta una donna*, a film made with contributions from Cesare Zavattini, Sandro De Feo and Ercole Patti, is instructive. As she would recall in 1963:

> It was an important premiere because the Federale [leading Fascist official] of Milan, the mayor and many others were there. The cinema was full. The lights went down and the screen lit up; at the appearance of the announcement 'La Scalera film presenta' there were whistles. The title came up: whistles again. My name appeared: more whistles. They whistled from the start to the finish of the film. My mother fainted and I got up to help her. A scandal blew up because the Federale offered me a bouquet of flowers at the very moment that I turned my back on him to attend to my mother. The next day I was summoned to the Casa del Fascio; I won't say how I was treated. And you know why they whistled so much? It was because two-thirds of the tickets – and this was established by the police – had been bought by a celebrated Fascist actress who I won't name because she is still alive and I don't want to bring this shame on her. She organised the whistling because she had wanted to star in that film. The friends of the hierarchs almost always took the best parts for themselves.⁵⁷

The film was the story of an unwed mother-to-be named Dina who is rejected by her lover and his family. After briefly contemplating abortion, she gives birth in a clinic whose doctor persuades her not to abort. In the clinic she meets a fashion model who procures work for her and seeks to encourage a friendship of interest with a rich industrialist. However, Dina encounters the doctor again and they decide to marry, ignoring the opposition of his parents. Despite his good intentions, the doctor is tormented by Dina's past. She gives up the child to its grandmother, hoping to save her marriage. But unable live with what she has done, she rushes out into the fog to the station and is hit by a bus. She is taken to hospital where she dies unidentified. The film was a melodrama, similar to those Mario Mattoli directed in the same period. It distantly echoed the human drama if not the theme of *La signora di tutti*, albeit corrected with a Fascist emphasis on reproduction. It was interesting on account of its realistic Milan setting, including location shots of the station, the Duomo, the foggy streets and neon lights.

The film confirmed Miranda as a fashionable figure. The demand that Italian actresses should be elegant and vehicles of good taste and of Italian fashion had long been fulfilled by the actress. As early as 1935 she was modelling Italian clothes and was praised for showing that it was not necessary to look abroad for models of elegance.[58] Dina is slim and stylish, despite her recent pregnancy, and she wears magnificent coats. There are frequent references in the film to her as a fashion piece, as having the physique of a model, a 'perfect figure'. Her allure is confirmed in some beautiful scenes, including one in which she models various versions of a wedding dress and is moved round like a doll for hours. Miranda is given numerous close-ups which highlight her blonde hair and plucked eyebrows. One of these presents her in tears behind a rain-spattered window. Initially, the film was intended to have a fantasy element in which the protagonist returned after her death as a ghost to watch over the son, but this Zavattinian touch was dispensed with at Freddi's behest.

Press reaction was mixed. *Tempo* said the film should have found its poetry in the everyday and ordinary but stardom and hyperbole had been grafted on to it.[59] Others saw it as a trite film and a clichéd story in which only Miranda sparkled by virtue of a measured and subtle performance. As in the past, she was seen as better than the material she had to work with. However, there were some who saw her as a tragic actress who did not have the plastic impressionability of the film star. Mario Gromo of *La Stampa* was among those who were unconvinced:

> Do we want to examine, very calmly and in a sympathetic way, what the 'Miranda case' might consist of? To me it seems to be a question of acclimatisation. The actress is always there, fortunately for us, but she has to be sought out and found under a strange patina, undoubtedly due to the American sojourn, with all its impositions and pretensions, its flattery and suggestions. It is a patina that renders the actress circumspect, studied, sometimes even worried, even of every minimal closing inflection: and it does not always help her adhere to her character and its states of mind. Compared to *Senza cielo*, the present test is certainly more convincing, but for her own good and that of our cinema it is to be hoped that all residual Hollywoodian encrustations soon disappear. I recall the trepid, anxious, human Nennele of *Come le foglie* and I cannot see her except in brief moments in the still Dietrich-style heroine of *E' caduta una donna*. With all the admiration that we have had for her, we ask only that she returns to being herself – because our cinema needs above all to be Italian, from the choice of subject to the style or the manner of a player.[60]

In the spy story *Documento Z-3*, critics thought she still had not found the spontaneity of her pre-Hollywood work. She adopted poses and was criticised for being mannered, in a way that was regarded as Garbo-esque. By contrast, Diego Calcagno, writing in *Film*, thought that at last Miranda was less pathetic and 'fatal' in the film. 'Actresses are like fizzy drinks; some prefer them sweet and some bitter. I am for a bitter Miranda', he observed.[61]

In 1941, the women's magazine *Grazia* commented that Miranda's down-to-earth screen image contrasted with an off-screen presence that was marked by great elegance. 'The public understood that she was a great actress but so much naturalism disturbed it, and it realised that it had discovered something truly ours, that could be appreciated without a lot of hullabaloo.'[62]

There was a permanent desire to read her as ordinary and human, made of flesh and blood, rather than as an idealisation, a fatal and fragile creature. She was the daughter of a tram driver who had worked as a shop assistant, model and typist before taking to cinema. In the eyes of her domestic admirers, she was national and homely; she did not have behind her the mythology of Paris or of the Berlin cabarets that had been the forging ground of Dietrich. There was something endearing and human about her. 'Isa Miranda was thought of as the woman's woman, surrounded by a certain mystery as far as her private life was concerned: in reality she avoided contact with the public out of shyness and she always felt ill at ease among people', Guarini observed years later.[63] She did not live in the smart Parioli district as many did; she avoided festivals, most gala evenings and social occasions. She even turned down an invitation from Hitler.

Inevitably, there were efforts to see her as the embodiment of Italian womanhood. For Arturo Locatelli, author of an admiring 'open letter', this was her true key: 'I like your beauty, which is that of an Italian woman, your calm expression which is that of a woman who could perfectly well have a good husband and delightful children ... Permit one of the crowd to tell you that you please him greatly and that he loves you'.[64] Ramperti, a long-time admirer, and another to regard her as a natural beauty, had remarked in 1936 that modesty and reserve were key traits of her persona: 'I recognise in her the Lombard woman of Manzoni. Decency of a type that Manzoni dubbed "severe" survives in her even in the crudest fictions of the most lost of souls ... The "Signora di tutti" is still the sister of Lucia'.[65] 'At the same time' he continued, 'I recognise the Lombard woman of Leonardo. If her shadowed cheek recalls those of Hepburn and Dietrich, more directly it reminds us of the women that the Tuscan painted, as young Madonnas or saints in Cisalpine land. That shaded face was born harmonious, between a damp field and a vaporous cloud of Brianza. Under the studio lights, a new Virgin of the Rocks appears.' Writing in *La Stampa* in 1941, Ramperti repeated that 'her unique sweetness on the screen is typical of the Lombard region'. 'Isa Miranda has been and is an Image admired by five continents ... a shadow, if you like, a ghost, a nothing: but one in whose face many thousands of remote eyes will have recognised, or thought they had recognised, Italy itself.'[66]

In 1942 she made two prestige films that would restore her reputation and would count among her best work. Both were period films. The first, directed by Mario Soldati, was *Malombra*, adapted from the novel by Antonio Fogazzaro. The second, *Zaza*, directed by Renato Castellani, gave her a chance to play the part she had been deprived of in Hollywood. Both were made by Lux film. Later Miranda praised the producer Gualino for paying no attention to the discouragement offered by the hierarchs of the Ministry of Popular Culture. These films only appeared in the tumult of 1943 and would make no great impact. But they were hailed for their quality, and after the war were regarded as two of the best examples of the 'calligraphic' school of costume film. Soldati had wanted Alda Valli, his favourite actress, for *Malombra*, but she was busy. He saw Miranda as 'good but getting a bit old and almost at the start of her decline'.[67] Under duress, he made a screen test of the actress that he later claimed was the best thing he ever shot. He convinced himself and all involved that Miranda was well suited to the film. Most required no convincing that the role of a woman who is taken over by the spirit of a woman who went mad and died seventy years previously was ideally suited to Miranda's talents. As an actress she grew over the years, and pained expression, anxieties and desperate reactions became part of her baggage. They were at one with her temperament, which was romantic with a latent hysterical side. In *Malombra*, she was ambiguous and complex, dark and aloof.

Zaza was, on the face of it, little more than a variant on *La Dame aux camélias*. A French singer-courtesan falls for a Parisian man, an engineer, who she renounces when she discovers that he has a wife and children. With this story Miranda was on familiar ground, once again playing a woman and a performer, with the former triumphing over the latter. This had been the theme of many of her films, from *La signora di tutti* onwards, and she had several times taken the roles of star, singer and model. However, over time she had refined her capacity for understated suffering to the extent that she could explore emotions through the smallest of gestures and glances. In the film, she is still within the recitative style of Marlene Dietrich; she looks and even sounds like Dietrich, and her gestures and walk, with her body thrust forward, recall the German actress. But she is more sentimental and less cynical than Dietrich. She brings a spiritual air to her pain that contrasts with the triviality of Zaza's world, which is one of bad taste and excess. Even Gromo praised the humanity and warmth of Miranda's performance.

To place Miranda in the star system of the Fascist period is not easy because much of that system was formed after she first emerged and established herself. Also, despite a handful of routine films, she avoided the prison cage of genre. Miranda was a star of drama, an 'actress'. She never worked seriously in the theatre but she began her career on the stage and it can be argued that her sense of herself as an actress derived from that. She never made a 'white telephone' film. She was intensely committed to her art and never learned to love the film industry at home or in Hollywood. She had quite a wide repertoire and played singers in several films, although mostly the singing voice heard by audiences was not hers. Curiously, for a performer who was so bound up with the idea of the rebirth of Italian cinema, she very rarely played Italians. More commonly she was French, German or Polish. But her off-screen image was familiar and homely. Although she was always likened to Garbo and especially Dietrich, she was never in the public mind a vamp.[68] A professional, with a mastery of her craft, people saw her as warm and friendly.

In relation to Fascist culture, Miranda performed a number of different functions. She was the national screen actress, the proof that Italy could give rise to a star of international allure. The aspects of her persona that were derivative grated, but were also, for some, worthy adaptations of an international trope. With her incarnation of a whole gallery of suffering, but also loyal and patriotic women, she can be seen as having provided a type of female representation that was not as ideologically ambivalent as it might appear. Yet the clashes and problems with the regime over her departure for America and after her return prove that she was anything but a simple vehicle for the Fascist project in cinema. As an erotic spectacle, Miranda perhaps provided an example of cultural hybridity, in that her scenes as singer and performer encouraged a mode of spectatorship that highlighted sexual difference in an unconventional way. She created an unstable synthesis of two of the poles of glamour, elegance and titillation.

As a performer, Miranda had more chance to exercise agency than many of her peers, mainly because she could work abroad, and because Guarini plotted her career with her. But she was obliged to do *Scipione l'Africano* and was subject to obstacles on her return to Italy. In Hollywood, she was fitted out with a Dietrichian frame that she could do nothing about. Overall, she was caught up in negotiations with different sources of authority that governed the processes of producing visual pleasure. It was through her resistance, compromises, surrenders and her determination to remain a private person that she confirmed her standing as the most emblematic Italian screen actress of the period.

Notes

1. O. Caldiron and M. Hockhofler. 1978. *Isa Miranda*, Rome: Gremese, 11.
2. G.P. Brunetta. 1979. *Storia del cinema italiano,1895–1945*, Rome: Editori Riuniti, 510.
3. S.M. White. 1995. *The Cinema of Max Ophuls*, New York: Columbia University Press, 199.
4. Ibid., 199.
5. Ibid., 200.
6. Ibid., 204.
7. Ibid., 207.
8. M.A. Doane. 1988. 'The Abstraction of a Lady: *La Signora di tutti*', *Cinema Journal* 28(1), 65–84, 66.

9. Ibid., 68.
10. Ibid., 70.
11. Ibid., 71.
12. M. Landy. 2008. *Stardom Italian Style: Personality and Performance in Italian Cinema*, Bloomington: Indiana University Press, 45.
13. X. 'Isa Miranda: l'arte, i film, la vita', *Film*, 5 February 1938, 12.
14. M. Walker. 1986. 'La Signora di tutti', *Movie* 36(200), 62–72, 65.
15. A.G. Majano and P. Negro. 1934. 'Argomenti d'attualità', *Almanacco cinematografico 1935*, page unnumbered.
16. L. Freddi. 1949. *Il cinema*, Rome: L'Arnia, 436.
17. F. Rosso, 'Miranda nostalgica e fiera', *La Stampa*, 14 December 1975, 18.
18. S. Masi and E. Lancia. 1994. *Stelle d'Italia: piccole e grandi dive del cinema italiano dal 1930 al 1945*, Rome: Gremese, 12.
19. M. Morandini, 'Era la diva dell'autarchia', *Il Giorno*, 27 August 1971, 7.
20. This struggle can be read in relation to the categories of celebrity, performer and professional elaborated in Christine Geraghty. 2000. 'Re-examining Stardom: Questions of Texts, Bodies and Performance' in C. Gledhill and L. Williams (eds), *Reinventing Film Studies*, London: Hodder, 183–201.
21. A. Baracco, 'Isa Miranda una fiaba', *Film*, 18 July 1942, 7–8.
22. Caldiron and Hockhofler, *Isa Miranda*, 14.
23. *Film*, 5 February 1938, 8.
24. G.C. Castello. 1957. *Il divismo: mitologia del cinema*, Turin: ERI, 414. On her being viewed as 'not beautiful', see Baracco, 'Isa Miranda'.
25. Caldiron and Hockhofler, *Isa Miranda*, 11.
26. A. Solmi, 'La Garbo all'italiana', *Oggi*, 8 July 1978, 20; A. Santuari, 'Isa Miranda la nostra Garbo', *Paese sera*, 24 September 1981, 14; M.Porro, 'Isa Miranda: un'attrice condannata diva', *Corriere della Sera*, 10 July 1977, 17.
27. L. Koepnick. 2002. *The Dark Mirror: German Cinema between Hitler and Hollywood*, Berkeley: University of California Press, Chapter 'Zarah Leander and the Economy of Desire'.
28. Caldiron and Hockhofler, *Isa Miranda*, 11.
29. I. Miranda, 'I miei registi', *Star*, 5 May 1945, 5.
30. F. Sacchi, 'Come le foglie', *Corriere della Sera*, 2 February 1935, 5.
31. Quoted in Caldiron and Hockhofler, *Isa Miranda*, 44.
32. Quoted in ibid., 53.
33. M. Doletti, 'Passaporto rosso', *Il Resto del Carlino*, 23 August 1935, 7.
34. Quoted in Caldiron and Hockhofler, *Isa Miranda*, 53.
35. A. Franci, *L'illustrazione italiana*, 15 November 1937. Quoted in Caldiron and Hockhofler, *Isa Miranda*, 78.
36. C. Costantini, 'Semplicemente vamp', *Il Messaggero*, 4 June 1978, 15.
37. M. Gromo, *La Stampa*, 25 November 1937. Quoted in Caldiron and Hockhofler, *Isa Miranda*, 29.
38. X. 'Isa Miranda'.
39. Castello, *Il divismo*, 414–15.

40. G.V. Sampieri, 'Isa di Hollywood', *Lo Schermo*, January 1938, 17–19.
41. L. Schiavi, '"Bis" della donna fatale', *Cinema illustrazione*, 2 February 1938, 3.
42. Quoted in Castello, *Il divismo*, 414.
43. Ibid., 415.
44. A. Phillips and G. Vincendeau (eds). 2006. *Journeys of Desire: European Actors in Hollywood – A Critical Companion*, London: BFI, 49.
45. Ibid., 'Introduction', 8.
46. Ibid., 368.
47. Miranda, 'I miei registi'.
48. The *velina* for 9 December 1939 read 'Do not accord any coverage to Isa Miranda until further notice. The order also applies to illustrated magazines'. Reproduced in S. Raffaelli. 1997. 'Le veline fasciste sul cinema', *Bianco & Nero* 4, 45.
49. Costantini, 'Semplicemente vamp'.
50. N. Marino and E.V. Marino. 2005. *L'Ovra a Cinecittà: polizia politica e spie in camicia nera*, Turin: Bollati Boringhieri, 227.
51. F. Callari, 'Isa Miranda è rimasta Isa Miranda', *Lo Schermo*, February 1940, 13–14.
52. Rosso, 'Miranda nostalgica e fiera'.
53. O. Fallaci, 'Bentornata Signora', *L'Europeo*, 2 August 1963, 56. This meeting remains vague but it is known that Mussolini met Miranda at Cinecittà in January 1940. 'Isa Miranda introduced herself with a fatal air; she is rather scrawny and on the mature side' is the transcribed comment that appears in Claretta Petacci's diary. C. Petacci. 2009. *Mussolini segreto: diari 1932–1938*, Milan: Rizzoli, 183.
54. Masi and Lancia, *Stelle d'Italia*, 13.
55. G.P., untitled article, *Tempo*, 15 December 1940.
56. Rosso, 'Miranda nostalgica e fiera'.
57. O. Fallaci, 'Bentornata Signora', *L'Europeo*, 2 August 1963, 56.
58. Marta, 'Il cinema e la moda', *Lo Schermo*, December 1935, 39.
59. Caldiron and Hockhofler, *Isa Miranda*, 95.
60. M. Gromo, *La Stampa*, 3 December 1941.
61. D. Calcagno, *Film*, 25 April 1942.
62. Anon., 'Isa Miranda', *Grazia*, 20 March 1941, 16–18.
63. E. Doni, 'Tra due miti', *Il Messaggero*, 16 January 1976, 17.
64. Caldiron and Hockhofler, *Isa Miranda*, 9.
65. M. Ramperti. 1981. *L'alfabeta delle stelle*, Palermo: Sellerio (first published 1937), 137.
66. Caldiron and Hockhofler, *Isa Miranda*, 10.
67. E. Monreale. 2006. *Mario Soldati: le carriere di un libertino*, Bologna/Genoa: Cineteca di Bologna/Le Mani, 282.
68. M. Mida, 'una vedette fatta in casa', *Paese sera*, 7 May 1978, 14.

6

The Matinée Idol
Vittorio De Sica

By the time of Italy's entry into the war, Vittorio De Sica's star status was in decline. In fact, in the *Cinema* poll of 1940, he finished a distant third in popularity (4,209 votes) behind Amedeo Nazzari (19,020) and Fosco Giachetti (5,481). It was perhaps some consolation that his films did well in the poll and were remembered even several years after their release.[1] Yet, for most of the 1930s, no name had been more guaranteed to draw audiences to the box office than that of the Neapolitan actor whose charm and enthusiasm outweighed what he lacked in terms of good looks. To this extent, he made a crucial contribution to the revival of the national star system.[2] Like most, if not all, of the male actors who worked in cinema in the interwar years, De Sica began his career in the theatre and he never left it definitively. Unlike most others, he remained attached to the stage and continued to perform regularly through the 1930s, reducing his appearances only in those years – notably in 1938 when he made six films – in which film work left little time for other activities. The reason for this attachment to a form that was certainly less remunerative and more physically taxing has never been properly explained. De Sica certainly enjoyed the family atmosphere of the theatrical company (he performed among others with Sergio Tofano and Umberto Melnati, and with Giuditta Rissone – who he would marry in 1937 and with whom he formed a company in 1933–36) and the contact with a live audience. It may also be argued that he did not regard film work highly; he played in many films of poor quality, in a wide range of roles, apparently without discrimination. He also, in a small number of films, revelled in sending up a certain idea of the star, just as he enjoyed imitating and ridiculing on stage some of the great names of American cinema. The irony with which these performances are infused reflects first of all a certain detachment from the cinematic medium and an awareness of the falsity of the image that was constructed through his most successful films. As Sergio Grmek Germani has argued, Italian cinema in those years was closer than others to Hollywood; 'the Italian star seemed for example fully aware that he was building his image artificially' with a marked separation of public and private aspects.[3] Image was a surface collage that amounted to a 'parody of stardom' sustained by actors who treated it as separate from themselves.[4] It is not necessary to accept this as a general argument to see it as relevant to the case of De Sica.

De Sica is in some respects a riddle. A protagonist of the light comedies of the 1930s who – uniquely among the actors of the period – would turn to directing, making at first films little different from those in which he had starred, before creating several of the most memorable works of Italian neorealism, he was a figure for whom cinema was only ever a part of his endeavours. He remained attached to the theatre but also to the street, to popular culture, and to humour. Not by chance, the two key influences in his long career were Mario Camerini and Cesare Zavattini. Lacking a formal education but a keen learner and an instinctive entertainer, he placed much emphasis on performance and naturalism. Although he was born in Lazio to a middle-class family, he always laid claim, through his father, to a Neapolitan identity in which the theatricality of everyday life was a source of inspiration.

The close link between theatre and cinema in the 1930s is crucial to understanding De Sica. In the early sound era, cinema drew extensively on theatre for its first stars (Elsa Merlini, Milly, Antonio Gandusio, Armando Falconi, Angelo Musco), who played in a series of films drawing on their stage repertoires. The main diet of Italian stage, beyond the classics and the occasional drama, consisted of elegant light comedies, which used high society settings and featured fatuous debonair men in tailcoats and languorous women in furs. The substitution of drama by comedy at this time has been linked to the desire for escape fostered by a small increase in living standards. While some texts were Italian novelties, by for example Aldo De Benedetti, many were adaptations of the Parisian Boulevardier theatre or by authors of the London West End like Frederick Lonsdale and Noel Coward.[5] 'It is not surprising therefore that national cinema in the fifteen years between 1930 and the end of the Second World War drew on comedy and tried out all its variants, all its sub-genres, often mechanically copying foreign models, sometimes attempting formulae more of our own that however lacked the necessary cultural, industrial and political oxygen to develop and prosper'.[6] Hungarian sources were especially useful not only on account of the popularity of the novels of Ferenc Kormendi and Lajos Zilahy but because they lacked the sexual explicitness of, say, the works of a Coward; they had a lightness to them for which they were superficially daring but within clear limits. They worked well both in the censorious context of Fascist Italy and the Hollywood of the Hays code.[7] Cosmopolitanism was a hallmark of these productions, a telltale sign almost of their foreign origins. In Italian cinema, a number of directors had worked extensively abroad and had built up wide experience – in the United States and Germany in the case of Alessandrini; in France in that of Genina. Even if original comedy ideas were scarce, men like these could bring a plausible air to imported material.

The quantity of comedies was striking. It has been calculated that 355 were filmed, around half the total production of the period 1930–1943.[8] Industrially, they were the strongest genre, not least because they were less costly to make than historical, musical or adventure films. Cines, and its directors Mario Camerini and Nunzio Malasomma above all, was alone responsible for around one hundred titles.[9] For Umberto Rossi, 'the comedies were the true motor of film production between 1930 and 1944'.[10] They were produced in series, often at great speed. Directors like Gennaro Righelli, Max Neufeld and Carlo Ludovico Bragaglia were renowned for rapid turnovers. Indeed, Giuseppe De Santis wondered of Bragaglia: 'Why such a hurry, why make ten films a year?'[11]

Camerini's films are acknowledged as the best products of the genre. More realistic than some, they frequently featured exterior locations and real settings. In several of them De Sica starred: *Gli uomini, che mascalzoni!* (Men, What Rascals!, 1932), *Darò un milione* (I'll Give a Million, 1935), *Ma non è una cosa seria* (But It Is Not A Serious Matter, 1936), *Il signor Max* (Mr Max, 1937) and *Grandi magazzini* (The Big Store, 1939). These films all counterposed to a world of the rich and the false a more genuine and simple world of the petite bourgeoisie. By contrast, *Batticuore* (Heartbeat, 1939) and *Centomila dollari* (One Hundred Thousand Dollars, 1940) were conventional 'white telephone' films. In critical work, De Sica's films with Camerini are often given pride of place. This reflects a contemporary evaluation. In the *Almanacco cinematografico 1935*, Camerini was praised for his ability to get the best from actors, 'ridding them of their congenital actorly defects or by creating a strong artistic individuality even in people new to the work'.[12] De Sica in *Gli uomini, che mascalzoni!* was deemed 'perfect', 'a very different De Sica from the affected and conventional actor that other directors of lesser standing have since palmed us off with'. This line has been adopted by Marcia Landy who, in her discussion of the actor, credits Camerini with 'launching major Italian stars of the 1930s and 1940s such as Assia Noris and Vittorio De Sica',[13] and proceeds to examine exclusively four of the five films he made under his direction.[14] Wider criticism, both under the regime (when comedies were heavily criticised in the press for their repetitiveness and artificiality, for example in constructing unlikely interiors, swanky imaginary nightclubs and so on) and more recently,[15] has also attributed a value to Camerini's work that was denied to that of directors including Mario Mattoli, Gennaro Righelli, Carlo Ludovico Bragaglia, Nunzio Malasomma, Amleto Palermi, Guido Brignone and Mario Bonnard. Yet all of these also directed De Sica on numerous occasions, Palermi and Mattoli some six times each.

Acknowledged as the only director with a distinctive personal style, Camerini drew on a humanitarian socialism to develop a critical approach to the upper bourgeoisie in *Il signor Max*. The criticism was at best satirical but, for all its lightness, the film and other works by the director were graceful and relatively sharply observed. In this sense, he carved out a personal path, distinct from the dominant trends in Italian cinema. 'With the Camerinian realistic comedy,' Ernesto G. Laura has argued, 'Italy, which was photographed sometimes outside of studio sets, began to be seen on the screen in ways that were neither the monumental and heroic one of the regime nor the evanescent and decadent one of the "white telephones".'[16]

This current of criticism positions De Sica as the creation of Camerini and as the participant in, or hero of, a realistic tendency that in some way was the prelude of neorealism. In fact, much of this may be questioned. Without taking anything from the importance of De Sica's films with Camerini in turning the actor into a screen performer of success and versatility, recognition needs to be given to others, notably Mario Mattoli, who in effect 'invented' De Sica as a performer in revue theatre and who

Fig. 6.1 Charming everyman Vittorio De Sica, pictured with Maria Denis in the film *Partire* (Leaving). (Author's own collection)

contributed decisively to his screen stardom.[17] He identified and exaggerated some of the hallmarks of De Sica (his gift for music, his smile, his ability as a romantic lead or hearthrob, his talent for physical comedy). Furthermore, the 'realism' of Camerini, or at least the idea of him as a director who looks up disdainfully or satirically at the glamorous and fatuous elite from the point of view of the petite bourgeoisie, is not quite right. Camerini was born and largely lived on the fashionable Via Veneto in Rome. He knew well the snobbish types who inhabited the road's exclusive bars. The news kiosk of *Il signor Max*, with its many international customers, is situated there. He was, in reality, a scion of the high bourgeoisie who regarded the upstart aspirations of the petite bourgeoisie as unwelcome and humorous. The somewhat patronising depictions of lower-class desires for individual social mobility contained in his films broadly matched the ethos of Fascism with its rigid concept of class hierarchy.

However, this is not to say that there was any overt coincidence of designs between the director and the regime. For Lino Miccichè, Camerini was 'a man who was avowedly not a creature of the regime'.[18] His family was wealthy but his father had been a socialist and he would himself join the Italian Socialist Party after the war. But he was also the film-maker 'who gave the regime least to worry about and who, in a way involuntarily, responded best to Freddi's project for a neutral, calming, in brief not militant cinema'.[19] The morality of *Il signor Max*, the story of a newsvendor who, after briefly being caught up on false pretences in cosmopolitan high society, returns, chastened, to his place, was: be content with what little you have for he who wants to pass for what he is not will be disappointed. The rich were depicted as bored and unhappy, while the poor have the happiness that is born of simplicity. In other words, spectators were encouraged to value their own social origins and sentiments.

Camerini's comedies reflected an idea of cinema that was technically of a high standard, furnished with a feel good factor, and in which a common morality always triumphed. As Stefania Parigi has argued: 'if the sentimental comedy genre represents, as is evident, a constant undermining of the heroic Fascist ideal, the elements which conflict with the dominant moral code, that is to say with the prevailing petit bourgeois customs, appear rather weak and generally are reconciled with the dominant norm'.[20] Critics including Umberto Barbaro railed against their 'imbecile optimism' and likened them to 'opium, morphine' and other drugs.[21] Others, of a more Fascist persuasion, deplored their triviality and foreignness. Raffaello Patuelli for example, launched an attack on the Cines company: '*Squadrone bianco* is made, *Scipione l'Africano, Giovanni dalle bande nere* [*Condottieri*] are prepared, and they continue to film nightclubs, tailcoats, platinum blondes and the young mopheads with which they populate their so-called little films'.[22] The young Michelangelo Antonioni saw Camerini as an artist but urged him to improve: 'We would just ask him to show a bit more courage and less subjugation to the superficially daring', he wrote.²³

A more recent critic, Alberto Farassino, takes a similar line. The definition of Camerini as the 'poet of the petite bourgeoisie is too narrow', he argues, as he also presented a richer and more complex picture of the aristocracy than is generally acknowledged. Aristocrats were not merely fatuous but modern, mobile, adventurous, cultured and quite humane in his films. 'As a filmmaker', he continues, 'he loves them ... He loves the places where one can meet them, or stage them, the Casino (of which he was a habitué, even if not as much as his friend De Sica) and the Grand Hotel, where he lived for a period in Rome, preferring it to private residences'.²⁴

One of the chief hallmarks of Camerini's films is transformation. Changes of identity, whether by accident or design, dressing up and disguise, aspirations to remake oneself, the interplay of surface impressions and deeper sentiments characterise much of his work. There was a Pirandellian influence here (*Ma non è una cosa seria* is an adaptation), which ran through the work of other directors, but also something that was peculiar to the social order of the Fascist period. As De Grazia has argued, one significant effect of the overthrow of the liberal order was 'widespread bewilderment about class position and sexual identity'.²⁵ 'Mussolini's own rapid changeover from left to right, his swift ascent from street-fighting bully to prime minister, his relinquishing of the black shirt for a morning coat were themselves causes and symptoms of this confusion', she adds.

De Sica suited the instability of this type of situation for his manner of performing was such that he could simultaneously be inside and outside a role, playing it in other words while ironically commenting on it. The insubstantial nature of the roles allowed him the freedom to sketch in many of their aspects with mannerisms and gestures of his own invention. De Sica, it has been said, was 'regarded by the critics as the prototype Italian actor, on account of the naturalness of a performance style resting on subtlety and introspection'.²⁶ At the time he made his debut as a lead in *Gli uomini, che mascalzoni!*, he was a theatre actor who had appeared in just three films in supporting roles. Camerini saw potential in his ability to be natural before a camera and to immerse himself fully into the fluffiest of characters. In other words, he appreciated his ability to act in cinematic way. This mattered as Camerini was one of few directors to understand cinema as an aspect of modernity and to explore its possibilities in terms of the developing urban landscape with its cacophony of sounds, variety of objects and myriad visual attractions. The issues of reality and illusion, identity, social flux, mobility and masquerade were addressed in relation to this.

De Sica was not a natural choice to play the young lovelorn chauffeur. He was known to theatre audiences as a suave and sophisticated entertainer who was most at home in evening dress. According to Mario Corsi, he was known as 'the Chevalier of the Italian stage' and as a 'heart-breaker'.[27] Despite not being thought of as handsome, due to his hollow cheeks and long teeth, he was often cast as the leading man. Luigi Almirante, who directed a company with Sergio Tofano, was the first to invite him to play the romantic lead. He protested that he could not: 'I am ugly ... I've got a long nose and a lanky figure!', he reportedly said.[28] Despite his success, Stefano Pittaluga, the founder of Cines, was unconvinced that he could take similar roles on screen. He felt that his face and especially his large nose were unsuited to cinema.[29] Ludovico Toeplitz, who joined the Cines board in 1930 as the nominee of the Banca commerciale italiana, which owned 80 per cent of the capital, and which took over the company after Pittaluga's sudden death, was sceptical about Camerini's casting choice but not opposed. In his memoirs, he happily took a share of the credit for this successful debut.[30] His only regret was not to have used the title of the song 'Parlami d'amore Mariù' (Speak to me of love, Mariù) for the film, since it became a huge hit and even featured in the repertoire of Bing Crosby. The actual film title, he noted 'was a phrase said in dialogue that no one heard because it was covered by the laughter of the audience from the previous gag'.

The runaway success of 'Parlami d'amore Mariù' tied the song to De Sica's name and ensured that in many of his roles over the following period he would be required to sing, and often play the piano too. The whole phenomenon was a product of a tie-in between cinema, radio and the gramophone industry. The development of sound cinema permitted new commercial synergies that all parties were keen to exploit. The song had been written by Bixio, a Neapolitan transplanted in Milan, but its appeal owed much to the cordial, warm and ironical mood that De Sica conferred on it. A love song positioned midway between melancholy and passion, it was inflected with nostalgia. For Gianfranco Vené:

> the "cad" for whom it was written, is a poor guy, a romantic type out to impress, who is in love with the simple Mariù. He addresses his girlfriend by drawing on the baggage of the past. He uses dated words like "maliarda" (seductress), concepts like that of disappearing in "the whirlpool of emotions ... with you" and even verses freely taken from the ultra-famous "Scettico blues" of the 1920s: "but what does it matter if the world pokes fun at me".[31]

The actor caught the atmosphere of the song and gave it the feel of a clumsy but honest confession that was not apparent from the words alone. In brief, he helped to make it memorable.

The film also established a screen image for De Sica. The title denoted him as a representative of *gli uomini* (men) and labelled him a *mascalzone* (rascal or cad). He was a bit of a rogue rather than a reliable type, but also somehow irresistible – a smiling charmer with the easy manner of a Maurice Chevalier. However, unlike the French actor, his persona was invested with a rash bravado; he was 'up for anything no matter how dodgy, for any sort of play acting'.[32]

Like many of Camerini's films, *Gli uomini, che mascalzoni!* was filled with symbols of modernity: several means of transport, communications, aspects of the urban experience, commerce, industry, advertising, machines. It offered a fictionalised but recognisable concentration of urban sensations while also having a conventional sentimental streak. The rhythm of the film was industrial and the soundtrack modern. The use of dissolves, fast editing, a fragmented screen, and unusual camera angles all gave it an avant-garde feel. But De Sica is positioned as being in conflict with these; he is clumsy (he crashes a car, over-indulges in perfume, is rendered absurd by advertising garb). Amid the flux, he incarnates familiar dreams of social promotion and sentimental fulfilment.[33] Landy has suggested that both De Sica and his screen partner Lia Franca '"speak" through ... gestures'.[34] Their performances owe a debt to silent film. This may be so, but none of their gestures have the pantomime quality of some silent-era acting. Indeed, Franca was selected for the part because she was of modest appearance and not at all 'actressy'.

Writing in 1949, Sergio Sollima argued that, 'with Camerini, De Sica learned how to act properly but above all he managed to do what very few Italian actors indeed had managed to do: that is, create a living persona, who had his origins in reality'.[35] Mario Soldati, who wrote the screenplay with Camerini, gave an insight into how the actor achieved this result. He recounted how he went with De Sica to a clothing store in Milan to purchase appropriate clothes for the role. Soldati was aiming for accuracy, seeking to secure a look that would be right for the first worker to be the protagonist of an Italian film. De Sica insisted that the jacket should be two sizes too small. As Soldati recalled:

> It was, to be sure, his comedy instinct, underscored by the formidable tradition of Neapolitan theatre; it was his already long training; it was his second nature, that influenced him and that made him refuse to give in to my rigorously realistic intentions ... In the final analysis, it was the model of the *guappo*, that was also linked somehow to Charlie Chaplin's tailcoat. And Vittorio had chosen it irremovably against my opinion. In his view the character should be true, but true with also a touch of the ridiculous, the comical; the too-tight jacket with too-short sleeves and the shirt cuffs sticking out were an indication of poverty and, as such, were funny. Besides, De Sica was so young and so likeable that he gave out a feeling of attractiveness even in the most absurd of situations and conditions. He was surely right; the film was perfect and full of grace, but with a good-humoured, smiling realism shaded with optimism and irony.[36]

This sense of the visual impact of costume derived directly from De Sica's stage experience. He carried on performing even after his film career took off because that was his milieu. Titta Rissone, his companion, was only sporadically involved with cinema. He also had strong personal links to Melnati and Tofano, who also acted less frequently on screen. The understanding with Melnati was an important one since the two men performed sketches together on the radio as well as adaptations of their stage plays. The radio was the main medium of light entertainment at the time. A novelty of the 1920s, it had, thanks to the support of the regime, become in short time a dispenser not only of news and culture but also an extraordinary diffuser of popular songs and witty comic sketches that were reliant on improbable intrigues and misunderstandings. According to the radio historian Franco Monteleone, 'the sketches of Vittorio De Sica and Umberto Melnati were in vogue when every Italian was whistling the appealing tunes diffused by the Trio Lescano and the Vocal Quartet of the Mida brothers'.[37] Tullio Kezich has argued that the stage was necessary to 'the effort to keep up the dignity of his own artistic image'.[38] 'Like many theatre people, until he passed to directing, De Sica continued to think that only the stage, with its burdens, its risks, the wearing routine of tours and repeat performances, was real work. By comparison cinema was a joke, albeit a very well-paid one'. If this is so, then it is not a view that was shared by all. Elsa De Giorgi wrote of the unbearable boredom of repeat performances, and recounted that De Sica and Rissone would combat this by quietly joshing with each other between the lines they uttered for audience consumption.

De Sica's experience in the theatre was built from the early 1920s when he joined the company of Tatiana Pavlova. After being recruited by Almirante and Tofano, he extended his repertoire as a young principal to Shaw, Pirandello and other modern masters. Then he moved from serious to light theatre, joining in 1931 the Za Bum revue run by the lawyer-turned-impressario and future film director Mario Mattoli. In this new setting, his success was so great, Maria Mercader wrote, 'that [he] was marked by it for the rest of his professional life'.[39] It established him as comedy actor and a singer of light and humorous songs. The song 'Ludovico, sei dolce come un fico' (without the rhyme: Ludovico, you are as sweet as a fig), sung in duet with Melnati, became his first hit. It was while working with Mattoli that he first asserted his ability to get inside the fatuous characters he embodied while also looking at them from outside. The Za Bum shows which Mattoli and Luciano Ramo staged from the late 1920s revolutionised Italian variety. Their careful choice of actors, all of whom had to be able to sing and dance properly, and sparkling, often satirical, texts marked them out. The shows began as revues and later included comedy and drama. Often they took a cue from a Hollywood film to elaborate a plot, stringing together various episodes and types of spectacle. The words of songs were partly composed by De Sica who emerged as a creative talent as well as a versatile performer.

Songs were a crucial factor in early sound cinema. Critics were attentive to their quality and audiences evaluated and compared them. Actors were often forced to become singers. Indeed, several early Thirties' stars were basically singing stars. This was a dimension of Italian-ness that cinema incorporated and used in its strategy of promotion. Elsa Merlini owed her success to her singing voice and so too did Milly. De Sica sang in every one of his early films as a contractual condition imposed by producers. His tenor voice turned songs into a sort of escapist opium. By means of it he spread a relaxed atmosphere of joy. His voice became the key marker of his star quality and also of his Neapolitan identity, which was not exhibited in the form of an accent or any other mannerisms in most of his films. 'He sings because he is Neapolitan', wrote Mario Corsi, having seen him in Palermi's *Napoli d'altri tempi* (Naples of Olden Times, 1937).[40] The lack of any obvious regional root distinguishes the pre-war De Sica from the post-war actor and is to be explained in relation to the regime's drive towards the Italianisation of dialect theatre and its exponents, including the De Filippo brothers, Edoardo and Peppino, and the Sicilian Angelo Musco, all of whom performed on screen with only the mildest of regional inflections. According to Farassino, De Sica's voice 'became the Italian voice to believe in, counterposed to the voice to be obeyed, the voice-off of Luce films that praised the genius, hardwork and power of Italians. It was smiling and tranquillising – more effective with audiences than the lugubrious masculinity of Giachetti and Nazzari'.[41] His songs caught the traditional charm and humanity of the Italian people.

Mattoli would direct De Sica for the first time in 1934 when he cast him in his debut film, *Tempo massimo* (Full Time). Unlike his later work with the stage comics Macario and Totò, who he directed in a detached manner without forcing the performer into a set of situations and rhythms typical of cinema, this film owed much to the method and style of Camerini. If 'the true Utopia of Mattoli was to dream of a cinema based solely on the cast', with few takes and a degree of improvisation, as Stefano Della Casa has argued,[42] then it was scarcely realised in this film, which was a fast-paced comedy that deployed many filmic techniques with striking assurance. Mattoli liked to work with stars, and the trust he placed in them freed him to concentrate on other aspects of the film's confection.

Tempo massimo is a film whose pace is set by means of transport. In the first few minutes, a bicycle, a boat, an aeroplane and a car all appear, to be followed by a train and, in a retreat from the modern emphasis of the action, horses. A number of events well known from *Gli uomini, che mascalzoni!* are repeated: a song, a car crash, a cycle chase and the lure of modern ways and inventions all feature. De Sica plays Giacomo Banti, an unworldly professor who lives cocooned in a sumptuous residence where he is mothered by his aunt and a valet. On this occasion too, his character is drawn to modern ways by a woman (higher class this time). His tranquil life is upset when the sporty socialite Dora, played by Milly, upends his rowing boat when she parachutes from a plane and lands directly on him. He is fascinated by the modern manners and Anglicisms of her band of friends. After a modern singalong by the group, he sings the same song alone at the piano. To win her affections and prise her away from a gold-digging fiancé, he takes up sport and enters a cycle race. The awkwardness of the chauffeur Bruno at the Milan trade fair is repeated when the lovelorn Prof. Banti takes, with his manservant, a series of humble jobs in Milan with the aim of forgetting the woman. He works first as a sandwich man advertising a Mickey Mouse film at the children's cinema, before, after getting fired, taking a job as a dishwasher, from which he is also dismissed after distractedly smashing plates. Finally, after being tipped off by a maid (Anna Magnani in a delightful comic supporting role) that Dora is about to marry her aristocratic but secretly broke fiancé, he hijacks first a taxi and then a tourist bus and drives madly through Milan, arriving just in time to steal her away from her intended.

De Sica would intersperse his celebrated work with Camerini with other, lesser known but often equally significant films with Mattoli. After *Tempo massimo*, he made *Amo te sola* (I Only Love You) in 1935, *L'uomo che sorride* (The Man Who Smiles) in 1936, *Questi ragazzi* (These Boys) in 1937, and *Ai vostri ordini signora* (At Your Orders, Madam) in 1939. Throughout this period, he refined his art, becoming the epitome of a new type of naturalistic, understated acting that made older performance styles seem outdated. According to the contemporary critic Remo Branca, film actors should not seem actors; they should appear real, through being measured and intimate, and should inhabit their characters. 'All this means,' he added, 'that of the film actor is required a certain correspondence between the type that he impersonates and his temperament so that the construction of the character seems like an unveiling of the subconscious of the individual'. The film actor had to have the right physical and psychological qualities to get inside certain human types and make them plausible. 'In this case, the interpretation, even if broken up by the needs of the shoot,' Branca continued, 'will always find its unity in the intrinsic qualities of the actor, who does not transfer himself outside of himself, but lives a reality that is potentially his.'[43]

All this corresponded to the requirements and expectations of modern audiences, who found the conventional mannerisms of theatre actors, and often even theatre itself, unappealing. For Branca, younger people felt less affinity for the theatre than earlier generations. 'Theatre as it is in Italy today belongs to history ... cinema is in touch with life and it reflects its general level', he observed.[44] 'So the old stage is dead. The actor who stalks the boards and gesticulates and shouts to make himself heard up in the gods is finished and has been substituted by the man who walks the roads of the world and acts in houses that are of or which we hope will be ours.' The public had transferred its interest to cinema; it 'can no longer identify with the traditional mode of acting of the theatrical performer; it identifies with the naturalism of the film actor. The former is artificial, static; the second succeeds in creating a multi-dimensional illusion of reality and satisfies with his dynamism the restless spirit of the crowd.'

Branca was referring especially to leading men and it was precisely in the area of the representation of masculinity that some of De Sica's specific traits can be identified. The performance of masculinity in Italian cinema in the 1930s took several forms, as will be seen also from the chapters dealing with Amedeo Nazzari and Fosco Giachetti. In relation to British cinema of the period, Andrew Spicer has written of the importance of the gentleman – gentlemanliness being a composite ideal incorporating the romantic, the ethical and the practical. Character formation was a central part of it and it was typically externalised in the forms of loyalty, teamwork, conformity, restraint, self-sacrifice and noblesse oblige.[45] The gentleman was not working class (only the postwar years would see examples of the ordinary man as hero), but he was nonetheless situated in relation to the collectivity, and cinematic versions of him were related to national identity. In Italy, pluralism took the place of hierarchy. The Fascist manly ideal was much less class specific although it incorporated elements of nobility as well loyalty, teamwork, conformity and so on. However, in the gender wars of Fascism, the supremacy of this model was never assumed; it was always seen as a process and in permanent conflict with other, older or alternative types of masculinity. In this sense, it was identified with the *nazione* (nation) but not, to use historian Ruggero Romano's distinction, with the *paese* (country).[46] The latter was a cluster of established values, attitudes and practices that was much older, usually more regional and more quotidian. De Sica's 'type' belonged to this substratum of Italian culture. Although his accent and gestures mostly did not bear the stamp of Naples, his peculiar mixture of melancholy and optimism, romanticism and skulduggery, inventiveness and resignation, introspection and taste for performance had a southern, and perhaps more specifically Neapolitan, aspect. Although his characters could be northern or southern, Italian or foreign, and upper class, middle class or working class, these features were rarely highlighted except by location, role or material attributes. Although he often took on different moods, guises, social roles and attitudes in the course of a film, intimately De Sica was always the same – a basically lower-middle-class individual who was provincial and quite conservative, who was drawn towards encounters with a larger modern world in which his sense of himself was challenged. 'De Sica often impersonated a benign, slightly awkward, but charming rogue who, after being tamed by circumstances, finally becomes a respectable member of the petite bourgeoisie', Landy has observed.[47]

In his analysis of the actor, Giovanni Calendoli recalled that Emilio Cecchi, artistic director of Cines in the early 1930s, saw De Sica the film actor as bearing the mark of the Commedia dell'arte tradition. His mobility, brio, rhythm, natural playing and versatility all dovetailed with this.

The wide range of expressions and moods he adopted belonged to the same character. 'This character is straightforwardly Italian', Calendoli judged.[48] The actor's success derived from his being true, spontaneous, and faithful to a way of being that was part tradition, part national spirit. While many of the characters of Italian cinema had little relation to reality, 'the persona of Vittorio De Sica took inspiration from the most common suggestions of the Italian character and found their reason for being and their limit in the immediate surrounding world'. It did not matter if he was plebian or aristocratic, since he was:

> cordial, eager for human contact, sociable, optimistic, loving of life, whose true meaning he discovers in simple, uncomplicated feelings; he is good, without giving this too much weight; he pays his dues as far as the collectivity is concerned and judges things accurately, weighing them up with intelligence, but without ever assuming the severity of a judge. He underlines sometimes with his irony the defects of the human race, but without ever embracing violent sarcasm or satire, precisely because he does not have the indelible mark of a personality who is carried to extremes by his exceptional qualities. Rather he is contented to stay within the vaster zone of common feeling.[49]

The De Sica character's modernity lay in this commonness, which verged on anonymity. Apart from his prominent nose, for Calendoli he had no distinguishing characteristics. 'His open, friendly, familiar image is in a way a common image, that of the nameless man who lives in the beehive of the contemporary city and who every evening is swallowed up by the apartment blocks of the suburbs without leaving any trace', he continued. 'Besides, it is the generic nature of his exterior appearance that constitutes the basis of the character, which is exactly that of the everyman, of the individual who is immersed up to the neck in the minute facts of every day and who will never rise above that, not even if he will, for a moment, be brushed by exceptional events.'[50]

The immersion in the everyday was a feature of many of De Sica's characters. In his films with Camerini, he is often inserted in working environments such as a garage, a news kiosk, a department store, the street. In his wider film work, identifiable streets and institutions in Milan, Rome and Naples figured. However, there were also a large number of fantasy locations such as nightclubs, cruise liners, ballrooms and international resorts. What enabled him to pass seamlessly from the banal to the desirable was the vivacity and freshness of his playing. He had a light touch, variety of pace and a fine sense of timing.

The delicious ordinariness of the De Sica persona is striking for its utterly depoliticised nature. If it is true, as Paola Valentini has argued, that he incarnated the Italian of 1930s and his aspirations, then those aspirations were simple and the Italian not at all the remoulded soldier type that Fascism propagated.[51] Indeed, she continues, he represented the other side of the Fascist coin; he was sentimental, inventive and individualistic where the former was unflinching, obedient and self-sacrificing.[52] His sole genre was light comedy in its various permutations and, unlike almost every other male actor of appropriate age, he never appeared on screen in a military role. In fact, in Gli uomini, che mascalzoni!, as in one of the films De Sica directed in the early 1940s, I bambini ci guardano (The Children Are Watching Us, 1942), uniforms (that of the chauffeur in the former, the boy's boarding school uniform in the final scenes of the latter) are used as symbols of dehumanisation.[53] His films usually have an ironical undertow, and varied costumes reflect the fluidity of his character and its capacity for transformation. Although he adopted some of the attitudes of the male seducer, it is usually, in the early films, the women who take charge of a romantic situation. De Sica rarely emerged with credit or footloose from these. For the standards of the time, his persona was a weak one, sometimes indecisive or tending to passing melancholy, and the aspect of change introduced a conventionally feminine element. He never played the hero or the leader.

De Sica's persona, then, was a-Fascist but it should be underlined that this does not mean it was anti-Fascist. Indeed, such a thing would have been inconceivable. Despite his occasional adoption of lower-class roles, his background was bourgeois and his characters never actively undermined the family, religion or respectability. He provided, in other words, the same sort of escape as some of pleasures of consumption referred to in Chapter 3. Fascism was based on compromise as far as the middle classes were concerned, and space was always allowed for conventional values, attitudes and distractions. It simply absorbed some behavioural models while carrying others, including patriotism and male supremacy, to extremes. Viewed in this light, De Sica provided not an antidote so much as a necessary safety valve, a link to a certain type of familiar and innocuous tradition. Bolzoni sees him as an artist who posed the regime no problems at all. 'He was elected the subtle and charming spokesman of that ideal type of Italian, or rather of the Neapolitan with the heart of gold and the pleasant smile, who, when faced with any difficulty, always finds a way out that is rarely dishonourable'.[54] Nevertheless, he received significantly more press coverage in commercial magazines like Cinema illustrazione, published by Rizzoli, than in publications that were more obviously subservient to official directives.[55]

Writing in 1946, the future director Steno (Stefano Vanzina) situated the actor with precision in relation to the main currents of popular culture. 'Beyond the Italy of Mussolini, there existed just below the surface, the Italy of Vittorio De Sica', he wrote:

> 'Official' Italy was that of the banners and speeches, of the heads shaved in the ancient Roman style and the demands; the 'unofficial' Italy, by contrast – that of Vittorio – was that of holidays on the Riviera or at Montecatini, that of the lottery or the Motta *panettone*, that of the puzzle weeklies that were devoured in

the second-class compartments and by servant girls who, while washing the plates, made the courtyards of the municipal housing blocks reverberate with the languid words of 'Today my heart is full of nostalgia'.[56]

There were two interlinked keys to the success of De Sica that unified his screen persona and wider star image. The first of these was his smile, which Landy identifies as both 'crooked' and 'quintessential to his popularity'.[57] The actor certainly had a dazzling smile, which spread broadly across his face and revealed his teeth. In the mid-1930s, the smile had not yet become either a fully fledged Hollywood trope, which it would do in the war years, or been given the predominantly female connotation it would acquire through the pin-ups of Rita Hayworth. Douglas Fairbanks though had almost single-handedly branded the smile, which in his case expressed optimism and the good life, while the brute force of Maciste had disappeared from the screens. For the journalist Mino Doletti, writing in 1929, it was precisely his inability to transcend fisticuffs that brought Maciste's film career to an end. 'If he had taken care to throw fewer punches at his adversaries on screen, today he would be less "popular" but more famous', he observed, adding that 'rough, fighting types do not have much success in cinema; they only garner the noisy backing of those spectators who get in at half price'.[58] Fairbanks, he observed, was the first to show the power on screen of a 'delightful smile that reveals perfect, white teeth'. With his suave, smiling manner, De Sica keyed into the softer, upbeat mood that typified light entertainment.

The film *L'uomo che sorride* (The Man Who Smiles, Mario Mattoli, 1936) was adapted from a stage play that De Sica had performed with Rissone and Tofano. From the moment he appears on screen, smiling broadly, elegantly attired and with Brillantined hair and pencil moustache, it is clear that De Sica is sending up himself and, perhaps more broadly, the very idea of the star. Partnered by Assia Noris, with whom he acted in several of the films he made with Camerini, he not only smiles from the beginning to the end of the film, he also turns his smile into an approach to life and especially towards women. Noris plays a spoilt and capricious young woman who, it is implied, needs to be taught a lesson or somehow brought to heel. Various male characters including her father threaten her with 'kicks' (*pedate*) or 'slaps'. De Sica, by contrast, uses modern methods to win and to tame her; he records her words to remind her what she has said, engages in various subterfuges, and ridicules her persistent former fiancé, played by Melnati – but he never resorts to the violent methods invoked by others. Finally, he brings out from his armoury, in addition to his smile, his ability to sing and play the piano. In a reference to the De Sica star image, which required the actor to break into song in every film, he declares to Noris that he had kept this talent hidden because 'I wanted you to like me even if I did not know how to sing'. After the pair have married and Noris, not yet completely cured of her infuriating ways, runs away, he keeps faith with his unconventional and charming method. Thrown by this, she exclaims, 'Treat me badly but command me! Order me to return home!' 'Come home!', De Sica finally orders, to which she meekly replies, 'Yes, dear, yes'. In the final scene the actor turns his smile knowingly towards the audience.

The smile connotes the star, the character and the actor. For Calendoli,

> Right from the time of *La segretaria di tutti*, *Due cuori felici* and *Gli uomini, che mascalzoni!*, Vittorio De Sica's smile was famous and this smile was really the emblem of the life that that actor has made his character live. It is a luminous, sweet, cordial smile, a positive, straightforward smile but a smile that is lit by a white and understated flame that does not arouse passions, that expresses exactly a peaceful, serene and detached happiness. It is a smile that is beautiful in its mediocrity and because of its mediocrity. It is the smile that says "He who is satisfied is happy".[59]

It said, in other words, that life should be accepted as it is and that dreaming should aid reconciliation rather than portend change.

The mid-1930s was a period that witnessed an outbreak of smiles in Italy. The years that historians have identified as corresponding to the zenith of Fascism's consensus were also marked by the first affirmation of mass culture. Cinema, radio, the press and advertising worked together to create a modern public of consumers. Advertisers were among the first to sense that new tools of communication and a new tone were needed. An editorial in the magazine *La Pubblicità d'Italia* (organ of the corporation of advertising agencies) entitled 'Sorridere' (smiling) called for a revival of cordiality: 'cordiality in advertising means psychological understanding, learning how to speak in a way that everyone can comprehend, asking for what one wants in a clear, polite and honest way, and a sincere desire to come over as useful and pleasant'.[60] 'What more than advertising should accept readily and fully the commandment to "go towards the people"? At the cost of renouncing certain cold and perhaps complicated intellectualisms, our art can draw great advantage for itself and for others from more humane, more smiling and felicitous expressions and concepts. The markets (not only in Italy but throughout the world) are in need of a ray of cordial optimism', it concluded. For the anti-Fascist Camillo Berneri, politicians were not exempted from this trend. 'The man of the day, the public man, whose fame is like a trumpet, is situated, in terms of ... glory, between the smile of Maurice Chevalier and the fists of Carpentier', he wrote.[61] Even Mussolini adapted his image at this time. Luisa Passerini notes that observers commented on how the Duce laughed but almost never smiled in the 1920s. As time passed, he developed a repertoire of 'discreet smiles' that added a gentle, cordial tone to his public persona.[62]

The second key to De Sica's success was his relaxed, detached manner. Unlike some of his male colleagues, he offered no pretence at being a great actor. With his light roles and easy manner, he was as accessible to seamstresses and shop girls as to his more bourgeois theatre audiences. The lack of pretence derived from a patchy education, a fact which would contribute to the complementary nature of his partnership with the more cultured Cesare Zavattini. Even the press stressed that he was a self-made man, who was self-taught and had no family background in the performing arts. He was a hit, Valentini argues, 'above all because his parabola as a star even beyond the screen mirrored the reality of the facts of those years', in underscoring that simple ambition and social mobility were desirable and attainable goals.[63] In the illustrated magazines, pictures from the family album of De Sica as a boy and a young man suggested, not unlike Mussolini, the destiny that awaited him. Contemporary pictures, however, typically showed him at leisure, with his dog or in the company of friends. The rewards of success were apparent in his elegant wardrobe and love of fast cars. The idea that ran through all of this was that De Sica was 'one of us', he was a 'plebeian aristocrat', as Margherita Sarfatti defined Mussolini in her biography *Dux*, who,[64] in contrast to the Duce – who was projected as advancing along the road of history – walked a more familiar, well-trodden path. It was 'a fusion of stardom and the quotidian [that constituted] De Sica's distinctive trait', Valentini has argued.[65]

It was this Italian ordinariness that provided the well-spring of one of his comic traits, which was a lightly mocking outlook on the modern fads of the Anglo-American world and their Italian devotees. The comedy was accented differently in different films and it never truly evolved into satire, but it was sufficiently consistent to mark De Sica himself as being simultaneously equally as modern and less modern than others. On stage, he had often parodied American actors, including Ramon Novarro and Garbo's partner John Gilbert, and several of his films, including *Tempo massimo*, *Darò un milione* and *Il signor Max* feature snobs whose affected anglicised mannerisms are both embraced and rejected. In only his second film, *Due cuori felici* (Two Happy Hearts, Baldassare Negroni, 1932), he played Mr Brown, the son of a magnate of the American car industry, who comes to Rome on business and falls for the wrong girl. The character is not drawn in an absurd or grotesque way, but with a gentle dose of irony. Mr Gold, the sad millionaire of *Darò un milione* who wants only to rediscover simplicity and goodness, is, beyond his money, barely given any 'American' attributes at all. De Sica's ease of manner and movement led to comparisons with Cary Grant, Fred Astaire or Chevalier. For this reason, some saw him as the equal of Hollywood actors and, when Vittorio Mussolini undertook a trip to the movie capital in 1937, he took with him a film test of De Sica and Milly performing in (terrible) English.[66] The American element, no matter how it was configured, incorporated an aspirational self-projection that, spectators through the persona of De Sica, could absorb. For Italians, he was not so much American as a local take on the Hollywood American; a Gary Cooper or James Stewart as seen by Italians.[67]

For Francesco Bolzoni, De Sica was not truly a star because he 'had difficulty believing fully in the fiction'.[68] The ability to be both inside and outside a role that was so important to his playing of multiple parts, necessitating changes of costume and identity, positioned him as insufficiently solid and resonant, not to mention not exceptional enough, to be embraced by the public or the industry as a source of envy and identification. He could not be presented seriously as a human ideal through fabulous photographs and admiring articles because the playful aspect inevitably would have turned these into parodies. In brief, he was too obviously 'playing' Vittorio De Sica. While it can be accepted that aspects of his persona placed him outside the conventional parameters of stardom, it would seem unnecessarily restrictive to deny him his status as a star because his uniqueness lay precisely in the fact that he treated his own image with amusement and that others did so too.

However, in the late 1930s the actor started to be dissatisfied with his established image and his long curriculum of light comedies. He expressed a desire to return to the theatre and abandon both his songs and his smile, as if he was aware that these were acting as collective narcotics. In an article in which he addressed his public, he critiqued his own smile:

> Some people smile because they are always happy. I am never content but I have long, shiny teeth and if you have noticed thin lips. Smiling is my way of being lazy, of resting, of letting my mouth do what it likes ... My smile, therefore, does not simply reflect my qualities but has often cordially betrayed them: its is a physical fact rather than a moral expression. It has given me a happy spirit that does not belong to me; it has enriched me with an ephemeral and transient appeal that too often has disturbed me.[69]

This reflection was the prelude to the shift that led to De Sica establishing himself as a director. Although his films were at first conventional in content, they soon began to acquire a depth that was novel. From an article he penned, after directing four films, for an official almanac, it was apparent that he had tired of amusement and sought a more serious engagement with reality. In an anticipation of neorealism, he declared: 'I like best of all faces that are, let us say, new, actors that are not actors, those who have not been corrupted by their trade and by experience and in which everything is genuine and straightforward. If it were possible, I would like to choose my players in the street, among the crowd'.[70]

Curiously, others took a different view. The writer Vitaliano Brancati remarked in 1950 that as public opinion became disaffected, irony rather than anger prospered:

> Between 1936 and 25 July 1943, providence armed the new generations with laughs rather than knives. And the reason seems clear to me. The authoritarian fanaticism had taken on such an aspect of madness that the words "heroism", "sacrifice of life",

"absolute dedication to the cause", "martyrdom" were so over used, and even practised, in a gross and mistaken way to be sure, but still a strongly deceptive one, that the only weapon against such things was the smile.[71]

Satire and ridicule certainly accompanied the final stages of Mussolini's regime. Giuseppe Bottai noted in his diary that even officials of the regime told each other jokes at Mussolini's expense, and artists privately lampooned the once all-powerful dictator, but other forms of detachment and reflection also prospered.[72] It was perhaps appropriate that the man most associated with the breezy entertainments of the period should have set aside his smile while others polished up theirs.

De Sica's change of direction came at the very start of the descendant phase of Fascism. By the time he made *I bambini ci guardano*, a film that has often been read in tandem with Visconti's *Ossessione* as a precursor of postwar neorealism on account of its unsentimental treatment of marriage and adultery, and the accusation it implicitly directed against the social order, he had acquired sufficient respect from producers to be allowed to pursue more original projects. However, it has been suggested that there was a strong personal element in the elaboration of this film as De Sica had left his wife Giuditta Rissone for the Spanish starlet Maria Mercader, who he had directed in *Un garibaldino al convento* (A Garibaldian Redshirt in the Convent, 1941). For Bolzoni, the timid and romantic persona De Sica played on screen, and which the public was induced to believe corresponded to his true personality, was in fact false since 'there was undoubtedly a lot that was autobiographical in the portrayal of a seducer in permanent active service'.[73] Like other male leads, he regarded the pool of young actresses of Cinecittà as a private hunting ground. Mercader later recalled that he 'was famous in Italian cinema for his capacity to perform and to get others to perform and, just after – or just before – that, for his female conquests'.[74] An inveterate gambler and Don Giovanni, he was also famed among colleagues for his frightening temper and extreme jealousy.

'De Sica cannot be defined a sympathiser of Fascism, even if he did nothing to oppose it. Like many other stars, he limited himself to conducting his own life and doing his job as well as possible, seeking not to get involved in political questions', Sergio Vicini has argued.[75] But the personal trajectory of De Sica was inseparable from Fascism even if he embodied the softer underside of the culture of the period rather than its overtly militaristic official dimension. That he should have struggled to free himself of this role was proof that even the lightest of entertainment, ultimately, served the purposes of the regime.

Notes

1. P. Valentini. 2002. 'Modelli, forme e fenomeni di divismo: Vittorio De Sica' in M. Fanchi and E. Mosconi (eds.), *Spettatori: forme di consumo e pubblici del cinema in Italia, 1930–1960*, Rome: Bianco & Nero, 108–33, 116.
2. G.P. Brunetta. 1991. *Cent'anni di cinema italiano*, Rome–Bari: Laterza, 204.
3. S.G. Germani. 1991. 'Introduzione a una ricerca' in M. Argentieri (ed.), *Risate di regime: la commedia italiana 1930–1944*, Venice: Marsilio, 81–98, 83.
4. Ibid., 85.
5. E.G. Laura. 1991. 'I percorsi intrecciati della commedia anni '30', in Argentieri, *Risate di regime*, 109–37, 110.
6. Ibid.
7. Ibid., 111.
8. U. Rossi. 1991. 'Le commedie: la debole forza della produzione italiana', in Argentieri, *Risate di regime*, 187–95, 189.
9. Ibid., 192.
10. Ibid., 194.
11. Quoted in S. Parigi. 1991. 'Commedie in rivista: la critica nella stampa specializzata 1930–1945' in Argentieri, *Risate di regime*, 213–50, 246.
12. A.G. Majano and P. Negri. 1934. 'Registi' in *Almanacco cinematografico 1935*, Edizioni Bella, Milan, page unnumbered.
13. M. Landy. 2008. *Stardom Italian Style: Personality and Screen Performance in Italian Cinema*, Bloomington: Indiana University Press, 46.
14. *Ma non è una cosa seria* is the missing title.
15. See Parigi, 'Commedie in rivista', 231.
16. Laura, 'I percorsi intrecciati', 133.
17. Parigi, 'Commedie in rivista', 248. See also F. Bolzoni. 1984. *Quando De Sica era Mister Brown*, Turin: ERI, 8.
18. L. Micciché. 1991. 'Il cinema italiano sotto il fascismo: elementi per un ripensamento possibile', in Argentieri, *Risate di regime*, 37–63, 42.
19. Ibid., 42.
20. Parigi, 'Commedie in rivista', 225–26.
21. Quoted in ibid., 226.
22. Ibid., 235.
23. *Cinema*, 25 September 1940. Quoted in ibid., 244.
24. A. Farassino. 1992. 'Camerini, au-delà du cinéma italien' in Farassino (ed.), *Mario Camerini*, Locarno: Yellow Now, 19.
25. V. De Grazia. 1994. *How Fascism Ruled Women: Italy 1922–1945*, Berkeley: University of California Press, 204.
26. Parigi, 'Commedie in rivista', 239.
27. M. Corsi. 1942. *Maschere e volti: sul palconscenico e in platea*, Milan: Ceschina, 81.
28. Ibid., 85.
29. G.C. Castello. 1957. *Il divismo: mitologia del cinema*, Turin: ERI, 402.

30. L. Toeplitz. 1964. *Ciak a chi tocca*, Milan: Edizioni Milano Nuova, 113.
31. G. Vene. 1982. 'La canzone e il cinema', *La canzone italiana*, no. 10, Milan: Fabbri, 109–20, 116–17.
32. A. Farassino. 1992. 'Il Signor Vittorio: un'interpretazione dell'octologia De Sica-Camerini' in L.Micciché (ed.), *De Sica: autore, regista, attore*, Venice: Marsilio, 107–14, 109.
33. Brunetta, *Cent'anni*, 9; S. Vicini. 2008. *Le stelle del duce*, Bresso: Hobby & Work, 126.
34. Landy, *Stardom Italian Style*, 48.
35. S. Sollima, 'Vittorio De Sica', *Cinema*, 30 January 1949, 108.
36. M. Soldati. 2006. *Cinematografo*, Palermo: Sellerio, 419–20.
37. F. Monteleone. 1976. *La radio italiana nel periodo fascista*, Venice: Marsilio, 115.
38. T. Kezich. 1992. 'Servitore di due padroni' in Micciché, *De Sica*, 3–18, 13.
39. M. Mercader. 1978. *La mia vita con Vittorio De Sica*, Milan: Mondadori, 73.
40. Corsi, *Maschere e volti*, 81.
41. A. Farassino, *La Repubblica*, 15–16 April 1979. Quoted in Valentini, 'Modelli, forme e fenomeni di divismo', 125.
42. S. Della Casa. 1990. *Mario Mattoli*, Florence: Il Castoro/La Nuova Italia, 7.
43. R. Branca. 1943. *Polemiche sul cinema*, Bergamo: I.P.L., 163.
44. Ibid., 158.
45. A. Spicer. 2001. *Typical Men: The Representation of Masculinity in Popular British Cinema and Society*, London: I.B. Tauris, 8–9.
46. R. Romano. 1997. *Paese Italia: venti secoli d'identità*, Rome: Donzelli.
47. Landy, *Stardom Italian Style*, 53.
48. G. Calendoli. 1967. *Materiali per una storia del cinema italiano*, Parma: Maccari, 166.
49. Ibid., 166–67.
50. Ibid., 165.
51. Valentini, 'Modelli, forme e fenomeni di divismo', 121.
52. Ibid., 120.
53. Bolzoni, *Quando De Sica*, 18.
54. Ibid., 5.
55. Ibid., 25.
56. Steno, 'Divi sottaceto: De Sica, ovvero l'amoroso qualunque', *Fotogrammi*, 10 August 1946, 3.
57. Landy, *Stardom Italian Style*, 53.
58. M. Doletti. 1929. *Cinematografo*, Bologna: Poligrafici Riuniti, 64–65.
59. Calendoli, *Materiali per una storia*, 172.
60. Anon. 1938. 'Sorridere', *La Pubblicità d'Italia* 11(15–16), September–October, 4–8.
61. C. Berneri. 1966. *Mussolini: psicologia di un dittatore*, Milan: Azione Commune (first published 1937), 30.
62. L. Passerini. 1991. *Mussolini immaginario*, Rome–Bari: Laterza, 132.

63. Valentini, 'Modelli, forme e fenomeni di divismo', 117.
64. M.G. Sarfatti. 1926. *Dux*, Milan: Mondadori, 63.
65. Valentini, 'Modelli, forme e fenomeni di divismo', 118–19.
66. The footage is among the extras featured on the RHV 2007 DVD edition of *Tempo Massimo*.
67. S. Ricci. 1992. 'Camerini et Hollywood' in Farassino *Mario Camerini*, 36–46, 41–42.
68. Bolzoni, *Quando De Sica*, 15.
69. V. De Sica, 'Il mio sorriso non basta a dir le mie virtù', *Scenario*, May 1940, 250–51.
70. V. De Sica. 1942. 'Volti nuovi nel cinema' in Direzione generale del cinema (ed.), *Cinema italiano anno XX*, Rome, 37–38.
71. V. Brancati. 1950. *I fascisti invecchiano*, Milan: Longanesi, 96.
72. G. Bottai. 1982. *Diario 1935–1944*, ed. by G.B. Guerri, Milan: Rizzoli, 163, 278. For Tono Zancanaro's grotesque sketches of a Duce-like figure, Il Gibbo, see R. Cremoncini et al. (eds.). 2010. *Against Mussolini: Art and the Fall of a Dictator*, London: Estorick Collection, 32–35.
73. Bolzoni, *Quando De Sica*, 36.
74. Mercader, *La mia vita*, 17.
75. Vicini, *Le stelle del duce*, 139.

7

Everybody's Fiancée
Assia Noris

Of all the female stars of the period, none embodied the idea of the conventional girl-next-door more fully or consistently than Assia Noris. While there was no shortage of young actresses playing subdued, shy, family-oriented young women, only a handful were fortunate enough to develop a screen persona that was reinforced over time in a series of lead roles in films which resonated with the public. With her doll-like features and blonde hair, exotic accent and ready tendency to tears, Noris appealed to young men who saw her as an ideal fiancée, to older women who wanted to mother her, and to girls for whom she was, if not a role model, then a projection of certain traits, hopes and limitations that were familiar to them. Her busy screen manner – often encapsulated in fast, high-pitched speech (in part an effect of the prevailing sound technology), brisk body movements, elaborate curled or wavy hair styles, innumerable little hats, and personalised costumes – provided a counterpoint to, and distraction from, the conventional nature of her characters' attitudes, values and behaviour.

Born in St Petersburg to a Russian mother and a Swedish father, in a year that is variously indicated as 1912 (*Enciclopedia dello Spettacolo*) or 1919 (her own claim),[1] Noris had no family connections to Italy. When she was still very young, she moved with her parents to the south of France, where she was brought up in an environment of Russian émigrés. Her entry into the world of Italian cinema was as casual as that of any of the actresses of the time, if not more so. Spotted by the producer Giuseppe Amato sitting with her mother while she took tea in the foyer of a Roman theatre – the two women had decided to sit out the show since neither understood Italian well enough to follow it – she was soon signed up and thrust before the cameras with only the barest minimum of preparation. The fact that Noris, who at the time of her discovery was known by her real name of Anastasia von Gerzfeld, was only in Italy at all because her parents had been invited to pay a visit to friends living in Naples adds a further element of chance to a star biography that was as romantic and mysterious as could be.

In fact, curiously, almost nothing was made of the actress's origins in promotional or press material. In contrast to Hollywood, where background elements were often mobilised in developing a specific identity and allure for an actor, Noris's foreignness was rarely mentioned and never played up. Her unusual Italian accent gave her away, of course, but, since she was a gifted linguist who knew four or five languages before she encountered Italian (Tullio Kezich remarked that no one ever understood precisely what her mother tongue was; to complicate matters, she claimed only to have learned Russian after moving to Rome),[2] it was a faint variation on the standard rather than a thick accent in the manner, say, of Greta Garbo's English (Kezich describes her as 'compensating with grace for ineradicable defects of diction'). To all intents and purposes Noris became naturalised as an Italian actress who was regularly and without problem cast in Italian parts. Her difference was merely an endearing quality that marked out her individuality. To explain this unusual phenomenon, account needs to be taken of the historical appeal of a series of actresses of Slavic extraction active in the silent era and, more particularly, of the cosmopolitan veneer that was an integral feature of Italian cinema in the era of Pittaluga's Cines and which persisted through the 1930s and beyond. Noris could plausibly play the parts of foreigners in films set either in Italy or in some foreign context such as France, Hungary, Russia or the United States. In fact, her first role was as a young American in *Tre uomini in frak* (Three Lucky Fools, Mario Bonnard, 1933), the first film to star two idols of Neapolitan popular theatre, Eduardo and Peppino De Filippo.

What did Amato see in the young girl who, if her own account is true, was aged no more than twelve or thirteen when he noticed her in Rome? Certainly, the producer saw something that struck him sufficiently for him to go to considerable lengths to persuade the girl's mother to allow her to make a film. Amato left no account but it is not difficult to guess that his eye would first have been drawn by her fair hair and the porcelain perfection of her features. Her face was slightly flat, her forehead wide and high, her eyes large and lively, and her smile broad. An expert could see immediately that she had the type of looks that would photograph well. In life, she probably had something of the look of a lollipop, with a head that was slightly larger than her diminutive body warranted. But, as Jib Fowles has argued, this is exactly the sort of physical proportion that many screen actors have.[3] In addition, Amato may have seen the future actress conversing animatedly with her mother. Indeed, the sound of a foreign conversation may have caught his attention first. Noris would have struck him as a lively, curious adolescent, with an intrinsic vitality that could potentially be captured by movie cameras.

A colourful figure who would remain active in Italian cinema into the 1960s, Amato gave Noris a new surname and also her second film role, this time as the lead actress, in *La signorina dell'autobus* (The Young Lady on the Bus, Nunzio Malasomma, 1933). However, it would be the encounter with Mario Camerini that would determine the trajectory of her screen career and lay the basis for her emergence as a star. The director had made a number of features and scored a big hit with *Gli uomini, che mascalzoni!* (Men, What Rascals!, 1932) when he first worked with her on *Giallo* (Mystery, 1933), a loose adaptation of an Edgar Wallace novel in which Noris plays a society bride who suspects her husband of plotting to kill her. Although Camerini, who was born 1895, was around twenty to twenty-five years older than Noris, he made her his wife as well as his protégée, and for some eight years (until they divorced in San Marino in 1942) they constituted a solid professional cinematic couple who worked both together and with others.

Camerini is often bracketed together with Alessandro Blasetti, the two men being widely recognised as the most talented Italian directors of the

Fig. 7.1 A stylised Assia Noris on the cover of women's magazine *Piccola*. The caption describes her as the 'number one example of photogenic charm'. (Author's own collection)

period – those who contributed most to the development of professional standards of film-making in Italy. The two shared little else, however, since Blasetti was for much of the 1930s a convinced Fascist and the author of some notable propaganda films, while Camerini was never aligned with the regime and only, under pressure, made one propaganda film (*Il grande appello*, 1936). Camerini developed a specific poetic that it would not be correct to label anti-Fascist but which was sufficiently distant from the rhetorical emphases of the regime for critics even to have seen him as a competitor with Fascism for ownership of the particular spirit and character of the petite bourgeoise.[4] 'Camerini the petit bourgeois', 'the confessor of the petite bourgeoisie' and 'the poet of the simple people' are a few of the epithets that Alberto Farassino notes have been applied to him, even though the director was born into a wealthy Roman family and lived for a time at the prestigious Hotel Excelsior.

Five films in particular established the director's reputation in this sense: *Gli uomini, che mascalzoni!*, *Daro' un milione* (I'll Give a Million, 1935), *Ma non é una cosa seria* (But It Isn't Serious, 1936), *Il signor Max* (Mister Max, 1937) and *I grandi magazzini* (The Big Store, 1939). Noris appeared in four of these taking the parts, respectively, of a circus wardrobe mistress, a socialite, a maid and a shop assistant. In addition, she made four other films with Camerini. *Batticuore* (Heartbeat, 1939), *Centomila dollari* (One Hundred Thousand Dollars, 1940) and *Una romantica avventura* (A Romantic Adventure, 1940) are films that in certain cases can be compared to the first five but which are also different due to their explicit foreign or period setting, or general lack of realism. Noris's own roles were sometimes of the same type (a telephonist in *Centomila dollari* for example), but not always – she played a poor girl turned society thief in *Batticuore*. Their final film together, *Una storia d'amore* (A Love Story, 1942), was a melodrama that had only superficial traits in common with the rest of the director's oeuvre.

The first five films mentioned above all starred Vittorio De Sica and therefore they have been discussed in Chapter 6. Noris's roles in the four in which she co-starred were not equal to De Sica's in terms of the amount of screen time or quantity of lines. Although she played the main romantic interest in all except *Ma non é una cosa seria*, she was essentially a supporting actress. Only in *I grandi magazzini* did her status and function in the film broadly equate to that of De Sica. This does not mean that it is mistaken to give emphasis to her contribution to the films or indeed that this was minor. On the contrary, it is significant that her contribution was so determinant given the limited nature of her parts. The point can be made by comparing Noris to Lia Franca, the actress who co-starred in the first of the series, *Gli uomini, che mascalzoni!* In the film, the petite, dark-haired actress plays Mariuccia, the daughter of a taxi driver who works first in a parfumerie and then at a perfume stand at the Milan trade fair. Despite some personal grace and the occasional spirited gesture, she is an anonymous presence, both visually and in terms of the film's narrative development. Barely distinguishable from the other female employees in the film, she is a foil for De Sica who brings no extra quality to her part or allure to the film.

On the face of it, as a type Noris was little different to Franca. The names of her characters are often diminutives (like Mariuccia – from Maria) such as Loletta, Angioletta, Lauretta, Arlette and so on. Moreover, she often plays dignified working girls of humble origins. Although her characters may occasionally transgress (though there is invariably an explanation for this, such as the poor girl who has been sucked into thieving by an unscrupulous Fagin character in *Batticuore*) they are always revealed to be fundamentally honest and moral. A happy ending is de rigueur. Yet Noris is always memorable in her films. No one could say that she was not a focus of visual interest. She was not an actress of any great range or subtlety – although she could bring different registers to roles – but through her appearance and screen presence she made ordinary, bland girls interesting and compelling. In part this was due to her particular photogenic qualities. These did not depend on the talents of any one cinematographer, since she worked with many different ones, although three of her Camerini films were shot by Anchise Brizzi ('I adored Brizzi because he was really talented', she later said).[5] There seems to have been a general understanding by directors, cinematographers, and surely Noris herself, that her features and hair could take a high degree of luminosity. She is often bathed in light and untroubled by shadow or complexity. Even though her parts are ordinary, she never looks as ordinary as she really should do. The actress's voice, moreover, apart from her distinctive pronunciation of Italian, was shrill and a little pathetic.

In addition, a comment on hair, make-up and costume is required. Noris's honey blonde (and occasionally platinum) hair was often kept quite short, brushed off the face, and waved in the manner that was fashionable in the 1930s. Only in period set films, such as *Un colpo di pistola* (A Pistol Shot, Renato Castellani, 1941) in which she plays a nineteenth-century Russian aristocrat with long curls, did she wear long hair. She did not innovate in this area so much as personalise existing trends. The same applies to her make-up. Her eyebrows are often highly plucked and arched well above her eyes, in the conventional international film star manner.

A wide variety of costume designers worked on Noris's films and thus the stylistic continuities can be said to be related more to the star persona of Noris than to the requirements of each part, although there were continuities here too. Almost always, she is dressed in dark garments, whether they be an evening dress (*Giallo*, *Batticuore*) or simple workwear (*Il signor Max*, *I grandi magazzini*). These serve to remove her body from the visual centre and focus attention on her head and neck. This was both because – unlike say with the full-figured Paola Barbara, or the breezier and more casual Alida Valli – her figure was not part of her appeal, and to take the eye directly to the focus of her persona. The neck is then framed typically by a light-coloured collar, which may be stylish or simple, adorned with lace or a decorative accessory. Finally, more than any other actress of the period, hats of many different sizes, shapes and styles – many designed specifically for the actress – lent an individual, bizarre note. In his history of the hat, Colin McDowell notes that, in Hollywood, costume departments 'created hats for the screen goddesses that were designed more to express personalities than to fit the needs of the plot', adding that 'the more sophisticated the actress the smaller and simpler the hat has been'.[6] Although hats became a Noris trademark, and many were small, they were not an indicator of sophistication since the actress and her main constituency were young. Rather it may be said that, more than any other actress in Cinecittà, she understood how characters, and characters' moods, could be defined through their headwear. Cumulatively, hats added to the glamour of her screen persona.

There were several actresses who enjoyed wearing sumptuous costumes, and one or two, notably Vivi Gioi and Clara Calamai, who were regarded in some quarters as elegant – but only one other actress styled herself with

Fig. 7.2 Magazine advertisement for *Centomila dollari* (One Hundred Thousand Dollars), starring Assia Noris (top left) and Amedeo Nazzari (second from right, bottom row). (Author's own collection)

such meticulous consistency as Noris, and that was Elsa Merlini. After winning fame as the buoyant and bubbly secretary in *La segreteria privata* in 1932, Merlini made several other films, few of them of note. Her main medium in any case was theatre and it was in fact at one of her performances that Amato first spotted the future star. With her round face and taste for eccentric hats and accessories, Merlini forged an identity through a personal use of fashion that found no equivalents until Noris evolved her own distinctive, if less ostentatious, signature style.

In the films that made her famous, Noris's winsome characters are never threatening or challenging. They belong to a world of quite limited horizons and expectations, where young women knew their place and, even if they had a degree of economic independence, knew that they could not live as they chose. The maids and shopgirls she played are romantic and hopeful but they are not ambitious or forward. 'For Camerini I was always Lauretta. So much so that in every film I made with him I was called Lauretta', she told Francesco Savio in the 1970s, exaggerating somewhat. 'This Lauretta became a symbol for the Italian audience; I was the fiancée of everyone, Lauretta'.[7] They may seem confident and may speak up when wronged, but they are also inclined to shed tears, appear vulnerable and be subject to the tyranny of a family or employer. Perhaps for this reason, Noris was not a difficult actress to cast opposite. The art of casting was not well developed in Italy but the top stars for the most part could work easily with each other. This had to do not only with the fact that the film community was small and everyone knew everyone else, but with the fact that the variety of gender types was limited and the trajectories of each character were defined as much by social norms as plot. As Noris would later say, 'In Italy in those days there were no women who betrayed their husbands, there were no thieves, there were no suicides'.[8] The area where difficulties could arise was with other actresses. Not known as a generous colleague, Noris would often persuade cinematographers to give her the best treatment.[9]

Noris's leading men included De Sica, Amedeo Nazzari and Fosco Giachetti. The dynamic in each case was quite different, even though the latter two actors were interchangeable for some parts. With Giachetti, a gloomy and grumpy colleague concerned to look younger than his years, according to various testimonies there was no screen chemistry at all. Although in *Un colpo di pistola* (A Pistol Shot, Renato Castellani, 1942), a Dostoyevsky adaptation, the two actors play characters who are passionate about each other and separated by misunderstanding, there seems little spark between the frivolous Mascia and the serious Andrei. With De Sica, the screen combination is more successful, although there is an imbalance between the authenticity Camerini attributed to the lower-class characters the actor convincingly plays (having previously played society men in the theatre) and Noris's evident artificiality. Not by chance, the most successful pairing occurred in *Darò un milione*, in which De Sica only feigns poverty, as a rich man who seeks to be loved for himself, a goal he achieves when Noris's circus performer falls for him. Here the intriguing dynamic between the Noris extradiegetic star persona (exemplified in the traits mentioned above) and the diegetic inauthenticity of De Sica makes for a touching and affecting comedy. Curiously, this film, more than any other according to the actress, caused men to mistake her for her screen character and write offering to save her from the sordid world of the circus.[10] With Nazzari, with whom she made *Centomila dollari*, the pairing also worked well, even though the plot (resembling that of *Indecent Proposal*, in which a rich man seeks to buy a night of love with another man's wife, here presented simply as a dinner date) hinged on an economic gulf between the telephonist Lily and the millionaire Woods. What is lost on the plane of comedy was gained in terms of a scintillating interaction limited to relatively few scenes that were interspersed by others that were carried by each actor alone, and an active and colourful supporting cast (Woods's employees, Lily's doltish fiancé and her family). To render their scenes most effectively, Camerini took the unusual step of narrowing the conventional distance between the two protagonists for close-ups and shot/reverse shot sequences.[11]

In all her films she required the support of an upstanding young man who would lead her back on to the straight and narrow if she had strayed, through no fault of her own, or had been the object of attentions on the part of an alternative suitor. In the films with De Sica, misunderstandings delay the resolution of the happy ending, while in those with Nazzari and Giachetti there is a second male character to provide dramatic tension. In *Centomila dollari*, this is Lily's hapless fiancé, who finally wins her back after failing at first to impede the material overtures of Nazzari's millionaire. In *Un colpo di pistola*, Antonio Centa, a handsome actor with a lantern jaw who transmitted an arrogant appeal, wins her briefly before she is finally united with the honest and lugubrious Giachetti. For the public of the mid-1930s, De Sica and Noris seemed the ideal couple, the bearers of humble dreams and modest aspirations. Each in their own way incorporated sufficient elements of ordinariness into their persona to bridge the gulf between the screen and the stalls.

It has been said that Italians in general under Fascism were reduced to the status of children compelled or induced to look up to an omnipotent father figure. This was especially true of women who were directly subjected to patriarchal authority in the home and workplace as well as society at large. Denied independence of spirit or action, they could only find in some of the modern pursuits and activities that escaped traditional ideas a measure of autonomy and self-definition. This is one explanation for the proliferation of young teenage actresses in the cinema of the period. In another view, the perfect, happy, uncomplicated faces of actresses like Irasema Dillian, Vera Carmi and Adriana Benetti provided an escape from the masculine emphases of the regime and its rhetoric, and the hardships of everyday life. The innumerable girls' college comedies of the period provided the perfect vehicle for this sort of emotion.

If, as she later claimed – passport to hand – she was born in 1919, then Noris was aged just sixteen in 1935 and twenty-one in 1940. She was just one year older than Alida Valli. Yet, unlike the latter, she never appeared in a schoolgirl comedy, even though her strong point was light entertainment. It may be suggested that Noris was insufficiently candid an actress to persuasively play a girl of school age. There was something knowing and refined in her image that clashed with the well-scrubbed and natural appearances required of the innocent girls of comedies including *Ore 9, lezione di chimica* (9 O'clock Chemistry Lesson, Mario Mattoli, 1941), *Maddalena zero in condotta* (Maddalena, Zero for Good Behaviour, Vittorio De Sica, 1942) and *Giorno di nozze* (Wedding Day, Raffaele Matarazzo, 1942). Despite her age and the simple, conventional nature of her characters, Noris simply would not have looked right in a tunic. The main reason for this is precisely that element of excess or fashion that marked her femininity. She looked styled; she looked as though she had been out in the world, even if only as the maid of a society woman or a shopgirl. To that extent she did not project a sheltered virginal aura or a child-like quality even if her characters were clearly connotated as virgins.

To what extent therefore was Noris's screen persona sexualised? In the Italian cinema of the time there was little room for ambiguity between the good girls destined for marriage and the fallen women or femmes fatales who invariably met a bad end. Most actresses played one type or the other. The former were certainly objects of desire for male members of the public, who often wrote to them proposing marriage. Noris herself claimed that she engaged several secretaries to deal with her fan mail,[12] and by universal recognition she was, at the height of her fame, the 'national fiancée', *la fidanzata d'Italia*. So it would not seem that there was anything about her that might have disrupted this reputation. Nonetheless, it is pertinent to ask if the Noris screen image was sexualised more than her persona. In other words, was her visual image organised and projected in such a way that it invited a sexual engagement denied at the formal level?

Sex appeal in cinema consists of a mixture of natural and artificial elements. The testimonies of Hollywood still photographers like George Hurrell, who were responsible for the most alluring photographs of the stars, suggest that some actors were perceived to have a natural sexual energy that transpired from their persons and which could be captured with little autonomous input from the photographer.[13] Others, who lacked this quality or had it in smaller measure, could be made to look sexy though the use of poses, gestures, backdrops and textures, and shadow. For Hurrell, glamour consisted simply of an aura of seduction;[14] 'you can create glamour totally, I think, but a woman in our business generally had some quality of it', he added.

Interestingly, Noris, unlike most of the other stars of the period, does not appear to have been photographed by the leading Roman studio photographers of the day. If she was, the photographs did not circulate widely and have not featured in collections or exhibitions, suggesting at the very least that they were not successful. In contrast to Hurrell and his colleagues, Luxardo, Ghergo and others did not try to confer a standardised and transferable look on their subjects even if their repertoire of effects and their personal hallmarks were identifiable. They aimed to enhance the allure of specific subjects whose individuality was crucial to the overall result. They employed shadow and contrast not to 'sex up' photographs but rather to add depth, intensity and sometimes mystery to the actors who sat for them. Clearly Noris was not an actress who sought this sort of treatment. Unlike her colleagues Maria Denis, Alida Valli and Vivi Gioi, all of whom made their names in light comedy and then progressed to contemporary drama (the last-mentioned only after the war), she remained confined to light comedy and period pieces. Her image was light and bright, frothy and unreflective, in keeping with a face that, Ennio Flaiano once remarked in *Cinema illustrazione*, 'recalled the sweetness of Viennese candies'.[15]

In life, Noris was not quite the sweet innocent she repeatedly played on screen. The extreme precociousness of her progression to adult roles, long before she reached the age of majority, suggests a range of experience and maturity that went beyond her years. By the time she married Camerini in 1934, at age 16 if her own assertion of her birth date is true, she had already been through two extremely brief marriages (one to Roberto Rossellini, before he had any involvement with cinema) that had each lasted a matter of days. Both had been annulled. She would deny, in interviews given to the press many years later – by which time she was married for the fifth time – that she had ever been a femme fatale.[16] But she was without doubt an impulsive young woman of some temperament. The fussy artificiality of her screen image was in this sense illuminated not only by the work of cinematographers but by the vitality and energy of the actress herself. Despite her limited range, she usually received good notices for her work. The writer and literary critic Giacomo Debenedetti remarked of her performance in *Il signor Max*: 'the great actor, the thoroughbred actor – and this is the case of Assia Noris – always manages, even in the most fast-paced story, to make space and time for himself [sic], transcending in some way, the part he plays'.[17]

Camerini adored Noris and in his films he conferred on her the ideal image of the sentimental ingénue that went over so well with the public. The names he gave her characters (Lauretta and variations) evoked that of his mother Laura who died when he was aged three. Her sweetness was ratcheted up to the highest degree and her youthful radiance projected with care and skill. Only once, in *Darò un milione*, did he explicitly turn her into an erotic object, clothing her in a sparkling and brief two-piece costume for a circus scene. The intention was to win sympathy for a girl constrained to exhibit herself in the course of her employment but, at a time when such outfits were rare and regarded as extremely daring, the scene provoked wide controversy. Later, the actress attributed this episode to Cesare Zavattini, Camerini's collaborator on the film, and proudly labelled it 'the first sexy scene in Italian cinema'.[18]

The final film he made with her, poignantly entitled *Una storia d'amore*, marked the end of his enchantment. For the first and only time in her career, excepting the highly theatrical *Giallo*, Noris took a dramatic role as a wayward and ill-fated woman in trouble with the law, who finally dies in childbirth. Noris's character, Anna, first encounters her future husband, Gianni, while she is hiding from the police. She smokes heavily, has a cynical air and thinks nothing of accepting hospitality from a man she does not know. As the pair fall in love, she renounces her past and finds regular employment in a confectionary shop. Eventually she falls pregnant and marries Gianni. Once respectability has been won, the past comes back to haunt her and witnesses to her former life threaten to undermine her happiness. When one implies that he will reveal that she spent a year in gaol for theft, she kills him with the pistol with which Gianni had been issued by his employer. Her doting husband does not desert her and, when it transpires that giving birth may risk her life, he begs doctors to save her at the expense of her baby. The film concludes with Gianni taking his newborn daughter in his arms while the baby's face is superimposed with a ghostly image of his adored dead wife as she assures him that, through the infant, 'I have come back'. A routine melodrama belonging to the current begun by Mario Mattoli,[19] the film was entirely centred on Noris who in essence played two different characters (old Anna and new Anna) while the male lead was played by a debutant, Piero Lulli. Noris's dominance is underlined by the fact that, although her wrongdoing is punished indirectly in the narrative by death, her husband never invokes traditional morality to reprove or leave her. Anna has captured him as completely as Noris was accustomed to captivate spectators, and his attitude thus serves to sanction her star persona.

Others saw her differently to the besotted Camerini. Having achieved fame at an early age, Noris had some of the qualities of the spoilt child and was known for her temperamental behaviour on set. Possessed of aristocratic antecedents on both sides of the family, she sometimes behaved in a haughty manner and affected the airs of a princess (on occasion even claiming, falsely, that she was entitled to use this appellative. In interview in 1969 she claimed, only slightly more modestly, 'I was born a baroness').[20] Unsurprisingly, she denied this. 'I never had the impression being a diva', she told Savio. 'Never, because first of all my mother would not have allowed it. Then, I don't know, I am not a diva by nature; I am very simple.'[21]

Several of the men who worked closely with Camerini saw a less attractive side of her character, and realised that it could be harnessed effectively on screen. Renato Castellani's debut film, the Russian-set period drama *Un colpo di pistola*, saw her take the part of a young aristocrat who unwittingly torments her guardian, played by Giachetti, who, on account of his *in loco parentis* role, represses his love for her. Flirtatious, coquettish and impulsive, Mascia is fundamentally sweet but also elusive and infuriating. The role was interesting because it did not deny or subvert Noris's established type but rather turned up a hitherto minor aspect, namely coquettishness, at the expense of the dominant thread. A different approach was practised by Mario Soldati in his film *Dora Nelson* (1939). A remake of a French original, the film involved the actress playing two parts, which corresponded to the two aspects of her persona. In the first instance, she is the way Soldati saw her: a cinema actress, a star of Cinecittà, with a marked inclination for diva-like behaviour. On the other, she is a simple girl, a sweet-natured seamstress who bears a striking resemblance to the famous diva and who is engaged to step into her shoes when the former storms off set leaving the production team in the lurch. It was to Noris's credit that she went along with this joke, even though she surely knew that it was at her expense. Soldati, who never got on well with her, and whose favoured actress was Alida Valli, later asserted in interview that the film was his way of 'getting my own back on Assia Noris. I didn't have to correct her at all. When she plays the part of this irritating woman, she is perfect'.[22] As one of very few films to actually feature Cinecittà itself (including some real technicians and the head porter, Pappalardo) and the social dynamic of stardom, albeit within a confection marked by a strong dose of unreality and artificiality, it provided spectators with an insight into the mechanics of illusion, not only within cinema but more broadly in society.

Noris was a gifted performer, one who, without any formal training or moulding, demonstrated a natural aptitude for screen acting. Precisely because she was exceptional in this regard, noted the author of an article in *Cinema illustrazione* in October 1938,[23] there needed to be a more serious investment in the grooming of actresses, who were often selected for roles for reasons that had little to do with their professional qualities and were then left to improvise or work off instinct. It was the balance between her innate talent and the artificiality of her image that made Noris so perfect in the roles she played. Every medium, like every communicative order, brings to the fore certain people who in other media or in a different age would not prosper. Cinema, notoriously, required youth and beauty more than theatre, in which the close-up was lacking and make-up could more effectively rejuvenate the aging performer. In Italy, there were many screen actors who seemed to carry the theatre within them and others who brought to the screen the precious qualities of youth and beauty but nothing else. Noris appeared fully at home in cinema to the extent that it was difficult to imagine her existing outside the medium or a social world shaped by it.

Still photographs of the actress invariably show her with her hexagonal head tilted slightly forward, a beaming smile stamped on her face revealing an upper row of perfect white teeth, her eyes highlighted by false lashes and the sweep of a set of arched eyebrows. Her large clear brow conveys a sense of intelligence, honesty and health, while her richly painted lips, the lower more generous than the gently undulating upper one, betray a hint of sensuality. If Noris was sometimes described as 'doll-like' (her character Lauretta convincingly pretends to be a shop dummy in one surreal scene of *I grandi magazzini*) then it was because her large eyes and broad smile dominated her face (thus distracting attention from a less appealing nose). But it was also because the very perfection of her features when prepared for the camera seemed slightly unreal and fixed. She was often drawn in caricature because she was a gift to sketch artists. In addition, it may be added that there was something glassy and inhuman about her appearance. Her smile was probably the most radiant and winsome of all the actors in Cinecittà. It was not exactly a Hollywood smile, in the understood meaning of this term. This, Edgar Morin has noted, was a halfway house between an openmouthed laugh and contained smile;[24] it was a smile with the mouth sufficiently open to show the teeth. It was a smile that conveyed a sense of euphoria, of complete contentment and even a hint of Utopia. It was the same smile that appeared in innumerable advertisements and which invited the public to share in the happiness that the stars seemed to have manufactured and patented. No Italian smile of this period or even the postwar years (when commentators still noted the difference between the 'false' American smile and the 'true' Italian one) achieved this.[25] But there was something 'exterior' and constructed in Noris's smile that brought it into the same field of reference as the Hollywood smile. It did not appear to be the reflection of an inner moral character, personality or culture but rather to be a constructed appendage shaped and stamped on the face in order to achieve a positive reaction from the spectator. The smile does not descend from the eyes, which are cold rather than warm. It is a commercial smile, modern certainly and profoundly related to image.

Within Italy's Catholic culture, the images of the stars that fans bought and collected inevitably took on some of the features of the *santino*, or saint's image.[26] The chocolate cards that were the local equivalent of cigarette cards in the English-speaking world were of roughly the same size as the images of saints that the devout obtained in churches and places of pilgrimage. Some of the church's hostility to the star system derived precisely from the fact that it saw it as a competitor; the lives of stars were tending to substitute the lives of the saints in the formation of youth, and the photographic images of screen favourites were more immediately appealing than the illustration of holy martyrs. Noris was not an actress who ever attracted criticism for the roles she played on the part of the Church's stern cinema watchdogs. The fundamentally conventional nature of her persona outweighed any concern that may have arisen over her evident vanity or modernity. Yet the saintliness of her image was unequivocally material and secular.[27] There is nothing transcendental in the characters she played and they project no desires or torments that cannot be satisfied within the temporal world.

The single feature about Noris that first drew the eye of Italian spectators was her brilliant blonde hair. In a nation in which brown hair, whether darker or lighter in tone, was the norm, her fair locks singled her out like a light in the dark. Given the Church's long-established custom of depicting saints and Christ himself with fair hair, a practice that had had an impact on Italian poetry and painting from the Middle Ages, with Dante's Beatrice and Petrarch's Laura being described as fair long before Botticelli and the masters of Renaissance Florence produced a catalogue of fair beauties that would set standards for feminine and pictorial beauty for centuries, there was an automatic association of the fair with rarity and virtue, both constituent elements of established ideas of beauty. The cult of the fair was cultivated in literature and painting through the nineteenth and early twentieth centuries and it thus fed into the development of the idea of photogenic beauty. There would be several natural blondes in the Italian cinema of the interwar years; the most prominent included Polish-born Irasema Dilian and the half-Swedish Vivi Gioi. There were also some Italian dull blondes of northern appearance and some bottle blondes as and when the occasion demanded it. Of all of these Noris was arguably the most blonde, in the sense that the sentimental type she made her own was possessed of just that element of ethereality to seem, in the context of the range of meanings that can be generated by film, like a close cousin of spirituality. Noris, in short, was blonde on the inside and as such always deserved and always won her man (unlike Dilian and Gioi, for example, who lost out respectively to Adriana Benetti in *Teresa Venerdi* and to Lilia Silvi in *Dopo divorzieremo*).

The Fascist attitude towards the foreign legion of Cinecittà was ambiguous. On the one hand, it was a matter of prestige that foreign actors, directors and technicians came to work in Rome. Many hailed from countries that were allies and their role aided the export of films. On the other hand there was a certain irritation with the way the foreign became a fetish of Cinecittà. The foreign-set 'white telephone' films may have served a purpose and may have come about due to the difficulty of tackling certain themes in an Italian context, but they were never liked by the regime. There was a preference for national themes and stories that contributed to the national spirit and, as a reflection, for actors whose positive Italian qualities were apparent from their names, appearance and morality. Cosmopolitanism was regarded as an unfortunate legacy of the period when the Cines company dominated production in the 1920s and early 1930s. In consequence, there were drives to 'Italianise' actors' names and to influence casting. Fair hair as such never seems to have attracted official comment though, perhaps because Mussolini was known to be sensitive to the allure of blondes (his wife Rachele was fair) but also because there were other fair Italians. In aesthetic terms, Noris was not in any serious way a troubling presence; rather her difference was seen as an unavoidable attribute of the cinematic process.

In contrast to Camerini, Noris never took on positions that might be described as anti-Fascist. 'I was not anti-Fascist ... but neither was I Fascist. I understood nothing of politics then just as I don't now', she remarked in 1969.[28] But as a prominent star she was subject to certain attentions and expectations. She met Hitler when she was in Germany, sent by the Ministry of Popular Culture to discuss a possible contract with the UFA studio, and she recounted with pleasure the anecdote of when Mussolini stopped his car during a visit to Cinecittà to offer her his compliments. As a foreign-born actress she regarded herself as extraneous to certain domestic pressures even though she had no life or career outside Italy. This caused some conflict with the authorities, as did her refusal to adopt the Fascist-approved 'Voi' form of formal address after this became required, or to succumb to expectations that she would take out Fascist Party membership. As a result, according to her own account, she was subjected to disciplinary measures on several occasions.[29] She never appeared in any military or propaganda films although it is not known whether this was because she refused such invitations or, more likely, because she was never cast in them.

Noris earned well and lived the life of a star. She had a weakness for fur coats and collected a remarkable quantity of them. For some of her audience, excess of this sort only contributed to her appeal. But she did not indulge demands for publicity, for news about her private life or domestic circumstances. A perusal of the leading film and women's magazines of the period reveals no interviews, no photographic features and precious few mentions outside the context of reviews and film-specific articles. This ostentatious privacy on the part of so popular a figure attracted comment. In *Cinema*, Gianni Puccini (writing under the transparent pseudonym Puck) remarked that fans found it impossible to find out anything about her childhood or mysterious family origins.[30] She may have been an extreme case but she was not unique. 'It is strange but we know more precise things about the far-off actresses of Hollywood than we do about those of the very close Cinecittà', Puccini added. Little had changed by the following March, when a journalist on *Film* was obliged to invent a series of musings on Noris to print in place of the envisaged interview. The article, which announced that 'Assia prefers to live her quiet and peaceful life far removed from any journalistic indiscretions or any form of publicity', was entitled 'Discussions with the Ghost of Assia Noris'.[31]

The exotic quality that she brought to cinema was not pronounced but it was sufficient to distinguish her from actresses who much more evidently belonged to a national typology of beauty and behaviour. While the darker beauties of Cinecittà, such as Maria Denis, Alida Valli, Doris Duranti and

Luisa Ferida, were blessed with official and popular approval, the foreign blondes brought an air of something different – like an imported aperatif or a poster advertising holidays abroad – to the Italy of autarky. 'For men, the fascination of the Slav still functioned', wrote the veteran critic Pietro Bianchi years later; 'that ardent little face, that blonde hair, those ankles that were a touch too big' struck home. 'Even her uncertain Italian seemed pleasant, and certain syrupy ways likeable'.[32] She was not an exceptional beauty by any standard, but an ordinary beauty whose pretty looks were rendered special by being out of context and through the alchemies of the photographic and cinematic processes. 'I have never been a great beauty, but I have always had five lire worth of charm', she confessed to an interviewer in 1981.[33]

In *Film* magazine's reflection, something further can be gleaned about her appeal:

> The audience, when it goes to the cinema, would perhaps not be able to define you precisely. People go to the cinema and when they see you on the screen they feel a special attraction to you; it is a strange link that you send back, like a reflection, from the screen canvas to them, due to which you are easily understood and admired. Because in your performances you are above all human and a woman in the smallest particulars, in the slightest expressions, in the shades of hinted and unsaid meanings.
>
> You are not a female type like the majority of actresses but something more human, true and logical, as a result of which the audience understands you immediately from your first lines and likes you straight away. While in others it 'sees' a woman, in you it 'feels' a woman. A simple woman, even if sometimes a bit mannered just as many girls can be that one encounters in life, perhaps the most beautiful, who lives her part with joy in her eyes, held back and then freed by her open, smiling lips, like a sigh, and with that little hand raised unsure whether it is so to act in defence or to give offence.
>
> Well done, little Assia. The pubic likes you because you do not descend from on high, or hail from another world, but because you go to meet it smiling, on the same street, with your hand stretched out. When girls see you on the screen, they are content because they see in you something of themselves, even if improved, and the young men feel a shudder of inexplicable contentment down their backs because they see in you the realisation of their type, even if a bit idealised, and when they step out of the cinema they will look around to catch sight of and approach a girl like you, ready to give flight if they follow them, ready to stop and look round with a worried look when they realise that you are not tailing them any more. Everyday tears, smiles, small dreams, disappointments and fears – that is what you represent for the Italian public.

There can be no doubt about her popularity. 'It was madness, every day I used to receive marriage proposals, everyone wanted to marry me. During the war, for example, everyone wrote me letters. I received around four to five hundred per day. It was massive; I had three secretaries to deal with it all'.[34]

Noris has been labelled 'the popular heroine, the symbol of an entire era, that of the clerks who dreamed of earning a thousand lire per month'.[35] 'With her romantic and ingenuous air' she has been seen as having contributed decisively to a cinema whose primary role was to keep people in the dark, 'with their eyes closed and ears blocked'. She was the heroine of a cinema that 'spoke as little as possible of serious matters and invented stories with which to distract the attention of spectators'. The fact that many of her films – notably those directed by Camerini – were set not in remote, unidentified or artificial locations but in places that seemed to be immediately familiar, meant that she could act as a vehicle of fantasies that were anything but false. The lower-middle classes constituted the bulk of the filmgoing audience in the 1930s and early 1940s, and the content of films was determined as much by their tastes and values as by the imperatives of the regime. In the poll which Vittorio Mussolini's magazine *Cinema* conducted in 1939–40 to determine the popularity rating of Italian actresses, Noris topped the ranking with 9,250 votes, some 260 more than the second-placed Alida Valli, who, however, had yet to make the films that would turn her into the national favourite. 'I was the best paid, the most adored', Noris later said, claiming that a producer merely had to have her signed up and he could get a bank to finance his film.[36] Yet, she insisted, 'you could not have everything like today, there wasn't all this stardom'. The scale of her success, she was keen to show, was huge, even though she well knew that it would not outlive the fall of the regime.

Notes

1. For Noris's own extended comment on the issue, see O. Ripa, 'Ho perso il mio piccolo angelo', *Gente*, 14 August 1969, 52. The article is the first installment of a two-part interview with her.
2. T. Kezich. 2006. 'Gli attori italiani dalla preistoria del divismo al monopolio' in O. Caldiron (ed.), *Storia del cinema italiano*, Vol. 5, 1934–39, Venice–Rome: Marsilio/Edizioni Bianco & Nero, 383–403, 396.
3. J. Fowles. 1992. *Starstruck: Celebrity Performers and the American Public*, Washington: Smithsonian, 32.
4. A. Farassino. 1992. 'Camerini, au-delà du cinéma italien' in Farassino (ed.), *Mario Camerini*, Locarno: Yellow Now, 11–35, 12–13.
5. F. Savio. 1979. *Cinecittà anni trenta*, Rome: Bulzoni, 844.
6. C. McDowell. 1992. *Hats: Status, Style and Glamour*, London: Thames & Hudson, 76 and 89.
7. Savio, *Cinecittà anni trenta*, 836.
8. Quoted in F. Faldini and F. Fofi (eds). 1979. *L'avventurosa storia del cinema italiano: raccontata dai suoi protagonisti, 1935–1959*, Milan: Feltrinelli, 13.

9. L. Pellizzari and C. Valentinetti. 1995. *Il romanzo di Alida Valli*, Milan: Garzanti, 46.
10. C. Mazza, 'Già a 12 anni avevo gli italiani ai miei piedi', *Eva*, 14 August 1969, 48.
11. S.G. Germani, 1992. 'Entretien avec Mario Camerini' in Farassino, *Mario Camerini*, 134.
12. Savio, *Cinecittà anni trenta*, 833.
13. See S. Gundle. 2008. *Glamour: A History*, Oxford: Oxford University Press, 190–91.
14. J. Kobal. 1993. *George Hurrell: Hollywood Glamour Portraits*, London: Schirmer, 15.
15. E. Flaiano, 'Una romantica avventura', *Cinema illustrazione*, 13 November 1940, reproduced in Farassino, *Mario Camerini*, 176.
16. Savio, *Cinecittà anni trenta*, 833.
17. G. Debenedetti, 'Il Signor Max', *Cinema*, 10 December 1937, reproduced in Farassino, *Mario Camerini*, 171.
18. Ripa, 'Ho perso il mio piccolo angelo', 54.
19. On the melodramas of the 1930s and 1940s, see L. Pellizzari. 1999. 'Melodramma e strappalacrime nel cinema dei telefoni bianchi', in O. Caldiron and S. Della Casa (eds), *Appassionatamente: il melò nel cinema italiano*, Turin: Lindau.
20. Ripa, 'Ho perso il mio piccolo angelo', 52.
21. Savio, *Cinecittà anni trenta*, 833.
22. Quoted in E. Monreale. 2006. *Mario Soldati: le carriere di un libertino*, Bologna/Genoa: Cineteca di Bologna/Le Mani, 255n.
23. A. Franci, 'Interpretazione della bellezza', *Cinema illustrazione*, 26 October 1938, 3–4.
24. E. Morin. 1972. *Les stars*, Paris: Seuil, 59.
25. See S. Gundle. 2007. *Bellissima: Feminine Beauty and the Idea of Italy*, New Haven and London: Yale University Press, 92–103.
26. See E. Detti. 1989. *Le carte povere: storia dell'illustrazione minore*, Florence: La Nuova Italia, for a selection of images.
27. For a general reflection on this issue, see Morin, *Les stars*, 65–97.
28. Ripa, 'Ho perso il mio piccolo angelo', 53.
29. Ibid., 54.
30. Puck, untitled article, *Cinema*, 10 December 1937, 10.
31. C.B., 'Colloqui con il fantasma di Assia Noris', *Film*, 26 March 1938, 5.
32. P. Bianchi, 'Un caro e domestico fascino slavo', *Il Giorno*, 13 August 1969, 17.
33. C. Silva, 'Riabbracciando Assia Noris', *La Domenica del Corriere*, 23 May 1981, 44.
34. Savio, *Cinecittà anni trenta*, 843.
35. G. Villa, 'Negli anni '40 era la fidanzata degli italiani', *Sorrisi e canzoni TV*, 27 July 1969, 34–35.
36. Savio, *Cinecittà anni trenta*, 844.

8

The Star as Hero
Amedeo Nazzari

In 1938 Amedeo Nazzari made the defining film of his career, the film that would establish him as Italy's leading male star and win an enduring place for him in the hearts of the country's women. *Luciano Serra pilota* (Luciano Serra, Pilot, Goffredo Alessandrini, 1938) was no ordinary film. It was the most successful and striking example of the type of propaganda that the Fascist regime regarded as most effective in the field of the feature film. It avoided any explicit reference to Fascism while making subtle and implicit connections to the social and political order. Organised and supervised by the Duce's son Vittorio, and directed by Goffredo Alessandrini, the film traces the story of the eponymous hero who, following a successful period of service as a pilot in the First World War, is reduced in the following years to taking tourists on air jaunts to scrape a living. He has lost the respect of his wife, whose pleas that he should accept a job in her father's company he rejects. When she leaves him, taking their son Aldo with her, he opts to emigrate and goes to work in a circus in Argentina, where his air stunts are given equal billing with a trained lion. Some years later, local businessmen try to persuade the fallen hero to undertake a sponsored marathon air journey from Buenos Aires back to Italy as a publicity ploy. He agrees only when he is struck by a fierce desire to see his son, who, now adult, has been accepted into the Italian air force. Using a false name, Luciano enrols in the legion of expatriate Italians engaged in the war in Ethiopia, hoping that this will bring him into contact with Aldo. When a train he is travelling on comes under fierce attack from Ethiopian forces, he learns that a plane piloted by the young lieutenant Serra has crash-landed nearby and that he is wounded. Luciano bravely reaches his long-lost son and manages to extract him from the plane and carry him to safety. In the course of this action, he is fatally wounded and, after sharing precious moments with his son, he dies. In the final scene, Aldo receives the gold military medal that has been awarded posthumously to his father.

Shown at the Venice Film Festival in 1938, the film was awarded, ex aequo with Leni Riefenstahl's *Olympia*, the Mussolini Cup (the prize would be renamed the Golden Lion after the war) for best film, while Nazzari took home the prize for best actor. It won universal favour among the Fascist elite, bringing Nazzari high praise from the Duce himself. 'Well done, Nazzari, you are the perfect incarnation of the new national hero: composed, rigorous, reflective, nobly generous and dismissive of danger', he is reported to have said.[1] Such enthusiasm was accompanied by an invitation to take out membership of the National Fascist Party, an invitation that the actor preferred to decline. 'Thank you Duce! I would prefer not to concern myself with politics, occupied as I am with ever more pressing artistic commitments', he is reported to have responded.[2] Unlike many of the films which the regime threw its weight behind, *Luciano Serra pilota* was a huge box office hit. Throughout Italy, people warmed to the story of the displaced war veteran who redeems himself and reclaims his paternal role shortly before dying a noble death. Most especially, they took to their hearts the actor who lent his handsome face and substantial physical presence to the role. For the very young, the adult Aldo, played by the fresh-faced Roberto Villa, was a more accessible idol, but women who were beyond their teenage years yearned for Nazzari, the courageous and no-nonsense man of action whose noble character was misunderstood by his wife. Men, for their part, found him enviable and admirable.

Fascist interest in the film was linked more to its theme than its cast. Aviation was regarded by the regime as a field with high propaganda value that dovetailed perfectly with its plans to turn Italy into a modern warrior nation. Actual investment in the sphere remained low, but on the symbolic plane the adventurous appeal of air endeavours was thoroughly exploited. The activities of pilots had been lauded during the war and were known to have a unique power to arouse mass interest and involvement. Mussolini himself was a keen pilot and the pioneer transatlantic team flights led by the leading Fascist Italo Balbo in 1930 and 1933 brought lustre to claims that, under a dynamic, forward-looking regime, Italy was achieving new primacies that rekindled past glories. What in the English-speaking world was termed 'air-mindedness',[3] which roughly meant a bold openness to new ideas and challenges as the corollary to a new and still mind-boggling means of transport, was in Italy given a distinctively Fascist inflection. Aviation served to fashion a pedagogy of the new nation. In fact, in the comic-strip version of the film that appeared in instalments in the Mondadori magazine *Paperino* (Donald Duck) in 1939, the ending was modified to remove the final dramatic twist. Instead of dying in the course of a tragically brief reunion with his son, Luciano's story ends with his triumphant arrival back in his homeland at the conclusion of his heroic solo transatlantic journey.[4] He becomes a sort of Italo Balbo in reverse.

Aviation was a popular theme in cinema that was encouraged by the Ministry of Popular Culture. Between 1938 and 1943 some nine feature films and several documentaries were made that used civil aviation or the air force as a backdrop or plot material. If *Luciano Serra* was the most successful of these it was due as much if not more to the performance of Nazzari as to the undoubted skill with which the action sequences were shot and the story structured. In the *Cinema* readers' poll of 1939–40, Nazzari emerged decisively as the most popular male actor, even though he had only made five previous films and still liked to think of himself mainly as a stage actor. The film itself scored highly and would remain in distribution for many years.

Nazzari's caution over cinema was justified by some early setbacks. In 1933 he lost out to Alberto Rabagliati in Twentieth Century Fox's contest to find a replacement Italian actor for Rudolph Valentino. The panel summarily dismissed him as too tall and thin, and too gloomy of expression, to fill the place of the dead idol. The Italian director Corrado D'Errico, who would eventually direct him in *I fratelli Castiglioni* (The Castiglioni

Fig. 8.1 Amedeo Nazzari, Italy's Errol Flynn or Clark Gable, was the top star in the country by 1939. (Author's own collection)

Brothers, 1937), gave him a screen test and found his cheekbones to be too high and too prominent to go over well on screen. 'Give it a miss, Amedeo, this is not for you. You are not cut out for the cinema', he is quoted as having said.[5] Moreover, the actor himself was known not to be satisfied with his first screen performances and was not planning to devote further time to cinema. However, there were some signs that, if they were not encouraging to Nazzari himself, did not go unnoticed by film professionals or the public.

His first film as lead actor, *Cavalleria* (Cavalry, 1936), also directed by Alessandrini, was a box office success that established some of the personal traits and themes that would be revisited and developed in *Luciano Serra, pilota* two years later. Nazzari plays a young cavalry lieutenant, Umberto Solaro, who will have a glittering career as a master horseman and trainer before abandoning the cavalry for the air force. The transition occurs after his horse dies following an accident in a competition. Solaro becomes a top First World War pilot before falling heroically in combat. The linear plot hinges on his devoted but unrequited love for Speranza di Frasseneto, a Piedmontese count's daughter, played by Elisa Cegani. She is drawn to him and their bond is sealed when she suggests the name Mughetto (Lily) for Solaro's horse after the two meet casually in a park in the opening scene. However, she is obliged to truncate their burgeoning love in order to enter a marriage with a rich Austrian baron that will save her family from financial ruin. After she disappears from his life, Solaro moves to Rome. Some years later he learns from Speranza's brother, who has joined his regiment, that she is in the capital. His hopes are revived only briefly when the pair meet again. After his death, his body is recovered and escorted by cavalry to its burial site in a field of lilies.

The film was seen at the time as a work of unusually high quality for Italian cinema. The intimate story is shot with ample use of close-ups, while spectacular elements including competition horsemanship, air combat and a high-society ball scene, all of which are filmed in full scale, give the film dramatic extension and strong visual interest. Nazzari was hailed for his interpretation of the romantic and heroic Solari, a man whose sense of loyalty and duty transpires from every pore. Press critics noticed the relative naturalness of his performance. 'Nazzari is a young actor, sober and devoid of any residual theatrical accents or gestures. To say that he talks and moves as though he were in his own home is the highest praise he is due', wrote the critic for the Milan paper *L'Ambrosiano*.[6] Writing in *Il Lavoro*, a Genoa paper, Guglielmina Setti dubbed him 'the most interesting male lead in our cinema'.[7] 'He possesses that secret, indefinable quality that we usually call personality that allows him to escape the constrictions of dull or not particularly decorative parts such as this pre-war cavalry officer with his moustache and outdated uniform', she continued.

Nazzari stands out physically for his height and vigour, and morally for his inflexible devotion. Some key elements of his physical appeal were established here, including a moustache that he would never abandon except in the role of the Renaissance hooligan Neri in *La cena delle beffe* (The Jester's Supper, Alessandro Blasetti, 1941). Thick wavy hair, here worn plastered down and combed back, broad shoulders, an upright, athletic posture (enhanced by a military uniform), controlled bodily movements and minimal hand gestures, warm eyes and an aura of quiet strength were established as signifiers of his screen persona. His exemplary character is emphasised by his white horse (all other horses in the film are of darker shades). An establishing shot not only introduces him astride the shortly-to-be-named Mughetto, but which is low angle, positioning the spectator at the level of Speranza and her family; and there is an absence of scenes of an informal nature, save those in which his undying love for Speranza (before and after her marriage) is developed.

The character has a backward-looking, almost nostalgic quality to him. He is a man of the old school, a one-woman man with strong and unwavering feelings and a pronounced sense of duty, who has little time for frivolity or amusement. The use during the opening credits of the same shots that conclude the film, of cavalry lined up before a field a lilies, announces the fact that he is doomed. Yet this sense of being out of time is balanced by a ferocious engagement with the present that is signalled by his passage from the cavalry to aviation; the chivalrous tradition is reinvented in the modern era through the application of technology and the willingness of men of spirit to preserve a valued sense of nobility.

The coverage received by some of the pilots of the First World War such as the late Francesco Baracca, Italy's top air ace, whose actual career trajectory formed the model for Solaro's fictional one, suggested to the Fascists that aviation possessed a pedagogical potential on several levels. The noble death in the service of the fatherland, that united Solaro and Serra, was accorded high value in the Fascist view of the world. In the rituals of its political religion, martyrs were regarded as living on in the memory and patrimony of the national community,[8] and the calling out of their names on ceremonial occasions was met with the orchestrated response 'Presente!' Thus the sacrifice of the two characters played by Nazzari resonated with audiences on an emotional level and in their eyes turned the actor into the guardian of their spirits.

An anecdote that was recounted in the press on numerous occasions in later years by the actor himself gave an idea of how Nazzari became aware of this. In 1938 the actor was enjoying his new-found fame and spending his nights carousing in Rome. One evening he took cocaine for the first (and, he claimed, only) time, in a quadruple dose. He seemed literally to go mad, he later said, bursting into more than one night spot, punching customers and smashing furnishings, all the while announcing that he would pay for everything. He loaded his car with women, only to dump them in the middle of Rome. Towards dawn, still in a state of euphoria, he acted out a solo march down the imperial route from the Colosseum to Piazza Venezia, where he began to remove his clothes beneath Mussolini's balcony. When he was down to his underwear, a passer-by recognised him and exclaimed, 'What! You, Luciano Serra, get up to these things?' Full of shame, Nazzari gathered his discarded clothes and went home to bed. 'What struck him in the astonishment of the passer-by', wrote journalist and author Patrizia Carrano, 'was not the irreverent gesture he had made towards Fascism ... so much as the fact that he, the spotless hero, had almost been caught without his underpants'.[9]

From that moment on, Nazzari became aware that many filmgoers mistook him for the parts he played, and even those who did not still expected him to maintain faith in his personal conduct with the ideal of the noble heroes who he brought to life on screen. For a young unmarried actor of not much more than thirty (he was born in 1907), who earned well, enjoyed the pleasures of life and found his closest friends among the artistic and theatrical circles of the capital, this was a tall expectation. However, it was one that Nazzari took to heart. With just a small number of exceptions, all the roles he played in his career before the fall of Fascism in 1943, as well as those he played afterwards, conformed to the same basic type. He rejected parts that departed from the positive template or which in some way detracted from his established screen persona. Consciously and steadily, through role after role, he was configured as a model and an example, an ideal figure who embodied not just the hopes of a film industry that was being reborn but of a nation that in the eyes of many of its citizens had been forged through the efforts of great and exceptional men. Moreover, never again did his private conduct result in scandal. Indeed he cast a veil over his entire private life, only lifting it when he married, at the age of fifty, in 1957.

Numerous Italian commentators have remarked on the different facets of the Nazzari persona. His generosity of spirit, nobility, sense of justice, respect for tradition, and loyalty have been analysed by those who have sought to explain the appeal of an actor whose popularity was as strong in the postwar years as in the 1930s, and as strong ten years after his death in 1979 as it was during the final stages of his acting career.[10] The only issue of controversy concerns the extent to which the model of Italian he proposed was specifically Fascist or not. In his memoirs, Luigi Freddi claimed part of the merit for building Nazzari up,[11] while, for Gian Piero Brunetta, the actor was seen as 'the Mussolinian hero par excellence' (albeit 'unjustly').[12] Giuseppe Gubitosi, by contrast, while acknowledging the 'complementary nature – within the collective imagination – of the myth of Mussolini and the personality of Nazzari',[13] prefers to highlight certain differences between the actor's persona and the man who was the primary embodiment of the 'New Italian'. Nazzari was 'gentle and delicate towards women whereas Mussolini was brutal and hard'; he showed 'respect for women, where Mussolini was anti-feminist and cultivated a deep disrespect for women'; he showed 'a propensity for understanding … while Mussolini was peremptory … and incapable of listening'; he exhibited 'transparency and openness of character where Mussolini was closed and mysterious; commitment where Mussolini was elusive; humility where Mussolini was haughty and authoritarian'.[14] These differences, Gubitosi argues, were 'opportune' since 'the star figure and characters of Nazzari were not intended to correspond to the figure of the chief of Fascism, but to the masses that the chief wanted to form and guide'. These qualities, he continues, not only rendered the Italians easy to manipulate; they showed that the potential was there to mould the national character along the lines the Fascists envisaged. The patriotism that was a hallmark of all Nazzari's characters – and a key feature of the plot of many of his contemporary and modern historical films – along with his sense of authority, was the guarantee that the values he stood for could be channelled into a palingenetic project of collective national re-foundation.

Gubitosi's argument has enriched the debate about the linkage between the Nazzari persona and Fascism. However, while plausible, it may be disputed in certain respects. First of all, Mussolini's public image in the 1930s and early 1940s was not at all as he describes it. Little or nothing was known outside senior Fascist and government circles about Mussolini's womanising and disrespect for women, inability to listen, moodiness and so on. In the public imagination, the dictator was authoritarian to be sure, but he was also painted as a family man and a man of the people who could mix easily with simple people. He enjoyed dialogue with the crowds during rallies, was a hard worker for the national cause and a decisive leader who invariably knew what was best. Off-duty pictures and newsreels portrayed him as an elegant man and an athletic sportsman. By the same token, Nazzari's screen character consisted of elements additional to the indisputably positive ones that Gubitosi lists. He was often haughty and solitary, ill-disposed to conversation or reflection, inflexible in his ideas and responses to people, traditionalist in his attitudes to women, occasionally bullying (although his exaggerated performance as an unsympathetic lout in La cena delle beffe was unusual), short-tempered and self-centred. In short, although the number of outright propaganda films Nazzari appeared in was small (four or five, with some others containing anti-American and/or anti-British aspects), the relationship between the Nazzari character and the projected Fascist masculinity was one of overlap and coincidence as much as it was one of complementarity and contrast.

Nazzari, it has been said, represented a super-Italian; he was an Italian as Italians would have liked to be. They were happy to see themselves in him; men wanted to be him and women wanted their men to be like him. If, as Christopher Duggan has argued, there was a direct line between the ardent missionary patriotism of the founder of the Italian national movement, Mazzini, and Fascism,[15] then it should not be surprising that a character whose virtues seemed to pre-date Fascism and be rooted in the national culture should so easily prosper under – and due to – Fascism. Nor indeed, should it be surprising that such a figure would continue to enjoy popularity in the years after the fall of the regime, when new political forces presented themselves as the best inheritors of a national tradition that was not itself subjected to any critical evaluation at all.[16]

In order to get a better handle on Nazzari, it is necessary to focus on some aspects that have not hitherto received much attention. These include his characters' relations with women and family, their social class and extraction, their regional identification and their links to the rural world or otherwise. Consideration of these aspects leads inevitably into discussion of Nazzari's working methods and way of being a star. These may be regarded as crucial, and not secondary, contributors to the place he acquired in popular affections as well as the national star system. Nazzari was born in Cagliari, in Sardinia, and originally bore his father's surname of Buffa. He migrated to the mainland with his widowed mother and siblings at the age of six, and was sent to a Catholic boarding school in Rome. Curiously, a picture of him in a school group aged eleven shows him to be the only boy standing decisively,[17] with his arms crossed – a pose that, when found in a photograph of Mussolini at age fourteen (reproduced in the official biographies that proliferated from 1925) was widely taken as a sign of his dictatorial destiny.[18] He completed high school and began studying engineering at Rome University before abandoning his studies and embarking on a stage career that saw him work in a supporting capacity in the companies of some of the leading actor-managers of the day, including Annibale Ninchi, Ruggero Ruggeri, Marta Abba and Tatiana Pavlova, all of which performed modern and classical texts. It was while he was appearing in a drama with Pavlova at Rome's Argentina Theatre that he was spotted by Elsa Merlini and signed up for his first film, a Renaissance period drama entitled *Ginevra degli Almieri* (Guido Brignone, 1935).

Following his successful second film, *Cavalleria*, for which he demanded and received payment of 50,000 lire, he stepped up his film work, in keeping with both his growing popularity and the increasing productivity of the film industry. Soon, he established himself as a workhorse of Italian cinema. In 1937 he made three films, three in 1938, six in 1939, four in 1940, an astonishing eight in 1941 and seven in 1942, and four in 1943 in the period up to the fall of Mussolini in July. He was directed by twenty-three different directors, seven of whom worked with him more than once (Nunzio Malasomma and Camillo Mastrocinque both directed him three times). His female co-stars included all the leading names of the day, although it is the actresses with whom he made several films who may be considered his best partners: these were Lilia Silvi (five times), Alida Valli (four times),

Luisa Ferida (four times), Mariella Lotti (three times), Assia Noris (twice), Vera Carmi (twice) and Clara Calamai (twice). By far his most frequent male co- or supporting star was Osvaldo Valenti, who worked with him on no fewer than seven films. Paolo Stoppa is second-placed with five collaborations, but in his case he was only ever a member of the supporting cast, albeit usually a leading one. As will be seen in the case of Fosco Giachetti, Nazzari's only real challenger for the title of leading male film actor of the period, the construction of masculinity in the cinema of the period often passed through some form of conflict between alternative models. Curiously, there was a degree of ambiguity in this conflict in Nazzari's case that was absent in Giachetti's.

In his varied career, Valenti played every type of role; he was leading man in drama and comedy, charmer and villain; he took cameo parts, and was at home with classical and modern texts. Physically much slighter than Nazzari, and possessed of an irrepressible ironical expression and a Mephistofolian air, he was often cast as a sneak, a cheat, a cunning schemer or usurper. His snake-like manner threw the god-like perfection of Nazzari into sharp relief. Perhaps the reason Nazzari accepted to play the unsympathetic Neri in Blasetti's *La cena delle beffe* (against type and, perhaps for this reason, without moustache) was because, in the final scene, the lout, who has been tricked into killing his own brother by Valenti's bullied and vengeful character Gianetto, goes mad and thus wins the sympathy that had previously belonged to the victim of his brutish pranks. The fact that the relationship between the two characters has been seen by postwar critics as fundamentally a homosexual one (Neri the gay basher attacks the effeminate Gianetto to exorcise his own unconfessed inclinations) may not be relevant to a contextual interpretation of the film.[19] But it is noteworthy that the Catholic Cinema Centre dubbed the film 'a tangle of lust, brutality and libertinism ... not recommended for any category of audience'.[20] If Valenti takes on certain attributes of a female co-star in this and other films, as Gori alleges, it opens up a range of possible interpretations of the masculinity of the Nazzari persona. The intended one, to be sure, is that of rigid and straight virility as opposed to perverse deviations. But the installation of a diegetic interaction dictated by plot brings to the fore possible displacements or repressions. Overall, however, no matter how much Nazzari the actor enjoyed playing negative figures, or – one of his favourite roles – a wayward genius like Caravaggio (*Caravaggio, il pittore maledetto*, Goffredo Alessandrini, 1941), these off-beat performances tended, by the simple fact of their being exceptions, to reinforce the mainstream characteristics of his dominant persona.

Nazzari's films were set in a variety of periods, but the most common by far were the nineteenth and twentieth centuries. The actor appeared in eight dramas and literary adaptations set in the nineteenth century, four dramas set in the early twentieth century, and some twelve films of various genres set in contemporary times. In other words, his character was on the face of it more a modern and contemporary one than a historical one. In fact, as has been seen above, his modern films often had a nostalgic air to them and were informed by an older order of values. The implication was that the best aspects of the modern experience were rooted in the historical experience of the Italian people.

This point can be considered in relation to women and family. Gender relations under Fascism were more rigid than they had been before the establishment of the dictatorship, even though the degree of female emancipation in the late nineteenth and early twentieth centuries was very limited compared to northern Europe.[21] Quite strict control was maintained over female representations in the press, advertising and cinema. Examples of female leadership or vitality in cinema tended to be confined to traditional or established female roles (such as actress or singer) or were found in remote places or vaguely unreal contexts of a wholly female type (such as the boarding school). It is difficult of think of a single drama in which Nazzari starred in which he was not fundamentally a man alone. If he is married, as in *Luciano Serra pilota* or the period drama *I mariti (tempesta d'anime)* (Camillo Mastrocinque, 1941), there is a strong likelihood that his wife will misunderstand or misjudge him. Sometimes, as in the latter film, she will come to her senses before the end. Women are often petulant, superficial, misled and wrong-headed. In the cinema of the period, the homosocial world (typically a military or military-influenced one) is the dominant one. Men act, decide and determine what is to be given value. Families tend to be rooted and static while men travel and move (to go to war, to improve or to redeem themselves). While women's concerns may be voiced, they are only likely to count where they reinforce a male viewpoint or bring a new aspect to it. The utter inflexibility of Solaro's devotion to Speranza results, it may be said, from an inability to accept that she may decide (albeit against her own will) to adopt a course of action, and embrace a destiny, that is different to what he had envisaged. Nazzari's characters are often solitary; they undergo personal unhappiness and rarely have friends. The woodenness that was occasionally attributed to the actor was more obviously a feature of the characters he played. They are usually men of few words who move deliberately. However, they are capable of expansive gestures, such as when Solaro, briefly reunited with his lost love in Rome, on seeing a flower stall selling lilies in the Piazza di Spagna, is seized by emotion and exclaims to the seller, 'Prendo tutto!' (I'll take the lot!).

Rarely, if ever, were Nazzari's screen relationships based on equality of age and experience, and consequently he was usually partnered by actresses much younger than himself. He always named Alida Valli as his favourite screen partner, perhaps because she was so confident of her craft that she dismissed his efforts to coach her.[22] The actress was some thirteen years younger than him and often brought a girlish counterpoint to his solid maturity in the films in which they co-starred, including *Assenza ingiustificata* (Unjustified Absence, Max Neufeld, 1939), in which she played a child-bride, and the satire of film fandom *Apparizione*. Valli was a subtle actress whose characters were often modern and sometimes ambiguous in their morality. Their complexity complemented the simplicity of Nazzari's. The actor is invariably a paternal presence who takes the role of correcting and guiding a young wife or admirer. Lilia Silvi, who partnered him more than any other actress, was also younger. Their five films together are mostly comedies or light drama. In several they marry. There was an effective chemistry between the pair that went over well with the public; his solid security was well balanced by her exuberant mobility. But such was the disparity of size between the minute Silvi and the massive Nazzari, and very often also of social status – for example in *Scampolo* (Remnant, Nunzio Malasomma, 1941) where Silvi is an illiterate servant girl and he is an engineer – that the type of equality that marked American screwball comedies or, in a different way, the French comedies of the period, was absent. Nazzari's least favourite screen partner was Assia Noris, who he later dubbed 'presumptuous and capricious'.[23]

The Nazzari persona could be of various social extractions. In several films, the actor played professional men. He was an engineer in *Scampolo*, a lawyer in *I mariti*, a pilot in some four films, a businessman in *Centomila dollari*, and a film actor in *Apparizione*. He also played a journalist and a professor. Yet his persona was not fundamentally modern or bourgeois. Although he was surprisingly good at comedy and very effective in a number of the lightweight 'white telephone' films, notably *Dopo divorzieremo* and *Centomila dollari*, he lacked the interiority and perhaps even the physical manner of the bourgeois. He seemed to belong to an order of society in which the land and inherited roles dominated. His character belongs primarily to the rural world, as noble proprietor or as rustic worker. The actor played up his Sardinian origins and, despite having moved to Rome as a young child, spoke with a slight Sardinian accent.[24] The fierce independence of the island's inhabitants, and their characteristic taciturnity, became a part of the Nazzari persona.

In Italy, in the interwar years and for decades afterwards, everyone came from somewhere; a birthplace was not simply a fact for official records; it was a mark of identity and an indication of character. The country was still predominantly rural at the time and, for Fascism, the rural world remained an ideological resource and a repository of Italian-ness, counterposed to alien, imported modernities. Thus Nazzari's embodiment of certain provincial and specifically rural traits, including physical strength and moral rectitude, only served to enhance his appeal to regime and people alike. The most modern and cosmopolitan of filmgoers surely preferred the big American stars to the home-grown Nazzari, but it was impossible to deny the verve and authenticity that he brought to his wide gallery of Italian noblemen, artisans and soldiers. He stood proudly in the Italian landscape like a great tree, a protective and unbending repository of given values. For Giulio Cesare Castello, who would claim that the actor 'became a sort of Clark Gable of the "backward regions"', 'he was an eminently popular personality in his transparency and refusal of compromise, in the fundamental, constitutional "health" of a man who was often better than his destiny'.[25] Because it was a part of his person as well as his persona, Nazzari brought feudal dignity, or more specifically, an assumption of natural and unchallengeable superiority, a respect for established roles and values, and a disinclination for debate or discussion to even his bourgeois roles. He was a virile man, with big hands and a big heart, who was not given to introspection or reflection. Even when he played noblemen, Nazzari was never a courtier; he was a minor aristocrat, at bottom a man of the people.

This rigidity and embeddedness might have worked against Nazzari's popularity, limiting his individuality; however, his characters' sense of justice and honour was never subordinated to social position. On the contrary, he was often prepared to abandon conventional expectations or easy comforts in order to do the right thing. This endeared him to audiences of all opinions, even if there was an austerity – severity even – to the persona that curiously matched the dominant Fascist ideal of masculinity. In both *Cavalleria* and *Luciano Serra pilota*, the protagonists do not disdain the realm of society and pleasure. Solaro attends a high-society ball and Serra, abandoned by his wife and forced to live in a house without electricity, takes himself off to a grand hotel for an evening of distraction. Yet, they have nothing to do with the order of values of these realms or with their habitual denizens. The scenes are there to establish a contrast between frivolity and seriousness. They set a benchmark that will then seal the detachment of the men from the regular bourgeois world when they enter the theatre of war, where they realise or rediscover their true selves.

The rustic quality to Nazzari explains why the female co-star with whom he shared most qualities was Luisa Ferida. A woman of humble origin from the Bolognese hinterland, she was often dismissed by journalists and colleagues alike as having no innate elegance or class. Yet, although no older than Valli and Silvi, Ferida was not a childlike inferior in her screen partnership with Nazzari. Even in the medieval fantasy *La corona di ferro* (The Iron Crown, Alessandro Blasetti, 1941), in which she plays a warrior queen, or a drama located in nineteenth-century Russia and France like *Fedora* (Camillo Mastrocinque, 1942), where she plays a vengeful princess, she brings intensity and feeling to her parts. While she lacked the excitable frothiness of Silvi or the emotional vitality of Valli, Ferida brought other qualities to the screen. She was a recognisable Italian type ('a brown-haired Bolognese beauty', Castello dubs her),[26] of the sort that was not common among the actresses of the period. With her coarse features and passionate nature, Ferida was a sensual and distinctively lower-class beauty whose earthy leanings were not disguised by occasional aristocratic roles. When journalists who were irritated by the proliferation of fair-haired actresses with foreign backgrounds demanded that there should be more actresses with familiar Italian looks, it was often to Ferida that they turned for an example.

From the start of his career, Nazzari was compared to leading American actors. He was likened to Errol Flynn on account of a slight resemblance and similar moustache, and equated with Clark Gable for the dominant position he occupied within the star system. His own favourite, he confessed to Francesco Savio in the 1970s, was Gary Cooper.[27] As was noted in Chapter 2, the American star system provided a lexicon of stardom and a gallery of star figures, that the reborn Italian cinema could not ignore. In many cases, the American models informed the screen type more than physical appearance; in others, comparisons were the fruit of journalistic fantasy (as when Gemma Bolognesi was termed 'the Italian Mae West' or the comic Macario dubbed 'our Mickey Mouse'). What distinguished Nazzari was his presence. Not only was he dashingly handsome (although his small eyes would always remain a bugbear), he was tall and broad-shouldered. He filled the screen in an American way. In a cinema where most of the other leading men were small or slightly built, this was no mean quality. In a typical scene in *Luciano Serra, pilota*, he barges into a room in which a gaggle of diminutive Argentinian businessmen are discussing how best to exploit commercially his forthcoming transatlantic flight. A giant amid pygmies, morally as well as physically, he briskly reproves them with a few well-chosen words and gestures before striding out, ignoring their desperate pleas to return. Nazzari's deep and resonant voice added indisputable authority to his physical stature. Sounding like it emerged 'from the bottom of a cavern' (to use the words of Assia Noris, who attributed this to the imperfect live recording of the time),[28] his voice, like that of the Americans to whom he was compared, was a key part of his individuality. It was sure, strong and unmistakeable. As Guglielmina Setti remarked, 'what is pleasing about Nazzari is his diction, a diction that for the moment is unmatched on our screens'.[29]

Nevertheless, it is important to note some differences between the actor and the American stars of the day. The comparisons with Flynn, for example, did not take account of the ironical, self-mocking air that often marked the latter's performances.[30] Only in the postwar years would Nazzari allow himself to parody his own image.[31] Flynn mocked authority when he played outsiders and rebels too, which was something Nazzari rarely did. Physically, the Hollywood star was more graceful and agile, and his features finer. He had a soulful dimension and a 'fabulous smile' that, Ina Hark notes, both charms and cons.[32] Duplicity was generally absent from the Nazzari persona. Only in the war propaganda film *Bengasi* (Augusto Genina, 1942) did he play an Italian engineer who fraternises and jokes with the enemy while in fact being an officer on a secret mission. As the engineer, he is physically attacked by Italian residents of the Libyan city, angry at his apparent betrayal, but the audience is not remotely surprised to learn that he had only been play-acting. Nazzari could never be anything but a true patriot. Gary Cooper probably appealed to Nazzari because he moved so comfortably on screen and projected an idealised masculinity. He often played military roles, and did so with flair, but had a wider range too. Equally at ease 'on the prairie or in the parlour', he was rugged and manly but also sensitive and thoughtful.[33] His 'abrasive exterior suggests a rich interior', Corey Creekmur writes. Nazzari aspired to the 'rugged elegance' of Cooper but was widely seen as 'not a refined man but an authentic one'.[34] He could inhabit sophisticated environments but not move with grace in them. He had romantic notions but fundamentally was not reflective.

In a number of films (*Centomila dollari*, *Dopo divorzieremo*, *Harlem*), Nazzari played American characters, and did so with more plausibility than others. It was perhaps an inevitable feature of the period that these films were typically anti-American. In *Harlem* (Carmine Gallone, 1943), he is an Italian-American who has done well but is nauseated by the materialism of his adopted society. At the end of the madcap comedy *Centomila dollari*, the millionaire Woods, whose money values and ostentation have been attacked in the course of the film, abandons his country for the love of the simple telephonist Lily (Assia Noris). In *Bengasi*, he easily exchanges banter in English and adopts the expansive mannerisms of the enemy officers, but, once his identity is revealed, he becomes more contained.

Fig. 8.2 Stars like Amedeo Nazzari were often inundated with fan mail and requests for autographed pictures. (Author's own collection)

Nazzari's appearance changed only minimally from film to film, as his characters aged or the settings changed. His moustache might grow thicker or bigger, it might be supplemented with a beard of one sort or another; his wavy light brown hair might be longer or shorter, it might turn grey or be shot through with fair highlights. Like Cooper and other stars, he was not an actor who underwent great transformations; audiences always saw him as Nazzari, and this stability contributed greatly to his star persona. The characters he played are often of indeterminate age. Some greying may occur when the plot unfolds over time, but even here the precise age is never clear. Typically, between 1936 and 1943, when Nazzari was aged from twenty-nine to thirty-six, his characters mostly demonstrated vigorous maturity rather than youthful energy, suggesting perhaps an age somewhere between thirty-two and forty-nine. Despite practising a range of sports, he never displayed a semi-naked body, unlike Fosco Giachetti, an actor of less imposing physique, or Massimo Girotti, a fit and muscular younger actor who had been a professional sportsman. According to his daughter, who was born in 1958, he believed his legs to be too thin and even refused to wear a bathing costume on holiday.[35] In compensation, his costumes were always superb, even his modern outfits obviously being beautifully tailored, if sometimes eccentrically styled. The actor insisted that, before shooting, he should have at least two weeks to wear-in modern costumes, and four weeks for historical ones.

As often occurred with Hollywood stars, his films included nods or occasional amusing reference to previous roles (as when the former aviator Serra, in his new guise as Woods, grabs the controls of a plane and diverts its course in *Centomila dollari*). They also generated catchphrases, notably Neri Chiaramantesi's intimidating invitation 'Chi non beve con me, peste lo colga!' (May the plague strike anyone who does not drink with me!), which resonated long after the film had been forgotten.

There were limits to Nazzari's versatility. Unlike, say, Gary Cooper or John Wayne, he did not have a distinctive walk or move with much grace. According to Lilia Silvi, he danced badly and was tone deaf.[36] Despite playing a musician, he is unconvincing in the musical scenes of the comedy *Dopo divorzieremo*. However, he was an actor who took his craft seriously; he was always utterly professional in his preparation and application. He knew that he was the best guardian of his persona and he brooked no fool in his determination to ensure that its integrity was maintained. Over the years, he acquired a reputation for interfering with the direction of films, rewriting dialogue and refusing to play scenes he found to be out of keeping with his persona. For producers, from whom he invariably extracted record cachets, this was a source of frustration and resentment. Directors too grew impatient with an actor who used his box office power to usurp their role and effectively take over the direction of some films.[37] It may be said that he had an active, interventionist conception of his trade as a screen actor that was related as much to the pedagogical view he took of the function of his persona as to a desire to preserve its commercial value. His unique position allowed him to exercise more agency than most actors. Fosco Giachetti later claimed, with a touch of envy, that 'Nazzari had a sort of "ideas office" and he even had someone whose task it was to buy them up for him; he then said to producers that he wanted to make this or that film and was willing to let them have the idea that he had bought'.³⁸

In keeping with his economic power, Nazzari lived in grand style. Like many stars of the period, he disliked publicity. However, he maintained a certain public image that matched the expectations the public had of a major star. He demanded and achieved cachets that went far beyond what any Italian actor had previously earned and he knew that this brought responsibility.³⁹ He drove magnificent cars, owning, among other vehicles, a red Alfa Romeo cabriolet with white leather interior that appears briefly in the documentary *Cinque minuti a Cinecittà*. The actor could be seen driving this car in Rome and also along the avenues of the Cinecittà complex before war restrictions ended this. He practised a range of sports including fencing, swimming, boxing, horse-riding (following a crash course in preparation for *Cavalleria*), and tennis. He possessed a large number of suits, ties and shoes as well as all his screen costumes, which by contract he kept, along with a copy of each film made. No gossip ever appeared in the press about his private life and it was not widely known that he lived with his mother and two sisters.

In the interwar years he lived near the centre of Rome and his socialising was more private than public. He did not enjoy high society and he avoided formal social occasions, preferring the company of film personnel and artists from Rome's Via Margutta. Although disciplined in his work, he led a less orderly leisure life. He was a keen poker player and enjoyed gambling. He was a prodigious consumer of whisky and a heavy smoker. He often dined out in the company of film friends, who included Osvaldo Valenti, a versatile actor who was given to pranks and outrageous behaviour. A known and self-confessed cocaine addict, he was likely to have been responsible for inducing Nazzari to indulge in the drug on the one occasion he admitted to having taken it.

All this was accompanied by magnanimity and generosity. Although he would not move into the substantial villa, a close approximation of which would appear in Fellini's *Le notti di Cabiria* (The Nights of Cabiria, 1957), until 1952, the actor was known for his generous tips and hospitality. Friends could dine out at his favourite restaurants on his account and the hard-up or unfortunate knew that no request for help would be refused. Like a feudal lord – and also not unlike Mussolini, to whom far larger numbers wrote requesting aid or assistance – he dispensed welfare and gifts.⁴⁰

In his relations with his fans, Nazzari was correct and solicitous. He told a journalist in the 1960s that in the pre-war period he used to receive hundred of letters from girls, who sent him their photographs, invited him to visit them or asked to join him on his yacht.[41] He employed a secretary to deal with the correspondence who he trained to forge his signature on the photographs that were sent without fail to everyone who wrote to him. He was sure that the particular pattern of relations between the sexes and the psychological atmosphere of the adolescent world of the time determined female attitudes towards him. 'In my time, girls did not fall in love with their classmates. They needed a romantic escape that was absolutely extraneous to the reality that surrounded them. That is why they asked me to run away with them', he said.[42] The lesson that the film star Nazzari teaches his ingenuous young fan Andreina, played by Valli, in *Apparizione* was intended to be seen and heard by the legions of fans who dreamed of escaping from their daily lives in his company. Curiously, in this film, the actor's ample apartment features, among various decorative objects, a bust of himself. This is perhaps the only ironical touch in a film that could, in other circumstances, have been laced with them.

For the critic Fernaldo Di Giammatteo, writing in 1958, Nazzari 'with his face, represents something the Italians would have liked to be and still would like to be, loving as they do their provincial and modest romanticism, which functions as a surrogate of those things that they do not have'.[43] In the Fascist period, he was not yet this. He was rather the image of what Italians, especially those who gave the regime their support, thought their country was in the process of becoming. The ideal man for legions of female fans, he was the guarantee that honesty and right would triumph. At the same time, he was the strong protective figure to whom they knew they could turn for comfort in the event that things were to go wrong. To this extent, there was in his persona a residue of Maciste, the strongman who had rescued damsels and righted innumerable wrongs in a long series of films of the 1910s and 1920s. Nazzari was surely bound up with Mussolini in the collective imagination, but he had independent strengths and qualities which meant that he would emerge from the debacle of the war and the collapse of Fascism better than nearly all his fellow stars. There was, in a way, an innocence to his persona. When the writer Milena Milani remarked, 'I always knew that, underneath, a boy's spirit was hiding in a man's body',[44] she was surely not entirely wrong.

Notes

1. Quoted in S. Casavecchia. 2007. 'Amedeo Nazzari: il divo, l'uomo, l'attore' in Casavecchia (ed.), *Amedeo Nazzari: il divo, l'uomo, l'attore*, Rome: Centro sperimentale di cinematografia, 4–18, 12.
2. Ibid.

3. See J. Korn. 1983. *Winged Gospel: America's Romance with Aviation, 1900–1950*, New York: Oxford University Press, vii; and S.W. Palmer. 2006. *Dictatorship of the Air: Aviation Culture and the Fate of Modern Russia*, Cambridge: Cambridge University Press, 2.
4. G. Gubitosi. 1998. *Amedeo Nazzari*, Bologna: Il Mulino, 28.
5. P. Pruzzo and E. Lancia. 1983. *Amedeo Nazzari*, Rome: Gremese, 18.
6. G. Altighieri, 'Cavalleria', *L'Ambrosiano*, 29 August 1936. Quoted in ibid., 41.
7. G. Setti, 'Cavalleria', *Il Lavoro*, 29 August 1936. Quoted in Pruzzo and Lancia, *Amedeo Nazzari*, 42.
8. See E. Gentile. 1993. *Il culto del littorio*, Rome–Bari: Laterza, 50–54.
9. P. Carrano, 'Nazzari, cavaliere d'avventura', *Il Giornale*, 4 December 1986, 3.
10. See Gubitosi, *Amedeo Nazzari*; Casavecchia, *Amedeo Nazzari*; S. Vicini. 2008. *Le stelle del duce*, Bresso, Milano: Hobby & Work, Chapter 5; M. Scaglione. 2005. *I divi del ventennio*, Turin: Lindau, 158–61; Pruzzo and Lancia, *Amedeo Nazzari*.
11. L. Freddi. 1949. *Il cinema*, Rome: L'Arnia, 425.
12. G.P. Brunetta. 1991. *Cent'anni di cinema italiano*, Rome–Bari: Laterza, 212.
13. Gubitosi, *Amedeo Nazzari*, 71.
14. Ibid., 72–73.
15. C. Duggan. 2007. *The Force of Destiny: Italy Since 1796*, London: Allen Lane, 413–14.
16. The lack of critique was expressed in the widespread use of the term 'second Risorgimento' to describe the Resistance. See P.E. Cooke. 2012. 'La resistenza come secondo risorigimento: un topos senza fine?', *Passato e presente* 86, 62–81.
17. Pruzzo and Lancia, *Amedeo Nazzari*, 17.
18. See A. Antola. 2012. 'Mussolini and Photography: Images and the Construction of a Personality Cult', University of London Ph.D. thesis, Chapter 2.
19. See G. Gori. 1984. *Alessandro Blasetti*, Florence: Il castoro cinema/La Nuova Italia, 71–73.
20. Quoted in ibid., 71.
21. M. De Giorgio. 1992. *Le italiane dall'Unità a oggi*, Rome–Bari: Laterza, 116.
22. A. Libonati. 1964. 'I digiuni allungano la mia giovinezza', *Gente* 28, 35. This is confirmed by Nazzari's daughter in 'Conversazione con Evelina Nazzari' in Casavecchia, *Amedeo Nazzari*, 25.
23. M.E. Buffa. 2008. *Amedeo Buffa in arte Nazzari*, Rome: Sabinae, 91.
24. This point, it should be said, is disputed by his daughter, who claims that his Italian diction was perfect and that the notion that he spoke with an accent was entirely due to a celebrated television parody. See 'Conversazione con Evelina Nazzari', 26–28. In fact a Sardinian accent, slight but nonetheless distinct, is evident in many of his films.
25. G.C. Castello. 1957. *Il divismo: mitologia del cinema*. Turin: ERI, 408.
26. Ibid., 417.
27. F. Savio. 1979. *Cinecittà anni trenta*, Rome: Bulzoni, 828.

28. C. Maza, 'Già a 12 anni avevo gli italiani ai piedi', *Eva*, 14 August 1969, 50.
29. Setti, '*Cavalleria*'. Quoted in Pruzzo and Lancia, *Amedeo Nazzari*, 42.
30. I.R. Hark. 2011. 'Errol Flynn and Olivia De Haviland: Romancing through History' in A. L. McLean (ed.), *Glamour in a Golden Age: Movie Stars of the 1930s*, New Brunswick: Rutgers University Press, 158.
31. Notably in Fellini's *Le notti di Cabiria* (The Nights of Cabiria, 1957), in which he played a character closely modelled on himself, and Dino Risi's *Frenesie d'estate* (Summer Excitements, 1957) where he played an aging Lothario.
32. Hark, 'Errol Flynn', 157.
33. C.K. Creekmur. 2011. 'Gary Cooper: Rugged Elegance' in McLean, *Glamour in a Golden Age*, 74.
34. Castello, *Il divismo*, 409.
35. Buffa, *Amedeo Buffa*, 35.
36. L. Silvi. 2005. *Una diva racconta se stessa e il suo cinema*, Florence: Aida, 28.
37. Nazzari indirectly confirmed that he was often impatient with directors when he said that Blasetti was 'the only director with whom I never clashed. During his films, I rested; I slept really soundly because I knew I was in safe hands'. Quoted in F. Faldini and F. Fofi (eds). 1979. *L'avventurosa storia del cinema italiano – raccontata dai suoi protagonisti, 1935–1958*, Milan: Feltrinelli, 31.
38. Savio, *Cinecittà anni trenta*, 585.
39. A police report from 1938 suggests that the actor's personal secretary, De Censo, boasted of the approval Mussolini and his ministers bestowed on him 'in order to obtain good roles for Nazzari, given that he gets a percentage [of box office]'. Archivio Centrale dello Stato, Ministero dell'Interno, Direzione generale Pubblica Sicurezza, Divisione polizia politica, B. 904 Nazzari, Amedeo. Note dated 20 September 1938. This is the only document in the Nazzari file.
40. On the letters Mussolini received from the public, see C. Duggan. 2013. 'Interiorising the Cult: the Evidence of Diaries and Letters' in S. Gundle, C. Duggan and G. Pieri (eds), *The Cult of the Duce: Mussolini and the Italians*, Manchester: Manchester University Press, 103–26.
41. M. Chierici, 'Con le donne divento timido', *Oggi*, 29 April 1965, 41.
42. Ibid., 41.
43. F. Di Giammatteo, 'Nazzari, eroe per tutti', *Radiocorriere*, 26 July 1958, page unnumbered.
44. Quoted in Castello, *Il divismo*, 409.

9

The Uniformed Role Model
Fosco Giachetti

Born in 1900, seven years before Nazzari, Fosco Giachetti enjoyed a career that was in many superficial respects similar to that of the man he would work with on just two films, the war film *Bengasi* (Augusto Genina, 1941) set in North Africa, and the postwar film version of the Risorgimento drama *Romanticismo* (Romanticism, Clemente Fracassi, 1950). An actor who became best known for his roles in uniform, he embodied the same sort of unflinching sense of duty and honour as Nazzari in his military films. He too was often a man alone, who either disdained the ties and obligations of family or whose wives and lovers misunderstood his commitment to duty above all else. He encountered the approval of the regime, which was expressed in numerous honours and prizes, as well as unofficial comments, and, like Nazzari, he was pressured to join the National Fascist Party, an invitation he too declined. Giachetti's popularity was inferior to that of his fellow actor, as was demonstrated by the *Cinema* poll of 1939–40, but his second placing was more than respectable, a testimony to the warmth with which the audience responded to his honest and steadfast characters. Although Giachetti was in some ways similar to Nazzari, he inhabited his roles with greater intensity, a quality that meant he was less versatile and in some respects more predictable.

Giachetti made his name with three films, all of which had military themes and all of which were directed by Augusto Genina. *Squadrone bianco* (White Squadron, 1936) was set in the Italian colony of Libya, while *L'assedio dell'Alcazar* (The Siege of the Alcazar, 1940) recounted a famous episode of the Spanish civil war from the Francoist point of view; and

Bengasi (1942), for which he would receive the Volpi Cup for best actor at Venice, tackled the final months of the empire from the point of view of the Italian population of the Libyan city which gave the film its title. The status of *Lo squadrone bianco* as a film enjoying the highest official approval was confirmed by the fact that on its first release it was preceded by a double issue of the Luce newsreel featuring the Berlin Olympics and scenes of colonial life in Addis Ababa. Laced with propaganda impulses, these dramatic war films were among the most expertly made of the entire period. Despite the obvious agenda informing them, they were sober and unrhetorical; only the portrayal of the British in *Bengasi* smacked of the crudest type of propaganda. More subtle altogether were the racial politics of the two colonial films, not least because, as Giorgio Bertellini has noted, very little visual space is granted to the colonised populations.[1] Under the guidance of one of Italy's most able and experienced directors, who after the collapse of the Italian film industry in the early 1920s had worked widely in Europe, Giachetti shone as a specific type of soldier, the officer (a captain in each film) whose leadership is accepted without question by his men and who is ready to sacrifice everything personal to the cause. Incommunicative and authoritarian, he is the very embodiment of Fascist masculinity – for Castello, 'a typical personality of Italian cinema in the Fascistic era'.[2]

In addition, Giachetti made several prestigious films including the biopic *Giuseppe Verdi* (Carmine Gallone, 1938), for which he won respectful notices for his performance as the composer, and the dark and atmospheric two-part adaptation of Ayn Rand's anti-Soviet novel *We The Living* (*Noi vivi – Addio Kira*, Goffredo Alessandrini, 1942), in which he played a political commissar who falls for the white Russian girl Kira. He also appeared in the best-known blockbuster financed directly by the regime, *Scipione l'Africano* (Scipio The African, Carmine Gallone, 1937), Renato Castellani's debut film, the Dostoyevsky adaptation *Un colpo di pistola* (A Pistol Shot, 1942), and a proto-neorealist melodrama set in the world of truck drivers, *Fari nella nebbia* (Headlights in the Fog, Gianni Franciolini, 1942), as well as many other more routine films.

Giachetti worked with exactly the same number of directors as Nazzari, over a slightly longer period, between 1933 and 1943. Six directed him more than once, including Genina three times, Carmine Gallone four times, and Goffredo Alessandrini twice. It is striking that neither Mario Camerini nor Alessandro Blasetti, the two most prominent directors, worked with him. The actor's productivity was lower than that of Nazzari, who reached a peak of eight films in 1942. Giachetti adopted a rhythm of four films per year, which he maintained from 1938 to 1942 (except for 1940 in which he made three). He appeared in a number of films with predominantly male casts, or played roles in which no actress was cast against him. However, he also worked with several leading actresses of the day, making three films each with Alida Valli, Maria Denis and Paola Barbara. His most significant male

Fig. 9.1 Fosco Giachetti first made his name as the inflexible Captain Sant'Elia in *Lo squadrone bianco* (The White Squadron, 1936). (Author's own collection)

co-star was Antonio Centa; the conflict between the high morality of Giachetti's characters and Centa's imperfect ones in *Lo squadrone bianco*, *Un colpo di pistola* and *Fari nella nebbia* constituted a significant thread of the plot of each film.

The key feature of all Giachetti's major characters was their strong, virile sense of duty and purpose. Typically, they were proud, courageous and introverted. Always, they were serious and quite severe. The actor became known for his intense, unsmiling expression, physical containment and the clarity with which he delivered his lines. In a period in which audiences everywhere 'revelled in the pleasure of hearing voices',[3] a distinctive vocal trademark was a great advantage. Giachetti's deep, warm voice, with its slight Tuscan inflection (he was born and raised in Sesto Fiorentino) was his strongest weapon. It contributed to the atmosphere of manly determination with which he infused his characters. An article in *Cine illustrato* in

1938 entitled 'Serietà di Fosco Giachetti' ('Seriousness of Fosco Giachetti') announced, referring to his first name's literal meaning of 'gloomy': 'He has a name that is an entire programme ... Fosco! That is to say gloomy, sad, dark, serious ... Fosco Giachetti is a serious type, for serious parts ... If we consider his films ... the sense of duty, the responsibility of the role impose on him a mask of strength, an imperious expression and words that are dry and precise orders or the inspired phrases of a born leader.' At a time when it was usual to compare Italian actors to supposed foreign counterparts, Giachetti was seen as the Italian Humphrey Bogart and a cousin of Jean Gabin. He was invariably solitary, often surrounded by tragedy, unlucky in love and in life, but with a sure moral compass and a fundamental, unflinching sense of purpose.

The lack of humour or irony in the Giachetti persona was a limit; it restricted the variety of genres in which he could play, led to insinuations that he was not a complete actor, and caused career problems in the post-war years. The journalist Flora Antonioni, who interviewed him in 1947, evidently admired him as an actor, while adding that 'we would not mind at all seeing [his persona] spiced with a pinch of irony and refreshed with the addition of the odd smile'.[4] Just a few years earlier, this supposed weakness had been a strength.

It is worth exploring how Fosco Giachetti's persona came to be that of the man of granite, his face cast in an attitude of rocky taciturnity and expressive closure. Through what procedures and what processes of elimination did this image come to be? It may also be asked what tensions existed between the actor's quite consistent screen persona and his wider star persona, taking in his press image, publicised private life and opinions. The issue of the political significance of the image that was associated with him should also be considered.

Like nearly all the male screen actors of the period, Giachetti began his career in theatre. He was active in amateur theatre in Florence in the 1920s before joining the company of Ermete Zacconi in 1927 and then passing to that of Tatiana Pavlova, a Russian-born actress-manager who would transmit to him a love for the literature of her homeland. He made his first film in 1933 after being approached in Rome by the producer Giuseppe Amato and the director Mario Bonnard; he then combined theatre and film work until 1936 when he finally left the theatre. Film critics at this time often lamented the way actors recruited from theatre transferred ways of speaking and moving from stage to screen without any adaptation. No one said this of Giachetti. Like Nazzari, he never abandoned a certain sense of his profession as a screen actor that gave value to the solid theatrical training and experience on which it was based. But his efficacy was not diminished by this. From the start he was good on screen. Fabrizio Sarazani noted in an article in *Film*:

He approached the screen with humanity and ease, marked by an anti-theatrical style. In other words Fosco Giachetti has understood how to play the game, despite coming to cinema from the stage. He has left behind in the dressing room of the theatre all theatrical affectations, every comical mannerism, blending the experience of art with a necessary and indispensable naturalness of attitudes. In other words he has left behind on the boards of the stage the play style for the screen style: two styles and two modes that are as distant from each other as the earth and the moon.[5]

Only in his role as Verdi was an overly theatrical performance style evident. The film's script had not met with the approval of Freddi who was of the view that it should be nothing less than 'the exaltation of an Italian genius'.[6] Instead, the insistence on certain problems of the composer's personal life subjected him to 'patent belittlement'. The screenplay was a cold series of staged scenes that, when intimate relations were brought into play, 'slipped into banality, mediocrity and even vulgarity'. The Verdi of the film was simply unappealing, Freddi concluded. As a result the screenplay was modified, but defects carried over into the finished film. Presented at the Venice Film Festival in 1938, it won the wide praise that was expected, while Giachetti's rendering of the subject gave rise to mild objections. The *Gazzetta di Venezia* said that with his Verdi 'perhaps the confrontational aspect of his personality is stressed too much', while *La Stampa* glossed the matter by saying that Giachetti was 'wrestling with the most difficult challenge of his career so far'.[7] The actor explained his approach as follows:

> Verdi was a solitary type, or at least he was a man who did not like to reveal himself; he was reserved and irritable, incapable of telling the woman he loved 'I love you'. Yet, beneath this rugged, grouchy exterior, there lay an extraordinary sensibility, the sensibility of an artist as perfect, as great as Verdi. Here lies the arduous task I set myself: never to betray with gestures or sentimental gushing Verdi's combative reserve and to transmit the creative sensibility of his spirit.[8]

In other words, Giachetti constructed him from outside; he was attentive to what to avoid and eliminate in terms of physical movements and delivery of lines and less focussed on building the character from inside through psychological insight. Years later he admitted, 'I wanted to find the exterior personality of Verdi ... I wanted to find the beast that Verdi might have resembled. With this ragged beard, this untidy moustache and this attitude of severity, I worked out that his animal was the lion'.[9] This made for a static portrayal in which none of the small gestures or facial expressions normally so important in bringing characters to life on the screen were present. Giachetti's Verdi might have worked well on stage but on the screen his creative energy and lively spirit are absent.

Giachetti's appearance altered little from role to role. Only when he went into black face (and body) for *Scipione l'Africano*, were various styles of beard for *Giuseppe Verdi*, or embraced the guise of a moustachioed, long-haired pirate in *La figlia del corsaro verde* (The Daughter of the Green Pirate, Enrico Guazzoni, 1941) and a handful of period roles, did he abandon his conventional coiffure of thick, backcombed dark hair and sculpted, clean-shaven face. For a leading man, he was not especially handsome; physically he did not have the impressive stature of Nazzari, the sinister fascination of Valenti, the sporting physique of Massimo Girotti, or the square and firm jaw line of Antonio Centa. He was often dressed in functional work clothes or uniforms, with no attempt to project a cinematic elegance or personal trademark. His period roles are those in which he is most impeccably attired. Yet he donned dark leather jackets with enviable insouciance in *Noi vivi* and *Fari nella nebbia*, and wore military uniforms like a second skin. When lit, as he often was, in a way that half of his face remained shadowed, the brooding melancholy of his persona was at its most alluring.

The actor constructed a strong screen presence in the absence of any of the hallmarks of personal charisma. He did not fill the screen with an imposing physique or draw the eye irresistibly. He was of average height and colouring, and lean without being obviously athletic. He had no characteristic gait or repertoire of gestures. Only his voice, rendered thick and smoky by years of tobacco consumption, was distinctive and beautiful. His diction was without parallel in Italian cinema. Thus it can be said that it was solely through the roles that Giachetti constructed a presence. To this extent he was more an actor than a star, but the unvarying nature of his basic character type meant that filmgoers saw a symbiosis between the actor and his roles. Given that the roles were not trivial, but touched on some of the most actual military challenges facing the country or issues from recent history, the context served to make him a star. He enjoyed public favour, box office success and considerable financial rewards, and his career was crowned with numerous tributes and awards. Precisely for this reason he preferred not to step outside his comfort zone, and probably no one (except journalists and critics in lighter moments) proposed that he should.

More than any other film, *Lo squadrone bianco* defined the Giachetti persona and brought him to public attention. The *Corriere della sera*, on 22 August 1936, judged that 'Fosco Giachetti is a magnificent revelation in the energetic, sober, sculpted figure of the captain'. Writing in *L'Italia letteraria*, 1 November 1936, Dario Sabatello affirmed that 'of the male players one can speak only very well. Fosco Giachetti especially is superior to every expectation; his performance as Captain Sant'Elia is superb, worthy of an actor of great class'. His character commands a native squadron in the Libyan desert. He has recently lost his trusted second in command in a military action and is exceptionally brusque when his replacement, a lieutenant who has suffered a disappointment in love, reveals himself to be distracted and spoilt. Lieutenant Ludovici is given an opportunity to prove himself when Sant'Elia leads a column of troops across the desert to suppress a band of rebels. After initially seeming unequal to the task, he stiffens his resolve and determines to do all in his power to win his captain's respect. This he achieves and he successfully leads the column back to base after the captain is killed in action. In the final scenes, a group of tourists, including the woman who had broken Lieutenant Ludovici's heart, visit the fort. He, however, having now become a soldier, is indifferent to her.

Shot mainly on location, the film, although set in Libya and based on a French literary source, was one of two made in 1936 to mark the proclamation of the new Italian empire (the other was Mario Camerini's *Il grande appello*).[10] The films were not directed at either colonised peoples or Italian settlers since, as Salvatore Ambrosino has explained, Freddi 'totally ignored any possibility of structural intervention in African territory' leaving film distribution in private hands.[11] Rather they were aimed mainly at the domestic audience that was the primary target of the regime's imperial propaganda. The film features many scenes, which are framed as extreme long shots, of columns of mainly black soldiers dressed in white riding dromedaries. These austere, if technically accomplished and visually striking, scenes add much to the film's exotic flavour and general appeal, but, according to Bertellini, they also constitute the military convoy as a sort of religious procession and establish Sant'Elia as a priestly master of ceremonies. A man who leads by example rather than words, he is 'a solitary and reserved, almost aphasic, officer',[12] who effectively converts Ludovici to a new sense of his identity and destiny.

The film establishes Sant'Elia's exemplary qualities in a number of ways. In the opening scenes, he is shown giving orders in the shadow of the Italian tricolour to the assembled ranks of native troops. Photographed from a low angle, in the customary style of Luce Institute newsreels, he stands squarely with his hands on his hips in a classic Mussolinian pose (Fig. 9.1). The scenes bring into evidence his leadership position, indirectly assert Italian superiority with respect to the indigenous population from among whom Sant'Elia's troops have been recruited, and make implicit reference to the Fascist project. To underline these points, Lieutenant Ludovici is informed by several supporting characters, including a native soldier and a doctor, that Sant'Elia is a 'great captain' and a true leader.

That he is a leader by example who brooks no fear of danger or defeat is immediately made clear by his unhesitating decision to risk all by crossing the desert to confront a band of rebels. His pedagogical role works in a double action. First, a conflict is established between his unflinching but sexless virility (there is no woman in his life in the film and no backstory is drawn) and Ludovici's self-indulgent, feminised masculinity. The latter undergoes a personal transformation until, by the end of the film, he has effectively stepped into Sant'Elia's boots. Second, the woman who has ruined Ludovici realises her mistake when she learns of his heroism and witnesses him leading the troops stoically back to the fort. As she leaves the encampment in tears following his rejection of her attempts at a reconciliation, she is forced to reflect on the wrong order of values that had governed her earlier conduct. Thus the colonial film, like the colonial war, became 'a catalyst for the consolidation of the national community and for the redemption of those Italians who had remained outside the fold'.[13]

The role called for Giachetti to establish a model of serious manliness and this he did first and foremost by never smiling. Smiles, of course, do not have to be jovial or to signify triviality. They may signify courtesy, inner peace, satisfaction, arrogance and many other attitudes. But, they are predominantly associated with pleasure and have traditionally been thought of as feminine. It is, after all, the Mona Lisa who is 'the single most famous representation of smiling in our culture'.[14] Often, moreover, there was a constructedness or potential falsity to the smile that was related to its place, first, in patterns of interpersonal relations and, second, in commercial culture. In Italian cinema, the smile was a property primarily linked with Vittorio De Sica, as was seen in Chapter 6. In several of Giachetti's early films, light society comedies of a 'white telephone' type, he was required to convey levity, a mood that he communicated by broad toothy smiles which were reproduced in film advertising. Sant'Elia's disinterest in the niceties of social intercourse and heterosocial relations led the actor to distance himself from this model. He abolished smiles and opted for a contained performance style in which gestures and facial expressions were reduced to a minimum.

The pedagogical dynamic of *Squadrone bianco* was repeated again and again in Giachetti's films. In *L'assedio dell'Alcazar*, he is again presented diegetically as a great captain: 'il più bell'ufficiale del nostro reggimento' (literally, 'the most beautiful officer in our regiment') a young lieutenant informs two well-dressed and stylish young women who will become involved in the siege of the Alcazar of Toledo. Misunderstanding the meaning of this remark, the older and more sensual of the women, Carmen Herrera, played by Mireille Balin, comments, 'In effetti è un bell'uomo' (Indeed, he is a good looking man), causing the lieutenant to clarify that he was not referring to his captain's handsome appearance so much as his noble embodiment of military values. Not grasping the full extent of the rigour of the austere Captain Vela, Carmen is rebuked when she tries to claim more comfortable conditions for herself inside the besieged citadel. Only by buckling down with her friend, the fearless Conchita, played by Maria Denis, to provide succour to the weak and wounded does she win his respect and even affection. She is deeply moved when Captain Vela confesses to her that he has noticed her transformation and that he has developed feelings for her. The couple face each other in a lingering close-up but do not kiss. When the siege is relieved there are shouts of joy, couples kiss, and men embrace. But there is no sign of Carmen. Captain Vela is evidently not destined for a happy ending but for future battles in a war that is not yet concluded.

In Klaus Theweleit's powerful exploration of the roots of Fascistic masculinity in Germany,[15] the key trait of the authoritarian male is fear of women or more particularly of gender confusion or contamination. The utter hostility to modern women and their invasion of male spaces and prerogatives, their appropriation of once exclusively masculine garments and attributes, was expressed in violence against a variety of targets. To insulate himself against deviations, the soldier explored by Theweleit adopts a dehumanised exterior carapace and sternly insists on the relegation of women to the domestic realm. There is something specifically Germanic or North European about Theweleit's woman-fearing subjects. But the different Mediterranean context presented some of the same concerns and responses.[16] After all, Futurists and others had openly advocated a masculinist agenda. From the mid-1920s Fascism had made the

Fig. 9.2 Fosco Giachetti signing autographs for fans in Florence, c.1941. (Author's own collection)

reversal of processes of female emancipation one of its platforms, and pursued a programme of educational and custom reform designed to turn virility into a cardinal national trait. The effective removal of women from the main narrative and *dénouements* of military and colonial films was the expression of an intrinsic misogyny.

In no fewer than three films the actor Antonio Centa took the part of the incomplete, deviated male who, despite being a close colleague of Giachetti's, has not yet become a full soldier, or a true man. In *L'assedio dell'Alcazar* it is Andrea Checchi who fills this part. Centa's suitability for this type of role was raised by Francesco Savio who, interviewing him in the 1970s, brought to his attention that his characters were often not fully rounded.[17] A tall man with firm features and cruel lips, Centa made arrogance and presumption his trademarks; he had a touch of the screen villain about him but was more of a lovable rogue or rascal. His characters appealed to women and enjoyed flirting with them but, as the actor acknowledged, they were incapable of 'profound feelings'.[18] Ultimately, despite their bravado, they were weak and subject to domination. Giachetti never enters into direct competition with Centa, not even in *Un colpo di pistola*, when the two men fight a duel with pistols. After Centa's Sergio has fired and missed, Giachetti's Andrea responds to his baiting by opting to save his shot for a future occasion. The asymmetry that marks their relationship (Giachetti is always older, more experienced, tougher) means that Centa must always bend to Giachetti's superior character. In this respect, his attitude takes on a filial connotation.

The only film in which Giachetti's own character undergoes a transformation in his convictions is *Noi vivi – Addio Kira*. Here the convinced Bolshevik Andrei, a political commissar in the new Russia, falls for the alluring but politically hostile Kira, played by Alida Valli. Unaware that Kira is linked to Leo, the son of an executed white Russian admiral, Andrei woos her and thinks his feelings are returned. In reality, Kira, although attracted to the Bolshevik, is disposing of his generous gifts to help to pay for medical treatment for Leo. Andrei's awakening from the sentimental delusion he has been suffering coincides with the final disintegration of his political faith. Lacking any way forward, he takes his own life.

The film was controversial on account of its subject matter. The denunciations of tyranny and references to personal hardship in the film may have been appropriately directed against the Soviet order, but later recollections suggest that some spectators noted parallels with Fascist Italy. The casting of Giachetti, who by 1942 was regarded as a jewel in the regime's crown, as an honest and incorruptible Communist, gave rise to disquiet among senior Fascists. This fact is only known thanks to the testimony of Giachetti himself several decades later. He revealed that Vittorio Mussolini told him, after the start of shooting, that his role would be reduced, a decision that was confirmed in a phone call by Eitel Monaco, then director general of cinema.[19] Indignant that his artistic reputation might be undermined, Giachetti threatened to abandon the film. He was summoned to a meeting with the Minister of Popular Culture, Pavolini, who told him: 'I am afraid that in the third run cinemas the public, seeing this character, might accord him a round of applause and that would be troublesome'.[20] Giachetti replied that his job as an actor was precisely to seek that applause. Later in the day approval was granted for the film to be shot as intended.

One is obliged to ask what precisely might have caused this unease given that Andrei has lost his belief in Bolshevism by the end of the film. It might be suggested that the actor's star persona had something to do with it. This persona was specifically Fascist in some of its important traits; a displacement towards Communism was confusing and unwelcome. To cast the actor as a Communist was inconvenient, since it suggested that the Giachettis of this world, with their rigid, constant and unwavering demeanour, were not necessarily Fascists but could embrace any radical, anti-bourgeois creed. The actor more or less admitted this when, in his meeting with Pavolini, he told him: 'I like Andrei because he is an idealist, not only a Communist. He could be a Christian or he could reflect – why not? – your programme of 1919'.[21] Moreover, it was alarming that the Giachetti persona, even if displaced, should be presented as open to alternative, oppositional ways of thinking, and subject to ideological crisis and deviation from his course by love for a woman. Andrei's self-questioning and detachment from Soviet ideology turned him into a critical hero. This was a startling development in itself but it also implied that some of Giachetti's other characters, captains Elia and Vela for example, might, in their own different contexts, similarly undergo personal crises. In Italy in 1942 this was a disturbing prospect to raise.

The issue was one that turned the strength of the Giachetti character into a potential weakness. If Nazzari and Giachetti are compared, the differences between the two emerge strongly, despite a certain overlap of values and loyalties. While Nazzari was provincial, rustic, pre-modern and fundamentally external to power, Giachetti was urban, bourgeois and enmeshed in hierarchy. The Tuscan actor's gloom betrayed a vital inner life, his reserve a certain lack of security, and his actions deep convictions. Where Nazzari was instinctive and commanding, Giachetti was intellectual and decisive. There was something modern and provisional about his persona. Although he hailed from neither the industrial north of Italy nor the capital, Rome, but from the hinterland of Florence, he was an urban type who commonly played professionals and workers rather than nobles, rural artisans or peasants. The courageous leadership displayed by his characters may at times have seemed impulsive or ill-considered (for example, in crossing the desert in *Lo squadrone bianco*), but in fact they were surely motivated by deep inner strength and conviction. The processes of reasoning were never on display in his films; the action began after his position was settled. Exposure of their existence implied that the settled orientation of his basic persona was not automatic.

Noi vivi was divided into two parts at the suggestion of Giachetti on account of its unusual length, some four hours. It was a prestige film that closed the 1942 Venice Film Festival. Critics seemed unsure what to make of it. The extensive use of close-ups and numerous scenes based on dialogue between Kira and Leo and Kira and Andrei were seen as creating a claustrophobic atmosphere. Francesco Pasinetti argued that the repeated use of dissolves, focussing on an object and an analogous object to pass from one scene to another 'in the long run is boring'.[22] However, he admitted that the heavy, grim mood of the film was dramatically engaging and that this was aided by a naturalistic style of photography 'that tends to create an atmosphere, a grey, foggy atmosphere in which the faces of the protagonists stand out'. *Cinema* magazine strongly criticised both parts of the film, repeating the distaste for 'the sugary excess of close-ups' and condemning the actors' performances as 'mediocre'.[23] 'Beneath their limpid faces ... there is no sign of understanding, no illumination and, to put it briefly, no talent or consciousness.'[24] Only Giachetti was partially exempted from attack since 'despite all his defects, he is a man, and he has an anguished face'.

The gender politics of *Noi vivi* was unusual in the actor's canon. Kira is a modern woman, an architecture student. She breaks with her family over her love for Leo and goes to live with him out of wedlock. She is repulsed by Andrei's politics but is not indifferent to him personally, and sleeps with him while Leo is away convalescing. For a period she seems genuinely undecided which of her two men is most worthy of her love. A figure of some ambiguity who is played with great subtlety by Valli, Kira is a fluid, changeable type who unsettles Andrei, who is shocked when he discovers her relationship with Leo. Both die in the concluding scenes of the film but Kira's death, while she seeks to escape over the Soviet border, is not a punishment so much as a final demonstration of the inhumanity of the revolutionary state.

By contrast, in Giachetti's other films the gender dynamic works on predictable lines. Female transgressions are repaired or corrected by reconciliation to a traditional role or, in cases that are beyond redemption, punished by death. Variations or departures are absent and inconstancy is never forgiven unless it is shown to be the result of misunderstanding. For example, in *L'ultima nemica* (The Final Enemy, Umberto Barbaro, 1938) he is Franco Rossi, a doctor committed to research rather than winning fame and prestige. Rejected by Anna, the woman he loves, who opts to marry a rich businessman, he persists with his research and develops a vaccine against 'Tasmanian fever'. As a guinea pig he takes a prostitute, who dies following the injection. Frustrated and remorseful, Rossi destroys his laboratory and goes to work as a simple country doctor. Recalled to Rome some time later by a request that he resume his researches, he learns that Anna, on the other side of the Atlantic, has caught the virus. He tests the vaccine on himself before sending it by plane to Anna, saving her life. There is no question of their love being reborn. Like Lieutenant Ludovici, he is not interested in a woman who has spurned him. He opts instead to dedicate his life to science.

A similar dynamic operates in *Fari nella nebbia*, although this time a marriage is at stake and the woman is redeemed. Giachetti is a truck driver, Cesare, whose wife Piera (Luisa Ferida) works in a store and conducts an active social life outside the home. Flighty and pleasure-oriented, she derides him for his serious attitude to life and desire for children. To console himself, Cesare takes up with an alluring woman of easy morals, who betrays him with his mate Carlo (Antonio Centa). Intent on teaching his wayward wife a salutary lesson, he returns home to find that Piera, who had never been sexually unfaithful, has seen the error of her ways and now wishes to establish a conventional ménage. Having left the job which had brought her into contact with temptation, she now works from home. Cesare's transgression is never discovered by, or mentioned to, the wife and nor, in line with convention, is it punished.

In several other films in which he starred, women change their minds and/or redeem themselves. These include *Napoli che non muore* (Naples Doesn't Die, Amleto Palermi, 1939), *Ridi pagliaccio* (Laugh, Clown, Camillo Mastrocinque, 1941), *Nozze di sangue* (Blood Wedding, Goffredo Alessandrini, 1941) and *La figlia del corsaro verde* (The Daughter of the Green Pirate, Enrico Guazzoni, 1941). Female loyalty and constancy is rewarded with love in *Luce nelle tenebre* (Light in the darkness, Mario Mattoli, 1941), while Giachetti's character kills a woman who mocks him in *La statua vivente* (The Living Statue, Camillo Mastrocinque, 1943). In *Inferno giallo* (Yellow Hell, Geza Radwany, 1943), when he falls for another man's wife he is killed in a native uprising before he can reveal his feelings to her.

Bengasi is a significant exception. In this film Giachetti is a devoted family man whose wife and son Sandro, aged four, live with him and form part of his everyday life. When he seeks to send them away as the British close in on the city, his wife at first refuses. The film is in some respects an ideal continuation of *Squadrone bianco*. Although Giachetti's character in that film dies, it is a photograph of the actor as Captain Sant'Elia that stands in a frame in the living room of Captain Berti's home. However, unlike the austere Sant'Elia, Berti is a devoted family man who dotes on his son. Indeed, he smiles broadly whenever his eyes lock with those of Sandrino. When the boy is killed during a plane attack on the convoy in which he and his mother are leaving Bengasi, the truth is kept from him. Giachetti himself loses an arm in conflict, and when his wife visits him in hospital she cannot bring herself to tell him what has happened. It is the loss of a limb which must symbolise the deeper tragedy. For the actor the scene in which he returns home and caresses the bed of his dead son as if he were still there is the most telling. These caresses, he later said, 'signify in a certain sense the truth of the character'.[25]

The film is the only one of the period in which Nazzari and Giachetti starred together although Giachetti was given higher billing as his role was bigger. The two only appeared on screen together for some five minutes. Nevertheless, the way in which the actors' characters are drawn tells us something of their star personae. Nazzari is first introduced as a bourgeois and, even after it is revealed that he is in fact a military man operating under cover, he remains in civilian clothing. His character is at first a playboy type, then noble. Captain Berti, by contrast, is in uniform throughout and never wavers, not even to deceive the enemy. It would be unthinkable for the two actors to have exchanged roles since Giachetti's persona was more restricted. In a film with a military element, he would never have been cast as a bourgeois. The two men encounter each other only after Nazzari's character, Filippo, has cast aside his frivolous mask. But in terms of the elaboration of explicitly Fascist attitudes, neither Giachetti nor Nazzari embody official positions. That is left to the actor Guido Notari, who plays the resolute *podestà* or mayor of Bengasi, who addresses the cheering crowds after the British have left from a balcony in pure Mussolinian style.[26]

Giachetti's female co-stars were not always as good as him. Often the critics pointed this out. Sabatello, for example, having praised the male cast of *Lo squadrone bianco*, went on to say, 'It is not possible to speak so well of the women. Fulvia Lanzi, the player, is frankly ugly: she is fragile and too thin, [she] gives off a disconcerting impression of sterility and sadness ... Her natural and lady-like distinction when she moves and walks only just mitigates the sense of antipathy she provokes'.[27] In *Bengasi*, Captain Berti's wife Carla is played by Maria De Tasnady (who was better known as Maria Tasnadi Fekete), a Hungarian and German-speaking actress who is considerably less compelling than Vivi Gioi in the role of Nazzari's love interest. Nevertheless, Giachetti's films included in their casts several prominent actresses. There can be little doubt that his most satisfactory screen partner was Maria Denis, a young Roman actress who became a firm favourite in light comedies before expanding her repertoire with some significant dramatic roles and appearances in moving melodramas. Denis was not necessarily Giachetti's love interest. In *L'assedio dell'Alcazar*, she marries in extremis the man with whom she has been since the start of the film. But she occupied, in her dramatic roles, a territory that was compatible with the field of action of Giachetti's men. She was conventional, serious, loyal and sacrificial. Moreover, these virtues were a part of her persona; she did not perform them reluctantly but with a ready smile. On screen, her radiance more than makes up for what she lacked in beauty. By contrast, Giachetti's pairings with Ferida were devoid of chemistry and those with Noris, notably in the fine *Un colpo di pistola*, marred by an imbalance between his brooding intensity and her sugary gaiety. Noris later recalled that the actor was very concerned that he should look 'young, handsome and desirable'.[28] 'He was always grumpy and he carried on his face, instead of a normal expression, an iron mask', she observed.[29] Born in 1900 (he claimed 1904), he was often twenty years older than his co-stars and not always was this gap irrelevant. In *Noi vivi* he is not only a political commissar but a student, supposedly more or less the contemporary of Kira, played by the twenty-one-year-old Valli. He was forty-two at the time. The paternal cast that was often given to romance in the cinema of the period was socially normalised and this served to contain any potential anxiety about the age gap. However, Giachetti often found himself cast as men whose effective age was lower than his own. Like many leading men, he was obliged after the age of forty to enter a losing battle against the ravages of time.

As an actor Giachetti was a thorough professional who relished his craft. Cautious and diffident by nature, he nonetheless was attracted by parts that gave him chance to extend his repertoire or in some way challenge the typecasting to which he was subjected. Apart from *Noi vivi*, the most unusual roles he played were as Captain Massinissa in *Scipione l'Africano* and a swashbuckling pirate in *La figlia del corsaro verde*. In the former film he appeared in blackface, while in the latter audiences were treated to the sight of the actor stripped to the waist and endowed with flowing locks and moustache. Reassurance comes with the revelation that his character is not a real pirate, but rather the son of the Spanish governor of South America who infiltrates the ranks of the pirates to bring about their defeat.

Fig. 9.3 Fosco Giachetti relaxing at home reading a screenplay, c.1942. (Author's own collection)

These 'betrayals' of his established persona no doubt brought the actor some satisfaction. Asked by Francesco Savio why he always played similar types, he replied that 'when at a certain point in the cinema one has established a role, all the screenwriters and producers try to propose that role to you, that is to say characters of the same sort'.[30] Although he was never offered lighter roles, he claimed he would have relished them. Nevertheless, these rare departures from the norm did not shift the perception of him as the embodiment of a certain type of masculinity that was not identified explicitly as Fascist but which was entirely explainable in terms of the Fascist system of values. The critic Fabrizio Sarazani remarked that he had 'the temperament of a typically Italian actor, serious, careful, unsuited to farce or to parts for young actors in romantic comedies'.[31] His masculine expression was completely natural and not an affectation. From this point of view, he would always be Captain Sant'Elia, just as Nazzari would always be Luciano Serra. In the 1941 film *L'amante segreta* (The Secret Lover, Garmine Gallone) his Libyan experience is evoked in his character Giorgio Amholt, dubbed 'the African', who lives in a colonial manner and is attended by a black servant. The actor moreover, dubbed this the film 'that I love most'.[32] The difference was that Luciano Serra was an outsider, a rebel of sorts, whose appeal went beyond the specific frames of time and place in which his story unfolds, while Sant'Elia was more organically inserted in the colonial project that Fascism took over and made its own.

Giachetti has been compared to Humphrey Bogart but, as so often, a comparison of this sort is only revealing in part. The tough guy attitude was there, and although the physical resemblance was slight, both men had a melancholy, lonely air. Neither was conventionally handsome but they both nonetheless played romantic leads and were paired with some of the most compelling actresses of their respective cinemas. As a screen type, however, Giachetti perhaps had more in common with John Wayne, an actor with whom he shared an economic control of the body and reputation for self-reliant authority. Wayne, Gary Wills notes, was never 'against', never a rebel. 'Most movie stars are glamorously pitted against authority', he observes, adding that 'Wayne, even when not playing an officer in the Seventh Cavalry, was usually on the sheriff's side'.[33] Giachetti too was always on the side of authority or of some sort of authority that needed to be restored or re-established.

In his discussion of Wayne, Wills argues that he should be thought of as a political figure. 'Wayne did not just have political opinions. He embodied a politics; or his screen image did. It was a politics of large meanings, not of little policies – a politics of gender (masculine), ideology (patriotism), character (self-reliance), and responsibility'.[34] It goes without saying that Giachetti was a very different figure in many respects to Wayne – his world was smaller and his heyday shorter. Physically, he lacked the imposing stature and, cinematically, the hollow centre that others could 'disappear into'.[35]

But Giachetti's screen image certainly embodied a politics and one that rested on values that, in their Italian inflection, were not too different to Wayne's. His body was erect and taut; it displayed no concessions to physical needs or to age. In his functionality, it conformed to the idea of the 'metallic man' explored by Jeffrey Schnapp in his discussion of Fascism.[36]

If Giachetti did not shape dreams or impinge himself on the imagination in the same sort of way, it was because he did not have open spaces and the frontier as his backdrop, but the imperial ambitions of the Fascist dictatorship. He did not create, or have created for him, a body of values that was independent of, while practically sustaining, the political order. He may nearly always have played the same role but he was not truly an individual or his own man. Giachetti's screen persona was closely bound up with the official emphases and priorities of the regime. He was the actor who most completely incarnated the Fascist idea of the Italian that was inherited from and moulded on the basis of the 'sacrificial and epic' image of the patriot that flowered during the Risorgimento.[37] His spartan modes, dedication, carefully chosen words and sense of the aesthetic as well as moral value of the heroic gesture ultimately derived from classical antiquity, but in modern Italy they formed a part of the nationalist tradition that Fascism had taken over. This incarnation of approved values brought the actor honours, prizes and orchestrated public approval. But, like Nazzari, Giachetti refused to be drawn into a closer embrace with Fascism. He did not join the party and did not consider himself to be of a Fascist persuasion.[38] Born into a family of Socialists, he thought of himself as a man of the left and as such he would give his support to the parties of the left after the war. Yet, Fabrizio Borghini writes, 'he underwent a process of identification with the manly model promoted by the regime: virile, heroic, generous, and dedicated to sacrifice for love of the fatherland'.[39] Even his understated, ostensibly unrhetorical style became, in this key, a form of rhetoric.

In his broader public image, Giachetti of course conveyed a less monolithic impression. A feature in the illustrated magazine *Illustrazione del Popolo* in 1938 showed him relaxing outdoors and reading a stage weekly.[40] Other articles showed him fishing, enjoying the company of his dog or enjoying horse racing, his favourite hobby. But there were limits to this. Like other stars of the period, he was not a fan of publicity. 'Giachetti does not like interviews, requests with notebook in hand. Above all he does not like to talk about himself. Direct and shy, even in private life like in his films, he is an anti-star. He enjoys his work but does not like to hear it puffed up; he likes the roles that are entrusted to him but does not want to receive praise', wrote 'Emmeci' in a Bergamo newspaper.[41]

Publicity material for the actor's films reveal a disjuncture between the conventional still photography of the star and the roles he played. There was nothing new about misleading movie publicity. In Italy, as elsewhere, posters like film titles often suggested erotic situations or dramatic encounters that barely featured in the films themselves. But in this case something different was going on. In a wide variety of still photographs the actor is shown smiling broadly in a Hollywood manner. His lips are parted and his upper and lower teeth are revealed in a merry expression. Moreover, his face is bathed in light and his hair is not only combed back but slicked down. His skin and hair glisten while his fashionably cut clothes give him a stylish, contemporary air. Such shots clearly served a publicity purpose for his civilian films where they turned the actor into a saleable commodity. They look less congruous where the film is a military one. The portrait shot that accompanied the release of *L'assedio dell'Alcazar* is the most startling of all, as this dramatic film includes almost no light relief and there is no scene in which Giachetti's character smiles.

What a shot like this aimed to do was to maintain the separate identity of Fosco Giachetti the player from the Giachetti persona. The military, patriotic types he impersonated may have had little reason to smile, and indeed appeared to have banished all pleasant expression from their countenances, but this was not the case with Giachetti the actor and civilian. It is noteworthy that by 1942 this dichotomy no longer prevailed. Publicity shots were no less atmospheric and intense than the film stills that were widely reproduced in magazines. He had become absorbed into his persona. This would prove fatal for his postwar career. Looking back years later, he attributed this process of absorption to the audience: 'When an actor is loved by the public, and I think I was, he is believed; he is no longer free to play a part without the sentiments of the role he has adopted being attributed to him'.[42] These tensions in his image attest to the conflicts between political and commercial impulses that ran through the cinema of the period. By contrast, Nazzari was absorbed not by his screen type so much as by his role as a film star.

Giachetti unquestionably enjoyed great popularity. He was often mobbed on the street and he revealed that he received hundreds of letters, many of them from Italians who had served in Africa. During the filming of *La statua vivente* (The Living Statue, Camillo Mastrocinque, 1943) in Trieste, he was kidnapped by a group of female fans and released only the next day.[43] Audiences loved the romantic, melancholy air that he brought to his characters, his utter dependability, and his simple, unfussy performance style. Although his regional origin was not stressed, people saw in his gruff manner not simply the stern Fascist but the brusqueness that was regarded as typical of Tuscans and especially Florentines.

Not all his films were of the same quality. The rhetoric and propaganda in *Tredici uomini e un cannone* (Thirteen Men and a Cannon, Giovacchino Forzano, 1936), *Sentinelle di bronzo* (Sentinels of Bronze, Romolo Marcellini, 1937) and *Carmen fra i rossi* (Carmen among the Reds, Edgar Neville, 1939) was crude. Other films were simply mediocre. But Giachetti was always superior to the texts he performed. He was credible, even if the films in which he played were not. A biographical pamphlet by Pietro Osso published around 1936 suggested that:

> he does not recite, he does not perform, but rather he expresses a theme that is a part of his own life, that is the synthesis of his own spirituality. What is downplayed in the film, he accentuates; that which is forgotten, he seeks and finds in the course of his performance. Everything that is doubtful he recreates with serene optimism in a simple attitude full of crisp radiance. Giachetti constructs a security, and whatever can be 'saved' in a film is certainly his doing.[44]

In terms of the manner in which Giachetti engaged spectators with his performances, it may be said that his reserve and unwillingness to concede too much of himself did not discourage his popularity but rather enhanced it. He was seen as an artist who revealed himself through his work. 'Part of his constant artistic improvement is to be attributed to that impenetrability that makes him beyond attack and behind which he conceals his true, unknown, aspirations. The success of a new film brings him for a brief time into a closer connection with the public, but soon he retreats into his gloom', Osso observed.[45] Giachetti would later admit to being timid and also to not having a comfortable relationship with the camera. 'The movie camera has always been my enemy', he told Savio,[46] revealing that he never watched rushes and had not seen the completed versions of many of his films.

Off screen, Giachetti was the opposite of the playboy Nazzari. The actor married a fellow artist, Vera Calamai, in 1922 and their son Luciano was born in 1926. Osso revealed that 'he has an intelligent boy of ten who brings him the greatest joys of his life. He responds rarely, indeed almost never, to the thousands of female admirers who write to him. He appreciates the nice things that are said about him and is pleased about the demonstrations of affection, but prefers to live for his Art to which he had dedicated his entire being'.[47]

Giachetti moved with his family into a large apartment on Rome's Lungotevere Marzio in 1940 but he indulged in few star-type habits. He dressed well, his preferred tailor being Duetti of the Piazza di Spagna; he had his shoes custom-made in Milan and he wore Borsalino hats. However, he did not socialise with people from the film world but instead preferred the company of male friends who enjoyed hunting and horse racing.

Notes

1. G. Bertellini. 2003. 'Colonial Autism: Whitened Heroes, Auditory Rhetoric, and National Identity in Interwar Italian Cinema', in P. Palumbo (ed.), *A Place in the Sun: Africa in Italian Colonial Culture from Post-Unification to the Present*, Berkeley: University of California Press, 255–78, 263.

2. G.C. Castello. 1957. *Il divismo: mitologia dell'attore*, Turin: ERI, 407.
3. D.M. Lugowski. 2011. 'Norma Shearer and Joan Crawford: Rivals at the Dream Factory' in A. McLean (ed.), *Glamour in a Golden Age: The Movie Stars of the 1930s*, New Brunswick: Rutgers University Press, 132–50, 135.
4. F. Antonioni, 'Fosco Giachetti: intervista a 2000km', *La cinematografia italiana*, 26 May 1947, 8.
5. F. Sarazani, 'Fosco Giachetti', *Film* (undated clipping from Fosco Giachetti archive, c.1937).
6. L. Freddi. 1949. *Il cinema*, Rome: L'Arnia, 198–99.
7. Anon., 'Caloroso successo del film italiano "Giuseppe Verdi" di Carmine Gallone', *Gazzetta di Venezia*, 22 August 1938, 2; Anon., 'Il successo di Giuseppe Verdi', *La Stampa*, 22 August 1938, 3.
8. Quoted in Anon., 'Caloroso successo del film italiano "Giuseppe Verdi"'.
9. F. Savio. 1979. *Cinecittà anni trenta*, Rome: Bulzoni, 593.
10. See R. Ben-Ghiat. 2001. *Fascist Modernities: Italy, 1922–1945*, Berkeley: University of California Press, 134–35.
11. S. Ambrosino. 1991. 'Cinema e propaganda in Africa Orientale Italiana', *Ventesimo secolo* 1(1), 127–50, 130.
12. Bertellini, 'Colonial Autism', 265, 263.
13. Ben-Ghiat, *Fascist Modernities*, 134.
14. A. Trumble. 2004. *A Brief History of the Smile*, New York: Basic Books, 22.
15. K. Theweleit. 1987. *Male Fantasies*, 2 vols, Minneapolis: University of Minnesota Press.
16. See B. Spackman. 1996. *Fascist Virilities: Rhetoric, Ideology and Social Fantasy in Italy*, Minneapolis: University of Minnesota Press.
17. Savio, *Cinecittà anni trenta*, 320.
18. Ibid., 321.
19. See Savio *Cinecittà anni trenta*, 586–87; and F. Borghini. 1989. *Fosco Giachetti*, Florence: Edizioni Play Time, 5–6.
20. Savio, *Cinecittà anni trenta*, 587.
21. Ibid.
22. F. Pasinetti, 'I film della Mostra di Venezia', *Cinema*, 25 September 1942, 545.
23. Anon., 'Addio, Kira!', *Cinema*, 10 November 1942, 654–55.
24. Ibid., 655.
25. Savio, *Cinecittà anni trenta*, 584.
26. Notari was best known as the voice of many Luce Institute newsreels.
27. D. Sabatello, 'Vita del cinematografo: *Lo squadrone bianco*', *L'Italia letteraria*, 1 November 1936, 5.
28. C. Maza, 'Già a 12 anni avevo gli italiani ai piedi', *Eva* 34, 1969, 48.
29. C. Silva, 'Riabbracciando Assia Noris', *La Domenica del Corriere*, 23 May 1981, 43.
30. Savio, *Cinecittà anni trenta*, 591.
31. Sarazani, 'Fosco Giachetti'.
32. *Illustrazione del Popolo* 8, 1938, 8.

33. G. Wills. 1997. *John Wayne: The Politics of Celebrity*, London: Faber, 13.
34. Ibid., 29.
35. Ibid., 27.
36. J. Schnapp. 1996. *Staging Fascism: 18BL and the Theater of Masses for Masses*, Stanford: Stanford University Press, 94–95.
37. A.M. Banti. 2006. *La nazione del Risorgimento: parentela, santità e onore alle origini dell'Italia unita*, Turin: Einaudi, 196.
38. Borghini, *Fosco Giachetti*, 12.
39. Ibid., 12.
40. *Illustrazione del Popolo* 8, 1938, 8.
41. Emmeci, 'Fosco Giachetti', *La voce di Bergamo*, 24 April 1941, 3.
42. Borghini, *Fosco Giachetti*, 6.
43. Ibid., 12.
44. P. Osso. Undated. *Fosco Giachetti: il nostro prototipo*, Milan: Albore, 10.
45. Ibid., 12.
46. Savio, *Cinecittà anni trenta*, 585.
47. Osso, *Fosco Giachetti*, 16.

10

The Photogenic Beauty
Alida Valli

Mille lire al mese (One Thousand Lire Per Month, Max Neufeld, 1939), a frothy comedy of errors set in a Budapest television station, is the film that more than any other has been taken to encapsulate the popular cinema of the Fascist period. With its pastiche Hungarian setting but comfortably familiar faces and relationships,[1] its theme rooted in petit bourgeois aspirations (the sum referred to in the title was the average salary of a white-collar worker) and gay atmosphere, it was a typical example of the unpretentious, workmanlike comedies that were churned out by the Cinecittà studios to divert the masses. Apart from the initial premise of a highly qualified technician, a television engineer no less, who is forced to migrate to find work in his field, no reference to reality is allowed to intrude in the pleasant confection that was crafted with appropriate attention to rhythm and bolstered by a colourful cast of supporting actors. The artificiality of the setting is confirmed by the meta-cinematic reference that follows the title song: Magda, the engineer's fiancée, turns off the radio following the announcement that she has been listening to the song 'Mille lire al mese' from the film of the same title. It is reinforced in the final scene, when the two couples who have been protagonists of the story link arms and break out into a dance.

Mille lire al mese was by no means the most ostentatious or costly of the so-called 'white telephone' films. Blasetti's *Retroscena* (Backstage, 1939), for example, a markedly less popular film made the same year, featured a much greater display of luxury in its settings of grand hotels, cruise liners, opera houses, superlative automobiles and costumes. If it holds a particular place in popular memory it is because it spoke, in comedic key, to a widely felt concern about the difficulties of finding a well-paid job and settling down, and because it was the film that first decisively brought to public attention an actress who would shortly emerge as a popular favourite and who would later be described as the best and most original creation of the cinema of the period. The script – by Luigi Zampa, who was also assistant director and who, in the postwar years, would direct several biting satires of the Fascist period – was one of the most ably crafted of the time.

As Magda, the enterprising girl who goes to Budapest alone to find work for her qualified but indolent fiancé Gabriele, played by Osvaldo Valenti, Alida Valli struck critics and spectators alike with her lively spontaneity. Aged only eighteen, she brought a fresh sparkle to the part and contributed to the overall success of the film. Male critics in the press commented on her 'gracious manner' and 'likeable face', the Turin-based *Gazzetta del Popolo* critic noting that she 'makes her mark with her lively, spontaneous and courteous personality' and her 'physical qualities – a mobile, candidly expressive little face situated atop an exquisite body – which well match her theatrical ones'.[2]

Fig. 10.1 Osvaldo Valenti and Alida Valli in the madcap 'white telephone' comedy *Mille lire al mese* (One Thousand Lire per Month). (Author's own collection)

Everyone predicted a radiant future for her in the expanding Italian cinema. A supplement to the magazine *Hollywood* published in 1949 still recalled the impact of 'the freshness of her personality, truly exceptional in the film world' at the time of this film.[3]

To look a little deeper, it may be said that Valli traced out in this film some of the traits of her screen persona. She is conventional in that she does not herself work and is seeking to create the economic conditions for her marriage, but also modern: she travels alone, accepts invitations out, invents plots and schemes, pushes her fiancé in his career, and is brusque with men she sees as nuisances or molesters. There is something spiky about her, as she meddles in others' business and does not mince her words. Yet she is also sweet and remissive when the occasion demands it. There are few close-ups in the film, but almost all of them are for Valli. The remarkable photogenic beauty that would win plaudits for years to come was highlighted in a scene in a restaurant in which the camera lingers on her top-lit face as she confesses her anxieties to Gabriele's new employer. In an unreal setting, she is believable; in a film whose characters have no deep significance, she brings a touch of emotional depth. Her costumes in the film are not at all elegant, and nor is her deportment (she wears flat shoes and strides when she walks) – elements that confirm the note of realism she brings to her character.

The director of the film, Max Neufeld (whose first name was Italianised in the credits as Massimiliano) was an Austrian Jew who had come to Rome from Vienna in 1938 in search of a more congenial working environment. A specialist in light comedies with a central European flavour, he directed Valli no fewer than six times, more than any other director. Although these films are not considered to be her best, they made a decisive contribution to establishing her as a star. All of them were released between 1939 and 1940. The settings and plots are quite varied: in *La casa del peccato* (The House of Sin, 1939), marital jealousy provides the spur to comical misunderstandings; in *Ballo al castello* (Dance at the castle, 1939), a young dancer shrugs off insinuations that she is the lover of a prince to win success and marry her suspicious fiancé; in *Assenza ingiustificata* (Unjustified Absence, 1939), a young girl abandons school and marries a medic, only to decide secretly to resume her studies when he spends too much time at the hospital; in *Taverna rossa* (Red Tavern, 1940), a girl marries a count after an interminable series of misunderstandings, tricks, lies and simulations; in *La prima donna che passa* (The First Woman Who Passes, 1940) the usual sequence of misunderstandings is transferred to the seventeenth-century French court. These slight films brought three things to Valli's career. First, they established beyond any doubt her ability to tackle light comedy, bringing an unusual naturalistic playing to the genre. Second, they reinforced the perception established in *Mille lire al mese* that Valli's photogenic qualities were exceptional. In this period several young actresses brought to Italian screens faces that were so perfect as to seem like they were sculpted from sugar. The success of Assia Noris was the inspiration for a sequence of young players of whom Valli was the most prominent and Irasema Dilian a further example. These *signorinette* contributed to the dream world constructed in the movies by means of their innocence and irresponsibility. Neufeld's cinematographers almost always came, like him, from Central Europe, and the most frequent was the Czech Vaclav Vich, who first understood that Valli's face was enhanced rather than diminished by an astute use of shadow. As Stefano Masi has noted, neither Vich nor his compatriot Jan Stallich 'employed the enormous quantity of light to which Italian cinematographers were accustomed';[4] rather, they created a single main source of light and directed shadows uniformly. As such, they mainly made more realistic films in Italy; and the rare comedies on which they were employed 'smell only vaguely of white telephones'. Third, these films saw the first pairings of Valli with Amedeo Nazzari, a cinematic couple that spectators immediately took to.

Neufeld's sophisticated films did not enjoy universal praise from critics. Some found them false and mannered. Cesare Zavattini, in his review of *Ballo al castello*, dubbed him 'a provincial aunt' who was incapable of originality. Everything in the film had been seen before in some operetta or old silent film, he commented.[5] Despite the derivative nature of their plots, they guaranteed a certain standard of quality that was not present throughout Italian cinema, and provided a platform for some emerging as well as established actors. The fact that Valli also made some four films with each of two Italian journeymen directors, Carmine Gallone and Mario Mattoli, means that her work with Neufeld established her as an adaptable actress suited to a range of popular genres as well as a box-office guarantee for producers.

The pairing with Amedeo Nazzari – which, after the two actors appeared in roles of different weight in *La casa del peccato*, was established with *Assenza ingiustificata* – was in a way a consecration. Nazzari was the most popular actor in Italy, a consummate professional who had starred with nearly all the actresses of note. That the pair evidently worked so well on screen, despite the difference of age and experience, showed Valli's potential and raised the prospect that she might displace Noris as the country's most popular actress. Noris was the first to see this danger and, during the filming of *La casa del peccato*, in which she played the female lead while Valli was a supporting player, made sure that she had the best shots and complained when Valli's costumes and hats resembled her own. Her lighting in the film is resolutely traditional, with the backlighting that was her signature style giving her fair hair a conventional angelic glow.[6] Together, Valli and Nazzari seemed like the ideal Italian couple; he was the most handsome of men, the embodiment of a certain physical and moral ideal, while she was winning recognition for her fresh, youthful beauty and confrontational personality. Despite her relative inexperience, Valli refused to accept any advice or coaching from Nazzari, and their screen relationship too was characterised by a certain friction.⁷ Only *Apparizione* – the 1943 film in which Nazzari plays himself; and Valli, a young fan who meets her idol, is tempted to dump her fiancé for him – situated them in a blatantly unequal way.

Like many young actresses, Valli was predominantly an ingénue. She played fiancées, schoolgirls, daughters of industrialists and taxi drivers, dancers, secretaries and students. She was one of the many new faces that lent their countenances to a gallery of female types that corresponded to roles available to young women at the time. In several screen roles, she is no different from many of her colleagues, notably the ensemble schoolgirl comedy *Ore 9 lezione di chimica* (9 O'Clock Chemistry Lesson, Mario Mattoli, 1941). In others, however, she was more than an ingénue. For her biographers, Lorenzo Pellizzari and Claudio Valentinetti, she captured something a little more complex. If the dominant female image that the era would transmit to successive generations was that of the oppressed mother and housewife, they argue:

> the existence of another model, present in every class and category, cannot be excluded; and it is to that model that Valli is close: no less functional to the regime, it is that of the girl who is independent, who combines exterior daring with a repressed sense of duty, desire for distraction with possible repentance, cheeky enterprise with a basic respect for hierarchy, and who manages to skirt convention while coexisting with it.⁸

The issue here concerns the meaning of the term ingénue. This is often used in discussions of the young female stars of the period but its meaning is rarely elucidated. In an article in *Cinema* in 1949, Alfredo Peroni reflected on a category that by then had disappeared. The ingénues of Italian cinema were 'the most simple and insubstantial personalities that have ever been seen, and of this lack of substance they died', he argued.⁹ In his view, this figure was invented by producers and directors who, with Cinderella in mind, sought out 'women endowed with big wide-open eyes' who could bring to the screen a fairy-tale flavour. The problem was that young women who believed that babies were brought by storks or were found under cabbage plants did not exist in reality and, even if they had, they were not likely to interest the public or provide a boost to national cinema. Whereas the real ingénue was instinctive, unreflective and uncaring about convention, Peroni continued, 'the woman who is unworldly is not ingenuous, rather she is inexpert; the woman who is capable of patiently waiting for a lover who is remote and maybe unfaithful is not ingenuous, she is good and honest'. This type was a feature of many films and reflected the demand that actresses were needed who were 'typically Italian girls, modest, healthy and virtuous'.¹⁰ These worked well on screen because, as Lidia Menapace has argued, 'the possibility of identifying with the dreams, desires and adventures of those faces was considerable'.¹¹ However, precisely because varied narratives needed to be woven around such figures, frequently ingenuousness was only a starting point for trajectories that led in the direction of temptation and daring. It was precisely in this area that the fortune of Alida Valli was affirmed, since she was, for Peroni, 'one of the few actresses who were thought to be capable of acting, as well as opening her eyes wide'.[12]

The regime placed great emphasis on youth. The Fascist movement had pitched youth against age, and Mussolini, as the youngest ever Italian prime minister at age 39 in 1922, sought to endow his regime with youthful vigour. In reshaping the customs and values of the nation, the education of the young was given a prominent part. The generation that was brought up under the regime was seen as embodying the hopes of the future. Young men, of course, were destined for the battlefront, since Mussolini believed that it was only through war that nations proved their mettle. Women were encouraged to see their roles as wives and mothers as in the service of the nation. The huge investment in health and welfare reform that occurred under Fascism was designed precisely to reduce infant mortality and ensure the health of the Italians of the future. Through propaganda and activities that lent themselves to visual representation, images of healthy and good-looking young Italians were generated and diffused.

Youth was also seen as the hope of Italian cinema. The creation and development of the Centro sperimentale was intended to form the personnel who would reinvigorate Italian cinema at a time when the regime was actively promoting its expansion.[13] It was hoped that a new generation of actors trained specifically for the screen would bring professionalism to films along with the moral and physical qualities that demonstrated the success of the regime's investments in the nation's future. For this reason pleasure was taken in the appearance of new talents who exemplified the dogma, articulated most forcefully and repeatedly by the publicist Umberto Notari, that the Italians were the best-looking people in the world.[14] The emphasis on beauty which had been an element of nationalist discourses since the Risorgimento was elaborated under Fascism into an aspect of the idea of Italy as the beacon of civilisation. In the modern era, no medium could communicate this more powerfully than the cinema.

Debates over the characteristics that defined Italian beauty bore witness to the difficulty of establishing a single, generally accepted model. But critics were agreed that women were anyway the main vehicle of beauty since they were everywhere considered to be 'the representatives of the general characteristics of the peoples they belong to' and functioned as 'the eyes of the race', as one critic wrote in a popular weekly.[15] In illustrated magazines and feature articles, examples of typical Italian beauties were presented to readers. Whenever Mussolini undertook visits to rural areas, he was pictured surrounded by a selection of young beauties. Cinema, however, remained a problematic area, because of the evident influence of foreign models and the presence of significant numbers of foreign or part-foreign actresses. It was also problematic because it was a modern medium, born in an urban context, that primarily dealt with urban themes and addressed urban audiences. It was part of a media system that included radio and the press which proposed its own ideas about feminine beauty that were not straightforwardly those of the regime. The most popular example of commercial beauty at this time was constituted by the *Signorina Grandi Firme*, a cover girl drawn by the illustrator Gino Boccasile who adorned the covers of the magazine of the same name between 1937 and 1938. The *Signorina* was a dark-haired, shapely young woman with full red lips, a narrow waist and long legs that were always prominently in view. She wore tailored suits, dresses, swimsuits, sportswear and demure office wear. Each cover depicted her engaged in some activity: applying sun lotion, cheering on a football team, enjoying an open-air opera, visiting a tourist site, dreaming about film stars, or, on one occasion, marching triumphantly towards Cinecittà. No angel of the hearth but a modern girl, she was energetic and extrovert, enterprising and cheerful, as well sometimes as clumsy and accident-prone. 'With her unaware beauty she was appreciated by everyone: to men she offered a reassuring image of womanhood, despite certain obvious sexual connotations, and to women a point of comparison that was so abstract as to never become a fearsome rival', Paola Biribanti has written.[16] She was, Biribanti continues, 'the symbol of an era, emblem of those multiform and contradictory 1930s, years of "white telephones", of Fascist rigour, ersatz products and great film stars from Alida Valli to Clara Calamai and Assia Noris'.[17]

The *Signorina* was a popular but controversial figure whose brief heyday was brought to a halt when Mussolini determined the closure of the magazine, without explanation, in October 1938. She was not inspired by an actress but rather by a girl Boccasile spotted one day on a street in Milan.[18] She is an ordinary girl who loves cinema and partakes of the dreams it peddles. Her beauty is not static or historical but contemporary, and in that sense it is inseparable from her way of life.

It is useful to think of the beauty of Alida Valli in relation to these prevailing ideas and representations. Although her father was born in Trento of Germanic stock and her mother was half Slovenian, she was never considered to be anything other than Italian. This was so because she was born in Pola, not far from the city of Fiume that D'Annunzio had consecrated to the nationalist cause with his temporary occupation of it in the aftermath of the First World War. Moreover, she had grown up in Como. The surname she was born with, Altenberger, was exchanged for the more acceptable Valli after her first screen role in 1936. Her appearance was more Italian than that of many of the actresses working in Cinecittà. With her light-brown hair, high forehead and frank smile, she seemed to match exactly the demand for fresh young talent that the regime expected. Yet she was not precisely 'una faccia da casa nostra' (a recognisably Italian face). Unlike Luisa Ferida, she did not have coarse features; she was not sweet and demure like Maria Denis or earthy and sensual like Doris Duranti; she was not sugary like Assia Noris or simpering like Irasema Dillian. Her face was not bland but intriguing, and the studio photographs that Arturo Ghergo took of her caught the intensity of her gaze and inner mystery as much as her beauty.[19] Seen in profile, she had a large forehead that was convex, a nose that curved up to a point, and prominent lips and chin. Caricaturists had no difficulty capturing and exaggerating her likeness. Her undulating features provided the light traps that made Valli the most photogenic of the new stars of the period.

Valli pleased traditionalists with her beautifully cinematic face, while bringing something distinctive and unusual that marked her out as an individual. Her looks seemed to conform to a conventional idea of beauty while also being modern. There could be no doubt that she was a modern urban girl of bourgeois extraction. She had a liveliness and practicality to her that marked her first steps towards cinema. At the age of fifteen, she was keen to go to work after her father's death. Rejecting the conventional paths of training to be a primary school teacher or waiting at home until she married, she resolved to try her hand as a film actress. 'My family sent me to Rome where an uncle was to take care of me. There I learned about the Centro sperimentale school', she later recounted.[20] Alessandro Blasetti, who had been its first director and was still a teacher there, received her and the uncle ('a tall, elderly and good-humoured man of few words') at his house one autumn morning.[21] 'No one "introduced" her – at that time "recommendations" were forbidden, as a nepotistic leftover of the bourgeois regime', Blasetti recalled. Although she spoke little, refused to sit down and stared at the floor, he suspected that she had 'a temperament waiting to be revealed':

> While she listened to the man who had accompanied her from the opposite side of the table, Alida turned towards me – I was not looking at her – and resolved not to lower her gaze or in any way give the impression of avoiding my eyes. When I suddenly turned my head and surprised her by looking directly into her eyes, my instinct was awakened as if by an alarm – not so much on account of her delightful figure or the deep blue intensity of those extraordinary pupils as because of the character that Alida demonstrated by not turning away. In that moment, her pride scored a hard-fought victory over her timidity. I immediately 'recommended' her to the Centro, and Chiarini [the then director] admitted her. He too was so convinced of her potential that he bypassed the procedural issues that arose over admitting a student to a course that had already commenced.[22]

Valli was anything but a model pupil. Her talent was undeniable and her photographs splendid, but her behaviour was erratic and disruptive, as though she was desperate 'to hasten her achievement of the status of actress and woman, with a fully independent life'.[23] Testimonies suggest that she was headstrong and tomboy-ish, and given to pranks. She was equally undisciplined on the sets of her two first films, to which various pupils of the

Centro were recruited to play small supporting parts. Although she got on well with some of the teachers, her behaviour eventually led to her expulsion from the school. 'Chiarini chucked me out as hopeless', she later admitted.[24] However, she maintained contact both with teachers and fellow students. Her lively personality and fondness for jokes meant she was ideally suited to playing spirited youngsters like Vera, the disobedient wife in *Assenza ingiustificata*, and Anna, a girl with just these qualities, in the school comedy *Ore 9 lezione di chimica*.

For this reason, it was quite easy to place her in some situations that were reminiscent of the *Signorina Grandi Firme*. There were other actresses who, in their manner as well as in the composition of some their film scenes, evoked more clearly and explicitly this visual cliché – for example the German actress Elena Luber as the daughter Nanà in *La famiglia Brambilla va in vacanza* (The Brambilla Family Goes On Holiday, Carl Boese, 1942). But Valli's prominence made them more memorable, especially in the film *L'amante segreta* (The Secret Lover) which presented her as Renata, a wealthy girl whose tutor has squandered her inheritance, forcing her to seek work to make ends meet. Dressed in a tailored suit of the type Boccasile's creation often wears, she finds employment as an encyclopedia salesperson before securing a more regularly remunerated post as a hotel secretary. There is a series of set-piece vignettes in the film which may plausibly have been taken from the life of a young woman like her character. She is shown ice skating; she is spied on as she takes the sun in a bathing costume; she is approached by a local painter who wishes her to pose for him; she takes a ride in a car; and she is subjected to the brusque manner and molestations of her employer. A variety of men, all older than her, some by many years, seek to win a place in her affections.

The theme of the film (whose alternative title was *Troppo bella*, Too Beautiful) is her beauty. Throughout the development of the narrative, men fall at her feet, attempt to charm her, stare at her, and comment on her appearance. She is constructed as a textbook example of the male gaze. Shot by Vaclav Vich, who by this time had filmed her on three previous occasions, her numerous close-ups bathe her in an idealising hazy glow that contrasts sharply with the crisp realism with which the men in the film are captured. The spectator is given numerous opportunities to dwell on her hair, face, eyes and mouth as well as admire her figure clothed in close-fitting city clothes and work wear. There is a dichotomy between her gracious, reserved manner and the desires she unleashes in all the men around her. Like Boccasile's creation, she seems unaware of the effect she has, at least until her employer feigns the theft of money from the hotel safe in an attempt to force her to give in to his beastly advances. Even the one man who has appeared kind but unmoved, Fosco Giachetti playing a colonial returnee, kisses and embraces her when she turns to him for assistance. On this occasion she presents no resistance.

The culmination of her trajectory as object of desire in the film comes when she is obliged, in order to replace the missing money and save her job and reputation, to pose nude for the painter for the sum of 3,000 lire. Later, when the finished painting is unveiled she is identified before a group of socialites as its anonymous subject, and she steps up and admits that she is the woman men desire and women hate. The scene in which she strips to pose, which is conveyed in *mise-en-abyme* and confirmed by the vision of a naked shoulder, was a daring invitation to the spectator to imagine the naked body of Renata and therefore of Valli. Although brief, it was played up in the marketing of the film and indeed the very title ('The Secret Lover' of the film title is the title of the painting). The film, in short, offered a poignant depiction of the affronts and compromises an honest working girl may face, while itself exploiting the physical charms of its protagonist.

Unlike the *Signorina Grandi Firme*, Valli is not constructed from the legs up in the film, a hallmark of Boccasile's creation that the critic Antonio Faeti has identified as a sign of her 'virility', that is to say her being a female pin-up in the hyper-masculine context of Fascism.[25] But she is constantly on the move between spaces and geographical locations. She is mobile in a way that few young protagonists in films of the time are. Renata in fact is no one's lover in the film, but the insistent construction of her as object of desire reflected, and contributed to, a sexualisation of Valli's own image. All younger women in the cinema of the time were presented as ingénues but the ways and degrees to which they were sexualised were various, as has been seen with Noris and Miranda. In the case of all three actresses, their very first significant role introduced an implication of sexual experience that was never wholly eradicated even in films in which they were virginal. The difference was that, whereas Noris in *Giallo* and Miranda in *La signora di tutti* were given sophisticated images older than their real ages, their characters were also – or became in the course of the film – married women. In *Il feroce Saladino* (The Fierce Saladin, Mario Bonnard, 1937), in which the sixteen-year-old Valli played a supporting part, she takes the role of an odalisque, the sexy dancer 'the beautiful Sulamita', whose costume of veils, bare midriff and harem pants is that of a fantasy *entraineuse*. Giacomo Debenedetti, reviewing the film, commented in conventional terms on 'the enchanting figure and the fresh grace of the girl ... the young actress Alida Valli who is revealed as an ingénue of uncommon quality'.[26] In reviews of another film of the same year, Raffaello Matarazzo's *Sono stato io!* (It Was Me!), the tone is already slightly different, with Dino Falconi describing Valli in the Fascist newspaper *Il Popolo d'Italia* as 'a gracious and spontaneous little lady' and Filippo Sacchi in the *Corriere della Sera* referring to her 'piquant photogenic' qualities.[27]

Valli's biographers note that the issue of her desirability was one that from 1939 was affecting casting.[28] Blasetti rejected pressure to cast her as a well-meaning duchess in his costume film *Un avventura di Salvator Rosa*

(An Adventure of Salvator Rosa, 1939) on the grounds that she would have disturbed the ending; the audience would have expected the painter to end up with the 'sexual' Valli instead of the 'gracious, delicious' peasant girl Maria Denis, and this was not the way the plot unfolded. Thus the predominant ingénue image was coloured and shaken by an alternative image, one that reached its culmination in *Noi vivi*, one of the actress's most powerful roles, in which she is simultaneously involved in sexual relationships with two men.

The sexy image that was worked into the Valli persona was one that derived from a number of sources: the roles the actress took, visual and narrative references to her body or appearance, and the adult nature of some of the situations in her films. But it also derived from the promiscuity of the contexts in which the actress found herself in her contemporary films. Only a handful of her roles were played in mainly domestic settings or in female-dominated ones such as the boarding school. More often she was located in working or commercial environments, or played characters belonging to these. *Il feroce Saladino* itself was a by-product of a hugely successful commercial tie-in with a comedy radio programme entitled *The Four Musketeers*. Two national companies, Buitoni and Perugina, which lacked the resources to stage a national advertising campaign alone, joined forces to launch a series of promotional cards depicting the characters of the radio programme, which included the beautiful Sulamita and the fierce Saladin – the latter being so rare and sought-after a card as to come to symbolise the entire promotion. In other films Valli played students, a beauty salon assistant, a socialite, a secretary and a dancer. Often the girlish enthusiasm of her characters was signalled by a little run, to pick up a telephone, answer a door or meet someone of her own age.

Valli herself was a commercial property of some importance. Her success with audiences led to situations like that described above, when the director Blasetti clashed with production and distribution companies over casting. In 1938 she became the first Italian actress to be signed up to a Hollywood-style five-year contract for the sum of 5,000 lire per month by the company Italcine, a sum that increased as her popularity grew.[29] However, the film company did little or nothing to mould and promote her. 'At that time', she recalled, 'an actress was not something that producers and costume designers shaped like Pygmalions, and actresses like me lived normally ... At a certain point, I was quite fat but no one told me to go on a diet.'[30] Later she was signed up to Minerva film. Despite being a valuable property, Valli's image was not subjected to broader commercialisation. Like most actors she continued to make an average of four films per year and, like most actresses of the time, she only did a small amount of advertising.

Her popularity grew exponentially. She participated with many others in the gathering organised by Vittorio Mussolini at Riccione in the summer of 1939 that was intended to cement a nascent Italian star system by bringing together the stars and their fans. A number of contemporary observers, including the cinematographer Aldo Tonti, have written how she became a model for young women who copied her Veronica Lake-style side parting and plucked eyebrows, while the most eager also drew inspiration from her masculine overcoats and berets.[31] According to Valli herself, this was entirely a spontaneous phenomenon:

> It seems I influenced the fashion of an era. At the time I never realised it because I wore my hair straight because that is the way it was and because I never managed to keep it neatly combed. It kept falling in my eye. The tartan skirt and shoulder bag were born by chance without any intention of creating a style. I never chose anything with the aim of creating a type and it did not even occur to the people at Italcine, to which I was contracted, to turn me into a type.[32]

At times, her popularity took disturbing forms. When the premiere of *Piccolo mondo antico* (Little Old World, Mario Soldati, 1941) was held in Vicenza in April 1941, a mob of students tried to force their way into her hotel.[33] At the Venice festival that year she was horrified to find herself the object of insistent attentions on the part of fans, who grabbed at her and ripped her clothes. Similar scenes repeated themselves when she returned to the city of her birth, Pola, after an absence of twelve years.[34] The journalist and press agent Vittorio Calvino described, in the magazine *Scena illustrata*, an actress who was deeply harassed by interviewers, autograph-hunters and fans who showed no respect for her person. As an acquaintance of the actress, he was able to quote from a few of the many letters she received.[35]

Valli's press image in fact presented her as highly accessible. The illustrated weekly *Tempo* ran a photographic article in October 1940 in which the actress is not only introduced by her private pet name (Kitty) but is shown in a series of everyday activities: waking, receiving the post and newspapers from her maid, performing some physical jerks, responding to letters, having lunch, taking a bicycle ride and going to bed early.[36] Of course, there was much here that was concealed. There was no mention of Valli's personal life or her long-distance relationship that had lasted since 1934 with the pilot Carlo Cugnasca, who would perish in combat in 1941. There was no description of her real living conditions or of the social relations she cultivated within and outside the world of cinema. But there was something true about this naturalist image. At no point in her pre-1945 career was Valli ever depicted as a woman of refinement of elegance. On occasion, for example in *Ballo al castello* or even *Mille lire al mese*, she wore eye-catching frocks but these were nothing compared to the studied elegance of, say, Clara Calamai, or the innate stylishness of a lesser actress, Rubi D'Alma. In part because of her young age, her relationship with fashion was an arm's length one, and it was left to admirers to imitate accessories or hairstyles. The beret she wore in *Noi vivi* became as popular in Italy as Michèle Morgan's in France.

No doubt this apparent accessibility contributed to her popularity among young women for whom she was not a remote figure and for young men and soldiers for whom she was an ideal figure of woman. Her pictures circulated widely. The passport photograph of her shown in an early scene of *Noi vivi* was put into circulation as a chocolate card, while her photograph features on the wall above a soldier's bunk in the war film *Giarabub* (Augusto Genina, 1942). Although increasingly reserved in her dealings with the public, Valli was not aloof. Her colleagues found her easy-going and she often ate in the second category restaurant at Cinecittà that was frequented by technicians and supporting actors.

Valli sealed her position with a series of popular films directed by Mario Mattoli and one splendid literary adaptation that would win her unprecedented acclaim as an actress. Mattoli was much appreciated by producers because he always turned in his films on time and to budget. Entertainment was his idiom and he never claimed to produce anything else. Between 1941 and 1942, he made four films that were conceived as speaking 'to your heart'.[37] These were unashamed tearjerkers inspired by popular literary texts that were mostly oriented towards a female audience. Released one after the other over a period of just fifteen months, they aimed not to make the audience laugh but rather to cry. They were precursors of a more famous series directed by Raffaello Matarazzo starring Amedeo Nazzari and Yvonne Sanson in the 1950s. Valli starred in the first three of these films. In *Luce nelle tenebre* (Light in the Darkness, 1941) the constancy of her affections is rewarded when the man she loves, who is engaged to her sister (played by Clara Calamai), is blinded in an accident. He only realises that it is Valli who has helped care for him when, thanks to an operation, he reacquires his sight. In *Catene invisibili* (Invisible Chains, 1942) she takes the part of an industrialist's socialite daughter who is taken advantage of by her late father's illegitimate son. The gruff manager of her late father's factory, played by the Bolognese actor Carlo Ninchi, falls for her but confesses his love only when he realises that the man she has been protecting is not her lover but her half-brother. The film is the only contemporary one in which Valli's modernity is given a mildly negative connotation. She is spoilt and frivolous; she smokes and drinks, and seems only to care about money. Her relations with her mother are poor. Her shallowness is indicated by some ostentatious costumes, including a magnificent mink coat and a dashing trench coat, which were supplied by the Milanese fashion designer Biki. Interestingly, she was photographed crisply by Anchise Brizzi, whose numerous close-ups are lit realistically until the point at which the attitude of Ninchi's character towards her changes. From then on, she is given the conventional backlit aura of the romantic heroine. Her role as Elena added a layer to her screen persona as, not for the first time, she played the spoilt young bourgeoise. In the end she is redeemed through the love of the initially paternal Ninchi (whose character is revealed as being forty-one, while

Valli's is twenty-two). In the final film in the series, *Stasera niente di nuovo* (This Evening Nothing New, 1942), Valli plays a prostitute who tries but fails to redeem herself. On her deathbed she marries a journalist with whom she has shared the low life. Mattoli later revealed that the production company did not want Valli's character to die, fearing it would be badly received at the box office. However, the director, whose hand was strengthened by the success of the previous films, insisted and got his way.

The morality of these films was highly conventional. The male protagonists were actors who brought rough authenticity to their playing, Fosco Giachetti in the first and Carlo Ninchi in the second and the third. Ninchi was a Roman-nosed bruiser with a deep voice who in his best roles had something of the avuncular feel of Spencer Tracy and on less good days was a local version of Wallace Beery. His best role was as the fearless major who commands the doomed Italian fortress in the film *Giarabub*, set in North Africa. His relatively unemotional performance style and maturity contrasted with the youthful radiance and mobility of Valli, an actress whose ability to convey subtle shades of mood and feeling was already well known.

Had Valli remained as the favoured heroine of films of this type she would surely have consolidated her popularity. But she would not have won the respect that she acquired playing in two films that would bring her the highest praise of her career. *Piccolo mondo antico* was a well-loved novel by the nineteenth-century writer Antonio Fogazzaro. The decision to make a film version of it in 1941 was a controversial one since Fascist opinion was sceptical about the quantity of nineteenth-century set films being made and was doubtful about the wisdom of reviving a story that evoked the domination of Italy by Austria.[38] Mario Soldati's film is one that is belongs to a current of so-called calligraphic films that dwelt on period detail and literary culture to escape the restrictions that weighed on films with contemporary settings. The story allowed for a careful exploration of the intertwining of individual destinies and spiritual inclinations with a careful evocation of landscape and place. Shot on location in the places described in the novel, the film was a demonstration of the highest quality film-making. Valli, who won universal praise and the award of best actress at Venice for her playing of Luisa, claimed that with this film cinema became for her a serious matter, an artistic means of expression.[39] The shoot was riven with sexual tension between her and Soldati, who, having only accepted her after seeing a screen test fell for her on set, and her and an assistant director, the future master of the *commedia all'italiana* Dino Risi, with whom she enjoyed a brief liaison.[40] It was her first serious dramatic role, her departure from comedy and melodrama. A great actress was revealed, a fact that was amply underlined by press criticism and the subsequent public response. However, the film was not a watershed. Just as before, when the actress had been offered 'role after role' and had accepted them all 'without stopping to reflect on what was required of me', so now she continued with comedies and melodramas.[41]

Fig. 10.2 Alida Valli (Kira) and Fosco Giachetti (Andrei) in a still from *Noi vivi* (We the Living), a controversial drama set in Soviet Russia (*Cinema*, 25 September 1942). (Author's own collection)

The second film which confirmed Valli's new status as a dramatic actress of emotional subtlety and depth was *Noi vivi – Addio Kira*. Released in 1943, this film did not have anything like the audience of *Piccolo mondo antico*. Its posthumous fame outstrips by far its significance as a box office phenomenon. Nevertheless the actors were paid for two films and Valli claimed that with the proceeds of 180,000 lire she bought an apartment in the fashionable Parioli district of Rome. The film brought confirmation of her talents and also signalled important developments in her persona. Once again she plays a modern young woman, in this case a student who aspires to become an architect; the only problem being that she is living in post-revolutionary Russia under an order with which she has no sympathy. She shares this attitude with her lover Leo, played by Rossano Brazzi. She nonetheless forms an association with the honest communist Andrei (Giachetti) whose political faith she gradually undermines. The studio-bound film is shot in dark naturalist tones with ample use of shadow and close-ups. The action is surrounded by an atmosphere of gloom and impending doom that is only briefly lightened by the burgeoning but impossible love affairs of the three protagonists. Valli's playing is a triumph of emotional ambiguity. Her eyes and face convey every shade of the inner torment of a woman who in Ayn Rand's novel is loosely drawn. Never was melancholy made so compelling.

Valli herself later said that that she occupied a median position, insinuating herself between the 'alignment of lively naughty Lilia Silvi-style girls and that of the super-sensual, sinister and vaguely ambiguous actresses of the Luisa Ferida or Clara Calamai type'.[42] Her biographers feel that this view, expressed in the 1950s, may have been influenced by hindsight, for in fact she was a little more complex, different from the norm and unusual. As the exuberant nature she displayed to colleagues was tempered by a reserve that returned following the expansion of her fame and personal loss, she became a subtle and mysterious actress with a distinctive screen personality of her own. While still only aged twenty-four at the time of the fall of Fascism, she has been seen as the only fully formed star produced by autarkic cinema.[43]

For this reason, she was a valuable asset to the regime, which aimed to harness her fame to propaganda. Like other actresses, Valli was drawn into the campaign of comfort for soldiers. She visited the wounded in hospital and met numerous requests for autographed pictures. Like Noris and Miranda, she was sent to Berlin, where she made *I pagliacci* (Giuseppe Fatigati, 1943) with the tenor Beniamino Gigli, a fluent German-speaker and admirer of Nazism. Valli took no part in the rituals of high society that flourished under the regime and always preferred to socialise privately, but her prominence made her a target for the sort of malicious gossip that flourished under the dictatorship. Natalia Marino and Emanuele Valerio Marino have shown that spies overheard comments that attributed sexual entanglements with high Fascist officials to the actress.[44] The discovery of her real surname of Altenberger led some to identify her as a German spy. One report found that a picture of Valli in a jeweller's shop widow in Rome, on which the actress had written in her own hand 'Ogni ora sia d'oro per la Patria' (That every hour be gold for the fatherland) gave rise to 'ironical remarks and some serious ones' on the part of passers-by.[45]

With Valli, the issue of glamour presents itself forcefully. At one level, some of the basic preconditions were lacking. Valli did not benefit from any special grooming or packaging on the part of production companies or others. Moreover, although she was the most popular screen actress in Italy in the early 1940s, she did not fully become public property. Nunzia Messina has argued that Italian cinema lacked the capacity to create a mythology around its stars. Italian actresses reflected official directives in their attitudes, and in interviews they tended to 'propose a model of femininity that conformed to criteria imposed from above in which – as journalists underlined – their mammas were assiduously present even in the most unexpected situations'.[46] 'The Italian star system, she continues, was not characterised by glamour, sex appeal or the erotic and sexual charge of American models.

It generated a popularity of modest proportions, that had its obligatory itinerary in the Venice Lido during the film festival, the Via Veneto, where the stars would congregate in the summer ... and finally the postcards sent by the actors, which testified to a presence of cinema in everyday life.'[47]

It is notable that Messina has nothing to say about screen image or cinematography which are no less a part of glamour than lifestyle and publicity. On this plane, other critics have concluded that 'the spread of a photogenic canon founded on glamour coincided with the adoption on the part of the national film industry, in accord with the aspirations of the regime, of the models of the American star system'.[48] Brunetta has argued that 'right from the start of her career ... Alida Valli "enchanted" the movie camera with the sweetness and regularity of her face, the delicacy of her features, the regal "aura" that transpired from her body and her gestures which, though still tender and childish, were already capable of profound and total passions'.[49] 'As for her photogenic qualities, her close-ups are the only ones that do not induce nostalgia for Great Garbo's', he adds. Valli was not an actress who took much interest in her own image. Mattoli claimed that 'la Calamai was very attentive to the way she was photographed, to her star persona. Valli could not have cared less about this, but in cinema she came over as much more spontaneous.'[50]

It is quite apparent from the films that Valli made in the 1942–43 period that her face had come to be one of the most compelling advertisements for Italian cinema. More than that of any other actress at the time, it was foregrounded in lengthy close-ups that reached their apotheosis in *Noi vivi – Addio Kira*, a film dominated by them. Stefano Masi has identified her as 'un-starish and cordial, without pretensions, endowed with a fresh-faced beauty that above all did not require too much artifice'.[51] As a result, he argues, she 'was photographed with greater realism than her colleagues: her face is not necessarily devoid of shadow and almost none of her cinematographers tried to minimise the line between the forehead and the nose despite her strong profile. The shadows are there and they remain ... They serve to reinforce the personality of a profile that was destined to become memorable.' At the same time, the natural way Valli moved on set was linked to a model of lighting that, if not realistic, was quite simple.

These remarks highlight the different aspects which contributed to the Valli persona. Natural and spontaneous, young and eager, she had nonetheless experienced pain and misfortune. Her face was candid and complex and her expressions were never, even in her frothiest roles, untainted by some secret strain of melancholy. Her face was no blank canvas but one that offered cinematographers and photographers opportunities to write meanings with their tools. Years later, the journalist Oriana Fallaci would tell the actress: 'how many times, Alida, looking at your face, have I had the impression that I was looking at the face of Europe: so tired and yet so alive, so bitter and yet so sweet, so aware of guilt, privations, hopes and virtues. Its history is ultimately our history.'[52] Fallaci was referring to the configuration taken by Valli's face in her forties, but even her young face can be subjected to symbolic reading. More than any other face of the period, Alida Valli's expresses the tribulations of an era in which all shadows and doubts were to be banished in favour of heroic dedication and obedient devotion. The shadows that adorn her photographic image had an aesthetic origin, but they served, for those who wished to see them, to flag up the falsity of the official optimism of the regime.

Notes

1. G.P. Brunetta. 1991. argues that 'Italian spectators were never thrown by the fake Hungarian setting; at every moment they found themselves in familiar, neighbourly environments', *Cent'anni di cinema italiano*, Rome-Bari: Laterza, 250.
2. Acer, 'Mille lire al mese', *Gazzetta del Popolo*, 27 January 1939. Quoted in E.G. Laura. 1979. *Alida Valli*, Rome: Gremese, 40.
3. Alida Valli, *I Quaderni di Hollywood*, n.11, supplement to *Hollywood*, n.200 (1949), 5, picture caption.
4. S. Masi. 1991. 'Il controluce nei capelli', in M. Argentieri (ed.), *Risate di regime: la commedia italiana 1930–1944*, Venice: Marsilio, 177–85, 182.
5. C. Zavattini, 'Ballo al castello', *Tempo*, 14 September 1939. Quoted in Laura, *Alida Valli*, 44.
6. Masi, 'Il controluce nei capelli', 178.
7. Nazzari quoted in A. Libonati, 'I digiuni allungano la mia giovinezza', *Gente*, 9 July 1964, 35.
8. L. Pellizzari and C. Valentinetti. 1995. *Il romanzo di Alida Valli*, Milan: Garzanti, 44.
9. A. Peroni, 'Le ingenue dai telefoni rosa', *Cinema*, 15 July 1949, page unnumbered.
10. N. Messina. 1987. *Le donne del fascismo: massaie rurali e dive del cinema nel ventennio*, Rome: Ellemme, 22.
11. L. Menapace. 1988. 'La giornalista, l'atleta, la star: immagini di donna durante il regime fascista', in A.M. Crispino (ed.), *Esperienza storica femminile nell'età moderna e contemporanea*, Rome: UDI, 153–59, 158.
12. Peroni, 'Le ingenue'.
13. S. Polando et al. 1985. *Vivere il cinema: cinquant'anni del centro sperimentale di cinematografia*, Rome: Presidenza del consiglio dei ministri, 10–11.
14. See U. Notari. 1933. *Dichiarazioni alle più belle donne del mondo*, Milan: Notari; and 1939. *Panegirico della Razza Italiana*, Villasanta: Notari.
15. O. Cerquiglini, 'Fiori dei campi, fiori della razza', *La Domenica del Corriere*, 3 September 1939, 8–9.

16. P. Biribanti. 2009. *Boccasile: la Signorina Grandi Firme e altri mondi*, Rome: Castelvecchi, 75.
17. Ibid., 106.
18. G. Boccasile, 'Io e le donne', *Le Grandi Firme*, 1 July 1937, 6–7.
19. See C. Domini and C. Ghergo (eds). 2012. *Arturo Ghergo: fotografie, 1930–1959*, Milan: Silvana, 138–39.
20. O. Fallaci, 'Lo specchio del passato', *L'Europeo*, 14 January 1965, 57.
21. A. Blasetti. 1982. *Il cinema che ho vissuto*, ed. by F. Prono, Bari: Dedalo, 72.
22. Ibid., 74–75.
23. Ibid., 75. For a fuller evaluation of this phase, see N. Falcinella. 2011. *Alida Valli: gli occhi, la bocca*, Genoa: Le Mani, 14–15. G.C. Castello (1957. *Il divismo: mitologia del cinema*, Turin: ERI, 416) states that the Centro sperimentale judged her 'unsuited to a film career because devoid of artistic qualities'.
24. Fallaci, 'Lo specchio del passato', 58.
25. A. Faeti. 1981. 'Introduction', G. Boccasile, *La Signorina Grandi Firme*, ed. by A. Faeti, Milan: Longanesi. See S. Gundle. 2007. *Bellissima: Feminine Beauty and the Idea of Italy*, London and New Haven: Yale University Press, 89–92.
26. G. Debenedetti. 1982. *Al cinema*, ed. by L. Micciché, Venice: Marsilio, 230.
27. D.F., 'Sono stato io!', *Il Popolo d'Italia*, 24 December 1937; and F.S., 'Sono stato io!', *Corriere della sera*, 24 December 1937 – both quoted in Laura, *Alida Valli*, 32.
28. Pellizzari and Valentinetti, *Il romanzo di Alida Valli*, 45.
29. Ibid., 39. In Fallaci, 'Lo specchio del passato', 57, Valli claimed her starting salary was 1,500 lire.
30. Fallaci, 'Lo specchio del passato', 57.
31. A. Tonti. 1964. *Odore di cinema*, Florence: Vallecchi, 95.
32. Fallaci, 'Lo specchio del passato', 57.
33. Bort, 'Alida Valli trova un personaggio', *Film*, 19 April 1941, 5.
34. Pellizzari and Valentinetti, *Il romanzo di Alida Valli*, 70–71.
35. V. Calvino, 'La "più brava" del cinema italiano', *Scena illustrata*, November 1941. Quoted in ibid., 70–71.
36. F. Pasinetti, 'Una stella si riposa', *Tempo*, 19 October 1940. The author had been her teacher at the Centro sperimentale. See Pellizzari and Valentinetti, *Il romanzo di Alida Valli*, 48.
37. S. Della Casa. 1989. *Mario Mattoli*, Florence: Il Castoro/La Nuova Italia, 35–41.
38. L. Freddi. 1949. *Il cinema*, Rome: L'Arnia, 194–97. Soldati later claimed that there was a political subtext to the film, since the Risorgimento theme highlighted the need to liberate Italy of foreign domination. See M. Soldati. 2006. *Cinematografo*, Palermo: Sellerio, 179–80.
39. Castello, *Il divismo*, 417.
40. See M. Scaglione. 2003. *Le dive del ventennio*, Turin: Lindau, 143–44; testimony of Alberto Lattuada in F. Faldini and F. Fofi (eds). 1979. *L'avventurosa storia del cinema italiano: raccontato dai suoi protagonisti, 1935–1959*, Milan: Feltrinelli, 54.

41. Faldini and Fofi, *L'avventurosa storia*, 54.
42. Quoted in Pellizzari and Valentinetti, *Il romanzo di Alida Valli*, 56.
43. Scaglione, *Le dive del ventennio*, 144.
44. N. Marino and E.V. Marino. 2005. *L'ovra a Cinecittà: polizia politica e spie in camicia nera*, Turin: Bollati Boringhieri, 234.
45. Ibid., 234–35.
46. Messina, *Le donne del fascismo*, 22.
47. Ibid., 23.
48. C. Domini. 2012. 'Di belle forme e moderne funzioni: l'opera fotografica di Arturo Ghergo' in Domini and Ghergo, *Arturo Ghergo*, 27.
49. Brunetta, *Cent'anni*, 212–13.
50. Faldini and Fofi, *L'avventurosa storia*, 34.
51. Masi, 'Il controluce nei capelli', 184–85.
52. Fallaci, 'Lo specchio del passato', 57.

11

The Duce's Whim
Miria Di San Servolo

Myriam Petacci, younger sister of Mussolini's lover Claretta, made her screen debut at the age of eighteen in 1942 in the drama *Le vie del cuore* (Ways of the Heart). Directed by Camillo Mastrocinque, who had previously made some thirteen features, the film was a costumed melodrama in which she played Anna, a young duchess who, having been diagnosed with scarlet fever, is sent to her father's villa to recover. There she attracts the attentions of her father's friends, in particular of Count Ermanno Navarria, played by the handsome and elegant Sandro Ruffini, who spurns his established lover, played by Clara Calamai, in order to marry her. Despite a certain implausibility in the main narrative and reservations about its quality, the film was selected for presentation at the Venice Film Festival. Soon after, Petacci was again cast in the lead role in *L'amico delle donne* (The Friend of Women, Ferdinando M. Poggioli, 1943). Once more the setting was historical, this time nineteenth-century Paris; and again she played a noblewoman, on this occasion a tormented wife whose husband, frustrated by his inability to count on her love, departs on an expedition to the North Pole. The film was released in April 1943 when war events were reaching the brink that would soon lead to the fall of the regime.

Although a great deal has been written about Mussolini's relationship with Claretta, there has been little analysis of Myriam's brief and less than luminous screen career under the *nom d'art* of Miria di San Servolo. Mussolini's biographers mention her only in passing, as a minor player in the larger drama involving her sister. Only Luigi Freddi has commented in any detail. In his memoirs he writes disparagingly of the various schemes and manoeuvres that were put in place to allow her to embark on a film career, and recalls the fears he felt concerning the 'political or speculative encrustations that would certainly have immediately developed' around her, 'creating new problems for an already shaky Italian cinema'.[1] It is not surprising that Freddi should have written in such negative terms about the efforts that were made to turn the Duce's lover's sister into a star. The Petacci family was the object of sharp criticism from various quarters from the later 1930s. Senior Mussolini loyalists deplored the way the Duce was distracted from his duties by his young mistress. Many were also appalled at the activities of members of her family as they pursued a strategy of personal enrichment and influence-building. The process of denigration became public from 1943 and continued after 1945, when the surviving members of the Petacci family sought refuge in Franco's Spain.

Freddi had done much to promote the development of Italian cinema and had worked ceaselessly to establish it on a sure footing. He had no time for amateurishness or for the false illusions that the cinema machine attracted. He claimed to be horrified that a young woman could be allowed to step before the cameras in a leading role in a film by a respected director solely on account of her connections.[2] However, when he proposed to an 'intermediate "higher authority"' (probably Eitel Monaco, then director general of cinema) that some professional preparation would be opportune, 'I was looked at as if I was stupid or mad', he later wrote. As the president of Cinecittà, Cines and ENIC, Freddi found himself with no choice but to oversee almost every step of Myriam's career. He gave expression to his displeasure by acting to ensure that all matters, including the financing of her films, were fully in order. He behaved 'in a way that was more severe than with any other producer', thinking as he did so of Mussolini and 'sure that he would have approved of my conduct'.[3] He even intervened to stop Myriam travelling by car along the avenues of Cinecittà in accordance with the general wartime ban on this practice. It annoyed him greatly that a small production company, Viralba, had been taken over and was used to make sure everything was formally legitimate, save then to expect certain favours, privileges and gestures of regard.

Freddi soon realised that a figure he had to beware of was Myriam's mother Giuseppina, who often accompanied her daughter to work and paraded around the studio complex behaving as though she owned it:

> Halfway between a boxer and a sculpted female architectural figure, she was the living expression of that determined and interfering matriarchy that still survives in certain provincial Italian families. The explanation for everything that was going on was very simple. Miria represented the domestic 'phenomenon', blossoming beside the fireplace, the 'revelation' flowering between the modernist drawing room and the

little garden she tended 'with her own hands'. She could sing – rather well, it was said – well-known opera arias and fashionable songs, she could dance, she had performed adequately in some charity show. Why then should she not be a star? And what, after all, were stars? It was clear that 'the family' believed that the Regime had 'built up' the cinema solely so that Miria could walk into it with hips swinging and her chest, a lot of chest, thrust forward. It was clear that, in evenings spent at home, the 'revelation' was cocooned in that slightly pathetic and a bit hypocritical type of affection with which children are regarded in many Italian families. The 'madro' (virile mother) coordinated the 'launch' motivated more by a sense of ownership than motherly love. It is natural that this artificial warmth reverberates beyond the family. 'Very well, if she has talent, let her demonstrate it', someone must have said. But no one seems to have thought that, in every trade, in every profession, in every art, you need to start at the beginning and complete the necessary apprenticeship and make a career with your own efforts and your own qualities. No. Miria had to begin at the end: star and protagonist. In the cinema: in the jaws of this Moloch capable of devouring all, of this merciless idol that does not recognise half measures and which grants either fame or ridicule![4]

The decision to send *Le vie del cuore* to the Venice Festival was, in his view, 'more than scandalous, idiotic'.[5] 'And idiots', he continued, 'were those who had allowed this, because I am sure that if anyone had dared to alert Mussolini to the inopportuneness of it, that person would have been rewarded with esteem and gratitude.'[6] Not only did he believe the film unworthy of this honour; there were political ramifications that had not been thought through. If the film were to be whistled, for example, that might be interpreted as a manifestation of political dissent. Freddi advised that policemen in appropriate civilian dress should be spread around the auditorium. For his part, Myriam's older brother Marcello – a naval officer and medic at that time stationed at the Sant'Anna hospital in the city[7] – recruited tens of sailors to attend the show and express their approval by loud applause.[8] Unsurprisingly, given that the forces of order and policemen were present in such numbers, the presentation went off without incident. 'The comments were made afterwards, in Piazza San Marco and in the shadows of the cafes', Freddi remembered.

With this danger passed, there remained the challenge of the regular premiere in Rome. The Barberini cinema, which was owned by the state distribution organ ENIC, was chosen for the event. Freddi resisted pressure to splash out on publicity and instead treated the film in a routine way. On the first day of exhibition, the early shows passed without incident. At the potentially more troublesome late evening show, there were a few 'murmurings, whispers and chuckles' but little else, until someone threw some stink bombs into the auditorium.[9] Freddi advised the police commissioner against action that could turn a minor episode into an embarrassing incident. Nothing further happened and the film fizzled out of its own accord after barely two weekends.

Fig. 11.1 Miria di San Servolo (Myriam Petacci) photographed at the start of her brief film career. (Author's own collection)

The matter, however, did not rest there as Myriam's second film, *L'amico delle donne*, went into production soon afterwards. It was shot in the small studios of the Centro sperimentale without any particular clamour or incident. Freddi, however, was again called to account when the Viralba production company sought to have ENIC handle the distribution. When it was pointed out that ENIC at this time normally only distributed films produced by the nationalised Cines company, pressure was brought to bear to include all the films made by Viralba in the Cines programme. This, he wrote, was tantamount to having them financed by the state. He made his objections to the representative of Viralba, who responded that he would refer his response 'to the ladies'.[10] A furious Freddi summoned all the functionaries in the vicinity and then challenged him to repeat his implied threat. Predictably, he declined to do so and the film was put into distribution by another company, Tirrenia, which, however, was controlled by Vittorio Mussolini and was also in the state domain.

According to his own account, Freddi adopted this detached, even hostile, attitude towards the whole Miria circus not because he was prejudiced, even though his distaste for 'the whole brouhaha created around the girl' was palpable.[11] It was based, he claimed, on his devotion to Italian cinema. 'I was, frankly, jealous of [it] and anything that was damaging to it infuriated me, just as by contrast everything that could be useful to it, *from whatever quarter it came*, carried me to seventh heaven.'[12] Had he been convinced of the talent of the actress, if her films had been good, and if there was the guarantee of a good return, he claimed that he would have been more than happy to be more flexible, to 'take on' the film to do good business for ENIC and gain some credit for the 'revelation'. This pragmatic attitude, he wrote, was not understood by those who, for reasons of personal opportunity or simply out of a desire for a quiet life, embraced the project, supported it tacitly or allowed it to progress.

The chief problem for Freddi lay in working out what the attitude of Mussolini himself was. He knew Mussolini well but was not among those who had daily contact with him. He was convinced that the whole matter was one with which he was not concerned or to which, at least, he was not inclined to give overt support, since, as he saw it, he was not a man to confuse 'his pastimes with his duties'.[13] This belief should by rights have been overturned when the latter's private secretary, Nicola De Cesare, urged him to adopt a more indulgent attitude towards 'the well-known actress'. However, De Cesare's strange demeanour and circumlocutions convinced Freddi that he had been got at by the Petacci clan and that the meeting was not taking place with the knowledge of the Duce. This conviction was confirmed when Claretta Petacci herself subsequently sought and obtained a meeting with him in an attempt to overcome his reluctance to assist with the realisation of her sister's dream.[14] 'This girl has talent, everyone says so, including actors and directors. We are convinced of it. Even the Duce is convinced', she told him, adding, 'So why should her path be blocked? What harm is there? Lots of people work in cinema, why shouldn't she too?'[15] After repeating his view that Myriam should first enrol at the Centro sperimentale, he warned her that malicious gossip and envy were rife in the world of cinema precisely because everyone, down even to the ordinary typist, aspired to savour the success, fame and riches it could confer. Thrusting Myriam before the cameras might subject her relationship with Mussolini to unwelcome scrutiny.

According to Renzo De Felice, who devotes nearly twenty pages of his multi-volume biography of Mussolini to the dictator's relationship with his lover in the period prior to July 1943, Claretta was widely assumed to be able to obtain favours, concessions, positions and subsidies for relatives and others.[16] Both Giuseppe Bottai and Galeazzo Ciano denounced in their diaries the ascendancy of the Petacci family. For Bottai, the whole situation was a sign of the deterioration of the regime. 'The Regime is becoming *pompadourised* – and with what a low species of Pompadour!' he wrote on 21 November 1942. 'Already instances arrive addressed "to the Noble Lady etc. etc.", and already there is gossip about Myriam's new film whose title alone seems like a satire of the man: *The Friend of Women*.[17] They felt that not only was the Duce being made to lose prestige in the eyes of the Fascists but that his judgement was clouded by his unusual devotion to a woman many years younger than himself. As his physical health declined, he became ever more dependent on Claretta. Withdrawn and cut off from longstanding ministers and advisors, he was prey to her views and to the information he received from De Cesare, who owed his position to her, and the Interior Minister Buffarini Guidi, who always cultivated close contact with her as well as the women of the Mussolini family.[18]

After the Petacci family moved in 1938 into La Camilluccia, a luxurious modernist villa on Rome's Monte Mario, it became a centre of power of sorts. Claretta may have been entirely focused on her relationship and without 'ulterior motives',[19] but the other members of her family – from her doctor father to her profiteering brother – were all aware of the possible benefits of their unusual position. For the most part, Mussolini 'turned a blind eye and sometimes two' to the behaviour of his lover's family, intervening only when someone grossly overstepped the mark. Myriam's screen career was taken to be entirely a consequence of family influence, but the measures taken to promote it did not cause wide offence, merely 'gossip and sarcasm'.[20]

For Myriam herself, her cinematic adventure was the best of many presents she received for her eighteenth birthday in May 1941. In her memoirs, published in 1988, she ingenuously or deliberately ignored the machinations that led to her being cast in her first film. The 'gift', she claimed, came from the director Mastrocinque 'who invited me to join the cast of a film';[21] 'for me a full role was envisaged in the sense that I was expected to act, sing and dance'. 'Mussolini was kept in the dark about my debut on set, even though it could not have displeased him', she added. 'Was it not he after all who discovered the politico-spectacular importance of the new muse, affirming that "cinema is the strongest weapon"? Was it not he who invented in 1924 – 1924, I repeat – the newsreel, with the Istituto Luce? And to have founded Cinecitta?' The implication is that, because the Duce had shown that he understood the power of cinema, he could not but have approved the attempt to conquer the medium of the youngest member of a family with which he was intimately involved. Private aspirations were confused with state policy, and the Duce himself assumed to regard the organs of the state as a form of personal property.

For an example of how the Petaccis learned to harness the Duce's authority to their ends, one need look no further than Marcello, who passed the professional examination in surgical pathology after officials in Mussolini's private office sent a letter of recommendation to eminent experts informing them that it would 'give great pleasure' if they were to help Dr Petacci to 'achieve his wishes'.[22] The officials set to work after Marcello himself informed them that, in pursuing this course of action, he was merely 'following the desire of the Chief'. At no point was Mussolini's name or position mentioned in the letter of recommendation, but can any of the recipients, on opening a letter from the Duce's secretariat, have been in any doubt that it expressed his wishes? By the same token, would the officials of the secretariat have sought confirmation from the Duce himself that the claim advanced by his lover's brother was true? If these are taken to be unlikely, it can be seen how a member of the Petacci family cleverly exploited the position of Claretta for personal gain, operating in the interstices of Mussolini's power. There is no archival evidence of promoters of Myriam's career having availed themselves of similar strategic opportunism, but Freddi's description of the visit he received from De Cesare suggests that very similar practices were put into play.

The matter, however, is complicated by that fact that Myriam enjoyed a much closer relationship with Mussolini than her brother. The dictator knew her well and he often used her as a messenger or sounding board for matters regarding Claretta. The younger woman seems also to have acted as go-between when the pair had a tiff. Doris Duranti described the Duce as having a 'paternally affectionate' relationship with Myriam,[23] but she also seems to have been party to some of his sexual boasting and allusions. She herself indulged in humorous banter with him about Margherita Sarfatti and other former lovers.[24] 'Yes, I told Mimi that I want another one [lover] who is very young and whose heart has never been touched by love', Mussolini told Claretta in 1940; 'she told me I needed to stoop further down; "you should take one who is four years old!" (he laughs)'.[25] Claretta was aware that her lover found her sister attractive and she occasionally wrote of her suspicions in her diary. The first such entry appeared as early as May 1938. She recounts how the couple were out walking when they were joined by the 15-year-old Mimi: 'he stops to talk to her and looks at her with different eyes, like a man, in a way he has never done before'.[26] On 3 April 1939, Claretta records how Mussolini took the opportunity presented by a skiing trip to Terminillo to inform the sisters of rumours that were circulating about a *ménage à trois*. 'Mimi, I am very sorry about this and I'll do everything to put a stop to them', he told her.[27] 'It's monstrous, sure', he lamented; 'you should not be angry with me; you must think that people are nasty and women in particular are fierce and badly intentioned gossips.' De Felice confirms that both sisters were indeed rumoured to be his lovers and that this opinion was shared by the U.S. ambassador.[28] The gossip became public in August 1943, when the *Corriere della Sera* published two articles denouncing the two sisters as the dictator's 'favourites'.[29]

Given Claretta's obsessive jealousy, it seems highly unlikely that she would have tolerated sharing the Duce with her sister. Yet, by several accounts, he maintained a keen interest in the progress of Myriam's artistic career. Pierre Milza argues that his 'support permitted the young sister of Claretta to "make a name for herself" – Miria di San Servolo – in the world of theatre and cinema'.[30] When she made her debut as a singer of the Theatre of the Arts in winter 1941–42, he ordered that it should be broadcast on the radio so he could hear it, and he was widely seen as her 'protector'. That Freddi was almost certainly wrong in his belief that Mussolini was not an active or covert promoter of Myriam is demonstrated by the way cinema formed a common sphere of interest between the women and Mussolini. The sisters were keen filmgoers and Claretta always informed the ever-jealous Mussolini of their trips ('Why did you not tell me you were going to the cinema? It's very strange', he asked her one evening in January 1938).[31] Films supplied by the Ministry of Popular Culture were not only shown in the cinema created by Vittorio Mussolini at Villa Torlonia, but also at the Petaccis' villa. When, in January 1940, Mussolini paid a visit to Cinecittà, he telephoned Claretta the same afternoon to recount his experience. She transcribed this as follows:

> I witnessed some film scenes; I saw how they prepare the scenes. I must say that the women (that I met) are not famous: all of them were rather plain and scrawny. There was just one who gave me the idea that they want to do what you always say. Finding the type ... The big stars were not there; it was just those from the school [i.e. the Centro sperimentale], all more or less insignificant young girls. I was always thinking of you; I thought about you the whole time, especially as this matter has often been at the centre of our conversations and I could see that you were right too in saying that it is necessary to 'find the type' and I believe that this school will achieve that aim.[32]

The revelation that Claretta had spoken to Mussolini of the way in which new talent should be identified, and the frequent presence of Myriam at the couple's meetings, suggest that it is unlikely indeed that Mussolini would have been unaware of, or uninvolved in backing, Myriam's artistic career. Indeed, they suggest that the whole idea may have been hatched or debated in exchanges between the three of them. If he had not supported her, why otherwise would Mussolini have been so apparently put out by the girl's sudden marriage to Armando Boggiano, a wealthy grower and importer of cotton, in June 1942? According to Ciano, he commented with irritation on the event to Pavolini, the Minister of Popular Culture: 'While we speak a wedding is taking place at Santa Maria degli Angeli. Good from an economic point of view but damaging for the art of the girl who had a sure future before her in cinema', he is reported to have said.[33] 'I hope, anyway,' he added, 'that the newspapers will have the good taste not to talk about it. Only *Il Messaggero* – which the father writes for – can report the event in the news pages.' The sum of money he allocated for a gift was so paltry that the family had to add to it to avoid the impression of a snub.[34]

The only other possible explanation for his attitude sees the wedding as a stratagem devised by Claretta to put Myriam definitively beyond his clutches. Writing in 1946, a journalist named Franco Rovere argued that in fact Claretta first thought of the artistic career of her sister in this light.[35] However, it seems unlikely that she would have seen Cinecittà as a substitute convent. Many senior Fascists regarded the studio complex as a sexual hunting ground or a tantalising prospect to be dangled before the eyes of gullible young potential conquests. Freddi tells how he was asked to arrange screen tests for various protégées of officials. This sort of conduct, Elsa De Giorgi argues, was inspired precisely by 'the Duce's affair with Claretta Petacci [which] was a great stimulus to get involved in the most audacious of virile liberties'.[36] So automatic was this idea of Cinecittà that Mussolini himself felt obliged to assure Claretta that, on the occasion of his January 1940 visit, he had not initiated liaisons with any actresses.[37]

It is more plausible that Myriam's wedding was the result of scheming. What Mussolini did not know was that this was no marriage of love. Myriam would write in her memoirs that it was arranged in short order at the urging of Buffarini Guidi in order to put an immediate stop to damaging rumours circulating in the capital to the effect that Mussolini was involved in a love triangle with the two sisters.[38] The potential damage was such that only a very clear gesture – either immediate marriage or departure abroad – could put an end to it. The minister explained that he was acting without Mussolini's knowledge and in the expectation that he would never discover the truth. 'Upset, embittered and confused, like the accused who awaits a sentence' is how Myriam described her reaction to this proposition. If Claretta was behind this, the solution was a short-lived one, however, for the couple proved ill suited and separated shortly after the honeymoon.

Formally, Myriam was given the most cordial welcome by the film community. Alida Valli evoked her debut at Cinecittà to highlight the atmosphere of Fascist complicity that reigned at the complex. No one, she said in 1965, ever imagined it could end. 'Oh, what a party Cinecittà threw in honour of Miria di San Servolo! "The sister of the Duce's friend is making her debut," they cooed, "the sister of the Duce's friend is making her debut!" Everyone was there, stars and Fascist officials. It was like the launch of a ship.'[39] Assia Noris was on good terms with the family since Dr Petacci was her mother's physician; Claretta personally told her of her sister's desire to become an actress.[40] Doris Duranti took a liking to her. 'I appreciated her punctuality on set, the intensity of her light blue eyes and her determination to make it that remind me of my younger self,' she recalled.[41] According to his own testimony, Fosco Giachetti turned down a role in *Le vie del cuore*, telling Mastrocinque that 'before she does a film with me she must learn to act'.[42] 'Oh, but you, you're mad', the director replied. Eitel Monaco also called him and warned that a refusal might bring about the end of his career.

Myriam was not without admirers. Luigi De Vincentis wrote in 1946 that she 'had marvellous eyes and she was so gracious and likeable that to have her close was a true delight for the spirit'.[43] The issue was whether her charm could be harnessed by cinema. For all his grumbling, Freddi claimed to be open-minded. 'I was curious to see the new actress at work', he wrote; 'if she proved to be an authentic "value" then I would have been happy, regardless of the relations that linked Miria di San Servolo to a determinate situation.'[44] However, he was not impressed. Myriam had shown promise in her singing but there was little evidence that she had the necessary talent or screen presence to carry a film. Freddi did not exercise his right to preview the material shot for *Le vie del cuore*, but instead inspected photographs from the set and consulted the film's cinematographer, Arturo Gallea. His conclusion was dismissive:

> [T]here was nothing to be done. The new star was nothing but the product of a petit bourgeois environment, full of mannerisms that were beyond correction, an artificial vivacity and an insipid gaiety, incapable of attaining an expressive style, and devoid of that congenital 'class' which can turn a lowly peasant into a great player, with an unfortunate if eye-catching physique, an inexpressive and defective face that no makeup artist could have adapted to the camera.[45] [She was] an ordinary girl without originality or character, maybe desirable up to a point, who was endowed with a conventional and servile elegance; [her only distinction was] that which distinguishes all those petulant girls spawned by wholesale traders, provincial public officials, backroom officers, lucky rather than capable professionals and so on who pass their vacations in Cortina or San Remo, in Stresa or Rapallo, on Capri or in Rimini, staying in second category hotels.

Even the admiring De Vincentis admitted that the cinema showed up Myriam's defects.

Le vie del cuore was a modest affair, 'a bloodless and slapdash work' in which 'the protagonist appeared and disappeared without either shame or merit'. Reviews, needless to say, were flattering. *Corriere della Sera* wrote that 'this actress shows the promise from her very first test that will ensure she plays a prominent part in the future of our cinema',[46] while the Fascist *Popolo d'Italia* observed that the debutante 'acted with natural ease and versatility'. The magazine *Cinema* dubbed Petacci 'a fresh comic talent'. The *Segnalazioni cinematografiche* published by the Catholic Cinema Centre described *Le vie del cuore* as 'a period film, not particularly brilliant, directed nevertheless with praiseworthy seriousness and acted by a good group of actors',[47] even if the satirical portrayal of nineteenth-century high society 'which contains and boasts a preponderance of negative elements' meant that the film was not suitable for any category of audience.

Although the films have not survived in their entirety and even fragments are difficult to see, more recent critics have cruelly highlighted the clumsy nature of Miria's screen debut. Masi and Lancia poke fun at her 'chubby profile' and matronly stockiness in spite of her young years.⁴⁸ She should have gone on a diet two years before the first take, they opine. They note the involuntary humour in some scenes. When the hero first meets her he mistakes her for the daughter of the stableman. Seeing her later in *pompa magna* at a grand ball, he realises his error and falls instantly under her spell. Yet, they argue, with her full cheeks, chubby arms, abundant double chin and some flowers in her curly hair, she still looks more rustic than noble. The absurd effect is magnified by the fact that her love rival is played by Clara Calamai, one of the most alluring of Cinecittà's leading ladies. 'You can see that love is blind', they comment. None of this, in their view, is redeemed by the playing.

In fact, Myriam was no worse that many other young debutantes, although she was well below the standard set by the best. However, it is interesting that it was decided to launch her in films that were adapted from literary sources dating from the previous century. 'Not by chance, when it was decided to launch the young and not very talented sister of la Petacci, a series of nineteenth-century stories were chosen, like *Le vie del cuore*, directed by that Camillo Mastrocinque who was experienced in costume films', Massimo Scaglione has written.⁴⁹ He writes 'not by chance' because melodramas were seen as ideal star vehicles since they featured sympathetic heroines. Although period films were not well regarded by Fascists, who found them worryingly escapist, they were culturally dignified.⁵⁰ The name chosen for Myriam, San Servolo, provoked smirks in Venice, since it was also the name of the municipal lunatic asylum, but it had a pleasingly aristocratic ring (*Cinema* labelled it 'D'Annunzian') and was drawn from some remote source in the Petacci family genealogy.

As a bourgeois family of recent elevation, the Petaccis sought, like many before them, to find noble antecedents and embellishments to legitimise their position. The snob, Francois Rouvillon observes, 'is someone who aspires to nobility, or to the appearance and to the prestige of it, to a status superior to his own; he is an intruder, an imitator and very often, in very different ways, vain'.⁵¹ Italian snobbery, particularly in Rome, where the tone was set by the papal aristocracy, was 'more grandiose and less frivolous'; it was elaborated 'in the most lavish way, without restriction, without camouflage'.⁵² As relatives of the Duce's fixed mistress, the Petaccis sought to flaunt high status in innumerable ways, from the eye-catching villa, Giuseppina's lording it at Cinecittà, Marcello's questionable doings, and the father's newspaper column. Precisely because little public recognition could flow directly from a relationship that could not itself be publicised, the idea of film stardom exercised a special allure for them as a modern mark of distinction to be conquered and exhibited. If, as Rouvillon argues, 'fundamentally, snobbery is a dream, the dream of a grandeur that is often illusory or imaginary',⁵³ then nothing suited it better than the sanction of the movies. Since cinema was new as a badge of status and therefore not a lesser version of others, it provided a way whereby the family itself could emerge fully and claim the privileges and status that it believed were its right.

Myriam never willingly followed the practice of austerity that was imposed on the stars of cinema during the war years. The frequent costume changes of the protagonist of *L'amico delle donne*, highlighting the art of costume designer Maria De Matteis, provided a pretext for a barbed lament by Carlo Lizzani that was surely intended to refer more to present shortages than to the period setting: 'It is a pity that these days one cannot dress up like that,' he wrote. Off screen, she appeared in public with all the trappings of the front rank star. Like the Paris courtesans of the nineteenth century, the Petacci sisters appeared to believe that immorality could be disguised and offset by material excess. However, few were taken in. By the 1940s, even the state-owned fashion magazine *Bellezza* could observe that furs 'are a fashion element that possesses a vast range of values, which support today, with surprising elasticity, the most varied exigencies'.[54] After the fall of Mussolini, tracts and articles appeared which crudely exposed not only these exigencies but the blatant erotic appeal they cloaked. A pamphlet published in Rome in 1944 ridiculed the appearance of Myriam at Venice. The premiere of her film was carefully prepared, the anonymous author wrote: 'at a certain point *she* appeared. Her body was enveloped in a luxurious cape of blue fox fur (a gift from the omnipotent). But, despite the shiny gems, despite the ostentatious costliness of the clothes and the precious objects, it was not difficult to catch sight in the opulent bosom, in the stupid smile and in the flashing eyes of the newly minted celluloid goose, the unambiguous traits of the "part-time waitress"'.[55] The issue of Myriam's supposed entanglement with Mussolini was highlighted in August 1943 in the *Corriere della Sera*, which observed of Myriam that, 'it was said that she too boasted of a friendship with the Duce and certainly she exhibited the high linkage with much more tastelessness than her sister'.[56] The snobbery of the Petaccis tended fatally towards kitsch. When bourgeois families acquire wealth and power, Broch notes, they acquire 'the right to create a grandiose and exuberant decorative apparatus designed to beautify life'.[57] However, 'the absence of middling values' often turns this to kitsch, and modern kitsch, especially in cinema, he added, 'is impregnated with blood and with saccharin'.[58] All this ultimately came back to Mussolini, for 'the gross and gauche taste of the man from Predappio was revealed in his erotic predilections'.[59]

It is for this reason more than her modest screen performances, Masi and Lancia write, that Myriam Petacci was 'one of the least-loved creatures of Fascist cinema'.[60] Although she never became a true star, she continued to work. In addition to her first two features, she appeared in two films which remained uncompleted in July 1943. One of these was *L'invasore* (The Invader, Nino Giannini), a modest historical drama that, however, was written and supervised by Roberto Rossellini and which featured Amedeo

Nazzari and Osvaldo Valenti in the cast. *Sogno d'amore* (Dream of Love) was being shot at Cinecittà at the very moment Mussolini was deposed. Once again the setting was an aristocratic one and Myriam was cast opposite the experienced Roldano Lupi. Along with several other films, shooting was interrupted instantly when news of Mussolini's replacement was announced. In 1944, a sum was made available from unspecified sources to settle the debts that Viralba had accumulated towards various state organs.[61] Freddi was assigned the task of giving the episode closure. However, Myriam's career did not meet a brusque end. In 1944 Claretta 'reminded Mussolini, seeing that he was there [Berlin], to recommend to Goebbels her sister Myriam, who would like to find a space as an actress in Berlin'.[62] Eventually, she would make several more films in Franco's Spain.

Notes

1. L. Freddi. 1949. *Il cinema*, Rome: L'Arnia, 355.
2. Ibid., 360.
3. Ibid., 357.
4. Ibid., 358.
5. Ibid., 359.
6. Ibid., 360.
7. M. Petacci. 1988. *Chi ama è perduto: mia sorella Claretta*, Gardolo di Trento: Reverdito, 204.
8. R. Gervaso. 1982. *Claretta: la donna che morì per Mussolini*, Milan: Rizzoli, 106.
9. Freddi, *Il cinema*, 361–62.
10. Ibid., 363.
11. Ibid.
12. Ibid.
13. Ibid., 354.
14. The meeting is recounted in ibid., 366–71.
15. Ibid., 369.
16. R. De Felice. 1990. *Mussolini l'alleato 1940–1945*, I. *L'Italia in Guerra 1940–1943*, tome 2: *Crisi e agonia del regime*, Turin: Einaudi, 1070–72.
17. G. Bottai. 1982. *Diario 1935–1944*, Milan: Rizzoli, 337.
18. De Felice, *Mussolini l'alleato*, 1071–72.
19. Ibid., 1075.
20. Ibid., 1070.
21. Petacci, *Chi ama è perduto*, 187.
22. The case is outlined in R.J.B. Bosworth. 2005. *Mussolini's Italy: Life under the Dictatorship, 1915–1945*, London: Allen Lane, 365–66.
23. D. Duranti. 1987. *Il romanzo della mia vita*, Milan: Mondadori, 123.
24. Ibid., 377.

25. C. Petacci. 2011. *Verso il disastro – Mussolini in guerra: diari 1939–1940*, Milan: Rizzoli, 337.
26. C. Petacci. 2009. *Mussolini segreto: diari 1932 – 1938*, Milan: Rizzoli, 333.
27. Petacci, *Verso il disastro*, 84.
28. De Felice, *Mussolini l'alleato*, 1070n.
29. P. Chessa and B. Raggi. 2010. *L'ultima lettera di Benito: Mussolini e Petacci – amore e politica a Salò 1943–45*, Milan: Mondadori, 43.
30. P. Milza. 2009. *Mussolini*, Rome: Carocci, 853.
31. Petacci, *Mussolini segreto*, 183.
32. Petacci, *Verso il disastro*, 271–72.
33. G. Ciano. 1980. *Diario 1937–1943*, Milan: Rizzoli, 632.
34. Gervaso, *Claretta*, 107. Myriam herself reports that Mussolini gave his attendant Navarra the relatively modest sum of 2,000 lire to buy a gift of silver tableware. Concerned, Navarra went to La Camilluccia to consult Myriam's mother, who gave him an additional 8,000 lire to buy the splendid present that was put on display at the Grand Hotel. See Petacci, *Chi ama è perduto*, 198.
35. F. Rovere. 1946. *Vita amorosa di Claretta Petacci*, Milan: Bolla, 76–79.
36. E. De Giorgi. 1992. *I coetanei*, Milan: Leonardo, 37.
37. Petacci, *Verso il disastro*, 271–72.
38. Petacci, *Chi ama è perduto*, 196–97.
39. O. Fallaci, 'Lo specchio del passato', *L'Europeo*, 6 January 1965, 58.
40. O. Ripa, 'Ho avuto cinque mariti ma ero tanto bambina', *Gente*, 14 August 1969, 21.
41. Duranti, *Il romanzo della mia vita*, 123.
42. Testimony of Fosco Giachetti in F. Savio. 1979. *Cinecittà anni trenta*, Rome: Bulzoni, 584–85.
43. L. De Vincentis. 1946. *Io son te ...*, Milan: Cebes, 30.
44. Freddi, *Il cinema*, 355.
45. Ibid., 357.
46. For reviews, see Gervaso, *Claretta*, 106; S. Masi and E. Lancia. 1994. *Stelle d'Italia: piccole e grandi dive del cinema itaiano dal 1930 al 1945*, Rome: Gremese, 80–81.
47. Centro cattolico cinematografico. 1942. *Segnalazioni cinematografiche*, Vol. XV, Rome: Centro cattolico cinematografico, 165.
48. Masi and Lancia, *Stelle d'Italia*, 80–81.
49. M. Scaglione. 1999. 'Melodramma e strappalacrime nel cinema dei telefoni bianchi' in O. Caldiron and S Della Casa (eds), *Appasionatamente: il mélo nel cinema italiano*, Turin: Lindau, 19–28, 24.
50. See M. Argentieri. 1995. 'Un Ottocento duro a morire: cronache di una polemica' in Argentieri (ed.), *Schermi di guerra: cinema italiano 1939–1945*, Rome: Bulzoni, 285–306.
51. F. Rouvillon. 2008. *Histoire du snobisme*, Paris: Flammarion, 18.
52. Ibid., 22–23.
53. Ibid., 27.

54. E. Robiola, 'Pellicce', *Bellezza* 1(7–8), 1941, 113. See also A. Municchi (ed.). 1992. *Signore in pelliccia 1900–1940*, Modena: Zanfi.
55. Calipso. 1944. *Vita segreta di Mussolini*, Rome: IEDC, 28.
56. The articles were reproduced in the magazine *Leggere*, issue of May 1993, 33–38.
57. H. Broch. 1990. *Il kitsch*, Turin: Einaudi, 185.
58. Ibid., 185.
59. Calipso, *Vita segreta*, 28.
60. Masi and Lancia, *Stelle d'Italia*, 81.
61. Ibid., 374–76.
62. Chessa and Raggi, *L'ultima lettera di Benito*, 98.

PART III

The Aftermath of Stardom

12

Civil War, Liberation and Reconstruction

With the fall of Mussolini in July 1943, the Fascist dictatorship came to an end and film-making in Rome was brought to a halt. Although work continued at several private studios, no new films would go into production at Cinecittà until 1948. Thus the machine that had furnished Italians with a regular stream of new movies came to a standstill. For the actors, these events were disorienting. Many of the young women were scarcely aware of the world beyond cinema. They had had no political education and considered themselves too young to take a serious interest in politics. 'I was stunned', wrote Maria Denis years later, referring to Mussolini's overthrow; 'I did not understand. What was Fascism for me? I had lived, grown up and, you might say, been born under Fascism. I did not know anything else. I thought everything was going fine.'[1] Alida Valli recalled that she and her colleagues accepted the cinema and the world as it was:

> I was a young girl, 16, 17, 18 years old and I was successful and privileged. Everything was easy and when things come to you easily you do not stop to ask if things are right or not. I made films as automatically as a secretary types a letter. If no one explains to you what evil is, how do you know what is evil? ... I never thought that a cinema like that [i.e. white telephone films] was wrong or that it would end, because no one thought that Fascism would end.[2]

Luisa Ferida, who had greeted the Allied landing in Sicily earlier in July 1943 with tears of emotion, was one of few to understand that their whole world was coming to an end.[3]

Since the opening of Cinecittà in 1937, the Italian film industry had expanded dramatically and actors had worked longer and harder than ever before. Despite restrictions imposed as the war progressed, the stars lived well. Now, suddenly, their livelihood was imperilled. While a few films remained in production through August 1943, most activity ceased. According to the actor Claudio Gora, the final end came on 8 September when the king and his prime minister fled the capital to place themselves under Allied protection. Before the Germans arrived in the capital, those technicians, clerical staff and workmen who were still engaged at the studio complex made off with equipment, costumes and other material.[4] During the Nazi occupation, the studios were sacked and turned into a camp for the displaced.

Following Mussolini's rescue by Hitler's paratroops and subsequent nominal restoration to power, Freddi, who had himself been detained, began to make plans for the creation of a new film industry to be located in Venice. None of the major stars considered in Part II gave in to pressure to get involved in the short-lived cinema of the puppet regime of the Italian Social Republic. Testimonies attest to the variety of excuses and reasons that were offered to escape Freddi's insistent invitations to join him.[5] Vittorio De Sica claimed he had a large family, Alida Valli took refuge at a friend's house, and Massimo Girotti pointed to his sick wife. The most prosaic excuse was offered by Roman comic actor Aldo Fabrizi who referred to his haemorrhoids, while the most honest was Mario Camerini who simply informed Freddi that his well-known political views were not compatible with acceptance of the invitation. Others, including Nazzari, Giachetti and Noris, simply refused. For her part, Clara Calamai missed her appointment with Freddi when he departed Rome for the last time in a hurry after the Allies landed at Anzio and began their advance towards the capital.

While the Nazis imposed their control of the capital, many leading actors and directors busied themselves with two film projects that remained in production until the middle of 1944 or after. Sponsored by the Vatican, these were genuine films that, however, were conceived explicitly to provide movie personnel with protracted protection against pressures to go north. The first was *La porta del cielo* (The Gates of Heaven, 1945), a film about a train full of pilgrims travelling to the sanctuary of the Madonna in Loreto in search of a miracle. Directed by De Sica in the most trying of circumstances, the film's cast included Carlo Ninchi, Massimo Girotti, Claudio Gora and many others.[6] Work progressed slowly, with the restrictions imposed by the occupying authorities, including curfews and power limitations, weighing heavily on production. On paper, the second film was more ambitious. Entitled *I dieci commandamenti* (The Ten Commandments, Giorgio Vittorio Chili, 1945), it consisted of a series of episodes, each one corresponding to a biblical commandment. Among those involved with this project were Amedeo Nazzari, Assia Noris, Mariella Lotti, Elisa Cegani, Massimo Girotti, Claudio Gora and Carlo Ninchi. According to Gora, no one protested about the shambolic nature of the production 'because we got paid a few lira'.⁷

Apart from the Vatican-sponsored productions, the theatre was an option for actors at a loose end. Many had some background on the stage and a few had maintained strong links with the world of live performance. Musical revues prospered under the Nazis despite censorship and the repression that marked the occupation. They did so once more after the Germans fled and the Allies entered Rome in June 1944. Although war would continue in the north and centre of the country for many more months, with the civil war taking on an increasingly brutal dimension, some sort of normality slowly returned to the capital. No matter how uncertain the present was, most stars, no less than directors and writers, looked to the future with some hope. They believed that they could count on the loyalty of audiences who had grown to love them after the withdrawal of the American companies in 1939. Few had developed ties with the regime that were so close as to be personally compromising. Those who stayed in Rome through the dark days of the Nazi occupation were sure that their professionalism and experience would soon be valued in a reborn Italian cinema. Many of them did not perhaps realise that factors other than their popularity would weigh on their future. They were well aware that Hollywood would present serious competition, but they understood little of the spirit of renewal that was being fostered. In the new climate, debates that had begun in 1941–42, mainly in the magazine *Cinema*, came out into the open. The aim of what would come to be called neorealism was, for Antonio Pietrangeli, writing in 1944, 'to give to individuals an awareness of themselves, as men and citizens'.⁸ This entailed a break with the past and the adoption of new methods of film-making. The extent to which stars could be part of this process was a matter of considerable controversy.

Judging the Stars

Critics and writers who, for several years, had been eager to see a reinvention of Italian cinema were determined to subject the whole previous experience to rigid evaluation and selection. A new cinema was, in their view, essential to a renewed Italy and renewal involved critique and some sort of purge. Founded in Rome in 1944, the magazine *Star*, edited by the writer Ercole Patti, bore an opportunistic name (Steno dubbed it 'in bad taste' in his diary, while acknowledging that the Fascist habit of banning words it disapproved of had gone for good),⁹ but its content was less compromising. It was ferocious in its denunciation of Cinecittà as 'the fat lover of Fascism' and 'the fat and bejewelled tart that every nouveau riche needs' in its first issue.¹⁰ It was seen as Fascism's 'leisured mistress … a bit ridiculous and very provincial'. These invectives tarred all those who had been involved with the industry under the regime. 'Italian cinema was the favourite pupil of Fascism; it had just the right amount of money, women and bad taste to please the high officials', Adriano Baracco wrote in one article.[11] This view implied the need for a wholesale renewal of personnel, methods and expectations. The regime was seen as having protected bad production 'to the point that it became ever easier to exchange the little simpers of Lilia Silvi and La Duranti's tits for respect for human rights'.[12]

The situation of the stars was one of several issues to be faced. Pietrangeli attempted a balanced overview.[13] New talents had been chosen on the basis of what he called 'extra-artistic criteria'. Some were good but they had become lazy and stylised, with no impulse to improvement or development. These general considerations were accompanied by very personal remarks. Amedeo Nazzari was deemed a 'wooden, clumsy star' who had never been given a real character to stretch him. Fosco Giachetti was viewed as an interesting actor, a 'worn and incisive' type, who had become 'ridiculous' due to the 'implacable' attitudes of his characters. Assia Noris was especially loathed; she was 'always equally and displeasingly syrupy, sugary and sticky' with her 'frenetic, sentimental little shouts and the unbearable bleating of her distinctive pronunciation between the exotic and the mannered'. Her 'stereotyped smile' was always the same, as were the mechanical movements of her monotonous doll-like persona.[14] Maria Denis was seen as a little better but her personality was devoid of any dynamic aspect. Patti hoped that the falsely carefree atmosphere seen so often on the screen in the past, symbolised by the ridiculous spectacle of Roberto Villa playing tennis in a T-shirt, would never be repeated.[15] Writing a little later, Fabrizio Sarazani suggested that 'the characters of yesterday, who wore clothes like dummies, should be sent to prison, that perpetual prison of the eternally forgotten'.[16] In his diary, Steno waspishly coined an identikit name to synthesise into one fictional persona the female stars who had enjoyed official backing under the regime: Alida Durante di San Servolo.[17]

Spies' reports from 1942 reveal that many people associated the stars with the regime,[18] regardless of the actual position of individuals. Thus some would find themselves the subject of malicious gossip. This only found a limited echo in the press but it was a marked feature of the atmosphere of civil war and liberation. Precisely because the links between the regime and the world of cinema in the public mind were strong, the sexual abuse and derision to which Mussolini was subjected after his fall from power touched a number of female stars. The Duce had been widely ridiculed for his affair with Claretta Petacci by pamphleteers, and artists of various types had mocked the lechery of the aging dictator.[19] The first target of particular bile was Myriam Petacci. Derided in the press as 'Eleonora Duce', a play on the name of the great actress Eleonora Duse, she was rumoured to have been Mussolini's lover as well as her sister. Alida Valli too was alleged to have been a lover of Mussolini, his son Bruno and a government minister. This was a story without foundation that was repeated in numerous anonymous letters of denunciation.[20]

As far as the Allies were concerned, Italian cinema had been profoundly shaped by Fascism and all protective legislation and subsidies needed to be abolished. The Allied Control Commission demanded a purge but was encouraged when the Associazione di circoli cinematografici italiani (ACCI, Italian Cinema Circles Association), a body started by Luchino Visconti, began to evaluate the real responsibilities of individuals and decide on their future. Initially a forum for intellectuals, the ACCI was gradually widened to include broader categories of cinema workers. Mario Camerini, who enjoyed the backing of the Allies, was president of the commission that was charged with reviewing the culpability of individuals. Other members included De Sica, Visconti, Cesare Zavattini and others. Pietrangeli and Giuseppe De Santis, the Saint Just and Robespierre of the situation, were there too. It held hearings over a period of weeks. De Santis opened the proceedings, as prosecutor, while Isa Miranda was among the first to testify.[21] She recognised the failure to take account of reality. 'I made lots of films', she stated, 'but only a part of me was involved in what I was doing'. De Sica, for his part, confessed that his characters had lacked human depth. They had worn tailcoats, had fabulous wardrobes and used white telephones. He had, he confessed, been lazy and unserious. As a director, he proposed to be more engaged. Most of the other witnesses were directors and writers. Although few actors stepped forward, they were not judged too severely. Overall, the film world was not as bad as it could have been. The fact that very few accepted the invitation to go to Venice was encouraging.

The intellectuals were severe but the public was less keen to judge individuals, and the magazines did not banish or ignore anyone. Soon there was a resumption of the sort of flattering coverage that the stars had been accustomed to in the past. *Star* may have printed serious analyses but it also ran features on the stars at home and offered its readers pictures of their favourites. For example, Clara Calamai was shown relaxing at home in December 1944.[22] Features were run on Alida Valli, Gino Cervi, Mariella Lotti, Vivi Gioi and Maria Denis, several of whom were given the cover. The aim was to issue to readers 'an invitation to re-establish contact with the faces of so many actors who for a long time now we have not seen in new films. It presupposes an act of sympathy or faith towards all those who for good or ill have decided to stay on the bridge of the sinking ship'.[23] Journalists on the magazine were aware that in liberated territories lots of old Italian films were being shown with success. Only those with propaganda content were banned along with the Luce documentaries and newsreels, which were replaced with Allied material. As far as the audience was concerned, Nazzari and Valli were still the king and queen of the screen.[24]

Proof of the goodwill that existed towards the stars can be seen in the response to the fate of Osvaldo Valenti and Luisa Ferida, the two most prominent performers to join Freddi in the north. As the Fascist Italian Social Republic entered its final months, the two stars were drawn more directly into the conflict. Uncaring about the drift of events, Valenti accepted an officer's commission in the Decima Mas regiment and the pair became involved in Milan with the notorious band led by the Italo-German Pietro Koch, who enjoyed an unsavoury reputation as a pitiless torturer of captured partisans. Their connection to Koch at the time was held to be sufficient reason for them to be condemned by a partisan tribunal and shot. As Anton Giulio Majano would write in the magazine *Star* in May 1945, they were 'good actors' but they had 'become two criminals'.[25] Curiosity about the way they met their end was high and, in an article published in the same magazine the following month, Adriano Baracco claimed to reveal 'finally the truth' on the basis of personal interviews. The couple had not personally tortured prisoners, he said, but they had been present when torture had taken place and had been part of the milieu at the Milan villa that was Koch's headquarters.

Their fate was decided in the aftermath of the execution at Dongo on 28 April 1945 of Pavolini, organiser of the black brigade militias, and other officials following that of Mussolini and Claretta Petacci at Giulino di Mezzegra. On 30 April the *Star* reported:

> After a week or so in prison, Valenti and Ferida were condemned to death and led before the firing squad. The scene was cinematic, illuminated by the headlights of a car since it was night. Valenti was performing, Ferida sobbing uncontrollably – so the actor came up with one of his typical remarks that was well attuned to the bold personality he had always wanted to play. 'Stop it Luisa,' he said, 'did you not always say that you would have been happy even to die to stay with me?' The the firing squad opened fire and the two fell. One of them unbalanced and intelligent, the other dishonest and stupid, they had wanted to play a game that was bigger than themselves; they were not content with success, money, their house with luminous crystals, cars and magazine photographs; they wanted a bit of romance and they ended up just like the protagonists of a film by Carmine Gallone.[26]

The execution had a notable impact on public opinion. Many could not believe that two well-known actors had met such a fate. *Film d'oggi* ran an article in August 1945 asking 'Are Valenti and Ferida dead?', taking up a query that had first been raised a few days before in the Socialist newspaper *L'Avanti*.[27] Since Valenti was a master of disguise, the article's author conjectured, surely he could have fled across the border with his friend and protector Freddi. Doris Duranti too had been helped to escape possible retribution, as she later said, because 'Pavolini did not want me to share his destiny and got me to Switzerland'.[28] By the end of 1945 attention had shifted to the child Ferida was alleged to have had prior to her death and whose name was rumoured to be Benito.[29]

The Return of Hollywood

With the liberation came the return of Hollywood films to Italian screens. Through most of the 1920s and 1930s, American movies had been enormously popular and there was a great desire to renew familiarity with them after the enforced interruption. Although the films shown were a mixture of old titles, propaganda films and, at first, relatively few genuine novelties, Hollywood symbolised the new order of things. It brought ideas of democracy, prosperity, excitement and beauty. Movie posters and pin-up girls were as much a part of the breezy hedonism of the liberation period as swing music, the boogie-woogie and chewing gum. Hollywood glamour provided hard-pressed young people with hope and escape. Amid the sea of smiling faces adorning film magazines, two stars made a special impact. Rita Hayworth was a new face, unknown to Italians from before the war, whose image was among the most polished and glamorous ever furnished by Hollywood. The alluring love goddess would define, for years to come, the very idea of the Hollywood smile; with her luxuriant hair and curvaceous figure, she embodied a mood of euphoria as well as a civilisation that was at the apex of its power.[30] The second was Tyrone Power, the heart-throb who had co-starred with Hayworth in the bull-fighting drama *Blood and Sand*. The boyishly handsome Power became a hugely popular public figure in Italy, and his regular stays in the capital, where he liked to relax, turned him into a fixture – the proof that the stars existed in flesh and blood. 'Italy had been liberated and everything was in American hands, newspapers, the radio, magazines, and on the screen there were only their films, to the great joy of the public which had never forgotten the stars of the only true cinema, that which provided entertainment, dreams, escape and adventure', Federico Fellini remembered.[31] 'Besozzi, Viarisio, Macario, Greta Gonda ... How could they compete with the return of Gary Cooper, Clark Gable, the Marx brothers, Charlie Chaplin and all the beautiful female stars, and their screenwriters and their directors?', he added, deliberately substituting for rhetorical effect the leading Italian stars with a string of second-rank names.

Enthusiasm for Hollywood was certainly great but Italians viewed the returning stars with a mixture of awe and curiosity. 'We admire not so much their elegance and grace', wrote Roberto Bertolozzi, 'but the fact that they are the representatives of a new world and a new way of living, a new human type or ethnic group.'[32] This attitude emerged as the quantity of Hollywood films increased. Although the initial return was welcomed like the first drops of rain after a drought, Gian Piero Brunetta has written, attitudes changed when the rain turned into a flood.[33] Intellectuals grumbled about the irresponsible escapism that American films peddled. Hollywood movies were as 'shiny, elegant and well made as before', one journalist wrote, but they had no connection with the real world.[34] 'The reckless indifference of these living puppets to our suffering disgusts us and offends us. They seem like men who are quite happy to revel in our misery,' he continued.

As Hollywood typologies of stardom took hold, Italian actors, in collusion with journalists, took on some behavioural traits of the Americans, not always with good judgement. Leisure shots abounded, with sex appeal being injected in odd ways. Clara Calamai was pictured in the bath and Elsa De Giorgi walking her dog, while Elli Parvo, dubbed 'the glamour star number one of cinema', was shown at Fregene looking rather plump in a two-piece costume. Fatuous question-and-answer features of the type that had featured in *Cinema illustrazione* were also revived, for example, with Massimo Girotti, Mariella Lotti and others being asked: 'What would you do if you were a man/woman?' One magazine, *Star*, ran a rubric in which Italian stars addressed letters, mostly in subservient tones, to their American counterparts.

Meanwhile the first new Italian films gradually began to appear. These were not yet the films conceived during the German occupation and imbued with the drama and suffering of war and liberation that would win worldwide acclaim. They were instead films that had been completed before the fall of Mussolini or shortly afterwards. Some had had a partial release in the spring of 1943, while others were only finished following the liberation of Rome. To the astonishment of those who were engaged in mapping out a new path for Italian cinema, it was not the most innovative films of the late Fascist period that were now shown. These included Visconti's path-breaking *Ossessione*, a melodrama based on an American pulp novel which had stirred up great controversy on account of its numerous subtle anti-Fascist motifs, and De Sica's *I bambini ci guardano* (The Children are Watching Us), an exploration of bourgeois hypocrisy and adultery that had also aroused wrath. The first new Lux film to be distributed in late 1944 was Macario's *Scandalo al collegio* (School Scandal, otherwise known as *L'innocente Casimiro*), a film that had been nearly finished in the summer of 1943. It was a schoolgirl comedy of a certain grace, but completely linked to the old context. Other films of the same type included Mario Mattoli's madcap comedy *La vispa Teresa* (The Lively Teresa), starring Lilia Silvi, Carlo Ninchi and Roberto Villa, in which a wealthy father's efforts to sabotage his son's plans to marry a beautiful manicurist backfire with hilarious consequences. Guazzoni's *La Fornarina*, featuring Goebbels' former lover Lidia Baarova, aroused special anger. Some suspected that the Allies were deliberately giving the go-ahead to poor or innocuous films while other better ones languished in storage.

Two of the films put into distribution stood out. Blasetti's *Nessuna torna indietro* (No One Turns Back), an adaptation of an Alba De Cespedes novel which had been virtually ready for release in 1943, functioned as a sort of memory lane for filmgoers. Although it was devoid of all moral or political tension, it featured no fewer than seven of the most prominent actresses of the period, among them Doris Duranti, Maria Denis and Mariella Lotti. Superbly photographed by Vaclav Vich, the leading ladies of Cinecittà appeared at their most photogenic for what must have appeared like one last bow. Evidence suggests that, like Jean de Limur's *Apparizione* (Apparition) in which Nazzari played himself and Valli a young fan, the film was popular with hard-pressed audiences who took pleasure in seeing their favourites once more.

Old Stars, New Times

In *Roma città aperta* (Rome Open City), released in the Autumn of 1945, Rossellini offered the first example of the new style of film-making that would mark the rebirth of Italian cinema. He famously accorded two variety stars of relatively limited cinema experience, Anna Magnani and Aldo Fabrizi, leading dramatic parts in his film. Neither at that point was an established film star, although their performances in the downbeat comedy *Campo de' fiori* (Mario Bonnard, 1942) had won good notices. Both were required to perform to some degree out of character. In his next film, *Paisà* (Paisan, 1946), Rossellini dispensed with stars altogether and employed just a handful of professional actors. In his films of the neorealist period, De Sica cast non-professionals in all the lead roles. However, other directors who shared the desire to make cinema reflect the recent experience of the nation did not seek to abolish the stars. Neither Blasetti nor Camerini had been part of the group that had been preparing neorealism; the former's active Fascist past weighed more than Rossellini's, while the latter's frothy comedies, although much admired, seemed remote from the engagement now being advocated. Both men adapted to the demand for socially aware cinema while also maintaining faith with established names. Camerini's Rome-set *Due lettere anonime* (Two Anonymous Letters, 1945), which explored the theme of betrayal and compromise under the Nazi occupation, was hailed as the 'second film on the Roman Resistance'.[35] However, as a film which exploded the myth of the compact anti-Fascism of the Italians that, for all its exploration of sacrifice and suffering, was rather comfortingly portrayed in Rossellini's film, it was controversial.[36] It starred Clara Calamai as a print worker who, in the absence of her soldier fiancé (played by Andrea Checchi) forms a relationship with an ambitious fellow worker who cynically advances his position by cultivating the Nazi occupiers. Calamai performed in the same de-glamorised guise that Visconti had imposed on her in *Ossessione*, while bringing a more markedly personal anguish to the role. Dark and normal, she had none of the elegance that had marked her Cinecittà persona. The final shot of the film is a lingering close-up of Calamai behind bars. Her patent anguish after shooting her lover is tempered by the hope, imparted to her by Checchi, that, following the recent liberation, she may soon be released. Shot partly on location, the film also included documentary footage of the liberation of Rome. While Rossellini's film, despite its subject matter, was forward looking, this was a film about guilt that was mired in the past. Pina's spectacular and pointless death in *Roma città aperta* opened the way to a new view of the nation, while Calamai's character had still to pay for her sins.

Blasetti opted to explore more explicitly the theme of resistance in *Un giorno nella vita* (One Day in Life, 1946). The film recounted the drama of some partisans, one of them seriously wounded, who take refuge in a convent where they are cared for by the nuns until they are in a position to leave. A choral work that was shot on a shoestring, partly on location, the film featured several stars, including Amedeo Nazzari, Massimo Girotti, Elisa Cegani and Mariella Lotti. After the film has explored the encounter and the partisans have left, all but one of the nuns are subsequently killed by the Germans as a reprisal. The hopeful final sequence shows the partisans making their way to safety and joining with the Allies. All concerned appear to have been aware that the film offered an opportunity to take their distance from the cinema of the Fascist era. The mood and performance style is notably subdued. For Nazzari to embrace the role of a former soldier turned partisan chief was a bold move, although care was taken not to accord his character the sort of heroic status he would have had in the past. For Piero Pruzzo, the actor seemed to be trying to achieve a new performance style: 'He knew full well that the period of three or four years that separated this film from the seasons of his full employment at Cinecittà and the apex of his personal star appeal was as long as a century, that cinema needed to turn over a new leaf. And he began again humbly, just like many others'.[37] Little is known of the actor's personal attitude towards recent events but he always took care to ensure that his characters were upright, well intentioned and deserving of respect. In this light, he cautiously sought to reorient his persona for new times. All Italians carried baggage, and Nazzari's task was to inhabit characters who embodied an awareness of this as they struggled to move forward with dignity.

He was given a further opportunity to play out the transition of his persona in Alberto Lattuada's *Il bandito* (The Bandit, 1946), in which a returning soldier finds that his family and moral world has been destroyed. Lattuada chose not to follow the burgeoning neorealist practice of discarding stars for improvised actors drawn from real life, but instead to cast the country's top male name in the lead role and to flank him with Anna Magnani. The film breathed the air of reality by being shot out-of-doors and featuring the human and physical devastation of the war. But it also bore the hallmarks of genre cinema. *Il bandito* more or less turns into a gangster movie in the second half, when Nazzari's character is forced to join a criminal gang and is eventually killed in a shoot-out. However, this outcome occurs after he has partially redeemed himself by saving the baby daughter of one of his former comrades-in-arms from danger. The film reflected some of the real dramas that had been experienced in Italy, and gave Nazzari the chance to reassert his persona as a man alone, albeit, for those who recalled his earlier roles, 'unusually contained, unusually self-controlled'.[38]

These films were commercial projects that were hybrids. As such they are often left out of discussions of postwar Italian cinema. But they present issues that deserve consideration. Ruth Ben-Ghiat has highlighted the added value that star casting could bring. 'The handsome and physically imposing Nazzari brought a sense of glamour as well as danger to his role, giving [*Il bandito*] its libidinal charge and its commercial viability', she argues, even though 'his popularity came in part from having starred in Fascist military films'.[39] Alluding to this ideological aspect of his persona, she concludes that, 'the sorry fate he meets ... as an unredeemable example of militarised masculinity ... has a performative meaning in several senses'. While all films belonging, broadly speaking, to the current of neorealism sought to set out a vision of the nation that was pluralist and democratic in contrast to the totalitarian one of Nazism and Fascism, Ben-Ghiat suggests that star casting 'opens up for public view and discussion an Italian manhood in crisis, as personified in the returned soldier-prisoner, who stood for both the hard heart of Fascism and for the ignominy of its defeat'.[40] *Il bandito*, in her view, 'draws parallels between injuries to national prestige and injuries to Italian manhood', and appears to locate solutions to both types of wound in the re-establishment of the family as the locus of responsible male roles.[41] Reflecting on the poor critical reception the film received, and taking the viewpoint of one contemporary reviewer, she suggests that it aimed not to speak to critics but directly to spectators, in recognition that the work of reconstructing Italian masculinity in a new context would necessarily be a collective one.[42]

The tactic of using the commercial power of established names to advance discourses of a novel type was problematic. It was not just that stars whose personas and appeal had been established in the past struggled to act plausibly as the bearers of new themes or ideals, although this was certainly an issue for actors whose personas had been bound up at some level with the regime. It was that the attempts to elaborate the new were inevitably tentative and were obstructed by the continued circulation of other, not yet fully defeated or rejected, ideas. Many Italians remained diffident about the course of events in the country. A large number of films of the Fascist period remained in distribution in the postwar years, while others, including *Giarabub* and a re-edited *Bengasi*,[43] benefited from relaunches after the end of the Allied occupation. Stars functioned as vehicles of a process of renegotiation rather than markers of a watershed. For cinema's radicals this was not enough.

Nevertheless stars dramatised issues in particular ways. One of the most prolific and successful commercial directors, Mario Mattoli, also made a film inflected with realism in which he cast leading names. Mattoli was a controversial figure in the immediate postwar years as he refused to engage in the sort of self-criticism the ACCI encouraged and, indeed, polemically defended his output.[44] He saw cinema as entertainment and claimed that he had only ever given the public what it wanted. Thus the innovative intent of his film *La vita ricomincia* (Life Starts Over, 1946) was minimal. It was shot amid the ruins of war-damaged Naples not for ideological reasons, but because these were the practical conditions in which the film was made. It stars Fosco Giachetti and Alida Valli in a drama about a returning soldier who discovers that his wife has been forced to prostitute herself with a wealthy man in order to obtain money to buy medicine for their sick son. The film explores Giachetti's reaction. His first response is conventional. His honour shattered, he repudiates his wife. However, the wise counsel of an avuncular neighbour, played by Eduardo De Filippo, induces him to review his behaviour and be less judgemental. When Valli kills the man who has exploited her need for help, he takes over responsibility for the act. In terms of its message, the film is one which, Ben-Ghiat has written, 'argues that hardness must give way to tenderness'.[45] In this way the Giachetti persona was also subjected to revision.

Stars for Export

Despite the gradual revival of film production in the late 1940s, established names struggled to obtain the sort of high profile roles they had commanded before 1943. Many of them continued to experience idleness or unemployment. For many of the women, who were still in their twenties, the enforced break offered an opportunity to think about their personal lives. Alida Valli, Clara Calamai, Vivi Gioi and Carla Del Poggio all got married between 1943 and 1945, as did Assia Noris (for the third or fourth time) to British officer Jack Pelster.[46] Maria Denis also married a British officer, while Valli and Berti both had children. Unemployed stars busied themselves in numerous ways, taking part in revues, playing at charity football matches, and writing for newspapers. Alida Valli ran a column replying to letters from readers in the Rome newspaper *Città*. When offers of work failed to materialise some, like Noris, decided simply to withdraw. Others opted for exile. Those who were most associated with Fascist cinema, for political, personal or aesthetic reasons, mostly accepted invitations to work in Spain or in South America. Miria di San Servolo, Paola Barbara and others left for Spain in 1944, while, after nothing of interest materialised in Italy, Irasema Dilian headed for Mexico and Adriana Benetti for Argentina. The popularity of Italian films in the Spanish-speaking world was also demonstrated by Nazzari, who made three films in Spain before making a further one in Argentina.

The most fortunate were courted by Hollywood. The studios were well aware of the state of development of Italian cinema and they set about cherry-picking the best talent in time-honoured manner. In the interwar years, Isa Miranda had had a bruising experience with Paramount, but that did not stop others being tempted, especially at a time when the film industry was inactive in Italy. David O. Selznick, the producer of *Gone With The Wind*, was the most prominent figure to set about signing up talent. His scouts supplied him with information about Alida Valli, Valentina Cortese, Rossano Brazzi and others, and he received reports and photos of them. After a protracted period of negotiations and difficulties with Valli, which concerned both the propaganda films the actress was alleged to have made and rumours about her private life, she eventually set sail for America where she would immediately begin filming *The Paradine Case* with Alfred Hitchcock.[47] Initially, Selznick had seen the part of the mysterious foreigner, Mrs Paradine, as ideal for Greta Garbo and had bought the rights with her in mind. He then moved on to Bergman, before trying to get Vivien Leigh to take the part, and Laurence Olivier the part of the lawyer. Hedy Lamarr was also considered.[48] Valli was in some respects a last resort, but this was also an opportunity for the producer to fashion a new American star from European source material.

Valli had not been cast in any neorealist films and knew that as a northerner of bourgeois social origin she would not have been suited to them. Nevertheless, it is striking that, while other Italian actresses were subjected to systematic de-glamorisation, she was groomed and polished in the conventional Hollywood fashion of the interwar years. Selznick decided that, from the outset, she was to be presented as sophisticated and adult. Hence a full programme of glamorisation was ordered. This was geared first to establishing a specific off-screen image for Valli. The key person in this part of the process was Anita Colby, a former model who had advised on the Rita Hayworth vehicle *Cover Girl*. As 'feminine director' of the Selznick company, her task was to make contracted actresses look sophisticated and poised. The level of Selznick's personal involvement in Valli's on-screen presentation was remarkable even for a producer who was notoriously interfering. He commissioned Travis Banton, who had made Dietrich's costumes at Paramount, to design clothes for the film, but rejected his first proposals as inadequate. 'Use every trick in the book to present her excitingly, as a photographic dream and as a woman who is different in every way', the producer urged Hitchcock, suggesting that a lesson might be learned from Dietrich's director von Sternberg who, he admitted with evident reluctance, was always very good on 'mood and theatrical lighting'. This process was designed to turn Valli into a 'coherent, saleable persona' – in other words into a fully fledged star.

While Valli was in America, Italy embarked on the first proper election campaign since the war. In the politicised climate of the postwar years, a number of stars set aside the relative independence of the political sphere that they had struggled to maintain under Fascism. Giachetti, for example, positioned himself on the left.[49] The actor who had incarnated the Fascist masculine ideal the most gave interviews to left-wing papers and talked of promoting theatrical experiences for young people. In 1947 he gave a clear statement of his views to the women's magazine *Noi Donne*: 'I am not a member of any political party ... but my sympathies are with the democratic parties. I think that, even from a Christian point of view, you should help the people, be close to them, and that fraternity and equality are indispensable conditions for a civil society'. In 1948 he declared his support for the Democratic Popular Front.

Valli, like many other actors, had come out in favour of the republic in the 1946 constitutional referendum, but she did not frequent left-wing circles. Although she had largely avoided propaganda in Fascist Italy, her position as an Italian star in Hollywood in 1947–48 inevitably brought pressure on her to join the campaign to persuade her fellow countrymen to save Italy from the threat of communism. She appeared in a number of radio discussions including one in March 1948 featuring several actors that tied in with a *Time* forum on the international situation. Once the election was over, and the U.S.-backed Christian Democrats had secured a big victory, requests for Valli's contribution multiplied. American Relief for Trieste won her support for its aim of withstanding 'the enslavement of Communism', while an endorsement was solicited – and granted – for the new Italian edition of *Reader's Digest*.

When Italian cinema continued to languish after the elections, several stars joined the public campaign to promote the defence of Italian cinema. Meanwhile others opted to work abroad, among them Isa Miranda. Miranda was an actress who justifiably had high hopes for her postwar career. She was referred to as 'Isa nazionale' in the press and enjoyed public favour. *Film d'oggi* reported in February 1946 that a Roman student by the name of Giorgio Ranieri had written to the magazine asking to meet the star. 'Isa Miranda, begged by us, invited him to lunch' the magazine reported, and the event was immortalised on the cover. *Bellezza*, the monthly of Italian style and fashion, described her in 1947 as 'incontestably the Italian film actress most endowed with personality, talent and, naturally, photogenic qualities'. Yet she received few offers of film work. In 1945 she made *Lo sbaglio di essere vivo* (The Error of Being Alive, Carlo Ludovico Bragaglia, 1945), a drama set in 1938 in which she co-starred with De Sica and Cervi, playing the ostensible widow of a man who pretends to be dead in order to pocket his life insurance. After this she only made one film in Italy, Luigi Chiarini's *Patto col diavolo* (Pact with the Devil, 1947), which, despite the prestige of its director, then still director of the Centro sperimentale, passed without notice. Fortunately France beckoned and, following one routine film, she was cast in 1949 in René Clément's *Au-de-là des grilles* (Beyond the Bars, released in Italy with the title *Le mura di Malapaga*). Largely shot on location in Genoa, the film cast Jean Gabin as a French stowaway who is fleeing justice after killing his wife. After he decides to go ashore at Genoa, where his ship is berthed, he is tricked and robbed. Miranda is the waitress who befriends him. Her downbeat performance, that evoked the current in her work that stretched back to *Passaporto rosso*, won wide acclaim and was crowned with the best actress award at Cannes. However, when it was shown at the Venice Film Festival in 1950, it was ignored, a reaction which led Miranda to write an indignant open letter to the jury and critics. Once the queen of Italian cinema, Miranda felt, at the age of forty-four, that she was no longer of interest. With hindsight it can be seen that the film was a curious hybrid of descriptive realism and French noir style, with numerous high-angle shots and shadowed interiors creating a mood of impending doom. Moreover, whereas Miranda's performance style had once been praised as understated and naturalistic, in comparison with the new realist idiom it was merely subdued and unengaging.

By 1950 things had moved on. New stars had started to emerge who suited the new stories and styles, as well as the new audience tastes, of the postwar era. Although interest in the old names did not disappear, it grew weaker and became tainted with nostalgia. With just very few exceptions, the one-time princes and princesses of Cinecittà had to reconcile themselves to taking supporting roles or finding some other purpose in life. Having once basked in official and popular acclaim, they began a long and pitiless slide towards oblivion.

Notes

1. M. Denis. 1995. *Il gioco della verità: una diva nella Roma del 1943*, Milan: Baldini & Castoldi, 35.
2. O. Fallaci, 'Lo specchio del passato', *L'Europeo*, 14 January 1965, 59.
3. Testimony of Elsa De Giorgi, in F. Faldini and F. Fofi (eds). 1979. *L'avventurosa storia del cinema italiano: raccontata dai suoi protagonisti, 1935–1959*, Milan: Feltrinelli, 73.
4. Ibid., 70.
5. A. Baracco, 'Cinema in licenza', *Star*, 30 September 1944, 7; Faldini and Fofi, *L'avventurosa storia del cinema italiano*, 70–73.
6. See V. De Sica. 2004. *La porta del cielo: memorie 1901–1952*, Cava De' Terreni: Avagliano, 87–89.
7. Faldini and Fofi, *L'avventurosa storia del cinema italiano*, 78.
8. A. Pietrangeli, 'Bilancio', *Star*, 2 September 1944, 3–4.
9. Steno. 1993. *Sotto le stelle del '44*, Palermo: Sellerio, 46.
10. A. Baracco, 'L'amante grassa', *Star*, 12 August 1944, 2.
11. A. Baracco, 'Motivi', *Star*, 9 September 1944, 7.
12. A. Pietrangeli, 'Bilancio', *Star*, 2 September 1944, 3–4.
13. A. Pietrangeli, 'Gli attori', *Star*, 23 September 1944, 5–6. See also the second part in issue of 30 September 1944.

14. Ibid.
15. E. Patti, 'Bilancio', *Star*, 12 August 1944, 2.
16. F. Sarazani, 'Personaggi in galera', *Star*, 20 January 1945, 3.
17. Steno, *Sotto le stelle*, 143.
18. N. Marino and E.V. Marino. 2005. *L'Ovra a Cinecittà: polizia politica e spie in camicia nera*, Turin: Bollati Borighieri, 233–34.
19. See S. Gundle. 2010. 'Satire and the Destruction of the Cult of the Duce', in R. Cremoncini et al. (eds), *Against Mussolini: Art and the Fall of a Dictator*, London: Estorick Collection, 15–35.
20. L. Pellizzari and C. Valentinetti. 1995. *Il romanzo di Alida Valli*, Milan: Garzanti.
21. Anon., 'Coraggiose confessioni di attori e registi', *Star*, 13 January 1945, 3.
22. Anonymous note, *Star*, 9 December 1944, 5.
23. Ibid.
24. V. Lilli, 'Dive in prima linea', *Star*, 14 October 1944, 7.
25. A.G. Majano, 'Le SS andavano al cinema', *Star*, 26 May 1945, page unnumbered.
26. A. Baracco, 'Valenti-Ferida: finalmente la verità', *Star*, 16 June 1945, 1–2.
27. *Film d'oggi*, 25 August 1945.
28. Quoted in S. Bertoldi, 'Sesso, droga, crudeltà: e l'amore diventò tragedia', *Oggi*, 15 March 1995, 87.
29. Anonymous note, *Star*, 1 December 1945, page unnumbered. In fact she never gave birth; she was pregnant at the time of her execution.
30. On Hayworth and her image, see A.L. McLean. 2004. *Being Rita Hayworth: Labor, Identity, and Hollywood Stardom*, New Brunswick: Rutgers University Press. See also S. Gundle. 2007. *Bellissima: Feminine Beauty and the Idea of Italy*, London and New Haven: Yale University Press, Chapter 5.
31. F. Fellini. 1983. *Intervista sul cinema*, ed. by G. Grazzini, Rome–Bari: Laterza, 49–50.
32. R. Bertolozzi, 'Le attrici americane', *Star*, 14 October 1944, 4.
33. G.P. Brunetta. 1991. 'La lunga marcia del cinema americano in Italia tra fascismo e guerra fredda' in D.W. Ellwood and G.P. Brunetta (eds), *Hollywood in Europa: industria, politica, pubblico del cinema 1945–1960*, Florence: Ponte alle Grazie, 75–87, 80.
34. F. Sarazani, 'Personaggi in galera', *Star*, 20 January 1945, 3.
35. D. Risi, '*Due lettere anonime*', *Milano sera*, 18 December 1945. Reproduced in A. Farassino (ed.). 1992. *Mario Camerini*, Locarno: Yellow Now, 181.
36. As Camerini told Sergio Grmek Germani, 'during the German occupation of Rome, I experienced the servility of the Roman bourgeoisie, and even of a part of the working class, towards the Germans. Lots of Italians denounced other Italians. With that film, I wanted to denounce Rome and people understood that. When I went to the premiere at the Corso, I saw that half the people got up and left; they were indignant because the film was directed against them.' Germani, 'Entretien avec Mario Camerini' in ibid., 87–146, 135.

37. P. Pruzzo and E. Lancia. 1983. *Amedeo Nazzari*, Rome: Gremese, 96.
38. C.A. Felice, 'Il bandito', *Film*, 16 November 1946. Quoted in ibid., 98.
39. R. Ben-Ghiat. 2005. 'Unmaking the Fascist Man: Masculinity, Film and the Transition from Dictatorship', *Journal of Modern Italian Studies* 10(3), 336–65, 355.
40. Ibid., 355.
41. Ibid., 356.
42. Ibid., 359.
43. See D. Baratieri. 2004. 'La riedizione di *Bengasi* e *L'assedio dell'Alcazar* negli anni Cinquanta' in S. Bernardi (ed.), *La storia del cinema italiano*, Vol. 9, 1949–1953, Venice and Rome: Marsilio/Bianco & Nero, 118–29.
44. S. Della Casa. 1990. *Mario Mattoli*, Florence: La Nuova Italia, 48–50.
45. Ben-Ghiat, 'Unmaking the Fascist Man', 354.
46. Pelster committed suicide in London eight months later, after she had left him. On 20 September 1947 *Tempo* reported that 'the most difficult little character of Italian cinema' was looking out for husband number five.
47. See S. Gundle. 2012. 'Alida Valli in Hollywood: From Star of Fascist Cinema to "Selznick Siren"', *Historical Journal of Film, Radio and Television* 32(4), 559–87.
48. L. Leff. 1999. *Hitchcock and Selznick*, Berkeley: University of California Press, 232.
49. Giuseppe Parlato alleges, without citing any source, that he was a police informer during the RSI; see G. Parlato. 2007. *Fascisti senza Mussolini*, Bologna: Il Mulino, 113.

13

Survival, Memory and Forgetting

The relationship between history and memory is invariably an unstable one since, while history has conventionally been seen as rigorous, documented and fundamentally truthful, memory has been regarded as subjective, unreliable and sometimes remote from the truth. As John Foot observes in his history of Italy's 'divided memory', twentieth-century Italian history has rarely, if ever, given rise to universally accepted versions of events and this applies most of all to the experiences of Fascism, war and civil war.[1] Dominant interpretations have not only taken shape in contrast to alternatives but also alongside and sometimes in opposition to a variety of personal and collective memories. Cinema in this respect has mirrored politics. Just as, in the ideology of the democratic republic, Fascism was branded a negative experience in national development, to be condemned in nearly all its aspects, while the Resistance and the liberation, by contrast, were celebrated as important chapters in Italy's reawakening, so the cinema of the Fascist years was liquidated as worthless except for those instances that were seen as harbingers of neorealism. Yet cinema played a formative role in diffusing ideas, dreams and aspirations that remained with spectators even as the years passed and the political context changed. Films, film advertising, coverage of cinema in magazines, filmgoing and peer group discussions all had an impact on the imagination and on the personal identity of the generations that grew up and reached adulthood in the prewar and war years.

Gian Piero Brunetta argues that stars only played a limited role in this process of shaping mentalities and aspirations. The most important legacy of the cinema of the Fascist years, he asserts, lay in the way it formed material desires that would fuel postwar consumerism. 'Often even the castle of stars – constituted, besides Valli and Nazzari, Merlini, Mercader, Roberto

Villa, Leda Gloria, by tens of faces that appear and disappear in memory – appears weak and elusive compared to the system of objects', he argues.[2] Nevertheless, the memories of cinema-goers included forgotten personalities. Film research has shown that stars function as 'personal Utopias' constructed by spectators which, as they slide into the past, become inflected with nostalgia.[3] However, unlike the leading personalities of the regime, some actors, including Valli and Nazzari, did not disappear. Rather they continued to appear in new films and were active for several decades after the war. It is necessary to consider the extent to which stars like these remained bearers of discourses or memories linked to the earlier period. Star personas are formed over time through performances as well as the personal readings that are imposed on them by spectators. Very few reinvent themselves so totally in the course of a career as to erase the memories of early roles and the meanings that were attached to them.

In the first two sections of this chapter, these issues will be considered, first in relation to the press and television, and then with reference to Nazzari, the one star who enjoyed continuing fame while still acting as the bearer of at least some of the values which had attached to him from the 1930s. In the final section, three films set in the world of Fascist cinema will be considered. Made with different intents by directors with very different personal histories and concerns, the films demonstrate well the ambiguities and interactions of memory and history.

Press, Television and Waning Celebrity

Illustrated magazines were one of the great media phenomena of the postwar years. Modelled on the American weekly *Life* and on pre-war Italian examples like *Tempo* and *Omnibus*, weeklies like *Oggi*, *L'Europeo*, *La Settimana Incom*, *Le ore*, *Epoca* and, later, *Gente* achieved huge circulations with their diet of celebrity, modern life features, international curiosities and crime. At a time when the fruits of a growing economy were coming within the reach of ever wider groups, the magazines played a key role in forming Italian mass culture. Unlike *La Domenica del Corriere*, a publication that had not changed its basic formula or its custom of front and rear cover illustrations over its long existence since the 1890s, the illustrated magazines were forward looking. They were geared towards a new world of longed-for prosperity that had the United States as its main reference point. Within this overall framework, however, there was ample room for evocations and recollections of the recent past. Catering mainly to a middle-class readership, the weeklies became vehicles of what Cristina Baldassini calls the 'indulgent memory' of Fascism, which was accompanied by 'a vague and ill-defined form of nostalgia as well as a way – it too, benevolent – of situating the Fascist period in the history of Italy in a manner that suggested continuity rather than a break with the preceding liberal period'.[4] In this outlook, the violence and destruction wreaked by Fascism were overshadowed by recollections of the climate of social order, numerous images of national progress, realisation of the dream of empire, gratifying collective activities and light music broadcast on the radio. Events, experiences and personalities were evoked uncritically as a pure exercise in nostalgia. At the centre of this there was constant attention to Mussolini himself, no longer seen as a bellicose dictator but rather as an ordinary man with foibles and weaknesses. There were also regular articles about the sports heroes, popular singers, and of course the film stars.

The Fascist period itself had witnessed the development of a formidable set of stimuli to distraction. At a time of war, hardship and setbacks, these functioned to maintain an illusion of normality, provide a range of satisfying pursuits and in general promote consent. Brunetta argues that escapism functioned on national screens during the early 1940s 'as a sort of symphonic theme that united middle-level production and interpreted the collective need to subtract oneself from the watchwords of Fascism and to reject a war that was devoid of real objectives or ideal motivations'.[5] The poor, petit bourgeois Italy that 'lacked primary goods and was forced to invent synthetic textiles like Filital, Cocafil, Lanasol and Cisalfa ... marched beneath banners that bore symbolic white telephones or displayed the faces of Alida Valli, Amedeo Nazzari, Lilia Silvi, Elsa Merlini, Assia Noris ...'. This was a country that was dissatisfied and whose expectations had been betrayed; one that, despite restrictions and a grim outlook, 'had no intention of giving up the small spaces in which it could dream of fur coats, clothes and silk stockings, luxury cars, environments dominated by the superfluous and the idea that not all cultural and communicative links with the rest of the world had been interrupted'. Brunetta sees this process as spectator-led rather than regime-imposed. Stars and light entertainment did not so much inculcate false optimism as create opportunities for mental islands of freedom from depressing realities.

In fact both aspects need to be borne in mind. The way in which the movies worked was complex and not reducible to any single pattern. Like the artificial fibres, the stars were produced by an industry whose economic purposes they served while also finding backing from government, especially in a phase of autarky. Yet, because they provided fodder for fantasy, they were remembered with a good deal more fondness than the late unlamented fibres. Around 1950 many actors who had hoped to continue with their careers gave up.[6] Almost immediately the illustrated magazines started to run articles laced with nostalgia for the stars of bygone days. 'Where have they finished up?', asked Enrico Lancia in a 1952 article.[7] In August 1953, *Oggi* jumped on the bandwagon, announcing that 'the forgotten stars miss the screen'.[8] Over the years many magazines and newspapers ran series of articles with titles like *La Nazione*'s 'Incontri con i semidei del tempo passato' (Meetings with the Demi-gods of the Past), *L'Europeo*'s 'Le attrici del regime' (The Actresses of the Regime) and *Il Giorno*'s 'Le amanti del regime' (The Lovers of the Regime). Such articles spoke to a particular generation of readers; they reminded them of past favourites, mused on their best-known roles, and provided information about their present whereabouts and activities. They allowed a minimum of dialogue between stars and their audiences to be maintained.

Among the once prominent names who featured in such series were Maria Denis, Isa Miranda and Fosco Giachetti. 'Everything is difficult for Isa', one article commented, noting that there was little place for an actress of her class in a cinema dominated by starlets who got by wearing a bathing costume or tight jersey. In 1954, she was accorded a rare cover by *Hollywood*. The magazine lamented that, despite being 'our best dramatic actress', she was hardly working.[9] Instead, she spent her time making dolls for charity. Fosco Giachetti made thirteen films between 1945 and 1950, but then just eight between 1951 and 1960, and none in a leading role after 1954. The magazine *Fotocronaca* dubbed him a 'great film actor, perhaps the most complete Italian cinema has had up to now', adding that 'with the passing of the generations, he has become illustrious but forgotten'.[10] When *La Nazione* interviewed the actor in 1965, he was treated as a period piece like his home. 'The home on Lungotevere Marzio where Fosco Giachetti lives can be dated with a certain precision: the style is "Novecento", a bit monumental, a bit rationalist, post-Piacentini, of the type that was typical of the apex of Fascism', it commented.[11] 'I wouldn't know if cinema abandoned me or I abandoned cinema', he responded when asked about his career. 'Perhaps both are partly true. I did not do much to stay afloat. It is my character ... I was not a narcissist. I did not cultivate the myth of myself. I felt a certain reserve, just as today it irritates me to hear anyone talk about me in an exaggerated way.' In 1970, *Radiocorriere* magazine also visited him at home and noted the presence of several *chinoisieries* from the 1930s, a few paintings (a Mafai, a Guttuso, two Carignanis), some silver cups among which the famous Volpi award for best actor and 'one that has nothing to do with cinema but which is equally important for the actor: a first prize won by him in a horse and cart race'.[12] Asked to nominate his favourite role, the actor cited *Lo squadrone bianco*, since it had brought him his first taste of success. It was in this retro key that Bernardo Bertolucci cast him, that year, in *Il conformista* (The Conformist). His part as 'the colonel' was, according to the *Enciclopedia dello spettacolo* 'almost a distant and vaguely ironical echo of the brusque and solemn characters of the 1940s'.[13]

Those who did not abandon the performing arts often returned to the theatre. For some actors television was a godsend. The new medium enjoyed a close relationship with theatre and old actors found themselves presented with opportunities to perform once more for a mass audience. Miranda and Giachetti were among those who benefited. Lacking film roles, Giachetti had formed his own company which in 1958 toured with the French drama 'L'Équipage au complet', an evocation of war at sea. In the 1960s, he performed in a number of television productions, while Miranda also appeared in several British television plays. Gino Cervi, who had won popularity as the Communist mayor Peppone in the film versions of Giovannino Guareschi's Don Camillo novels, secured a wider following with his small-screen interpretations of Georges Simenon's creation Inspector Maigret.

Television also broadcast old films, sometimes grouping titles into personal retrospectives. In 1969 the RAI-1 channel broadcast four of Assia Noris's best films: *Grandi magazzini, Una romantica avventura, Una storia d'amore* and *Un colpo di pistola*. Each broadcast was preceded by a conversation with the actress, who was still only aged around fifty. The series was assembled by Giulio Cesare Castello, author in 1957 of a substantial book about stars.[14] *Sogno* magazine reported that 'she still receives many letters containing passionate declarations of love'.[15] The showing of her films 'has given rise to enormous interest among the public, many of whom relive through her face the dreams of their youth', it commented, adding that 'she is blonde, still has those green eyes that enchanted the generations of the 1930s and 1940s, and is slim like a girl'. In the years that followed, Noris enjoyed regular coverage in the illustrated weeklies. She tantalised readers with tales of her upbringing, her life in cinema, the famous people she knew, her husbands and the tragedy of losing her only son, who died at the age of four.[16]

The female stars of the past were a classic 'indulgent memory'. As the journalist Arturo Lanocita remarked in 1974, 'the beauties of the 1930s and 1940s remain a memory for some that is a bit of a fetish'.[17] This was surely true of the novelist and critic Alberto Arbasino, who waxed lyrical about them in a festival catalogue.[18] Working from personal memory, he wrote of seven stars he considered 'fully fledged'; he then categorised further names according to the character types they typically played. Interestingly, he selected only female stars. It is possible that the women created a deeper impression on him because they were more distinctive with respect to the dictates and models of the regime. The men, with the passing of the decades, merged in memory into a broad current of masculine models that culminated in the image of the dictator. The younger female stars were typically healthy, sweet and conservative, but they could also be cheeky, enterprising, resourceful and funny. Perhaps because of the regime's stress on reproductive femininity, such images evoked simply playful youth with a light erotic touch like Proust's *jeunes filles en fleur*.[19] As Stefano Masi has observed, 'there is an abyss between the little lamb Adriana Benetti, who emerged at the start of the 1940s, and the tiger Silvana Mangano, who emerged at the end of the same decade'.[20] The war represented a watershed in values, needs, aspirations and ideas of feminine beauty. Compared to the assertive, sexualised femininity of postwar screens, the fiancées and girls-next-door of the earlier period, representatives of an 'angelicised femininity', provided, especially for men of a certain age, a pleasant memory of female innocence.

The lighter side of cinema remained popular to some degree, thanks to periodic articles and memoirs. Lilia Silvi's memoirs consisted mostly of inconsequential anecdotes and impressions.[21] Roberto Villa's were more interesting and insightful, not least because they were occasioned by and jointly authored with Sergio Micheli, who had earlier published a study of the actor.[22] In both works there was an evident pleasure in recalling a time in their youth when they had been famous. However, there were also those who tended the memory of the period's stronger figures and femmes fatales. For the Peruvian author Manuel Puig, Isa Miranda loomed large in his imagination. He speculated, adopting the narrative voice of a producer, that she was a 'protagonist':

> La Miranda is ambiguous, she has sensitive eyes, but a certain tension in the lips that can herald who knows what nastiness ... La Miranda has in-built, interiorised suspense. A character played by her can be permitted any sort of surprise: if she decides to be nasty you believe her, if she decides to be good that is alright too. Ambiguity, in other words, is natural in her and for this very reason she can be very human if used properly.[23]

The darker side of the regime and its cinema was also something of a fetish. Doris Duranti was the most notorious of the actresses of the Fascist period, after the ill-fated Luisa Ferida. After sojourns in Switzerland, Brazil and Cuba, and periodic returns to Rome, Duranti moved to the Dominican Republic. She gave interviews at regular intervals, and in 1987 she published her memoirs for the leading publishing house Mondadori, an event which garnered her extensive publicity.[24] It was later turned into a television mini-series, *Doris, una stella del regime*. The actress revelled in the status of dark diva that she had first acquired in the 1940s. Unrepentant and feisty, she waxed lyrical about dictatorship, boasted about her famous topless scene in *Carmela*,[25] and remembered with pleasure the shoes, fur coats and jewels she amassed.

Other memoirs were tinged with bitterness. Maria Denis's book about Rome in 1943–44 included reflections about the pleasures of being a film actor but was mostly concerned with the period of her imprisonment on suspicion of having been an associate of the torturer Pietro Koch. When she attended the 'Il Cinema Ritrovato' festival in Bologna in 2006, she was keener on setting the record straight about this episode than anything else. For Myriam Petacci, whose memoirs *Chi ama è perduto* (He Who Loves Is Lost) appeared in 1988, it was imperative not only to salvage her own reputation but that of her sister.

For other actresses, revisitations of the past were less welcome because they consigned them to the past. Perhaps for this reason, Lorenzo Pellizzari and Claudio Valentinetti received no assistance or encouragement from Alida Valli for their sympathetic biography of the actress.[26] Even though she would win, in 1954, the prestigious role of Countess Livia Serpieri in Visconti's *Senso* and from there build a career in international art house cinema, she knew that she was no longer a star. When she was interviewed by Oriana Fallaci in 1965, she lamented the fact that she was seen 'solely as a museum piece, of interest for her past and nothing else'.[27]

> 'Do you remember her in *Assenza ingiustificata?* Do you remember her in *Ore 9 lezione di chimica?*' I am still young and I am an actress, but for most people I only have value as a memory, the melancholy of their lost youth ... I don't understand, Deborah Kerr is still Deborah Kerr; Simone Signoret is still Simone Signoret; Michele Morgan is still Michele Morgan; Ingrid Bergman is still Ingrid Bergman. And Alida Valli is still the Alida Valli of the white telephones.

By the same token, Clara Calamai, who only made a handful of films after 1950 and made no further films at all after Dario Argento's *Profondo rosso* in 1975, was evoked as a mysterious presence, more of an absence, by Italo Moscati and his fellow authors of *Clara Calamai: l'ossessione di essere una diva*.[28] In 1986 and 1989 the actress had been happy to evoke her past experiences in cinema for the weekly *Gente*, but after that preferred silence. Just as Pellizzari and Valentinetti were obliged to make recourse to their imaginations and therefore to call their work a 'novel', so Moscati and company evoked a mystery around Calamai's star status to compensate for the lack of input from the actress herself.

Survivors

Amedeo Nazzari, the most prolific, well-paid and popular star of the Fascist era, enjoyed a new heyday thanks to the popular cinema of the 1950s. With audiences booming, especially in the centre and south of the country, there was a demand for genre films with a strong Italian flavour. Under the direction of Raffaello Matarazzo, who directed him in eight films between 1949 and 1958, he adapted his established persona to a new situation in which women were more independent and visible than before, if no less enmeshed in and constrained by given ideas of honour and shame. In the early 1950s, he even renewed his screen partnership with Alida Valli. Before she won the role of Countess Livia Serpieri in the Risorgimento drama *Senso*, mentioned earlier, she appeared in *Ultimo incontro* (Last Meeting, Gianni Franciolini, 1951) and *Il mondo le condanna* (The World Condemns Them, Gianni Franciolini, 1953). In both films Valli played the part of a prostitute while Nazzari took that of an upright professional. Critics found them backward looking (*Ultimo incontro* was based on a novel written nearly fifty years earlier) and neither was as successful as *Assenza ingiustificata* (Unjustified Absence, Max Neufeld, 1939).

However, there was a much greater continuity between Nazzari's pre-war and postwar personas than there was with the other actors. He carried with him the legacy of past roles; he would always remain at some level Luciano Serra, despite the significant readjustment that he had effected, playing a soldier turned partisan chief in Blasetti's *Un giorno nella vita* and a displaced returning soldier in Lattuada's *Il Bandito*. Nazzari remained the embodiment of the idea of the film star. In the postwar years this idea, which had been vague and informed by fantasy in the pre-war era, was filled out in the public mind. Nazzari appeared with a certainly regularity in magazine features in the 1950s and 1960s. In keeping with the greater openness about personal and domestic lives, he was photographed at home, in his cars and, after his marriage in 1957 and the birth of his daughter Maria Evelina in 1958 in family contexts. These always presented him as the seasoned professional who had starred in more than a hundred films. In 1952, he moved into a massive 35-room villa on the Via Cassia a few kilometres from Rome (dubbed a 'house-museum' or 'Technicolor-magazine-house' in the press) that was no less fabulous than the stars' homes of Beverly Hills. It included a small cinema, a massive wardrobe housing thousands of garments and over eight hundred costumes that he kept by contract from his films, as well as a bar, a billiard room, outside games area, lodgings for seven servants, garages for five cars, and landscaped gardens, plus an entire separate wing for his sister. While all this would have been scarcely less than his fans would have expected, they might have been surprised by his hobbies: raising chickens, table tennis and entomology. The man who was regarded as almost an anti-star on account of his reserve and dislike for publicity had evidently decided that there was nothing to be lost, and perhaps something to be gained, by expanding the insight into his private realm that had first been conceded, in fictionalised form, in the film *Apparizione* in 1943.

There came a point at which, for directors and producers, Nazzari's film star persona overshadowed his talents as an actor. This happened at a number of levels. First, he always preserved something of his persona as fashioned in the 1930s. Although gradually modified by a number of critical and family-oriented roles, his moral and physical rigidity provided a bridge from the warrior ideal of the Fascist era to the democratic, domesticated model of the postwar era. In the context of masculine redefinition that witnessed a far greater emphasis on ineptitude and inadequacies than had been the case before,[29] he came to be something of a fossil. 'It is easy to smile at his characters, these good, upright men', commented the critic Fernaldo Di Giammatteo in 1958 while acknowledging their appeal to 'the popular public'.[30] Second, his style of acting, while still effective, lacked physical mobility and verbal complexity. Third, publicity about his lifestyle ensured that people no longer thought about him as a fluid and evolving screen persona but rather as a monument; a figure on the landscape whose stardom was encapsulated in his visible symbols of status. While Nazzari's popularity with the public did not undergo any obvious decline, the most significant part of his career was behind him. When he was asked about his fan mail by Maurizio Chierici of *Oggi* in 1965, he observed that from 1946 to 1947 there was a change of tone. 'I was still young and still the most famous Italian actor', he remarked; 'I used to receive sacks of letters, but they were very tepid compared to those that I used to get from admirers in the 1940s.'[31]

In 1957 Nazzari was still only fifty years old, some six years younger than Clark Gable (the actor to whom he was often likened) who in that year played the romantic lead opposite the twenty-five-year-old Sophia Loren in the comedy *It Started in Naples*. But he was already turning into a monument to himself. According to Fellini, the actor was wary when he invited him to play himself for the second time but acceded when he realised that the director viewed him, and what he stood for in Italian cinema, with great affection. His part in *Le notti di Cabiria* (The Nights of Cabiria, Federico Fellini, 1957), laced as it was with irony, was a genuine departure. As the mature film star, he breaks up with his young lover on the Via Veneto and picks up a diminutive prostitute named Cabiria who he takes to a club and then escorts in his sports car to his home. Nazzari was not in fact a habitué of the Via Veneto, the Roman road that was known for its colourful and celebrity-laden night life. But he knew that in the public mind he had to be. The public could accept that he was a little reserved and solitary but not that he was a comfortable homebody. The star's house as seen in the film closely resembled his own, save for the fact that the huge electronically operated wardrobe that so impresses Cabiria was considerably smaller.

The descendant phase of Nazzari's film career was marked by a number of performances laced with satire and self-irony. His role as an aging male model in Luigi Zampa's film *Frenesie d'estate* (Summer Excitements, 1964) was imbued with a certain melancholy, but it was also a light comedy of the quality of *Dopo divorzieremo*, in which he had appeared in 1942. In *Il gaucho* (Dino Risi, 1964), he repeated the stunt as a rich emigrant of residual Fascist sympathies who falls over himself to befriend Italian visitors to Buenos Aires. These were not at all the last sad gasps of a declining star. Press reviews were full of admiration for the 'verve and intelligence' with which he played; 'and there is the evergreen Amedeo Nazzari, for whom the years seem not to pass, and it seems as though he only just finished yesterday *Luciano Serra pilota*', wrote the Venice paper *Il Gazzettino*.[32] Nevertheless, the last remark attests to the nostalgia with which the actor's work was increasingly laced. Roles referred back to other roles, self-citations were numerous, and reunions with old colleagues inevitably evoked earlier times. Reprises and revisitations were common. In press interviews he was often asked about the past. In 1964, a year in which he won recognition for *Il gaucho* and *Frenesie d'estate*, he was asked: 'If you were to decide to produce a film and you allowed yourself to be guided only by nostalgia in the choice of the cast, which artists would you opt for?' He replied as follows:

> I would entrust the film to Alessandro Blasetti, a director I hold in very high esteem and I would sign up immediately: Fosco Giachetti, a great actor who has been unjustly overlooked as well as a very good friend; Elisa Cegani, a formidable actress; Alida Valli, a star who is still fascinating and loved by the adult audience; and Irasema Dilian, the sweet adolescent now forgotten by the Italian public. It would not be a flop. And this would, in the end, be a way of permitting those who are no longer twenty-year-olds, to reacquire, even if only for an evening, their youth.[33]

Far from getting the chance to make the film of his dreams, Nazzari found that opportunities of all types became fewer despite the acclaim won for his self-parodies. To his dismay he was passed over for roles that he coveted, like that of the prince in Visconti's *Il Gattopardo* (The Leopard), and soon not even lesser parts came his way. But his place in popular affections and the collective memory was sure. For Italians of two or three generations, he had embodied the nation's virtues, its best idea of itself. Even as times and tastes changed, that would ensure that he enjoyed a prominent place in the popular imagination.

Three Films

The world of Fascism hung like a shadow over the cinema of the post-war years. At first it was a taboo topic. Then, in the 1960s and 1970s, Fascism was dealt with in cinema in a variety of different, complex ways. The treatments of that period and of the decades that followed took different forms with drama, comedy, biography and parody all figuring. Yet only three films set in the Fascist period take cinema as their theme: Dino Risi's *Telefoni bianchi* (White Telephones [internationally released as The Career of a Chambermaid], 1976), Tinto Brass's *Senso '45* (Black Angel, 2002) and Marco Tullio Giordana's *Sanguepazzo* (2008). These works need to be assessed as perceptions of a reality that by the mid-1970s was already quite remote, if still part of living memory, and which by the mid-2000s had in most respects been consigned to history.

Dino Risi was one of the masters of the *commedia all'italiana*. By 1976, the year he made *Telefoni bianchi*, he had won acclaim for a long series of films dealing with the servitudes of Italians, including *Il sorpasso* (The Easy Life, 1962), *La marcia su Roma* (The March on Rome, 1962), *I mostri* (The Monsters, 1963) and *Il gaucho* (The Gaucho, 1965), the last of these starring Nazzari. He had established himself as a sharp critic of the complacent way in which his countrymen passed from situation to situation – be it poverty to prosperity or democracy to dictatorship – without ever facing up to their responsibilities or duties. A striking number of his films (nine in all) feature cinema itself to some degree, and his *Il viale della speranza* (Boulevard of Hope, 1953) is entirely centred on the dreams and illusions of young people who hope to embark on a career in the movies.

Telefoni bianchi, as the title suggests, evokes the lost world of Italian cinema of the Fascist era. It was made when many of the stars of the era were still alive. The subject was created by Risi and his co-writer on the film, Bernardo Zapponi, but it was one that was not unfamiliar to Risi, who had begun his career at the age of twenty-five as assistant director of Soldati's *Piccolo mondo antico* – an experience that remained with him, he later recounted on several occasions, because the film's star, Alida Valli, had rejected the advances of the smitten but mature director in order to conduct a brief affair with him.[34] The film recounts the story of Marcella (Agostina Belli), a chambermaid in a luxury hotel in Venice who is enamoured of cinema. Through a series of comic picaresque adventures, we follow her progress as she passes from influential lover to influential lover, all the while claiming she is emotionally faithful to her hapless platonic fiancé Roberto (Cochi Ponzoni), who is successively despatched to the war front in Africa, Spain and Russia. Finally, while seeking to rescue Roberto, who has surprised her with yet another lover, from a failed suicide attempt at Ostia, she encounters Mussolini himself and is summoned for a meeting at Palazzo Venezia. Following an obligatory sexual encounter, a screen test is arranged for her at Cinecittà and she embarks on a movie career as Alba Doris. Her fame grows until the fall of the regime when suddenly it all comes to an end.

The film implies that the female film stars of the era were no better than prostitutes (at one point Marcella is put to work in a brothel), that they had no talent and that their progress was entirely due to sponsorship from on high. A series of ridiculous vignettes evoke film genres of the period, the schoolgirl comedy, the colonial epic, the pseudo-American crime film and the German co-production. Doris has the look of a film star; she is platinum blonde, heavily made-up and dresses in fine gowns and extravagant furs. Evidently, she is a composite of several names of the period: first of all Assia Noris, whose hair, eye movements and voice she has; then, on account of her peasant origins and relationship with a leading male star, she recalls Luisa Ferida; and finally, her affairs with Fascist officials are a nod to Doris Duranti. Discreetly, Risi avoided any reference to Valli, although Marcella's encounter with the Duce would have reminded some spectators of the rumours on her account that circulated in 1943–46.

In the film, Vittorio Gassman, one of Risi's favourite actors, plays the vain, pompous and cowardly Franco Denza, a composite film star of mature years who she first sees driving a magnificent open-top blue and white sports car. Tanned, moustachioed and permanently smiling, Denza appears to be made of a dose of Amedeo Nazzari, a pinch of Fosco Giachetti and a large helping of Osvaldo Valenti. Reference to the latter is marked in a party scene on the eve of Fascism's collapse. The elegant company is gathered in Denza's villa and is enjoying the party, animated by jazz discs procured, the host says, from Vittorio Mussolini, whose filo-Americanism was still widely known in the 1970s. Suddenly Denza undoes the ribbon holding up the dress of a seated guest and reveals her breasts. He then invites Doris to expose hers in order that a competition may be held. The quotation of the notorious 'breast war' engaged by Doris Duranti on Clara Calamai incorporates a further note of reality, albeit of a salacious and anecdotal type. As Doris brushes him off, Denza proceeds to provoke the guests with off-colour and politically dangerous remarks, a practice for which Valenti was famous. He also snorts cocaine and offers it to the guests in the manner of the actor. As Risi admitted, 'naturally it [the film] is full of suggestions that come from my memory; it is full of my recollections'.[35]

The film is a parody, and as such it includes grotesque situations as well as references to real persons and events. For Zinni, the film, 'presented the spectator with a series of Fascist personalities including Mussolini himself, that were characterised by a strong recourse to the most classic stereotypes of the film comedy about Fascism'.[36] Critic Tullio Kezich found numerous errors of fact and chronology in the film and criticised the figure of Alba Doris who, he said, resembled a Hollywood star more than an Italian one. But as a comedy the film is entitled to evoke and mess with the past that it makes no pretence to present accurately. In many respects the film and its marketing played directly on notions that were part of popular consciousness already rather than seeking to examine or overturn them. The film poster reproduced a well-known cover of the magazine *Le grandi firme*, in which the cover-girl *signorina*, illustrated by Boccasile, hugs a pillow and dreams of the film stars whose photographs appear next to her, and on whose images she has placed lipstick kisses. The *signorina* stands in for Marcella, implying that she was a typical modern girl of the era, while the star images are no longer those of Robert Taylor, Errol Flynn and so on but the actors of the film: Vittorio Gassman, Cochi Ponzoni, Ugo Tognazzi and Renato Pozzetto. Risi's principal aim, he said, was to enjoy himself by 'putting in the film two generations of actors, Gassman and Tognazzi alongside Cochi and Renato, who here had one of their first chances'.[37] By 1976 the first two were in their fifties, while the television double act Cocchi and Renato was made up of men in their mid-thirties.

For Zinni, Marcella is 'the not very well concealed personification of a nation that, out of superficiality and in good faith, passes through the storms of history, adapting each time to circumstances in order to survive'.[38] This may be true, but, the 'superficiality' of the film itself derives from the fact that Risi's aim was not solely to draw a fresco of a period he knew well.

Like Fellini in *Amarcord*, made three years earlier, he preferred to make recourse to his personal sensations and recollections rather than base the film on research of a conventional type.

The film is not devoid of tragedy; Italian soldiers are seen dying in Spain and embarking on the tragic invasion of Russia. Tognazzi plays a vile trader who sells Jews to the Nazi authorities. But the overall tone is one of caricature. The execution of Denza, who is surprised in Fascist uniform by partisans who decide that he should be shot, is played as tragi-comedy. Unlike Valenti, he is alone, Alba having left him shortly before. Like Valenti though, he recites lines from his films as he is ordered to face the wall. Instead of shooting at him, however, the partisans aim at the sky and laugh at his evident relief as he realises it has been a joke. As they turn and leave, he is struck by a heart attack and dies. Evidently Risi felt that this would have been a more fitting end for an actor like Valenti who was guilty mainly of having mistaken his fantasies for real life.

By the time he made *Senso '45*, Tinto Brass had long established himself as the master of the Italian erotic movie.[39] Born in 1933, he had limited personal experience of the period but a sure sense of the box-office appeal of period erotica. He had set a string of films in the decades between the 1930s and the 1950s, and in this film he returned to the period and the environment of two earlier films, *Salon Kitty* and *La chiave* (The Key). Accustomed to adapting his narratives from literary texts, on this occasion he took as his starting point Camillo Boito's novella *Senso*, which had been filmed by Visconti in 1954. By updating the action to 1945 while maintaining the setting of Venice, he substituted the Austrian occupation of the pre-unification period with the Nazi occupation. Countess Livia Serpieri becomes Livia Mazzoni, the restless wife of a senior government official, while her lover, in the novella an Austrian officer, becomes a decadent SS officer. The film industry and its personalities feature in the film as a backdrop and a justification for a variety of citations and references as well as some meta-cinematic devices. One scene centres on the final take of a film entitled *Betrayal*. The director is played by Brass himself, although the name on the clapper board is that of Flavio Calzavara, the director of many of Doris Duranti's films. The lead actress in the film within a film appears briefly and is named only as 'Elsa', which is closer to 'Luisa' than 'Doris', although there is no physical evocation either of Ferida or Duranti. The scene takes place in what is announced as the new Scalera studio using equipment salvaged from the machinery the Germans had appropriated and sent to Poland. The walls of the studio are decorated with black and white portraits of actors of the period, with only those of Alida Valli, Osvaldo Valenti and Vivi Gioi being identifiable. Neither Valli nor Gioi took part in the brief experience of film-making in Venice, and it may be assumed that the relative prominence accorded to Valli's portrait served simply to reference the film stardom of the period and also to acknowledge her role in Visconti's film. An orgy in an aristocratic palace sees Livia try cocaine, the addiction to which has sometimes been indicated as the reason for Valenti's willingness to go to Venice. Overall Brass's interest in the film world and its personalities is small and these serve to provide period and location detail, as well as satisfy a certain conventional fetish for the aesthetics of Fascism and Nazism. The final scene is a mirror image of Visconti's, and accurately reflects Boito's ending: an angry and anguished Livia betrays her unfaithful lover, reporting his desertion to the authorities, and thereby prepares the way for his execution by firing squad.

Sanguepazzo is also largely located in Venice. It portrays some of the same situations and characters as *Telefoni bianchi* but it forsakes comedy for a hybrid of biopic and drama. Born in 1950, Giordana had no personal recollection of the period and nor did anyone involved with the production. Grotesque or salacious aspects are exchanged for serious engagement with the events as history. At the film's heart is the tragic odyssey of the two actors, Valenti and Ferida, who are merely alluded to or presented in composite form in the previous two films.[40] Their true story had been revisited several times in the 1980s and 1990s in popular history books and a television drama. In its broad outlines it was therefore well known. For Giordana, a director with a record of exploring the tragedies and mysteries of the postwar period, the subject offered an opportunity to investigate how and why two of the most popular actors of Cinecittà came to be caught up with the desperate final struggle of Fascism as the Allies advanced up the peninsula and the Resistance established an alternative source of authority to the crumbling state.

The film is constructed around a main narrative dealing with the last few weeks of the couple as the circle closed around them and they fell into the hands of the Resistance. Their fate is the subject of dispute between different individuals but in the end a tribunal condemns them to death. This is punctuated by numerous flashbacks to various moments in the 1930s and 1940s, beginning with Ferida's first attempts to break into the world of cinema. In the parts of Valenti and Ferida, Luca Zingaretti and Monica Bellucci bring a measure of authority to the proceedings, the former hamming it up in a manner that recalls the actor's exhibitionism and the latter bringing the necessary erotic charge to her character. But neither the casting nor the playing is perfect. Zingaretti and Bellucci were around ten years older than their subjects and as a result the story is inflected with middle-aged maturity instead of the last fireworks of waning youth. Although his drug addiction is highlighted, Valenti's Mephistofelian charm is largely missing, while Bellucci's reserved elegance prevents her from persuasively conveying the coarse streak that distinguished Ferida. Indeed, in her bearing and some of her costumes, she bears a closer resemblance to Doris Duranti than Ferida.

Sanguepazzo and *Telefoni bianchi* have several scenes in common. In both films, male actors deride starlets as stupid and talentless, and insinuate they have only reached their position by sexual favours. Both feature moments in which an actor identified broadly or specifically with Valenti mocks Mussolini and Fascism. Like *Senso '45*, both conclude with an execution, feigned in the case of Risi's film, real in Giordana's. It is also worth noting that Rossellini is appropriated by both Brass and Giordana to provide a momentary dramatisation of war. The former restages Anna Magnani's tragic final run from *Roma città aperta* in the streets of Venice, while the latter uses the opening of the final episode of *Paisà* – the dead body floating down the Po river with the placard indicating 'partisan' – to highlight the tragedy unfolding around his protagonists.

In the latter film the Fascist context is sketched in without regard to accuracy but in a way that mobilises well-known episodes or creates composite personalities to lend a feel of authenticity. None of this is unusual, as compression, invention and metaphor are all acknowledged features of biopics and historical films.[41] An important secondary character is Golfiero Goffredi, who is introduced as a wealthy aspiring film director whose desire to cast Ferida in his first film is mistaken by the actress for sexual interest. In fact Goffredi is homosexual but this does not prevent him from loving Ferida platonically or her from reciprocating his feelings even as she develops an intense relationship with Valenti. The film they make together is acclaimed and Ferida is rewarded with a best actress prize. However, they cannot work together again as Goffredi's anti-Fascist activities lead to him being despatched to internal exile. When they encounter one another again, the director is a member of a Resistance band that takes the screen couple into its custody. In a skirmish he is shot and mortally wounded. The character is intended to evoke Luchino Visconti, although he never directed Ferida, let alone discovered her, was not sent into internal exile and, of course, was not fatally shot in an armed action.

A further secondary character is Attilio Cardi, the director general of cinema and therefore a fictionalised Luigi Freddi. Cardi inhabits an enormous office that is dominated by a large sculpted head of Mussolini. He takes an obsessive interest in the sex lives of actors, and especially Ferida, for whom he evidently cultivates feelings. When Bellucci visits him to ask for a favour in the way to which movie personnel were accustomed, he plays a tape of her moaning during a sex act. In his final scene, set shortly after he has announced his intention to refound Cinecittà in Venice, Cardi tells Valenti that all is lost. He hands him a letter of resignation as director general, to be delivered to the minister, in which he recommends that the actor be appointed as his successor. The purpose, he explains, is to provide the actor, and above all his lover, with the means to escape to Latin America. As soon as Valenti steps outside his office, he hears a gunshot – Cardi has killed himself.

This treatment of the Freddi character is controversial but functional to the film's purpose of conveying a wide range of personalities and events in summary form.[42] It serves to establish three things: the important role of the Fascist state in cinema, the sexual entanglements of high officials and some actresses, and the sense of utter disorientation that some Fascists felt at the deposition of Mussolini. To this end, Freddi's specific role is rewritten and his activity in Venice cancelled. The suicide of the head of the Fascist press agency, Manlio Morgagni, the only man to kill himself in July 1943, is attributed to Cardi, who thereby becomes a composite.

Luce newsreel footage is employed at several junctures in the film to lend authenticity and to provide information about the course of events. Mussolini's declaration of war in 1940, the destruction of monuments that followed his overthrow in 1943, his rescue by German paratroops, and finally footage of the macabre spectacle of Piazzale Loreto, provide a powerful frame for the events of the narrative. This device is a common one in biopics, along with having supporting characters play themselves and creating fake original newsreels or manipulating real ones. No extracts from any of the films of the two actors are used or re-staged in this film, although Valenti is portrayed playing up on set, and black and white footage of Bellucci is spliced into a period newsreel about the Venice Film Festival.

One striking feature of the film is the absence of any attempt to portray the milieu of cinema. Few actors are seen other than Valenti and Ferida, and none are named. Two directors figure and both are fictionalised composites. There is in this sense a leap from the larger historical context to the intimate reality of the two doomed stars. Everything that intervenes between these two narrative levels is either minimised or fictionalised to some degree. This, ultimately, turns the drama of Valenti and Ferida into a tragedy that is somehow emblematic of the stardom of the Fascist period and that asserts the two stars as its most representative figures. If, as Dennis Bingham claims, the aim of the biopic genre is not to locate a subject in context so much as 'to enter the biographical subject into the pantheon of cultural mythology, one way or another, and to show why he or she belongs there', then this is achieved.[43]

Endings

By the time *Sanguepazzo* was released, all the major stars explored in this book were dead. Giachetti and De Sica died in 1974, Nazzari in 1979, Miranda in 1982, Noris in 1997 and Valli in 2006. Most of them had been out of public view for some time and, at the time of death, only De Sica, who continued to act and direct into the 1970s, was still a major player in Italian cinema. Obituaries evoked not only the stars' careers and their major films, but also what they meant to spectators. Their names conjured up a time and an idea of cinema that had long since passed, but the hopes and dreams that attached to them, the physical and moral ideals they embodied, the black and white contours of their features, the timbre of their voices, and the joys and sufferings of their characters all resonated in the memories of spectators old enough to remember them in their heyday.

As Italian cities expanded in the 1970s and 1980s, some new roads and squares were given – alongside the names of political and religious figures, writers, inventors, musicians, martyrs and film directors – the names of stars. A walk down via Fosco Giachetti in the EUR district of Rome leads past via Aldo Fabrizi and veers near via Gino Cervi. A few dozen metres to the north lie via Elsa Merlini and via Isa Miranda. Both Milan and Rome have a via Vittorio De Sica, while Amedeo Nazzari's name adorns roads and squares in his native Sardinia as well as Caserta and Anzio. For the authorities in the capital and other municipalities, the stars were professionals working in an industry that had brought lustre to Italy. No one blamed them for Fascism or for contributing with their glamour to the pattern of consent on which the regime rested. Rather they were seen as men and women who, through their screen personas, had shared with their fellow countrymen and women the most tragic and divisive period in twentieth-century Italian history and, in their best moments, granted some relief from the deadly beat of the Fascist war drums.

Notes

1. J. Foot. 2011. 'Introduction' in *Italy's Divided Memory*, New York: Palgrave Macmillan.
2. G.P. Brunetta. 1997. 'Il cinema' in M. Isenghi (ed.), *I luoghi della memoria: strutture ed eventi dell'Italia unita*, Rome–Bari: Laterza, 223–52, 239.
3. J. Stacey. 1994. *Star Gazing: Hollywood Cinema and Female Spectatorship*, London: Routledge, 63–66.
4. C. Baldassini. 2008. *L'ombra di Mussolini: l'Italia moderata e la memoria del fascismo (1945–1960)*, Soveria Mannelli: Rubettino, 4.
5. Brunetta, 'Il cinema', 237.
6. On the decline of the old stars, see S. Masi. 2003. 'Destini diversi dell'attore: l'ascesa del divismo femminile', in C Cosulich (ed.), *Storia del cinema italiano*, Vol. 7, 1945–1948, Venice: Marsilio/Bianco & Nero, 330–35.
7. E. Lancia. 'Dove sono finiti?', *Hollywood*, 7 June 1952, 15.
8. A. Lusini, 'I divi dimenticati rimpiangono lo schermo', *Oggi*, 13 August 1953, 39.
9. *Hollywood*, 10 July 1954. Picture and caption.
10. *Fotocronaca*, 18 February 1956, 3.

11. *La Nazione*, 22 September 1965, 15.
12. *Radiocorriere*, 5 December 1970, 8.
13. S. Alovisio. 2003. 'Fosco Giachetti', *Enciclopedia del cinema*, Rome: Treccani, 673.
14. G.C. Castello. 1957. *Il divismo: mitologia del cinema*, Turin: ERI. Noris had briefly returned to cinema in 1964, when she produced and cast herself in *La Celestina PR*, a film directed by Carlo Lizzani. Adapted from a popular French play about a stylish and cynical woman who pimps for rich businessmen, the film offered an unusually caustic portrait of the Milan of the economic boom.
15. E. Solari, 'Abbandonai Rossellini dopo due giorni di nozze', *Sogno*, 7 September 1969, 14.
16. Her fullest interview was published in *Oggi* in 1969 in two parts: n.34, 52–55 and n.35, 19–21.
17. A. Lanocita, *Corriere della Sera*, 24 December 1974, 17.
18. A. Arbasino. 1979. 'Piccolo lessico morfologico degli anni trenta italiani' in A. Aprà and P. Pistagnesi (eds), *I favolosi anni trenta: cinema italiano 1929–1944*, Milan: Electa, 10.
19. B. Gaudenzi. 2011. 'Commercial Advertising in Germany and Italy, 1918–1943', University of Cambridge, Ph.D. thesis, 161–62.
20. Masi, 'Destini diversi dell'attore', 331.
21. L. Silvi. 2005. *Una diva racconta se stessa e il suo cinema*, Florence: Aida.
22. R. Villa. 2000. *Sono nato a Casablanca ... ma non sono Humphrey Bogart*, ed. by S. Micheli, Florence: Aida; S. Micheli. 1996. *Roberto Villa: attore e divo*, Florence: Manent.
23. M. Puig. 1991. *Gli occhi di Great Garbo*, Milan: Leonardo, 35–36.
24. D. Duranti. 1987. *Il romanzo della mia vita*, Milan: Mondadori.
25. This episode is explored in depth in D. Forgacs. 2002. 'Sex in the Cinema: Regulation and Transgression in Italian Cinema, 1930–1943', in J. Reich and P. Garofalo (eds), *Re-Viewing Fascism: Italian Cinema 1922–1943*, Bloomington: Indiana University Press, 141–71, 159–61.
26. The transcription of the bizarre telephone call recording their attempt to persuade her to talk to them is recorded on pages 307–9 of their 1995 volume, *Il romanzo di Alida Valli*.
27. O. Fallaci, 'Lo specchio del passato', *L'Europeo*, 14 January 1965, 57.
28. 1996. Venice: Marsilio.
29. See J. Reich. 2004. *Beyond the Latin Lover: Marcello Mastroianni, Maculinity and Italian Cinema*, Bloomington: Indiana University Press.
30. F. Di Giammatteo, *Radiocorriere*, 26 July 1958.
31. Maurizio Chierici, *Oggi*, 29 April 1965.
32. *Il Gazzettino*, 6 October 1964.
33. A. Libonati, *Gente*, 9 July 1964.
34. D. Risi. 2004. *I miei mostri*, Milan: Mondadori, 69–70.
35. F. Faldini and G. Fofi (eds). 1979. *L'avventurosa storia del cinema italiano: raccontata dai suoi protagonisti, 1935–1959*, Milan: Feltrinelli, 296.

36. M. Zinni. 2010. *Fascisti di celluloide: la memoria del ventennio nel cinema italiano (1945–2000)*, Venice: Marsilio, 232.
37. Faldini and Fofi, *L'avventurosa storia*, 296.
38. Ibid., 232.
39. See S. Gundle. 2007. *Bellissima: Feminine Beauty and the Idea of Italy*, London and New Haven: Yale University Press, 205–11.
40. See R. Bracalini. 1986. *Celebri e dannati: Osvaldo Valenti e Luisa Ferida storia e tragedia di due divi del regime*, Milan: Longanesi; O. Reggiani. 2007. *Luisa Ferida, Osvaldo Valenti: ascesa e caduta di due stelle del cinema*, Milan: Spirali; I. Moscati. 2007. *Gioco perverso: la vera storia di Osvaldo Valenti e Luisa Ferida*, Turin: Lindau.
41. D. Bingham. 2010. *Whose Lives Are They Anyway? The Biopic as Contemporary Film Genre*, New Brunswick: Rutgers University Press, 5.
42. Ibid., 11.
43. Ibid., 10.

Bibliography

A. Primary Sources

Archival Sources

Archivio Centrale dello Stato (ACS), Rome:
  Ministero dell'Interno, Direzione generale publica sicurezza, Divisione polizia politica 1927-1944, B. 175 bis, f. M 39/1 Ente nazionale per la cinematografia; B. 904 Nazzari, Amedeo. Note dated 20 September 1938.
  Ministero della Cultura Popolare, Gabinetto, Fasc. Cinematografia, sottofasc. 17 'Film' giornale.
  Segreteria Particolare del Duce, carteggio riservato, B. 48, Pavolini Alessandro.
Centro documentazione Rizzoli, Milan.
Fondo Mainardi, Trieste.
Fosco Giachetti archive, Rome (private).
National Archives and Records Administration (NARA), Washington DC:
  U.S. Department of Commerce, Bureau of Domestic and Foreign Commerce, Motion Picture Division, *Motion Pictures Abroad*, 1930–1938.

Newspapers and Magazines

Bellezza
Bollettino 20th Century Fox Film
Cinema
Cinema illustrazione
Cinematografia italiana, la
Corriere della Sera

Domenica del Corriere, La
Eco del cinema, L'
Europeo, L'
Eva
Film
Film d'oggi
Fotocronaca
Fotogrammi
Gente
Grandi Firme, Le
Grazia
Hollywood
Italia letteraria, L'
Messaggero, Il
Oggi
Primi piani
Pubblicità d'Italia, La
Radiocorriere
Rivista del Cinematografo
Scena illustrata
Scenario
Schermo, Lo
Si gira
Sogno
Sorrisi e canzoni tv
Stampa, La
Star
Stelle
Tempo

Autobiographies, Memoirs and Testimonies

Arbasino, A. 1979. 'Piccolo lessico morfologico degli anni trenta italiani' in A. Aprà and P. Pistagnesi (eds), *I favolosi anni trenta: cinema italiano 1929–1944*, Milan: Electa, 2–22.
Ciano, G. 1980. *Diario 1937–1943*, Milan: Rizzoli.
De Giorgi, E. 1992. *I coetanei*, Milan: Leonardo.
Denis, M. 1995. *Il gioco della verità: una diva nella Roma del 1943*, Milan: Baldini & Castoldi.
De Sica, V. 2004. *La porta del cielo: memorie 1901–1952*, Cava De' Terreni: Avagliano.
De Vincentis, L. 1946. *Io son te …*, Milan: Cebes.
Duranti, D. 1987. *Il romanzo della mia vita*, Milan: Mondadori.

Faldini, F. and G. Fofi (eds). 1979. *L'avventurosa storia del cinema italiano: raccontato dai suoi protagonisti, 1935–1959*, Milan: Feltrinelli.
Fellini, F. 1983. *Intervista sul cinema*, ed. by G. Grazzini, Rome–Bari: Laterza.
Freddi, L. 1949. *Il cinema*, Rome: L'Arnia.
Mercader, M. 1978. *La mia vita con Vittorio De Sica*, Milan: Mondadori.
Petacci, C. 2009. *Mussolini segreto: diari 1932–1938*, Milan: Rizzoli.
———. 2011. *Verso il disastro – Mussolini in Guerra: diari 1939–1940*, Milan: Rizzoli.
Petacci, M. 1988. *Chi ama è perduto: mia sorella Claretta*, Gardolo di Trento: Reverdito.
Puig, M. 1991. *Gli occhi di Great Garbo*, Milan: Leonardo.
Risi, R. 2004. *I miei mostri*, Milan: Mondadori.
Savio, F. 1979. *Cinecittà anni trenta*, Rome: Bulzoni.
Silvi, L. 2005. *Una diva racconta se stessa e il suo cinema*, Florence: Aida.
Steno. 1993. *Sotto le stelle del '44*, Palermo: Sellerio.
Tebano, N. 1983. *La scatola magica: tra i fantasmi del cinema e della memoria*, Bari: Dedalo.
Toeplitz, L. 1964. *Ciak a chi tocca*, Milan: Edizioni Milano Nuova.
Tonti A. 1964. *Odore di cinema*, Florence: Vallecchi.
Villa, R. 2000. *Sono nato a Casablanca … ma non sono Humphrey Bogart*, ed. by S. Micheli, Florence: Aida.

Contemporary Published Works

Anon. 1949. *Alida Valli, I Quaderni di Hollywood*, n.11, supplement to *Hollywood*, n.200.
Anon. 1934. *Almanacco cinematografico 1935*, Edizioni Bella, Milan.
Berneri, C. (1937) 1966. *Mussolini: psicologia di un dittatore*, Milan: Azione Commune.
Branca, R. 1943. *Polemiche sul cinema*, Bergamo: I.P.L.
Calipso. 1944. *Vita segreta di Mussolini*, Rome: IEDC.
Corsi, M. 1942. *Maschere e volti: sul palconscenico e in platea*, Milan: Ceschina.
De Sica, V. 1942. 'Volti nuovi nel cinema' in Direzione generale del cinema (ed.), *Cinema italiano anno XX*, Rome, 37–38.
Doletti, M. 1929. *Cinematografo*, Bologna: Poligrafici Riuniti.
Freddi, L. 1935. 'Arte per il popolo' in *40 anniversario della cinematografia*, Rome: Sottosegretariato di Stato della Stampa e Propaganda.
Notari, U. 1933. *Dichiarazioni alle più belle donne del mondo*, Milan: Notari.
Notari, U. 1939. *Panegirico della Razza Italiana*, Villasanta: Notari.
Osso, P. Undated. *Fosco Giachetti: il nostro prototipo*, Milan: Albore.
Rabagliati, A. 1932. *Quattro anni fra le stelle*, Milan: Bella.
Ramperti, M. (1936) 1981. *L'alfabeta delle stelle*, Palermo: Sellerio.
Ridenti, L. 1931. *Il traguardo della celebrità*, Milan: Ceschina.

Rovere, F. 1946. *Vita amorosa di Claretta Petacci*, Milan: Bolla.
Sarfatti, M.G. 1926. *Dux*, Milan: Mondadori.
Soldati, M. 1981. *24 ore in uno studio cinematografico*, Palermo: Sellerio; first published 1935, under the pseudonym Franco Pallavera.
Varaldo, A. 1926. *Profili di attrici e di attori*, Milan: Barbera.

Collected Writings and Reviews

Bianchi, P. 1978. *L'occhio di vetro: il cinema degli anni 1940–1943*, ed. by O. Del Buono, Milan: Il Formichiere.
Blasetti, A. 1982. *Il cinema che ho vissuto*, ed. by F. Prono, Bari: Dedalo.
_____. 1982. *Scritti sul cinema*, ed. by A. Aprà, Venice: Marsilio.
Bottai, G. 1982. *Diario 1935–1944*, ed. by G.B. Guerri, Milan: Rizzoli.
Debenedetti, G. 1983. *Al cinema*, ed. by L. Micciché, Padua: Marsilio.
Soldati, M. 2006. *Cinematografo*, Palermo: Sellerio.
Zavattini, C. 1979. *Diario cinematografico*, Milan: Bompiani.
_____. 1991. *Cronache da Hollywood*, Rome: Lucarini.

B. Secondary Sources

Albano, A. 1979. 'Hollywood: cinelandia ...' in Redi, *Cinema italiano sotto il fascismo*, 219–31.
Almeida, F. d'. 2008. *High Society in the Third Reich*, Cambridge: Polity.
Alovisio, S. 2003. 'Fosco Giachetti', *Enciclopedia del cinema*, Rome: Treccani, 673.
Ambrosino, S. 1991. 'Cinema e propaganda in Africa Orientale Italiana', *Ventesimo secolo* 1(1), 127–50.
Antola, A. 2011. 'Ghitta Carell and Italian Studio Photography in the 1930s', *Modern Italy* 8, 249–73.
_____. 2012. 'Mussolini and Photography: Images and the Construction of a Personality Cult', University of London Ph.D. thesis.
Aprà A. and P. Pistagnesi, 1979. *I favolosi anni trenta, 1929–1944*, Milan: Electa.
Argentieri, M. 1995. 'Un Ottocento duro a morire: cronache di una polemica' in Argentieri (ed.), *Schermi di guerra: cinema italiano 1939–1945*, Rome: Bulzoni, 285–306.
_____. (ed.). 1991. *Risate di regime: la commedia italiana 1930–1944*, Venice: Marsilio.
Baldassini, C. 2008. *L'ombra di Mussolini: l'Italia moderata e la memoria del fascismo (1945–1960)*, Soveria Mannelli: Rubettino.

Banti, A.M. 2006. *La nazione del Risorgimento: parentela, santità e onore alle origini dell'Italia unita*, Turin: Einaudi.
Baratieri, D. 2004. 'La riedizione di *Bengasi* e *L'assedio dell'Alcazar* negli anni Cinquanta' in Bernardi, *La storia del cinema italiano*, 1949–1953, 118–129.
Ben-Ghiat, R. 2000. 'The Fascist War Trilogy' in D. Forgacs, S. Lutton and G. Nowell-Smith (eds), *Roberto Rossellini: Magician of the Real*, London: BFI, 20–35.
———. 2001. *Fascist Modernities: Italy 1922–1945*, Berkeley: University of California Press.
———. 2005. 'Unmaking the Fascist Man: Masculinity, Film and the Transition from Dictatorship', *Journal of Modern Italian Studies* 10(3), 336–65.
Benjamin, W. 1970. 'The Work of Art in the Age of Mechanical Reproduction' in Benjamin, *Illuminations*, ed. by H. Arendt, London: Fontana.
Bernardi, S. (ed.). 2004. *La storia del cinema italiano*, Vol. 9, 1949–1953, Rome and Venice: Marsilio/Bianco & Nero.
Bertellini, G. 2003. 'Colonial Autism: Whitened Heroes, Auditory Rhetoric, and National Identity in Interwar Italian Cinema', in P. Palumbo (ed.), *A Place in the Sun: Africa in Italian Colonial Culture from Post-Unification to the Present*, Berkeley: University of California Press, 255–78.
Bingham, D. 2010. *Whose Lives Are They Anyway? The Biopic as Contemporary Film Genre*, New Brunswick: Rutgers University Press.
Biondi, D. 1973. *La fabbrica del duce*, Florence: Valecchi.
Biribanti, P. 2009. *Boccasile: la Signorina Grandi Firme e altri mondi*, Rome: Castelvecchi.
Bisoni, C. 2010. 'Il cinema italiano nelle riviste e nei settimanali popolari' in O. Caldiron with A. Baldi (eds), *Storia del cinema italiano*, Vol. 6, 1940–1944, Venice–Rome: Marsilio/Bianco & Nero, 509–21.
Boccasile, G. 1981. *La Signorina Grandi Firme*, ed. by A. Faeti, Milan: Longanesi.
Bolzoni, F. 1984. *Quando De Sica era Mister Brown*, Turin: ERI.
Bono, F. 2010. 'Verso un gruppo di Stato: Cinecittà, ENIC and Cines' in O. Caldiron with A. Baldi (eds), *Storia del cinema italiano*, Vol. 6, *1940–1944*, Venice–Rome: Marsilio/Bianco & Nero, 365–82.
Borghini, F. 1989. *Fosco Giachetti*, Florence: Edizioni Play Time.
Bosworth, R.J.B. 2005. *Mussolini's Italy: Life under the Dictatorship, 1915–1945*, London: Allen Lane.
———. 2009. 'Dictators Strong or Weak? The Model of Benito Mussolini' in R.J.B. Bosworth (ed.), *The Oxford Handbook of Fascism*, Oxford: Oxford University Press, 259–75.
Bracalini, R. 1985. *Celebri e dannati: Osvaldo Valenti e Luisa Ferida storia e tragedia di due divi del regime*, Milan: Longanesi.

Brancati, V. 1950. *I fascisti invecchiano*, Milan: Longanesi.
Broch, H. 1990. *Il kitsch*, Turin: Einaudi.
Brunetta, G.P. 1979. *Storia del cinema italiano 1895–1945*, Rome: Editori Riuniti.
———. 1989a. 'Il sogno a stelle e strisce di Mussolini' in M. Vaudagna (ed.), *L'estetica della politica in Europa e America negli anni trenta*, Rome–Bari: Laterza, 161–76.
———. 1989b. *Buio in sala: cent'anni di passioni dello spettatore cinematografico*, Venice: Marsilio.
———. 1991a. *Cent'anni di cinema italiano*, Rome–Bari: Laterza.
———. 1991b. 'Mille e più di mille (lire al mese)' in Argentieri, *Risate di regime*.
———. 1991c. 'La lunga marcia del cinema americano in Italia tra fascismo e guerra fredda' in D.W. Ellwood and G.P. Brunetta (eds), *Hollywood in Europa: industria, politica, pubblico del cinema 1945–1960*, Florence: Ponte alle Grazie, 75–87.
———. 1997. 'Il cinema' in M. Isnenghi (ed.), *I luoghi della memoria: strutture ed eventi dell'Italia unita*, Rome–Bari: Laterza, 223–52.
———. 1999. 'Divismo, misticismo e spettacolo della politica' in Brunetta (ed.), *Storia del cinema mondiale, L'Europa*. Vol. 1 *Miti, luoghi, divi*, Turin: Einaudi, 535–42.
Buccheri, V. 2009. *Stile Cines: studi sul cinema italiano 1930–1934*, Milan: Vita e Pensiero.
Buckley, R. 2009. 'The Emergence of Film Fandom in Postwar Italy: Reading Claudia Cardinale's Fan Mail', *Historical Journal of Film, Radio and Television* 29(4), 523–59.
Buffa, M.E. 2008. *Amedeo Buffa in arte Nazzari*, Rome: Sabinae.
Burchielli, R. and V. Bianchini. 2004. *Cinecittà: la fabbrica di sogni*, Milan: Boroli.
Caldiron, O. and M. Hockhofler. 1978. *Isa Miranda*, Rome: Gremese.
Caldiron, O. and S. Della Casa (eds). 1999. *Appassionatamente: il melò nel cinema italiano*, Turin: Lindau.
Caldiron, O. (ed.). 2006. *Storia del cinema italiano*, Vol. 5, 1934–1939, Venice–Rome: Marsilio/Bianco & Nero.
Calendoli, G. 1967. *Materiali per una storia del cinema italiano*, Parma: Maccari.
Campi, A. 2007. *L'ombra lunga di Napoleone: da Mussolini a Berlusconi*, Venice: Marsilio.
Cannistraro, P.V. 1975. *La fabbrica del consenso: fascismo e mass media*, Rome–Bari: Laterza.
Caranti, C. 2003. 'La diva e le donne: Francesca Bertini nella stampa popolare e femminile' in G. Mingozzi (ed.), *Francesca Bertini*, Genoa: Le Mani, 112–24.

Carter, E. 2004. *Dietrich's Ghosts: The Sublime and the Beautiful in Third Reich Film*, London: BFI.
Casavecchia, S. (ed.), 2007. *Amedeo Nazzari: il divo, l'uomo, l'attore*, Rome: Centro sperimentale di cinematografia.
Castello, G.C. 1957. *Il divismo: mitologia del cinema*, Turin: ERI.
Catania, A. 1996. 'Luigi Freddi e il libro della solitudine' in M. Biondi and A. Borsatti (eds.), *Cultura e fascismo: letteratura, arti e spettacolo di un Vnetennio*, Florence: Ponte alle Grazie, 291–308.
Chessa, P. 2008. *Dux: una biografia per immagini*, Milan: Mondadori.
Chessa, P. and B. Raggi, *L'ultima lettera di Benito: Mussolinie Petacci – amore e politica a Salò 1943–45*, Milan: Mondadori.
Cicchino, E. 2010. *Il Duce attraverso il Luce*, Milan: Mursia.
Colarizi, S. 1991. *Le opinioni degli italiani sotto il regime, 1929–43*, Rome–Bari: Laterza.
Cooke, P.E. 2012. 'La resistenza come secondo risorigimento: un topos senza fine?', *Passato e presente* 86, 62–81.
Corner, P. 1975. *Fascism in Ferrara, 1915–1925*, Oxford: Oxford University Press.
———. 2009. 'Fascist Italy in the 1930s: Popular Opinion in the Provinces' in P. Corner (ed.), *Popular Opinion in Totalitarian Regimes: Fascism, Nazism, Communism*, Oxford: Oxford University Press, 122–46.
Corsi, B. 2001. *Con qualche dollaro in meno: storia economica del cinema italiano*, Rome: Editori Riuniti.
Cremoncini, R. et al. (eds). 2010. *Against Mussolini: Art and the Fall of a Dictator*, London: Estorick Collection.
Dagna, S. and C. Giannetto (eds). 2009. *Maciste l'uomo forte*, Bologna: Cineteca di Bologna.
Dalle Vacche, A. 2008. *Diva: Defiance and Passion in Early Italian Cinema*, Austin: University of Texas Press.
De Felice, R. 1974. *Mussolini*, Vol. 3. *Mussolini il duce*, I. *Gli anni del consenso 1929–1936*, Turin: Einaudi.
———. 1990. *Mussolini l'alleato 1940–1945*, I. *L'Italia in Guerra 1940–1943*, tome 2: *Crisi e agonia del regime*, Turin: Einaudi.
De Giorgio, M. 1992. *Le italiane dall'Unità a oggi*, Rome–Bari: Laterza.
De Grazia, V. 1981. *The Culture of Consent: Mass Organization of Leisure in Fascist Italy*, Cambridge: Cambridge University Press.
———. 1992. *How Fascism Ruled Women: Italy 1922–1945*, Berkeley: University of California Press.
Della Casa, S. 1989. *Mario Mattoli*, Florence: Il Castoro/La Nuova Italia.
Detti, E. 1989. *Le carte povere: storia dell'illustrazione minore*, Florence: La Nuova Italia.
Di Marino, B. 2010. 'Gli interpreti maschili tra commedia, drama, film storico e realismo' in Laura and Baldi, *Storia del cinema italiano*, Vol. 6, 1940–1944, 264-84.

Doane, M.A. 1988. 'The Abstraction of a Lady: *La Signora di tutti*', *Cinema Journal* 28(1), 65–84.

Domini, C. and C. Ghergo (eds). 2012. *Arturo Ghergo: fotografie, 1930–1959*, Milan: Silvana.

Duggan, C. 2007. *The Force of Destiny: Italy Since 1796*, London: Allen Lane.

———. 2013. 'Interiorising the Cult: the Evidence of Diaries and Letters' in Gundle, Duggan and Pieri, *The Cult of the Duce: Mussolini and the Italians*, 103–26.

Dyer, R. 1979. *Stars*, London: BFI.

Eckert, C. 1991. 'The Carol Lombard in Macy's Window' in Gledhill, *Stardom: Industry of Desire*, 30–39.

Falcinella, N. 2011. *Alida Valli: gli occhi, la bocca*, Genoa: Le Mani.

Farassino, A. 1992a. 'Camerini, au-delà du cinéma italien' in Farassino, *Mario Camerini*, 11–35.

———. 1992b. 'Il Signor Vittorio: un'interpretazione dell'octologia De Sica-Camerini' in L.Micciché (ed.), *De Sica: autore, regista, attore*, Venice: Marsilio, 107–14.

——— (ed.). 2001. *Mario Camerini*, Locarno: Yellow Now.

Fogu, C. 2003. *The Historic Imaginary: Politics of History in Fascist Italy*, Toronto: University of Toronto Press.

Foot, J. 2011. *Italy's Divided Memory*, New York: Palgrave Macmillan.

Forgacs, D. 2002. 'Sex in the Cinema: Regulation and Transgression in Italian Cinema, 1930–1943' in Reich and Garofalo, *Re-Viewing Fascism: Italian Cinema 1922–1943*, 141–71.

Forgacs, D. and S. Gundle. 2007. *Mass Culture and Italian Society from Fascism to the Cold War*, Bloomington: Indiana University Press.

Fowles, J. 1992. *Starstruck: Celebrity Performers and the American Public*, Washington: Smithsonian.

Gaudenzi, B. 2011. 'Commercial Advertising in Germany and Italy, 1918–1943', University of Cambridge, Ph.D. thesis.

Gentile, E. 1993. *Il culto del littorio*, Rome–Bari: Laterza

———. 2002. *Fascismo: storia e interpretazioni*, Rome–Bari: Laterza.

Geraghty, C. 2000. 'Re-examining Stardom: Questions of Texts, Bodies and Performance' in C. Gledhill and L. Williams (eds), *Reinventing Film Studies*, London: Hodder, 183–201.

Germani, S.G. 1991. 'Introduzione a una ricerca' in Argentieri, *Risate di regime*, 81–98.

Gervaso, R. 1982. *Claretta: la donna che morì per Mussolini*, Milan: Rizzoli.

Gledhill, C. 1992. *Stardom: Industry of Desire*, London: Routledge.

Gomery, D. 1992. *Shared Pleasures: A History of Movie Presentation in the United States*, London: BFI.

Gori, G. 1984. *Alessandro Blasetti*, Florence: Il castoro cinema/La Nuova Italia.

Grandi, S. and A. Vaccari, 2004. *Vestire il ventennio: moda e cultura artistica in Italia tra le due guerre*, Bologna: Bonomia University Press.
Gribaudi, M. 1987. *Mondo operaio e mito operaio*, Turin: Einaudi.
Gubitosi, G. 1998. *Amedeo Nazzari*, Bologna: Il Mulino.
Gundle, S. 2001. 'Visions of Prosperity: Consumerism and Popular Culture in Italy from the 1920s to the 1950s' in C. Levy and M. Roseman (eds), *Three Postwar Eras in Comparison: Western Europe 1918 – 1945 – 1989*, London: Palgrave, 173–95.
———. 2002. 'Film Stars and Society in Fascist Italy' in J. Reich and P. Garofalo, *Re-Viewing Fascism: Italian Cinema, 1922–1943*, Bloomington: Indiana University Press, 315–40.
———. 2006. 'Divismo' in V. De Grazia and S. Luzzatto (eds), *Dizionario del fascismo*, Turin: Einaudi, 439–42.
———. 2007. *Bellissima: Feminine Beauty and the Idea of Italy*, London and New Haven: Yale University Press.
———. 2008a. 'Un Martini per il Duce: l'immaginario del consumismo in Italia negli anni Venti e Trenta' in A. Villari (ed.), *L'arte della pubblicità: il manifesto italiano e le avanguardie 1920–1940*, Milan: Silvana, 46–69.
———. 2008b. *Glamour: A History*, Oxford: Oxford University Press.
———. 2012. 'Alida Valli in Hollywood: From Star of Fascist Cinema to "Selznick siren"', *Historical Journal of Film, Radio and Television* 32(4), 559–87.
———. 2013a. 'Mass Culture and the Cult of Personality' in Gundle, Duggan and Pieri, *The Cult of the Duce*, 72–99.
———. 2013b. 'Mussolini's Appearances in the Regions' in Gundle, Duggan and Pieri, *The Cult of the Duce*, 110–28.
Gundle, S., C. Duggan and G. Pieri (eds). 2013. *The Cult of the Duce: Mussolini and the Italians*, Manchester: Manchester University Press.
Harris, T. 1991. 'The Building of Popular Images Grace Kelly and Marilyn Monroe' in Gledhill, *Stardom: industry of Desire*, 40–44.
Harris, W.G. 1998. *Sophia Loren: A Biography*, New York: Simon and Schuster.
Hay, J. 1987. *Popular Film Culture in Fascist Italy: The Passing of the Rex*, Bloomington: Indiana University Press.
Jewell, R.B. 2007. *The Golden Age of Cinema: Hollywood 1929–1945*, Oxford: Blackwell.
Kezich, T. 1992. 'Servitore di due padroni' in Micciché, *De Sica*, 3–18.
———. 2006. 'Gli attori italiani dalla preistoria del divismo al monopolio' in O. Caldiron, *Storia del cinema italiano*, Vol. 5, 1934–39, Venice–Rome: Marsilio/Bianco & Nero, 383–403.
Klaprat, K. 1985. 'The Star as Market Strategy: Bette Davis in Another Light', in T. Balio (ed.), *The American Film Industry*, Madison: University of Wisconsin Press, 351–76.

Kobal, J. 1993. *George Hurrell: Hollywood Glamour Portraits*, London: Schirmer.

Koepnick, L. 2002. *The Dark Mirror: German Cinema between Hitler and Hollywood*, Berkeley: University of California Press.

Koon, T.H. 1985. *Believe, Obey, Fight: Political Socialization of Youth in Fascist Italy, 1922–1943*, Chapel Hill: University of North Carolina Press.

Korn, J. 1983. *Winged Gospel: America's Romance with Aviation, 1900–1950*, New York: Oxford University Press.

Landy, M. 1986. *Fascism in Film: The Italian Commercial Cinema, 1931–1943*, Princeton: Princeton University Press.

———. 1998. *The Folklore of Consensus*, Buffalo, NY: State University of New York Press.

———. 2008. *Stardom Italian Style: Personality and Performance in Italian Cinema*, Bloomington: Indiana University Press.

Laura, E.G. 1979. *Alida Valli*, Rome: Gremese.

———. 1991. 'I percorsi intrecciati della commedia anni '30', in Argentieri, *Risate di regime*, 109–37.

———. 2000. 'Cinegiornali e mito del "Duce"' in Laura (ed.), *La stagioni dell'aquila: storia del Istituto Luce*, Rome: Ente dello spettacolo, 101–6.

Laura, E.G. and A. Baldi (eds). 2010. *Storia del cinema italiano*, Vol. 6, 1940–1944, Venice–Rome: Marsilio/Bianco & Nero.

Leff, L. 1999. *Hitchcock and Selznick*, Berkeley: University of California Press.

Lippmann, W. (1922) 1949. *Public Opinion*, New York: The Free Press.

Lotti, D. 2008. *Emilio Ghione – l'ultimo apache: vita e film di un divo italiano*, Bologna: Cineteca di Bologna.

McDowell, C. 1992. *Hats: Status, Style and Glamour*, London: Thames & Hudson.

McLean, A.L. 2004. *Being Rita Hayworth: Labor, Identity, and Hollywood Stardom*, New Brunswick: Rutgers University Press.

———. (ed.). 2011. *Glamour in a Golden Age: Movie Stars of the 1930s*, New Brunswick: Rutgers University Press.

Mancini, E. 1985. *Struggles of the Italian Film Industry during Fascism, 1930–1935*, Ann Arbor: UMI Research Press.

Marino, N. and E.V. Marino. 2005. *L'Ovra a Cinecittà: polizia politica e spie in camicia nera*, Turin: Bollati Boringhieri.

Mariotti, F. (ed.). 1989. *Cinecittà tra cronaca e storia 1937–1989*, Vol. II, *I film*, Rome: Presidenza del Consiglio dei Ministri.

Marshall, P.D. 1997. *Celebrity and Power: Fame in Contemporary Culture*, Minneapolis: University of Minnesota Press.

Martinelli, V. 1993. 'La Borelli' in J. Pantieri (ed.), *Lyda Borelli*, Rome: MICS, 27–28.

Masi, S. 1991. 'Il controluce nei capelli', in Argentieri, *Risate di regime*, 177–85.

———. 2003. 'Destini diversi dell'attore: l'ascesa del divismo femminile', in C. Cosulich (ed.), *Storia del cinema italiano*, Vol. 7, 1945–1948, Venice: Marsilio/Bianco & Nero, 330–43.
Masi, S. and E. Lancia. 1994. *Stelle d'Italia: piccole e grandi dive del cinema italiano dal 1930 al 1945*, Rome: Gremese.
Menapace, L. 1988. 'La giornalista, l'atleta, la star: immagini di donna durante il regime fascista', in A.M. Crispino (ed.), *Esperienza storica femminile nell'età moderna e contemporanea*, Rome: UDI, 153–59.
Messina, N. 1987. *Le donne del fascismo: massaie rurali e dive del cinema nel ventennio*, Rome: Ellemme.
Miccichè, L. 1991. 'Il cinema italiano sotto il fascismc: elementi per un ripensamento possibile', in Argentieri, *Risate di regime*, 37–63.
Micheli, S. 1996. *Roberto Villa: attore e divo*, Florence: Manent.
Milza, P. 2009. *Mussolini*, Rome: Carocci.
Monreale, E. 2005. *Mario Soldati: le carriere di un libertino*, Bologna/Genoa: Cineteca di Bologna/Le Mani.
Monteleone, F. 1976. *La radio italiana nel periodo fascista*, Venice: Marsilio.
———. 1992. *Storia della radio e della televisione in Italia*, Venice: Marsilio.
Morin, E. (1957) 1972. *Les stars*, Paris: Seuil.
Moscati, I. 2007. *Gioco perverso: la vera storia di Osvaldo Valenti e Luisa Ferida*, Turin: Lindau.
——— (ed.). 1996. *Clara Calamai: l'ossessione di essere diva*, Venice: Marsilio.
Municchi, A. (ed.). 1992. *Signore in pelliccia 1900–1940*, Modena: Zanfi.
Neale, S. 1999. *Genre and Hollywood*, London: Routledge.
Nowell-Smith, G. 1986. 'The Italian Cinema under Fascism' in D. Forgacs (ed.), *Re-thinking Italian Fascism*, London: Lawrence & Wishart, 142–61.
Paciscopi, L. 1986. *Cinefollie: miti e sregolatezze del "muto"*, Milan: Lucini.
Palmer, S.W. 2006. *Dictatorship of the Air: Aviation Culture and the Fate of Modern Russia*, Cambridge: Cambridge University Press.
Parigi, S. 1991. 'Commedie in rivista: la critica nella stampa specializzata 1930–1943' in Argentieri, *Risate di regime*, 213–50.
Parlato, G. 2006. *Fascisti senza Mussolini*, Bologna: Il Mulino.
Passerini, L. 1987. *Fascism in Popular Memory*, Cambridge: Polity (Italian edition 1984).
———. 1991. *Mussolini immaginario*, Rome–Bari: Laterza.
Peiss, K. 1998. *Hope in a Jar: The Making of America's Beauty Culture*, New York: Metropolitan.
Pellizzari, L. and C. Valentinetti. 1995. *Il romanzo di Alida Valli*, Milan: Garzanti.
Pellizzari, L. (ed.). 1982. *Hollywood anni trenta: le pratiche produttive e l'esibizione del private*, Venice: la Biennale di Venezia.
Phillips, A. and G. Vincendeau (eds). 2006. *Journeys of Desire: European Actors in Hollywood – A Critical Companion*, London: BFI.

Piazzoni, I. 2009. 'I periodici italiani negli anni del regime fascista' in R. De Berti and I. Piazzoni (eds), *Forme e modelli del rotocalco italiano tra fascismo e Guerra*, Milan: Monuzzi, 83–122.
Polando, P., et al. 1985. *Vivere il cinema: cinquant'anni del centro sperimentale di cinematografia*, Rome: Presidenza del consiglio dei ministry.
Pruzzo, P. and E. Lancia. 1983. *Amedeo Nazzari*, Rome: Gremese.
Raffaelli, S. 1997. 'Le veline fasciste sul cinema', *Bianco & Nero* 4, 15–63.
Redi, R. 2009. *La Cines: storia di una casa di produzione italiana*, Bologna: Persiani.
_____ (ed.). 1979. *Cinema italiano sotto il fascismo*, Venice: Marsilio.
Reggiani, O. 2007. *Luisa Ferida, Osvaldo Valenti: ascesa e caduta di due stelle del cinema*, Milan: Spirali.
Reich, J. 2004. *Beyond the Latin Lover: Marcello Mastroianni, Maculinity and Italian Cinema*, Bloomington: Indiana University Press.
_____. 2010. 'Slave to Fashion: Masculinity, Suits, and the Maciste Films of Italian Silent Cinema' in A. Munich (ed.), *Fashion in Film*, Bloomington: Indiana University Press, 236–59.
Reich, J. and P. Garofalo (eds). 2002. *Re-Viewing Fascism: Italian Cinema, 1922–1943*, Bloomington: Indiana University Press.
Rentschler, E. 1996. *The Ministry of Illusion: Nazi Cinema and Its Afterlife*, Cambridge, MA: Harvard University Press.
Renzi, R. 1992. 'Intervista con Vittorio Mussolini' in Renzi (ed.), *Il cinema dei dittatori: Mussolini, Stalin, Hitler – immagini e documenti*, Bologna: Grafis, 43–47.
Ricci, S. 1992. 'Camerini et Hollywood' in Farassino, *Mario Camerini*, 36–46.
_____. 2008. *Cinema & Fascism: Italian Film and Society, 1922–1943*, Berkeley: University of California Press.
Richards, J. 1984. *The Age of the Dream Palace: Cinema and Society in Britain 1930–1939*, London: Routledge.
Romano, R. 1997. *Paese Italia: venti secoli d'identità*, Rome: Donzelli.
Rositi, F. 1967. 'Personalità e divismo in Italia durante il periodo fascista', *IKON* 17: 62, 9–48.
Rossi, U. 1991. 'Le commedie: la debole forza della produzione italiana' in Argentieri, *Risate di regime*, 187–95.
Rouvillon, F. 2008. *Histoire du snobisme*, Paris: Flammarion.
Scaglione, M. 1999. 'Melodramma e strappalacrime nel cinema dei telefoni bianchi' in O. Caldiron and S. Della Casa (eds), *Appasionatamente: il mélo nel cinema italiano*, Turin: Lindau, 19–28.
_____. 2003. *Le dive del ventennio*, Turin: Lindau.
_____. 2005. *I divi del ventennio*, Turin: Lindau.
Scarpellini, E. 2011. *Material Nation: A Consumer's History of Modern Italy*, Oxford: Oxford University Press.
Schnapp, J. 1996. *Staging Fascism: 18BL and the Theater of Masses for Masses*, Stanford: Stanford University Press.

Soldati, M. (1964) 1979. *Le due città*, Milan: Garzanti.
Spackman, B. 1996. *Fascist Virilities: Rhetoric, Ideology and Social Fantasy in Italy*, Minneapolis: University of Minnesota Press.
Spicer, A. 2001. *Typical Men: The Representation of Masculinity in Popular British Cinema and Society*, London: I.B. Tauris.
Stacey, J. 1994. *Star Gazing: Hollywood Cinema and Female Spectatorship*, London: Routledge.
Storchi, S. 2006. '*Valori Plastici* 1918–1922: le inquietudini del nuovo classico', supplement to *The Italianist*, 26.
Sturani, E. 2003. *Le cartoline del duce*, Turin: Edizioni del Capricorno.
Theweleit, K. 1987. *Male Fantasies*, 2 vols, Minneapolis: University of Minnesota Press.
Thorp, M.F. 1939. *America at the Movies*, New Haven: Yale University Press.
Torri, B. 2010. 'Il caso "Ossessione"' in Laura and Baldi, *Storia del cinema italiano*, Vol. 6, 1940–1944, 176–84.
Trumble, A. 2004. *A Brief History of the Smile*, New York: Basic Books.
Turroni, G. 1980. *Luxardo: l'italica bellezza*, Milan: Mazzotta.
Valentini, P. 2002. 'Modelli, forme e fenomeni di divismo: Vittorio De Sica' in M. Fanchi and E. Mosconi (eds.), *Spettatori: forme di consumo e pubblici del cinema in Italia, 1930–1960*, Rome: Bianco & Nero, 108–33.
Vene, G. 1982. 'La canzone e il cinema', *La canzone italiana*, no. 10, Milan: Fabbri, 109–20.
Ventavoli, L. (ed.), 2001. *Il cinema del ventennio raccontato dai manifesti*, Turin: Bolaffi.
Vicini, S. 2008. *Le stelle del duce*, Bresso: Hobby & Work.
Walker, M. 1986. 'La Signora di tutti', *Movie* 36(2000), 62–72.
White, S.M. 1995. *The Cinema of Max Ophuls*, New York: Columbia University Press.
Wills, G. 1997. *John Wayne: The Politics of Celebrity*, London: Faber.
Willson, P. 1993. *The Clockwork Factory: Women and Work in Fascist Italy*, Oxford: Oxford University Press.
_____. 2002. *Peasant Women and Politics in Fascist Italy: The Massaie Rurali*, London: Routledge.
Zagarrio, V. 2006. 'Schizofrenie del modello fascista' in O. Caldiron, *Storia del cinema italiano, 1934–1939*, Venice–Rome: Marsilio/Bianco & Nero, 37–61.
Zinni, M. 2010. *Fascisti di celluloide: la memoria del ventennio nel cinema italiano (1945–2000)*, Venice: Marsilio.
Zocaro, E. 1993. '"Prima donna" del teatro italiano' in J. Pantieri (ed.), *Lyda Borelli*, Rome: MICS, 12–23.

Index

1860 30

Abba, M. 191
Addio giovinezza 56
Adventure in Diamonds 134
Ai vostri ordini signora 154
Albani, M. 32
Alessandrini, G. 24, 30, 51, 56, 62, 79, 115, 146, 184, 187, 192, 204, 215
Alfieri, D. 20, 27
Amante segreta, L' 218
Amarcord 290
Amato, G. 109, 166, 167, 168, 206
Amico delle donne, L' 244, 247, 249
Amo te sola 154
Apparizione 2, 3, 104, 114, 194, 200, 269, 285
Arata, U. 61, 270–71
As You Desire Me 134
Assedio dell'Alcazar, L' 56, 203, 210, 216, 220
Assenza ingiustificata 57, 226, 227, 232, 285
Au-de-là des grilles 274
audiences 69, 70, 73–74
aviation in film 185, 186, 188
Avventura di Salvator Rosa, Un 56, 273

Baarova, L. 268
Bagolin, S. 85
Balbo, I. 185–86
Balin, M. 210
Ballo al castello 226, 227, 235
Bambini ci guardano, I 75, 157, 268
Bandito, Il 270, 285
Baracca, F. 188
Barattolo, G. 27
Barbara, P. 55, 59, 77, 80, 88, 116, 170, 204, 272
Barbaro, U. 148
Batticuore 146, 169, 170
Beaton, C. 83
Beery, W. 237
Beghi, L. 88, 100
Belli, A. 288
Bellini, V. 34
Bellucci, M. 293
Benassi, M. 137
Benetti, A. 173, 179, 272
    compared to S. Mangano 282
Bengasi 196–97, 203, 204, 215, 271
Bertini, F. 41, 43, 45
Bertolucci, B. 281
Besozzi, N. 53, 54–55, 268
Biki 77, 79, 236
Bisbetica domata, La 75

Blasetti, A. 20, 22, 24, 30, 32, 34, 49, 56, 57, 58, 76, 168–69, 192, 195, 224, 231, 233–34, 268, 269, 285
Blue Angel, The 131
Boccasile, G. 230, 232–33
Boese, C. 75, 232
Bogart, H. 206, 218
Bolognesi, G. 196
Bonnard, M. 22, 147, 167, 206, 233, 269
Borelli, L. 41–43, 45, 47, 97
Bottai, G. 20, 25, 32, 162, 248
Bragaglia, C.L. 146, 147, 274
Brass, T. 13, 290–91, 292
Brazzi, R. 55, 62, 101, 238, 273
Brent, G. 135
Brignone, G. 35, 147
Brizzi, A. 61, 62, 170, 236
Buffarini Guidi, G. 249, 252

Cabiria 43
Caesar Film 27
Calamai, C. 6, 54, 80, 82, 85, 171, 192, 220, 235, 236, 239, 240, 244, 254, 262, 265, 268, 272, 289
Calvino, I. 100–1
Calvino, V. 111, 235
Calzavara, F. 57, 290
Camerini, M. 24, 30, 33, 36, 44, 56, 57, 70, 73, 74, 75, 83, 129, 146, 147–49, 204, 209, 262, 265, 269
Candiani, C. 56, 102
Cantor, E. 23
Cappello a tre punte, Il 36, 84
Capra, F. 23
Caravaggio, il pittore maledetto 192
Carell, G. 82, 83
Carmen fra i rossi 220
Carmi, V. 173, 192
Casa del peccato, La 226, 227
Castellani, R. 140, 170, 172, 177
Catene invisibili 236
Catholic Church 7, 178–79
Catholic critiques of stars 91, 114
Cavalleria 24, 56, 61, 79, 187, 196, 199

Cecchi, E. 155
Cegani, E. 57, 85, 187, 262, 270
Cena delle beffe, La 57, 188, 190, 192
Centa, A. 173, 205, 212, 215
Centomila dollari 32, 146, 169, 173, 194, 197, 198
Centro sperimentale di cinematografia (Experimental Film Centre) 6, 20, 56, 59, 82, 88, 229, 231–32, 247, 248, 274
Cervi, G. 10, 12, 54, 55, 56, 57, 107, 265, 274, 282, 294
Chaplin, C. 35, 45, 151, 267
Checchi, A. 87, 137
Chevalier, M. 150, 159
Chiarini, L. 20, 231–32, 274
Chiave, La 290
Ciano G. 19, 20, 87–88, 248
Cinecittà 3, 19–22, 23, 24, 27, 31, 54, 57, 63, 82, 87, 88, 103, 171, 177, 179, 180, 224, 230, 245, 251, 252, 254, 256, 261, 270, 275, 289, 291
  postwar criticism of 263
  as sexual hunting ground 252
Cinema 1939–40 poll 2, 116, 144, 182, 186, 203
Cines 8, 20, 27, 48, 51, 57, 58, 128, 146, 148, 150, 155, 167, 245, 247
Cinque minuti a Cinecittà 3, 85, 88, 103, 199
Clément, R. 274
Colbert, C. 59, 134
Colman, R. 48, 100
Colpo di pistola, Un 170, 172, 173, 204, 212, 216
Come le foglie 129, 131, 134, 138
Condottieri 24, 148
Contessa di Parma, La 76
Cooper, G. 160, 196, 197, 198, 267
Corona di ferro, La 195
Corradi, N. 84
Cortese, V. 102, 273
cosmetics and cinema 79–80
Crawford, J. 48

Crosby, B. 150
Cukor, G. 134

D'Alma, R. 235
D'Annunzio, G. 41, 134, 230
Dapporto, C. 91
Darò un milione 32, 74, 160, 169, 172, 175
Davis, B. 100
De Benedetti, G. 175, 233
De Cesare, N. 248
De Cespedes, A. 268
De Filippo brothers 36, 153, 167, 272
De Giorgi, E. 56, 85, 152, 252, 268
 and propaganda work 88–90
De Limur, J. 4, 104
De Mille, C.B. 32
De Matteis, M. 255
De Robertis, F. 30
D'Errico, C. 186
De Santis. G. 265
De Sica, V. 6, 9, 12, 53, 54, 55, 56, 57, 74, 80, 87, 101, 104, 114, 174, 210, 262, 265, 268, 269, 274, 293, 294
 appearance of 144, 150, 156
 and Camerini 145, 147–49, 151, 158
 and Fascism 156–57, 160, 162
 and *Gli uomini, che mascalzoni!* 146, 149, 150–51, 157
 image 145, 149–50, 161
 and masculinity 150, 155, 155–56, 157
 and Mattoli 147–48, 152, 153–54, 158
 and music 150, 152–53, 158
 and Naples 144–45, 153, 155, 157
 and Noris 158
 screen persona 154, 155–56, 160
 smile 158–59, 161
 and the stage 144, 152, 154, 160
 and Zavattini 145, 160
De Tasnady (Tasnadi Fekete), M. 216
Del Poggio, C. 102, 272
Denis, M. 10, 55, 56, 58, 62, 77, 82, 85, 86, 88, 111, 117, 175, 180, 204, 210, 216, 230, 234, 261, 264, 265, 269, 281, 283
Di San Servolo, M. (see Petacci, M.)
Diario di una donna amata, Il 131
Dieci commandamenti, I 262
Dietrich, M. 9, 36, 52, 61, 128–29, 131, 132, 134, 139, 140, 141, 273
Dilian, I. 57, 102, 173, 179, 227, 272
Direzione generale di cinematografia 4, 82
diva (Italian female stars of the silent era) 41–43
Documento Z 3 136, 138
Doletti, M. 91–92, 112, 130, 135, 158
Dopo divorzieremo 179, 194, 197, 198, 286
Dora Nelson 63
Due cuori felici 159, 160
Due lettere anonime 269
Duranti, D. 10, 56, 57, 59, 77, 86, 87, 89, 101, 231, 180, 250, 252, 264, 266, 269, 283
 and *Carmela* 288, 290
Durbin, D. 102
Duse, E. 41, 42

È caduta una donna 75
earnings of stars 79, 85, 87–88, 180, 191, 234, 238
economy, Italian 68–71, 75, 87
Elena, Queen 86
ENIC 27, 29, 245, 246, 247, 248
Excelsa film 58

Fabrizi, A. 10, 91, 262, 269, 294
Fairbanks, D. 45, 106, 135, 158
Falconi, A. 53, 145
Famiglia Brambilla va in vacanza, La 75, 232
fan letters 101, 104, 111, 199–200, 235
fan magazines 102–3, 106, 107
fan practices 104, 112, 113–15, 116–17, 234–35, 274

fans 96
Fari nella nebbia 56, 204, 215
Farinacci, R. 27, 32
Fascism and totalitarianism 7–8, 24
fashion and cinema 76–79, 88, 235–36, 274
Fatigati, G. 239
Fedora 195
Fellini, F. 267, 289
Ferida, L. 10, 12, 56, 58, 82, 84, 111, 116, 181, 192, 195–96, 215, 216, 288, 290, 291, 292, 293
    death of 12, 13, 265–66 (see also *Sanguepazzo*)
Feroce saladino, Il 22, 233
Figlia del corsaro verde, La 215, 217
film theatres 68–69, 74
films and consumerism 70–73
Fiume, O. 56, 60, 80, 111
'Five thousand Lire for a Smile' competition 108–9
Flaiano, E. 175
Flynn, E. 196, 289
Fontana, E. 57
Ford, J. 135
foreign film actors in Italy 179, 196
Fornarina, La 268
Forzano, G. 30, 220
Flynn, E. 2, 4, 47, 281
Franca, L. 51, 54, 155, 169
Franciolini, G. 56
Fratelli Castiglioni, I 186–87
Freddi, L. 8, 19, 20, 21, 24, 25, 27, 33, 34, 35, 37, 55–56, 113, 127, 130, 138, 189
    and censorship 28
    and Cines 8, 28
    and Italian Social Republic 262, 292–93
    and Mussolini 87–88
    and Myriam Petacci 244–48, 253
    and propaganda 31–32
    and publicity 28

    and stars 40–41, 48–50
Frenesie d'estate 286, 287

Gabin, J. 206, 274–75
Gable, C. 2, 4, 47, 100, 196
Gallea, A. 253
Gallone, C. 22, 30, 196, 204, 218, 227
Gandusio, A. 145
Garbo, G. 10, 36, 47–48, 52, 61, 103, 106, 128–29, 131, 134, 150, 167, 240, 273
Garibaldino al convento, Un 162
Gassman, V. 288–89
Gaucho, Il 286, 287
Gelli, C. 102
General Directorate of Cinema (see Direzione generale di cinematografia)
Genesi, V. 136
Genina, A. 30, 56, 57, 146, 196, 203, 204
genre in Italian cinema 32–34
Germany, Federal Republic of (see also Nazi Germany) 11, 12
Ghergo, A. 82, 105
Ghione, E. 43–44
Giachetti, F. 9, 54, 55, 56, 57, 61, 82, 101, 114, 116, 137, 144, 153, 155, 172, 198, 199, 232, 238, 252, 262, 264, 272, 281, 289, 293, 294
    appearance of 207–8, 217, 218
    and female co-stars 204–5, 210, 216–17
    and *Il conformista* 281
    and *L'assedio dell'Alcazar* 210
    and *Lo squadrone bianco* 205, 208, 209, 213, 218
    and masculinity 205–6, 209, 210–12, 214, 215, 219
    and Nazzari 213–14, 216
    performance method and style 207, 217–18, 220–21
    personal life 219, 221
    and political left 270–72
    and prizes 204, 206

and publicity 219–20
screen persona 203, 205–6, 208, 213, 219–20
screen persona and Fascist regime 203, 204, 212–13, 216, 218–20
and theatre 206, 281–82
voice of 205, 208
Giallo 168, 170, 176, 233
Giannini, N. 255
Giarabub 236, 237, 271
Gigli, B. 132, 239
Gilbert, J. 160
Ginevra degli Almieri 191
Gioi, V. 77, 80, 85, 86, 87, 171, 175, 179, 216, 265, 272, 290
Giordana, M.T. 13, 291–92
Giorno di nozze 174
Giorno nella vita, Un 270, 285
Girotti, M. 10, 55, 56, 82, 198, 262, 268, 270
Giuseppe Verdi 204, 208
glamour 75–80, 174–75, 239–40 , 294
criticism of 268
glamour of Hollywood 267
Gloria, L. 55, 56, 80, 101, 111, 279
Goebbels, J. 11, 25, 26, 31, 37, 86, 256
Gonda, G. 267
Gora, C. 137, 262
Gori 79
gossip 83–84, 107, 113–14
Gramsci, A. 42
Grand Hotel 71–72, 103
Grande appello, Il 24, 30, 169, 209
Grandi Firme, Signorina 109–10, 230–32, 233, 289
Grandi magazzini, I 70, 72, 146, 169, 178
Grant, C. 160
Gualino, R. 136
Guarini, A. 75, 131
Guazzoni, E. 215, 268
Guida, G. 79

Harlem 197
Harlow, J. 47, 51

Harvey, L. 100
Hayworth, R. 267, 273
Head, E. 135
Hepburn, K. 52, 100, 139
Hitchcock, A. 273
Hitler, A. 11, 26, 34, 86, 139, 180, 262
Hollywood stars (see also glamour) 40, 46–48, 53, 59, 61
and consumption 68, 73
negative view of 51, 52, 79, 81
Hotel Imperial 134
Hurrell, G. 83, 174, 175

Inferno giallo 215
Invasore, L' 255
Italcine 58, 234

Jachino, S. 84, 90
Jones, J. 102

Keaton, B. 45

Lake, V. 235
Lamarr, H. 273
Lamour, D. 59, 136
Lanzi, F. 216
Lattuada, A. 270, 285
Laurel and Hardy 35, 45
Leander, Z. 61, 129
Leigh, V. 273
lifestyles of stars 81, 82, 84–115
Lizzani, C. 255
Lombard, C. 47, 48
London Film 24
Loren, S. 106
Lotti, M. 56, 192, 262, 265, 268, 269, 270
Loy, M. 47
Luber, E. 232
Luce Institute 20, 23, 61, 249, 265
Luce nelle tenebre 215, 236
Luciano Serra pilota 56, 57, 102, 184, 186, 193
Lulli, P. 176

Lux film 58, 140
Luxardo, E. 82, 83, 105, 108

Macario, E. 10, 91, 153, 196, 268
Maciste 43–44, 45
Maciste contro lo sciecco 44
Maciste imperatore 44
Maddalena zero in condotta 174
Mafalda, Princess of Savoy 86
Magnani, A. 154, 269, 270, 292
Malasomma, N. 146, 147
Malombra 139
Maltagliati, E. 79
Marcia su Roma, La 287
Mariti, I 193, 194
Marx brothers 267
Mastrocinque, C. 56, 191, 193, 195, 215, 220, 244, 249, 252, 254
Mata Hari 134
Matarazzo, R. 174, 233, 236
Mattia Pascal 131
Mattoli, M. 75, 147, 174, 176, 236, 237, 215, 227, 228, 271–72
Melnati, U. 144, 152, 158
Menichelli, P. 41, 43, 45
Mercader, M. 86–87, 152, 162, 278
Merlini, E. 10, 48, 51–53, 54, 59, 62–63, 79, 87–88, 115, 145, 153, 172, 191, 278, 280, 294
Mille lire al mese 224–25, 235
Milly 48, 51, 52, 145, 153, 160
Minerva film 234
Ministry of Popular Culture 20, 27, 57, 81, 89–91, 140, 180, 185, 213, 251
Miranda, I. 9, 52, 54, 56, 58, 59, 62, 78, 79, 80, 85, 86, 101, 104, 116, 233, 239, 265, 273, 274, 275, 281, 294, 297
 early career 123
 European films 131
 and fashion 138–39, 274
 as forgotten star 281
 and Guarini 131–36, 139–41
 and Hollywood 132–35
 image of 128–30
 Italianness of 139–41
 and *La signora di tutti* 123–30
 Manuel Puig on 283
 and Mussolini 136
 return to Italy 135–37
Monaco, E. 87, 91, 212, 252
Monopoly Law 29
Morelli, R. 58
Morgagni, M. 293
Morgan, M. 235
Mostri, I 287
Musco, A. 22, 145, 153
Music in the Air 74
Mussolini, B. 7, 24, 25, 30, 31, 34, 49, 61, 80, 82, 86, 87, 114, 130, 149, 157, 159, 160, 162, 180, 185, 189, 191, 229, 238, 244, 245, 248–50, 255–56, 280, 288, 292, 293
 and Cinecittà 19–22
 and cinema 34–37
 and Claretta Petacci 9, 264, 266
 and consumption 68
 fall from power 4, 261–62, 268
 and Maciste 44
 and Myriam Petacci 249, 250–51, 255
 at Piazzale Loreto 293
 as star 9, 26, 41, 45, 90–91
 and stars 60
 and Valli 264
Mussolini, E. 83
Mussolini family 11
Mussolini, V. 22, 27, 35, 55, 112, 161, 182, 184, 212, 234, 247, 289

names of stars 82, 128
Napoleon (Bonaparte) 36
Napoli che non muore 215
Napoli d'altri tempi 153
Nave bianca, La 31
Nazi Germany 11, 21, 24, 25, 26, 37, 72
Nazi occupation of Rome 262–63, 269–70

Nazzari, A. 5, 6, 9, 12, 54, 55, 56, 57,
    62, 63, 82, 85, 86, 87, 103, 104, 114,
    115, 116, 144, 153, 155, 171, 172,
    173, 203, 204, 213, 216, 218, 221,
    227, 256, 236, 262, 264, 269, 270,
    278–79, 280, 289, 293, 294
  and American screen actors 196–97
  and *Apparizione* 2, 3, 194
  appearance of 188, 194, 196, 198
  and *Cavalleria* 186–88, 193, 195
  costumes of 198–99
  difficult early screen career 186–87
  and directors 198
  fan letters to 199–200
  as Fascist ideal 30, 189–91, 200
  and female co-stars 191–94, 195, 227
  as film star 285–86
  and Giachetti 213–14, 216
  lifestyle 199
  and *Luciano Serra pilota* 184–85,
    188–89, 193, 195, 196, 198, 285,
    286
  and masculinity 192, 193, 197
  and militarism 115
  and Mussolini 185, 189–90
  personal life 189, 198
  and postwar film roles 284–87
  prizes 185
  Sardinian origins of 191, 194–95
  screen persona 187–89, 192–93,
    194–95, 199–200
  and Valli 284–88
  voice of 196
Negri, P. 134
neorealism, origins of 263
Nessuna torna indietro 268
Neufeld, M. 57, 146, 224, 235
Neville, E. 220
Nina Petrovna 131
Ninchi, A. 191
Ninchi, C. 236, 262, 268
Noi vivi – Addio Kira 5, 57, 62, 217, 240
Noris, A. 9, 54, 55, 56, 57, 62, 63, 74,
    80, 82, 84, 85, 86, 104, 111, 112, 116,
    141, 262, 264, 272, 280, 288, 293
  appearance of 166, 167, 170, 171,
    179, 180–81
  blondeness of 179–81
  and Camerini 168, 169, 170, 172,
    175–76, 182
  characters' names 170, 175
  costumes of 170, 171, 172
  and De Sica 169, 170, 172–73
  personal life 175
  photography of 170, 172, 175, 178
  and politics 180
  and postwar television 282
  and publicity 180
  screen persona 166, 171–72, 174,
    178–79, 181
  smile 178
  temperament of 176–77
Notari, G. 216
Notari, U. 229
Notti di Cabiria, Le 199, 286
Novarese, N. 78
Nozze di sangue 56, 215
Nucci, L. 55, 56, 84, 85, 88, 111
Nuovo cinema paradiso 69

Olivier, L. 273
Olympia 185
Opera Nazionale Dopolavoro (OND)
    (National Afterwork Organisation)
    31, 69,
Ophuls, M. 9, 52, 123, 125, 128
Ore 9 lezione di chimica 174, 228, 232
Ossessione 31, 162, 268
OVRA 31

Pagano, B. (see Maciste)
Paisà 269, 292
Palermi, A. 77, 147, 153, 215
Palio 84
Paola, D. 51, 52, 53, 84
Paolieri, G. 52, 84
Partito Nazionale Fascista (National
    Fascist Party) 32, 36

Parvo, E. 268
Passaporto rosso, 35, 130, 131
Pastrone, G. 43–44
Patto col diavolo 274
Patti, E. 263
Paulucci de Calboli Carbone, G. 21, 27
Pavlova, T. 152, 191, 206
Pavolini, A. 57, 87, 90, 135, 251, 266
Peccatrice, La 77
Peresutti, G. 22
Perugina chocolates (including Buitoni promotion) 79, 80, 105
Petacci, C. 9, 60
    and Mussolini 248–50, 252
Petacci family 245–46, 248, 249, 254
    and villa La Camilluccia 249, 254
Petacci, G. 245–46, 254
Petacci, Marcello 246, 249–50, 254
Petacci, Myriam (M. Di San Servolo) 9, 244, 264, 272, 283
    appearance of 253–54
    Freddi view of 244–48, 253
    marriage of 251–52
    and material excess 255
    and Mussolini 249, 250–51, 255
    name of 254
    and snobbery 254–55
photography and stars 83, 214
Piccolo mondo antico 235, 237–38, 288
Pickford, M. 23, 106
Pietrangeli, A. 264, 265
Pilota ritorna, Il 31
Pirandello, L. 149
Pittaluga, S. 44, 48, 150
Poggioli, F.M. 56, 57, 75, 244
Pola, I. 51, 53, 84
Ponzoni, C. 288–89
Porta del cielo, La 262
Power, T. 59, 267
Pozzetto, R. 281
Prima donna che passa, La 226
Promessi sposi, I 107
    and hunt for 'Lucia' 107–8
promotion of films 74, 80, 81, 82, 108

propaganda and stars 88–90

Questi ragazzi 154

Rabagliati, A. 106
radio and stars 112
Radway, G. 215
Ramperti, M. 47, 52
Rascel, R. 10, 91
Re Burlone 74
recruitment of stars 111
Redenzione 32
Righelli, G. 146, 147
Rinascente, La 74, 107
Risi, D. 13, 288–90
Rissone, G. 144, 145, 151, 152, 162
Rizzoli, A. 52, 123
Roma città aperta 269–70, 292
Romantica avventura, Un 169
Roncoroni, C. 14, 28
Rossellini, R. 30, 175, 255
Ruffini, S. 244
Ruggeri, R, 191

Salon Kitty 290
Sanguepazzo 13, 287, 291–93
Sanson, Y. 236
Sassoli, D. 56, 108
Sbaglio di essere vivo, Lo 274
Scampolo 194
Scandalo al collegio (L'innocente Casimiro) 268
Scarpe al sole 74
Scipione l'Africano 23, 24, 31, 32, 132, 141, 148, 207, 217
Segretaria privata, La 51, 79
Selznick, D.O. 273
Senso 290
Senso '45 13, 287, 290–91
Sentinelle di bronzo 220
Senza cielo 136, 138
Serato, M. 101
Signor Max, Il 57, 107, 146, 148, 160, 176

Signora di tutti, La 52, 123–30, 233
Signorina dell'autobus, La 168
Silvi, L. 62–63, 85, 191, 194, 195, 198, 239, 264, 280
Sogno d'amore 256
Solari, L. 56, 85, 111
Soldati, M. 23, 53, 57, 58, 63, 103, 112, 140, 151, 235, 237
Sole 30
Squadrone bianco, Lo 24, 56, 61, 148, 203–4, 213, 215, 216
Stallich, J. 227
Stanwyck, B. 100
Starace, A. 21
star lighting 60–2 (see also Noris and Valli)
stars leaving Italy from 1945 272–75
stars in postwar memory 278–81
Stasera niente di nuovo 237
Statua vivente, La 215, 220
Steno (S. Vanzina) 263–64
Stewart, J. 160
Storia d'amore, Una 169, 176

Telefoni bianchi 13, 287–90, 291
Temple, S. 74
Tempo massimo 75, 153, 154, 160
Tenebre 129, 132
Terra madre 30, 84
Toeplitz, L. 150
Tofano, S. 144, 150, 152
Tognazzi, U. 281, 290
Tonti, A. 235
Tornatore, G. 69
Totò (A. De Curtis) 10, 91, 153
Tracy, S. 237
Tre uomini in frak 167
Trenker, L. 24
Trio Lescano 152

UFA 19
Uomo che sorride, L' 154, 158
Uomini, che mascalzoni!, Gli 75, 146, 149–51, 157

Uomo della croce, L' 31

Valenti, O. 10, 12, 84, 86, 192, 199, 203, 224, 225, 256, 289–90, 291, 292–93
death of 12, 13, 265–66
Valentino, R. 53, 97, 106
Valli, A. 4, 5, 6, 9, 12, 54, 55, 56, 57, 58, 62, 80, 82, 88, 90, 101, 103, 104, 112, 114, 116, 140, 171, 174, 175, 180, 182, 191, 193, 195, 200, 204, 214, 210, 217, 230, 231, 233, 262, 265, 269, 272, 273, 278–79, 280, 288, 290, 293
and *Apparizione*, 3–4, 228
appearance of 225, 230, 235, 240
and beauty 229–30, 232
as commercial property 234–35, 238
early life 230–31, 235
and elegance 235, 236
and Fascism 239
and glamour 239–40
in Hollywood 273–74
and *Il feroce saladino* 24
as ingénue 228–29, 232–33, 239
and melodrama 236–37
and Mussolini 264
and Nazzari 227, 284–88
and Neufeld 226–27
and *Noi vivi – Addio Kira* 238–39
personal life 235
photography and 226, 227, 233, 236, 240–41
in popular memory 284
popularity of 234–35
and postwar politics 274
publicity and 235
screen persona 226, 240
temperament of 231–32
Vecchia guardia 30
Venice Film Festival 59, 79, 91, 112, 207, 246, 237, 240, 275, 293
Verdi, G. 34, 207
Viale della speranza, Il 288
Viarisio, E. 268

Vich, V. 227, 232
Vie del cuore, Le 244, 246, 252, 253, 255
Villa, R. 6, 10, 55, 56, 59, 85, 101–2, 264, 268
Viralba film 245, 247, 256
Visconti, L. 13, 31, 162, 265, 268, 287, 290, 291, 292
Vispa Teresa, La 268
Vita ricomincia, La 272
von Sternberg, E. 273

Wayne, J. 198, 218
'white telephone' films 48, 70, 75, 147, 179, 194, 210, 224–25, 227

Young, L. 59

Zacconi, E. 206
Zampa, L. 225, 286
Zavattini, C. 47, 63, 109, 137, 138, 176, 227, 265
Zazà 139, 140
Zingaretti, L. 291
Zukor, A. 134

www.ingramcontent.com/pod-product-compliance
Lightning Source LLC
Chambersburg PA
CBHW072144100526
44589CB00015B/2079